America: The Framing of a Nation

Volume 2 – since 1865

Hugh C. Bailey

Samford University

Generously Donated to

The Frederick Douglass Institute

By Professor Jesse Moore

Fall 2000

CHARLES E. MERRILL PUBLISHING COMPANY
A Bell & Howell Company
Columbus, Ohio

For Joanie, Debbie, and Laura

Published by
Charles E. Merrill Publishing Company
A Bell & Howell Company
Columbus, Ohio 43216

This book was set in Palatino.
The Production Editor was Linda Gambaiani.

ISBN: 0–675–08749–X

Library of Congress Catalog Card Number: 74–33745

1 2 3 4 5 6 7 8 9—83 82 81 80 79 78 77 76 75

Photo Credits: World's Work VII (February 1904): 4404, p. 78; *World's Work* XLVI (September 1923): 533, p. 195; U.S. Army, pp. 260, 265, 271, 275, 276, 278, 285, 365, 367; U.S. Navy, pp. 116, 255; United Nations, pp. 274, 299, 353; The White House, pp. 323, 341, 344; NASA, p. 360; U.S. Department of State, p. 373; Wide World Photos, p. 231; in The National Archives: U.S. Signal Corps, No. 111-BA-97 (Brady Collection), p. 13; No. 111-SC-94980, p. 176; No. 111-SC-50081, p. 177; No. 111-SC-61127, p. 178; U.S. Office of War Information, No. 208-PU-219G-1, p. 47; No. 208-PU-222L-4, p. 243; No. 208-YE-15, p. 263; No. 208-YE-129, p. 266; U.S. War Dept. General Staff, No. 165-WW-448A-4, p. 58; No. 165-WW-441F-6, p. 139; No. 165-UM-4, p. 166; No. 165-WW-444B-1, p. 182; U.S. Information Agency, No. 306-NT-87817C, p. 60; No. 306-NT-727-5A, p. 201; No. 306-NT-150110C, p. 208; No. 306-NT-123924, p. 227; No. 306-NT-901-23, p. 243; No. 306-NT-355-B-2, p. 295; No. 306-55-77A-84-7, p. 315; Navy Dept., No. 19-N-19917, p. 115; No. 19-N-7936, p. 175; No. 80-G-26854, p. 251; No. 80-G-87990, p. 257; Work Projects Administration No. 69-N-2304, p. 222; Bureau of Agricultural Economics No. 83-G-41387, p. 229; Tennessee Valley Authority No. 142-RS-2E-1, p. 230; War Relocation Authority No. 210-G-2A-523, p. 259; World War II Collection of Seized Enemy Records No. 242-GAP-181A-4, p. 261; Gift Collection No. RG-200S-HK-1, p. 307; The National Archives, pp. 272, 312; all other photos reproduced from the collections of the Library of Congress. The Pullman Company, p. 57.

Printed in the United States of America

Preface

The saga of American life continues to interest not only the people of the United States but other peoples of the world as well. The uniqueness of our American experience, the diversity out of which our civilization has emerged, the incredible growth and marvelous achievements of so relatively young a nation—these are the framework of our history to date and, almost certainly, the promise of our future. To emphasize this fact, *America: The Framing of a Nation* seemed a most appropriate title for a text to survey our progress as a nation.

This text is designed for students in college courses which survey American history from its beginnings to the present. Its two volumes, taken in combination, cover the period from the late middle ages to 1974; chapter 13, on Reconstruction after the Civil War, is printed in each volume for the convenience of those who may choose to end one quarter's or semester's work or begin another with that material.

A number of guidelines have been followed in writing *America: The Framing of a Nation,* but one principle has been given special attention throughout: this book is designed for *students.* Hopefully, a book that is as clear and readable as it is thorough and accurate will also aid the instructor by producing better-read, better-prepared, and better-motivated students who are more eager to discuss the material and share interpretations of it.

The text strives to present major historical facts in as precise and clear a manner as possible for the novice of American history. Likewise, an intense effort has been made to include the latest historical scholarship, but without burdening the reader with the jargon of professional historians. The study of history has benefited, of course, from generations of the most intense research and writing; thus, the differences of opinion among very able scholars are included in an effort to convey the complexity and diversity of views on the American experience.

In addition, a number of aids specifically created for the student are included in the body of the text. First, each chapter opens with a brief chronology of the major events of the period under study. Second, each chapter includes a brief summary of what have been termed "Long-Range Developments"; these were selected to give the student at least some sense of how events or individuals in one period of history may influence the lives of succeeding generations of individuals and institutions. Third, the volumes have been richly illustrated with photos and artwork from the times as well as a number of explanatory maps, in the hope of giving students still another medium of information about our growth as a republic. Finally, as an aid to those students who wish more detailed knowledge, bibliographies at the end of each chapter cite both classic studies and the latest publications.

In writing this work the author received the help of innumerable people, most of whom cannot be mentioned due to space limitations. However, he would like specifically to thank the following Samford University personnel: Professor David M. Vess, who furnished constructive suggestions for treating the European background of American history; the late Professor Mary McGriff Washington, who read chapters 1–23; Professor Leah Atkins, who criticized chapters 24–25; and his secretary, Lynn B. Walker, who aided in preparing the manuscript. He is deeply indebted to Professor William Zornow of Kent State University and Patrick Foley of Ohio State University who read the entire manuscript and saved him from many errors, but, of course, he assumes full responsibility for the final work. A special debt of gratitude is due Tom Hutchinson of Charles E. Merrill Publishing Company and Linda Gambaiani, production editor at Merrill, for their extraordinary interest in this book and aid in its publication. Lastly, the author is most indebted to his wife whose cooperation in editing and typing the manuscript makes the work as much hers as his own.

Contents

Maps and Charts

America:
The Framing of a
Nation

Volume 2 – since 1865

Major Developments

1863	Lincoln's Reconstruction Plan announced
1864	Wade-Davis Bill
1865	Johnson Reconstruction Plan presented
	Thirteenth Amendment approved
1866	Unalterable break of president with Congress
	Ku Klux Klan organized in Pulaski, Tennessee
	Radical triumph in congressional elections
1867	First Congressional Reconstruction Acts
	Tenure of Office Act
	Alaska purchased
1868	Fourteenth Amendment approved
	Impeachment of President Johnson
	Election of Ulysses S. Grant
1869	Johnson-Clarendon Convention
	"Black Friday" episode
1870	Fifteenth Amendment ratified
1870–71	The Force Acts
1872	Amnesty Act
	Alabama Claims settlement
	Liberal Republican revolt
1873	Depression
1874	"White Man's" Movement began
1875	Civil Rights Act
	Resumption Act
1876	Disputed election
1877	Compromise of 1877
1883	Civil Rights Act invalidated

13

Reconstruction, Southern and National

Long-Range Developments

For Economics and Corporate Enterprise

Unwholesome business connivance with government to obtain private advantages became broader and more pervasive during the Grant era, a trend that has continued to the present.

The defeat of the Ohio Idea and passage of the Resumption Act of 1875 committed the United States to a conservative monetary policy for generations.

For Democratic Government

The Compromise of 1877 demonstrated the value to both sides of northern Republican-southern Democratic cooperation and resulted in each group largely refraining from infringements on questions the other considered of paramount importance.

For Civil Liberties, Freedom, and Reform

Federal intervention on behalf of southern blacks followed by national withdrawal intensified the problems of blacks.

The civil rights acts of the early postwar years, though limited in their immediate results, have in some cases been applied recently and have served as precedents for the far-reaching laws passed since 1957.

The Fourteenth Amendment has come to affect many aspects of American life, and in the twentieth century more cases reach the Supreme Court under it than under any other segment of the Constitution.

The failure to remove President Andrew Johnson by impeachment prevented another serious movement for presidential impeachment until 1974.

The State of the Union

The war, which dominated American life and thought for four years, left little time for concern with postwar plans. The termination of hostilities, followed soon afterwards by the assassination of President Lincoln, resulted in widespread turmoil and confusion. For example, the sudden ending of government contracts and rapid demobilization caused temporary northern unemployment until business readjustment was completed in 1868, but in the following five years rapid expansion and growth brought prosperity to many.

Unfortunately, a happy resolution of the nation's black problem was not achieved. The North was pervaded, to a lesser degree, by the same racist attitudes as the South, and men of the best will believed in black inferiority. Despite some progress in the immediate postwar years, the economic role of northern blacks showed no notable improvement, and a number of states, including Ohio, Michigan, Pennsylvania, New Jersey, and Connecticut, refused to grant blacks suffrage. A number of Radicals, many of whom were former abolitionists, constantly sought to reverse that trend, and the more zealous, who looked to Senator Charles Sumner for leadership, demanded full political and social equality for blacks. Other Radicals, such as Pennsylvania's Representative Thaddeus Stevens, were equally committed but were willing to accept less immediate gains. Many northerners who heartily disagreed with the Radicals on racial policy at home had a different attitude toward the South. Some were willing to follow Radical policies to remake and reform it, while others simply wished to see that former rebels did not reverse the results of the war.

In the South, where the losses sustained seemed unbelievable to many, destitution was

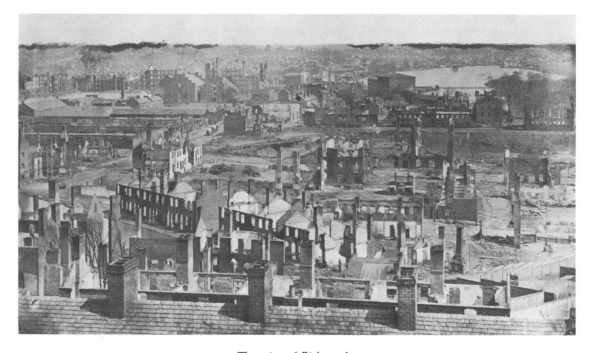

The ruins of Richmond.

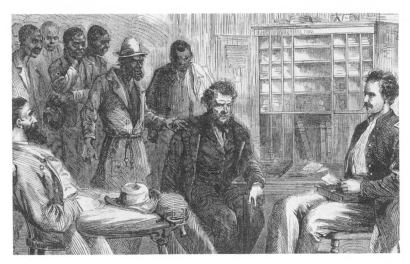

An office of the Freedmen's Bureau in Memphis, Tennessee.

widespread. Four million slaves, the greatest economic asset of the planters, and all the money invested in Confederate securities had been lost. Invading armies and years of inadequate maintenance had destroyed the region's railroads and many of its factories. One out of every seven men had been killed in the conflict, which was one of the highest casualty rates of all times, and innumerable women were left as heads of households. Lack of food was so great that thousands of whites as well as blacks owed their very lives to grants from the Freedmen's Bureau, an agency established in March, 1865, to care for the newly liberated blacks. Most of the five million bales of southern cotton in storage in 1865 were confiscated by government officials with little of the returns reaching the U.S. Treasury, and a heavy cotton tax siphoned away the profits from early postwar production. Innumerable difficulties including lack of capital, labor, and adequate transportation inhibited agriculture, and it was not until 1879 that cotton production exceeded its prewar record, while some other crops lagged even further behind.

Southern Treatment of the Freedman

The economic dilemma of the South was partially responsible for the harsh treatment received by many freedmen. With the former sources of plantation labor and capital gone, a method to cultivate the soil had to be found. The solution came with the development of various forms of farm tenancy including a leasehold arrangement known as "tenancy" for the poor farmer who could salvage some degree of independency and the "sharecrop" system for the poorest. Under the sharecrop system small units of land were parceled out to blacks and poorer whites and, in place of rent, the landowner received one-third to one-half of the crop, depending on the quantity of equipment and supplies he provided. The proportion of sharecroppers increased each year in the South until the 1930s, strengthening a system which limited rewards and encouraged the most wasteful practices.

The crop lien system, which emerged concurrently with sharecropping, was another system that victimized many southerners. Under it, to obtain necessary goods, a farmer mortgaged his crop to a merchant before it was produced. Thus he was forced to buy goods from only one merchant, often at exorbitant prices, and to sell to him at the lowest prices. The merchant also demanded the maximum production of a staple crop, usually cotton in the deep South, which prevented diversification.

Sharecropping and the crop lien system were economic vices from which much of the predominantly rural South suffered for generations. In the early postwar days, however, they were only beginning to emerge, and their full effects on the blacks were not realized. However, some Radicals urged that the federal government confiscate property of former planters and endow each black man with a forty-acre farm. This very practical suggestion, which many freedmen approved, was not acceptable to most Americans and was not acted upon.

In dealing with the serious economic and social consequences of emancipation, a united nation was sorely needed, but, unfortunately, the problems themselves produced greater chasms between the sections. The North became suspicious of the motives for southern actions, assuming that an effort was being made to reenslave the blacks, while southerners failed to assess the northern commitment to reform in the South and pursued policies which were easily misinterpreted. The most notable example of these came in the enactment of Black Codes, which varied in intensity but limited the freedom enjoyed by blacks. They prohibited blacks carrying weapons, marrying whites, serving on juries, and working in most fields other than agriculture. Special features practically forced blacks to sign labor contracts, whose violations were punished by strong penalties. Many southerners, familiar with vagrant blacks gathering in towns during early prewar days, saw nothing

harsh in these laws, but to distant northerners they looked like remodeled slave codes. Southern intentions came to be increasingly questioned as stories of mistreatment and murder trickled into the North from soldiers, ministers, school teachers, newspaper reporters, and others. Bloody race riots in New Orleans and Memphis in 1866 only reinforced the bad image.

Johnson's Reconstruction Plan

National policy regarding the freedman began to be formulated as early as 1862 when federal troops first moved into the South and the practical-minded, nonvindictive Lincoln established provisional governments under federal control. This action became the basis for a plan of reconstruction announced on December 8, 1863, whose leniency immediately drew the Radicals' fire since they distrusted turning the blacks' fate over to southern whites. Lincoln's plan provided amnesty for all southerners, except for leading Confederate officials, who would take a loyalty oath to the Constitution. When 10 percent of the number of 1860 voters in a state had taken the oath, they were authorized to form a state government which the president would recognize, provided it was republican in form and accepted the end of slavery. During 1864 Arkansas, Louisiana, Tennessee, and the government established in western Virginia complied with these terms, but, ominously, Congress refused to seat their representatives.

In July, 1864, Congress under Radical leadership passed the Wade-Davis bill, which provided for a much sterner reconstruction plan. Under it, a state was authorized to hold a constitutional convention only after a majority of its white, male citizens took an oath to the U.S. Constitution, and any person who had voluntarily fought for the Confederacy or served as its official was disfranchised and excluded as a convention delegate. Moreover, all new southern governments were to continue the prohibition on ex-Confederate voting, forbid slavery, and repudiate the Confederate debt. Lincoln, who felt the Wade-Davis bill was too severe, used his pocket veto on it and continued with his own program. The president's congressional opponents responded with the Wade-Davis Manifesto, which charged Lincoln with attempting to retain the electoral votes of the South at the expense of the blacks, and, after the 1864 election, they excluded the votes of the four states which had complied with Lincoln's terms. Partially in response to this action, Lincoln, who was a political realist, indicated a desire to have "very intelligent" blacks and black veterans given the vote, and, at the time of his death, he was obviously modifying his attitudes toward reconstruction.

Andrew Johnson's accession was hailed by many Radicals who felt his severe indictment of the southern planter class indicated he was a kindred spirit, but their confidence was misplaced. Johnson, a native of Raleigh, North Carolina, belonged to the most plebeian white class and rose to prominence politically by appealing to their fears and aspirations. After his father's death, when he was fourteen, he served an apprenticeship as a tailor and began his efforts at self-education. Moving to Greeneville, in East Tennessee, he was elected a city alderman at twenty and subsequently served as mayor, state representative and senator, U.S. representative, governor of Tennessee, and from 1857 to 1862 as U.S. senator. Through the years he was intensely loyal to the class interests of the less affluent, trying repeatedly to obtain enactment of a homestead law. When the Confederate states seceded, Johnson alone of the southern senators refused to resign. Lincoln appointed him military governor of Tennessee in March, 1862, and, even

though he was a Democrat, tapped him as the vice-presidential candidate for the 1864 Union ticket.

Once in power, Johnson's strong state's rights tendencies and anti-black prejudices guided many of his policies. He shocked the Radicals by adopting much of Lincoln's reconstruction plan and by pressing for an early return of the southern states to full participation in the Union. Johnson's program included a general amnesty, issued in May, 1865, to those who would take a loyalty oath to the Constitution. High Confederate officeholders and those whose property was valued at more than $20,000 were excluded, but provision was made for them to petition the president for special par-

Andrew Johnson

dons. Yet blacks were not given the vote nor guaranteed protection of their rights.

Johnson recognized the four state governments complying with Lincoln's terms and began the organization of provisional governments in the seven other southern states. In each of these the provisional governors were instructed to call conventions to repeal the secession ordinance, repudiate the war debt, and ratify the proposed Thirteenth Amendment, which prohibited the existence of slavery. When these things were accomplished, the president proposed to recognize the state as the legitimate government of its region. By December, 1865, when the new Congress convened, the southern states had complied with these terms to Johnson's satisfaction, but Congress prevented their readmission by refusing to seat their representatives.

The Radical Opposition

After Congress refused to accept Johnson's reconstruction program, it began to create its own by establishing a Joint Committee on Reconstruction composed of six senators and nine representatives. The Committee's chairman was seventy-three-year-old Thaddeus Stevens, a most successful Pennsylvania ironmaker and attorney, who had gratuitously defended many fugitive slaves in the antebellum period. He served in Congress from 1849 to 1853 and from 1859 until his death in 1868, during his last three years dominating the operations of the Joint Committee on Reconstruction and the Republican party. His position was always used to promote concern for the blacks and to advocate a stern southern policy.

Stevens contended that the southern states were conquered provinces, a position somewhat different from that of Senator Charles Sumner who held they had committed suicide

Thaddeus Stevens

and did not even have the status of territories. Others, including most Radicals, believed that the southern states still existed but required federal intervention to maintain a republican form of government. The joint Committee on Reconstruction did not officially espouse any of these views but simply declared that no true state governments existed in the South and that it was Congress' responsibility to establish conditions for readmission.

The motives for Radical action were complex and diverse. Many feared the return of an agrarian-dominated South, where all of the blacks instead of three-fifths would be counted in determining representation in the House of Representatives. Quite possibly in such a reconstructed Congress the Republicans would be a minority, losing not only the prizes of office but the wartime legislation attained after the South seceded. At the same time, great uncertainty existed as to the South's intentions to comply with federal policies regarding the freedman. Prominent Confederate leaders, including Vice-President Alexander H. Stephens, who was elected to the Senate, were chosen for high office, but there was no assurance acceptable to northerners that the South truly acceded to the war's results.

The Critical Year—1866

The inevitable conflict between President Johnson and the Radicals was fully projected in 1866, and the Radicals were sustained in the elections of that year. In February, Congress passed a new Freedmen's Bureau bill, designed to counteract the influence of the Black Codes, which gave the bureau military-type authority to try persons alleged to have deprived the black of his civil rights. Johnson vetoed the bill, asserting Congress could not legislate for the reconstructed southern states when they were unrepresented and that the bill violated the Fifth Amendment which declared that "no person shall be held to answer for a capital, or otherwise infamous crime, unless in a presentment or indictment of a grand jury, except in cases arising in the land or naval forces, or in the militia, when in actual service in time of war or public danger; . . . nor be deprived of life, liberty, or property, without due process of law. . . ." Johnson's reasoning was in accord with the prevailing concept of the Fifth Amendment based on Chief Justice John Marshall's 1833 decision in *Barron* v. *Baltimore* which held that the ten amendments in the Bill of Rights gave the individual protection only against the federal government but did not bind the states. Though initially sustained, the president's veto of a similar bill was overridden in July, 1866.

Earlier, in April, 1866, for the first time in American history, Congress passed a bill over the president's veto and made the Civil Rights Act a law. This action was a congressional declaration of independence which, with Johnson's intemperate attack on the Radicals, increased the conflict inside and outside the government. The Civil Rights Act made all persons born or naturalized in the United States national citizens and forbade the states to infringe on the legal rights of U.S. citizens. Radicals, who feared the law might be invalidated by the courts after the *Ex parte Milligan* decision declared martial law could not be imposed when civil courts were open, made the Civil Rights Act the basis of the Fourteenth Amendment which was submitted to the states in June, 1866. It was designed to make the Bill of Rights limitations apply to the states as well as to the federal government and provided that no state "shall abridge the privileges or immunities of citizens of the United States; nor shall any State deprive any person of life, liberty, or property, without due process of law; nor deny to any person within its jurisdiction the equal protection of the laws." It attempted to compel the states to permit black suffrage by providing for a reduction in representation in the House of Representatives when the right to vote was denied to men. This stipulation was never applied since it would have reduced representation for all restrictions on voting, not merely for racial exclusion. In an important provision, the amendment denied officeholding to anyone who had as a congressman, U.S. officer, state legislator, "or as an executive or judicial officer of any State" broken an oath to the U.S. Constitution by insurrection or rebellion or by giving "aid or comfort" to the nation's enemies. Congress was authorized to remove this disability by a two-thirds vote, but, in general, denial of officeholding meant that former local leaders were to be excluded from government. Though it did not go as far as many Radicals wished in protecting the freedman, the amendment achieved many of their objectives and became a basic feature of Radical reconstruction.

Of all the southern states, only Tennessee, which had passed under Radical control, immediately approved the Fourteenth Amendment and escaped the rigors of Radical reconstruction. The others, encouraged by the president's attitude, chose to remain outside the Union rather than accept its harsh restrictions, but, as sterner reconstruction laws were passed in 1867, approval of the amendment was made mandatory for readmission. With the aid of southern votes, the amendment was ratified in July, 1868. At the time few realized that it would fall hopelessly short of guaranteeing the freedman his civil rights and that for generations it would be utilized mainly for the protection of the civil rights of corporations which had the legal status of persons.

President Johnson chose to make the 1866 elections a plebiscite on his reconstruction plan and Congress' emerging program as revealed in the Fourteenth Amendment. A National Union Convention which he endorsed merely repulsed many northerners due to the prominence of former Confederates who attended. In an eighteen-day speaking tour, the president lost prestige when he replied to hecklers in terms inappropriate to his office. Average voters in the North, many of whom were deeply committed to the guarantee of equal rights for blacks, were fearful that the freedman was being abused in the South, and in the elections the Radicals obtained two-thirds of the seats in both houses, a position which enabled them to implement their policy.

The Radical Program

As a result of the Radical triumph, in March, 1867, the first of the Reconstruction Acts was passed. It divided the Confederate South except Tennessee into five military districts and placed a major general over each with extensive powers to protect civil rights. Before military control could end, each state was required to adopt a new constitution guaranteeing black suffrage and disqualifying from voting those ex-Confederates who were denied officeholding under the proposed Fourteenth Amendment. The amendment, of course, also had to be approved.

Since the southern states chose to remain under military rule rather than comply with Radical requirements, other reconstruction laws were enacted in March and July, 1867, and March, 1868. They authorized military commanders actually to conduct the registration of voters and to supervise the elections. When Alabamians attempted to defeat a proposed constitution by failing to vote on it, a law was passed reducing the requirements for approval from a majority of registered voters to a majority casting votes in the election.

Under the new Radical policy, constitutions were formed similar to those in the North except in their provisions for universal suffrage, disfranchisement of former rebels, and guarantees of black civil rights. Under these constitutions Arkansas, Louisiana, Alabama, Florida, South Carolina, and North Carolina returned to the Union in 1868. Georgia was readmitted at the same time but was soon expelled when blacks were ejected from its state legislature. It was readmitted in 1870 with Texas, Mississippi, and Virginia, which at last agreed to accept the disfranchisement clauses of their proposed constitutions.

Those states readmitted after 1868 were also required to approve the Fifteenth Amendment which prohibited the states denying or abridging the right to vote because of "race, color, or previous condition of servitude." Republicans had been reluctant to propose this amendment until the elections of 1868 in the North con-

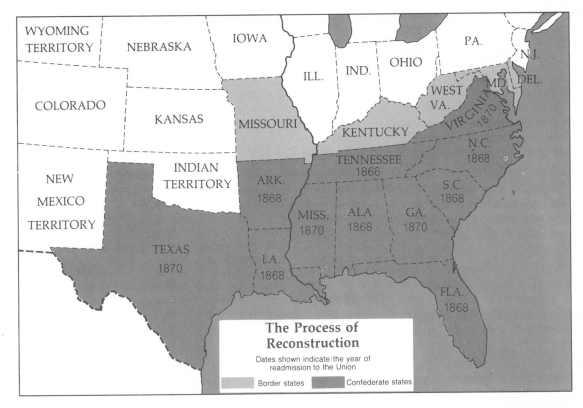

The Process of Reconstruction

Dates shown indicate the year of readmission to the Union

Border states Confederate states

vinced them that the party had more to gain than lose by insuring that blacks everywhere had the right to vote. No difficulty was experienced in obtaining approval in the Radically controlled South, but spirited contests took place in several northern states before approval was obtained in early 1870.

Under Radical policy, the votes of southern blacks were used to run the governments in the former Confederacy, and those states' electoral votes were safely secured for the Republican party nationally. The strategy combined the loftiest of moral motives with the basest of political rewards. Unfortunately the changes wrought were not fundamental enough to insure permanently blacks' political rights but were sufficiently galling to southern whites to raise a profound reaction. Indeed many Radicals were quite conservative in their economic views and would not consider reforms threatening property rights nor the position of those whose success was ascribed to hard work. Even the initiated changes came to be unacceptable to the average northerner who had a limited commitment to black rights and who greatly distrusted military rule and white proscription.

The Congress Dominates the Government

The struggle between President Johnson and Congress resulted in a congressional assertion of power which almost destroyed the balance between the three branches of government. Congress, as early as July, 1866, forbade the president to appoint new justices of the Supreme Court, and in March, 1868, it denied the

Supreme Court jurisdiction over certain civil rights cases, a decision which the Court did not challenge. In important decisions the Court itself assumed an ambivalent attitude toward its prerogatives and federal power unlike the strong stand it was to take in the 1870s. In the Test-Oath Cases of 1867 (*Cummings* v. *Missouri* and *Ex parte Garland*), it held both state and federal oaths of past loyalty were invalid since they were ex post facto laws and bills of attainder. The same year Mississippi attempted to enjoin President Johnson in *Mississippi* v. *Johnson* and Georgia tried to enjoin Secretary of War Edwin M. Stanton in *Georgia* v. *Stanton* from enforcing the Reconstruction Acts; however, the Court refused to intervene, holding that executive and political functions were not subject to judicial restraint. In 1869 the Court did accept Lincoln's concept of the enduring nature of the Union, holding in *Texas* v. *White* that, since secession was inadmissible, Confederate financial transactions were illegal. Moreover, without passing on the legality of the Reconstruction Acts, it recognized that Congress had the duty to guarantee republican governments in the states.

Largely unbridled by judicial restraint, Congress practically took the army from the president's control by stipulating that all military orders were to be issued through the general of the army, Ulysses S. Grant. It also assumed the traditional executive privilege of calling special sessions, but its greatest challenge to the division of powers came when the president was impeached. Had he been removed, the president pro-tem of the Senate, the Radical Benjamin Wade, would have become president, and Congress' control would have been complete.

Johnson was indicted by the House on eleven counts, most of which pertained to violation of the Tenure of Office Act. This law, enacted in March, 1867, provided that those officials confirmed by the Senate could only be removed with its approval, but the guaranteed tenure extended only through the term of the appointing president and one month afterwards. The measure was specifically designed to protect Secretary of War Stanton, the only cabinet member friendly to the Radicals, but President Johnson, who knew he was personally disloyal, deliberately chose to test the law by dismissing him. Since Stanton had been appointed by Lincoln, it was obvious that Johnson had not violated the Tenure of Office Act in removing him, but the Radicals applied sufficient pressure to make the House doubtful.

Chief Justice Salmon P. Chase presided impartially over the trial, one of the greatest dramas in the nation's history. Representative Thaddeus Stevens, who led the prosecution, used the most bitter invective against the president and contended that, since impeachment was a political not a legal matter, it did not

Salmon P. Chase

require evidence of guilt for conviction. When the vote was taken on May 16, 1868, seven Republican senators joined twelve Democrats in voting not guilty. By one vote the Radicals failed to attain the two-thirds majority of thirty-six votes necessary for conviction and removal. The nation was saved by the narrowest of margins from a fundamental alteration of its governmental operation.

Grant's Election

When the Republican national convention convened within a week after Johnson's acquittal, no one seriously considered his renomination. Instead, the knowledgeable politicians and novices alike turned to General Grant, whose wartime sacrifice of men had been forgotten and who was probably the most popular man in America. To many he had become the symbol of a united nation and of efficiency and determination in the face of adversity. He had come increasingly under the influence of the Radicals and endeared himself to them by his role in a controversy which occurred before Johnson's impeachment. The president had given Grant an interim appointment as Stanton's successor in April, 1867, with the expectation that this action would provide a basis for testing the Tenure of Office

Ulysses S. Grant and family at their New Jersey summer resort.

Act in the courts. When the Senate refused to sanction Stanton's removal, Grant resigned and returned the office to Stanton, forcing Johnson to appoint General Lorenzo Thomas, a relatively unknown person, as the basis for his test of the Tenure of Office Act.

Although he had never voted Republican in a presidential election, Grant was nominated on the first ballot as concern with victory led the delegates to discount his political inexperience, a mistake many came to regret. Schuyler Colfax, an Indiana Radical, was chosen as the vice-presidential candidate.

The Democratic convention, which met in early July, 1868, was confronted with great problems since many of the party's southern members were disfranchised and in the North the Republicans depicted all Democrats as disloyal. The party platform indicted Radical reconstruction as unconstitutional but attempted to raise an economic issue which could change the campaign's nature. In a direct appeal to the debtor class, it endorsed the "Ohio Idea," which proposed to repay the interest on government bonds in greenbacks, thus preventing a great accrual to those who had purchased bonds with depreciated paper. However, a hard-money man, former New York Governor Horatio Seymour, was nominated for president in an effort to retain conservative eastern support, and Missouri's Francis P. Blair was selected as his running mate.

In the presidential campaign, Seymour was mercilessly and unfairly attacked as a rebel sympathizer, but, despite numerous disadvantages, the Democratic candidates polled 47 percent of the popular vote and were defeated only by black ballots. Though Grant received 214 electoral votes to Seymour's 80, the surprisingly close election alarmed many Radicals, who resolved to retain political control in the South.

Black Reconstruction

As president, Grant gave his warm support to Radical reconstruction which reached its crest and declined during his administrations. Critics of the Radical regimes in the South referred to them as "black," but in many ways this was a misnomer. Only the lower house in South Carolina had a majority of black members, while the highest state offices held by blacks were those of lieutenant governor and supreme court associate justice. The largest number of blacks to serve in Congress from the South at one time was only eight out of delegations totaling more than one hundred. Two blacks from Mississippi reached the U.S. Senate— Hiram R. Revels, who for a few months filled the seat formerly occupied by Jefferson Davis, and Blanche K. Bruce, who effectively served a full term from 1875 to 1881.

Some of the white politicians holding office in the South during reconstruction were known as "carpetbaggers," northerners whom the southerners vilified by depicting them carrying most of their worldly possessions in a carpetbag when they first came south. These men varied greatly in their talents and ethics; some were brilliant, others dullards; some were moral zealots, others charlatans.

The majority of successful southern politicians were neither blacks nor carpetbaggers but belonged to a group unjustly stigmatized as "scalawags," native whites who cooperated with the Republican machines. At least in the earlier years of Radical reconstruction, many of these men were anything but the ne'er-do-well whites tradition has depicted. Some were former Whigs, planters, merchants, and industrialists who wished to align with the successful regimes and to end civil conflict quickly. As time passed, however, many of the abler scalawags, finding themselves eclipsed by carpetbaggers, became disillusioned and abandoned the Republican governments. Their loss was a critical one since the whites, even at the height of reconstruction, had a majority of votes in all the southern states except Louisiana, Mississippi, and South Carolina.

The black vote was increasingly organized and manipulated by carpetbaggers who utilized the Union League clubs as centers of indoctrination and intimidation and marched blacks to the polls where they voted in blocs. Scores of men posing as General Grant appeared on horseback to lead the new citizens in the correct exercise of their rights. Amazingly enough, the calibre of officeholders during the period was not appreciably different from those before or after it. The quality of local civil service had never been high except in limited areas, and only very able blacks reached higher positions.

Charges of corruption and inefficiency contributed to ending the reconstruction experiment in the South and to decades of government retrenchment following it. Certainly the cost of government increased enormously, and frequently corruption was involved in housekeeping operations. At the time, corruption was a national, not merely a southern, phenomenon, and irregularities of a similar nature continued in the succeeding era.

Most of the increase in state expenditures was due to a growth of government services and subsidization of capital improvements. In a number of states, support was given for the first time to public education, which became an obsession with the freedman. Although travesties were present, including some states with illiterate superintendents of education, systems of permanent importance were created. Charity hospitals and other similar institutions were erected, often for the first time in the South. Thousands of miles of railroad were underwritten, the state guaranteeing bonds in return for mortgages on railroad property.

Although much watering of stock took place and the eastern financiers openly bribed legislators, railroads were built, and the related corruption was no greater than in other sections of the nation.

Perhaps the Radical governments' greatest achievements were the constitutions drafted for the southern states. Ultimately, when white disabilities were removed, they would have provided for universal male participation in government. Even after their abandonment, their appeal haunted some dreamers who envisioned a new day in the South.

The shortness of Radical control, if nothing else, would have seriously impeded southern changes. Conservatives returned to power between 1869 and 1871 in Tennessee, Virginia, North Carolina, and Georgia; in 1873–75 power was regained in Alabama, Arkansas, and Texas. Radical control lasted beyond 1875 in only four states, Mississippi, South Carolina, Louisiana, and Florida. Few permanent results could be expected from only four to five years of Radical rule.

Return of Home Rule

Radical reconstruction ended when northern public opinion became less concerned with black rights in the South and a new unity emerged among southern whites based on a desire to restore local control. As the controversy over reconstruction lengthened into years, many northerners became weary of the struggle, and the Amnesty Act of 1872 removed the political disabilities of all but a few hundred southerners. After President Johnson's retirement, a personal villain was removed, and awareness of increasing northern corruption led many liberals to believe that injustices perpetrated in the South were spreading home.

In the South many of the most conservative and law-abiding citizens were repulsed by the Ku Klux Klan, which had been formed in 1866 in Pulaski, Tennessee, and spread throughout the South as a tool to intimidate blacks, carpetbaggers, and scalawags. Its first head, General Nathan B. Forrest, formally disbanded the organization in 1869 when it began to use violence, and soon many others withdrew also. By 1872 the Klan had practically disappeared, due in no small measure to the Force Acts passed by Congress. The Force Act of 1870 levied heavy penalties for interference with voting, and that of 1871 permitted the president to suspend habeas corpus in dealing with armed movements. Under it, Grant suspended the writ in nine South Carolina counties and made hundreds of arrests.

Ironically, use of the Force Acts led many southerners who had formerly cooperated with the Radical governments but who were fearful of despotic rule and unwise federal action to join the opposition. Friction between the races increased greatly as sterner carpetbag leadership emerged, and large numbers of whites began to reevaluate their positions. Many who a few years earlier would not have cooperated with Klan-type organizations began to do so. Beginning in Mississippi in 1874 and following later in other "unredeemed" states, partisans played leading roles in the dynamic "white man's" movements which were soon successful as northern concern with black rights crumbled.

The Legacy of Reconstruction

Although Radical reconstruction ended early, formal segregation did not arise in the South until the poorer whites increased their influence in government in the 1890s. Also it was not until then that disfranchisement by race

Mississippi Ku Klux Klansmen in the disguises in which they were captured.

occurred; before that time, many blacks continued to vote in much of the South. Yet the collapse of the Radical governments brought the end of national attempts to protect black rights in the South, and the blacks, with a declining voice in politics, had no means of self-protection. Perhaps these developments should have been expected as memories of the war cooled and racism continued unabated in the North where, except for a small segment of advanced thinkers, black inferiority was as widely accepted as in the South and economic opportunities were severely limited.

The last major Radical effort to protect the blacks by law came in March, 1875, when a Civil Rights Act was enacted. The law was drafted by Senator Charles Sumner, who believed that blacks would never be secure as long as even informal segregation existed, but the law was passed after his death. It guaranteed citizens equal rights in public places, including railway trains, theatres, and hotels, and prohibited the exclusion of blacks from jury duty. However, in 1883 the Supreme Court invalidated the act on the grounds that the Fourteenth Amendment did not protect the invasion of civil rights by individuals unabetted by the states. Discrimination in social areas and by private persons was held to be constitutional. No great moral reaction greeted this decision, and the black man, legally unprotected in basic human rights, continued his decline.

Reconstruction also left a southern white political cohesiveness which had not been known before. It was true that the various third parties emerging nationally in the late nineteenth century had southern wings which often fused temporarily with local Republican groups, and except for a brief period in the 1880s, no "solid Democratic South" emerged before the early twentieth century. Yet each southern political group attempted to use the black vote, but the Democrats not only used it more successfully, they also effectively appealed to white fear of national intervention in the blacks' behalf. Regardless of other issues, divisions which might menace white control or bring a renewed reconstruction became intolerable. Ultimately, reconstruction resulted in an abandonment of the southern black and a hitherto unknown southern legacy of distrust and fear which resulted in sectional alienation. Since it neither brought fundamental reforms in the southern black's status nor reunited the great majority of both sections spiritually, it was as tragic as the war itself.

The Business Mentality and Social Darwinism

Failure to channel reconstruction adequately was only one shortcoming of the Grant administration which also failed to diagnose the ills of the nation's rapidly industrializing society and propose legislation to deal with them. A portion of Grant's incapacity came from his novice status as a politician, a disadvantage which could have been overcome by adequate advice, but initially he chose to forego this necessity. In selecting his cabinet, the president did not consult leading Republican politicians, and, except for Secretary of State Hamilton Fish, it was composed of nonentities or unqualified men. Alexander T. Stewart, the New York merchant prince and one of the nation's largest importers, was nominated for secretary of the Treasury, but, fortunately, he was prohibited from serving by a law excluding men engaged in merchandising from the post. Once his administration was established, Grant obtained advice from a kitchen cabinet composed mainly of Radical politicians, such as Senators Roscoe Conkling of New York and Oliver P. Morton of Indiana, whose views were neither broadminded nor widely representative.

In choosing advisers and formulating policy, Grant was influenced by individuals' wealth, whose accumulation he equated with success. He was not alone in this approach, which reflected the gross materialism of the postwar period, well portrayed by Mark Twain and Charles Dudley Warner in *The Gilded Age,* a novel published in 1873.

Neither Grant nor his contemporaries realized the consequences of unbridled competition and lavish exploitation of the nation's natural resources. Although most of them probably never heard of the term, they were advocates of Social Darwinism, an application to society of Charles Darwin's concept of the survival of the fittest. The most effective American exponent of the theory was William Graham Sumner, who in 1872 at the age of thirty-two began a long career as Yale University's first professor of political and social science. Sumner vigorously opposed government regulation, social legislation, and trade unions, contending that unregulated competition always results in the destruction of the less efficient and dominance of the abler forces in society.

Neither Sumner nor less scholarly advocates of laissez faire adequately assessed the contemporary situation. Without government controls, men concerned only with acquiring wealth unfairly rigged the game, competition was eliminated, and corruption became a fine art.

As president, Grant offered little executive leadership, allowing Congress to formulate policy while he merely executed the laws. Without pressure from above, the war-levied income tax was repealed, and the tariff, which remained at an average rate of 47 percent in 1869, was reduced by 10 percent in 1872 but continued to be very high. Though provision was made for a civil service commission, no money was appropriated for its use. Realizing the unwholesomeness of conditions, those people sensitive to public need deplored the president's abandonment of responsibility but with little effect.

Achievements in Foreign Affairs

Concern with foreign affairs was far from a dominant interest with Grant, but the administration's major success came in this field. Under President Johnson's leadership, Secretary of State William H. Seward had inaugurated an expansionist policy which culminated in the purchase, attended by much criticism, of Alaska from Russia for $7,200,000 in 1867. Seward also urged the annexation of Hawaii and negotiated a treaty for the purchase of the Danish West Indies, the modern Virgin Islands. Although a plebiscite demonstrated

that the citizens of the Danish West Indies wished annexation, the U.S. Senate rejected the treaty.

Grant continued Seward's expansionist policies by proposing the annexation of Santo Domingo which he correctly believed would have strategic value for the United States, although he was partially influenced in reaching his decision by speculators who stood to gain from annexation. Senator Charles Sumner, chairman of the powerful Senate Committee on Foreign Relations, was primarily responsible for the treaty's defeat, and, in revenge, Grant obtained Sumner's removal as committee chairman in March, 1871.

In contrast to this defeat, the able Secretary of State Fish successfully resolved disputes with Spain and Great Britain. Difficulties with Spain emerged in the wake of the civil war which raged in Spanish Cuba for a decade after 1868. In 1873 the *Virginius,* which was trading with the rebels and illegally flying the American flag, was captured by the Spanish who shot fifty-three members of its crew, some of whom were Americans, for piracy. Secretary Fish, who had kept Grant from recognizing the rebels, averted war by demanding and getting an $80,000 indemnity for the heirs of the executed Americans.

An even greater triumph came in the resolution of the Alabama Claims, which arose from damages inflicted on U.S. commerce by the eleven British-built Confederate cruisers. President Johnson contended that 100,000 tons of U.S. merchant shipping had been lost to the cruisers and negotiated the Johnson-Clarendon Convention in 1869 providing British payment for the losses. The Senate, which rejected the settlement as inadequate, was greatly influenced by the arguments of Senator Sumner who held British aid had extended the war two years and that Britain owed the United States an indemnity of over $2 billion. He knew Britain would not pay such a sum and obviously was attempting to gain Canada as compensation.

Under Grant, new negotiations with Great Britain were begun by Secretary Fish, whose experience as a congressman, governor, and commissioner for the relief of prisoners had perfected his naturally tactful disposition. In May, 1871, the British, who were fearful of U.S. support of Irish rebels, agreed to the Treaty of Washington which provided for the submission of all differences to arbitration including disputes over the Canadian fisheries, the boundary between Vancouver Island and the mainland, and the Alabama Claims. For abandoning certain rights, in 1877 a mixed commission on the fisheries question meeting at Halifax awarded Great Britain $5.5 million which the United States paid. The German emperor arbitrated the boundary dispute recognizing the United States claim to the San Juan Islands. The Alabama Claims were settled in Geneva in 1872 by an international tribunal composed of representatives from Brazil, Italy, and Switzerland as well as those from Britain and the United States. This board refused Sumner's demands for indirect damages but awarded the United States $15.5 million for specific losses since the British failed to exercise proper diligence in allowing the cruisers to escape.

The settlement of the Alabama Claims provided an excellent example of arbitration and greatly improved Anglo-American relations. It removed one of the most bitter issues in American politics and enabled the Grant administration to claim one resounding victory.

Corruption in the Administration

Domestic problems, unlike foreign affairs, proved the bane of Grant's years in office. Though personally honest and never know-ingly involved in direct corruption, Grant allowed his administrations to become infected with the graft commonplace at the time. Symptomatic of general conditions were the activities of the Democratic leader of New York's Tammany Hall, "Boss" William Marcy Tweed who, through the use of a Board of Audit, milked the city of sums estimated at $75 million to $200 million. His downfall came as the result of an investigation by a New York Democratic State Committee headed by Samuel J. Tilden, who also helped in his prosecution and was aided by the superb cartoons of Thomas Nast appearing in *Harper's Weekly.* From 1869 to 1872 Nast produced a series of remarkable illustrations that awakened the

"Boss" William M. Tweed

HARPER'S WEEKLY.
A JOURNAL OF CIVILIZATION

Vol. XX.—No. 1018.]   NEW YORK, SATURDAY, JULY 1, 1876.   [WITH A SUPPLEMENT. PRICE TEN CENTS.

Entered according to Act of Congress, in the Year 1876, by Harper & Brothers, in the Office of the Librarian of Congress, at Washington.

POLITICAL "CAPITAL"

IT HAS BLOWN OVER

WANTED REFORMERS OF THE TAMMANY CLASS.

WANTED REFORMERS EDUCATED IN THE TAMMANY HALL SCHOOL OF REFORM.

REFORMED THIEVES WANTED TO TAKE CARE OF THE PEOPLES MONEY.

REWARD AND NO QUESTIONS ASKED.

ANYBODY WHO WILL BRING A FEW PLUNDERERS OF THE STATE TO JUSTICE WILL BE REWARDED BY THE HIGHEST OFFICES IN THE GIFT OF THE PEOPLE

O. D. LORD CONVICTED. ONE OF THE CANAL RING.

TAMMANY HALL SCHOOL OF REFORM. SCHOLARS WANTED FOR REFORMERS

REWARD TO THOSE THAT H HAVE ASSOCIATED WITH THIEVES, AND GIVE STATE EVIDENCE.

REWARD TO ALL PUBLIC THIEVES WHO HAVE ENOUGH AND CAN STOP OTHERS FROM CHEATING AND STEALING. THEY WILL BE REWARDED BY HONORABLE POSITIONS AND FAT OFFICES.

IT TAKES A THIEF OR ONE WHO HAS ASSOCIATED WITH THIEVES TO CATCH A THIEF.

TWEED-LE-DEE AND TILDEN-DUM Reform Tweed: *"If all the people want is to have somebody arrested, I'll have you plunderers convicted. You will be allowed to escape; nobody will be hurt; and then Tilden will go to the White House, and I to Albany as Governor."*

semiliterate public to the corruption of the Tammany organization, which he depicted as a greedy tiger preying on unsuspecting citizens. Although Tweed was sent to prison in 1872, no such drastic fate came to the unholy alliance of Daniel Drew, Jim Fisk, and Jay Gould, who used wholesale bribery and stock watering to filch millions from the Erie Railroad and prevented its stockholders from receiving a dividend until World War I.

Fisk and Gould used their contacts with Grant, partially through his brother-in-law, Abel R. Corbin, to engineer the "Black Friday" episode of September 24, 1869. They planned to corner the gold market by persuading the government to withhold sales and, by buying low and selling high, schemed to make a tremendous profit. The president, by instructing the secretary of the Treasury not to recall U.S. bonds and redeem them in gold, cooperated temporarily in the belief this action would increase the price of farm products sold to Europe. When gold skyrocketed creating a Wall Street panic on "Black Friday," the conspiracy was broken by the Treasury releasing $4 million in gold.

In September, 1872, another scandal surfaced when the public learned that Vice-President Schuyler Colfax, the Republican vice-presidential candidate Henry Wilson, Representative James A. Garfield, and other prominent congressmen had received shares of Crédit Mobilier stock, apparently to influence their votes. The Crédit Mobilier, a dummy company established by promoters of the Union Pacific Railroad to build the line, charged exorbitant prices for its services and in some years paid dividends of over 300 percent. When Congress investigated, only two of its members, one of whom was Oakes Ames, the purveyor of the stock, were censured for their conduct.

Knowledge of the most serious scandals directly involving members of the administration came only in Grant's second term, and six members of his official family, including five cabinet members and his personal secretary, were implicated. Secretary of War William W. Belknap was impeached by the House for receiving bribes to grant Indian trading post commissions in the West and was saved from removal by his resignation. The investigation also revealed that Grant's brother, Orvil, had received trading rights at four Indian posts, and, when General George A. Custer testified against him, he was relieved of his command. Secretary of the Treasury W. A. Richardson

defrauded the government of large sums by refusing to collect taxes in order that private contractors, who retained a portion of their collection, could be used. Richardson's honest successor, Benjamin H. Bristow, uncovered a "Whiskey Ring" in which a network existed to defraud the government of revenue from distillers. Among the 238 indicted was General Orville E. Babcock, Grant's secretary, to whom the president furnished a deposition which aided in his acquittal.

In a number of scandals, Grant was victimized by his friends, but he left himself vulnerable when he did not righteously renounce them. At best, he could be charged with ineptitude and stupidity in choosing associates whose conduct lowered the tone of public life and the confidence of the people in government.

Congress also came in for intense criticism when in 1873 it passed the "Salary Grab Act" which increased the salaries of congressmen and other government officials from $5,000 to $7,500 a year with the increase retroactive for two years. The salary of the president was doubled from $25,000 to $50,000. Public awareness of the grab act came at a time when the nation was aroused over the Crédit Mobilier scandal, and many were especially incensed over the retroactive lump sum payment of $5,000. As a result, Congress repealed all increases in January, 1874, except those for the president and Supreme Court justices.

The Liberal Republican Revolt

A disenchantment with the power politics of the Grant administration led to the revolt of the Liberal Republicans in 1872. As they surveyed the political scene, a number of Republicans, including many former Radicals, concluded that corruption and unrepresentative government in the South not only were unworthy of America but also spawned similar conditions in the North. Uniting behind a common program, they advocated a milder southern policy, reform of the civil service to bring governmental efficiency, and a downward revision of the tariff. While not state's righters, many Liberal Republicans were frightened by the centralizing effect of the war amendments and believed the nation's future demanded a concern with present issues, not a "waving of the bloody shirt" as a diversion.

The origin of the Liberal Republican movement dated from Senator Charles Sumner's break with Grant over Santo Domingo and the victory of the insurgents under Carl Schurz's leadership in Missouri's gubernatorial election of 1870. Supporting the movement were many of the morally sensitive leaders of the party, such as Charles Francis Adams, the journalist E. L. Godkin, Lincoln's able Navy Secretary Gideon Welles, and Schurz, who had played a vital role in converting antislavery Germans to Republicanism.

At the Liberal Republican convention in May, 1872, the erratic protectionist, Horace Greeley, was nominated for president and Missouri's B. Gratz Brown nominated for vice-president. In addition to civil service reform, the platform advocated use of the public domain by actual settlers only but was silent on the tariff. The regular Democratic convention swallowed its pride and nominated Greeley and Brown also, despite Greeley's high tariff views and his long, prominent role as a Republican partisan. Grant, of course, was renominated by the Republicans.

The eccentric, vacillating Greeley was an absurd candidate who did not convey the intense fervor of the Liberal Republicans and was repulsive to many Democrats. In the election, he carried only six southern states with 66 electoral votes to Grant's 286. Brokenhearted,

he died on November 29, 1872. Yet the Liberal Republican vote weakened the Republican party, and two years afterwards, in 1874, the Democrats won control of the House of Representatives.

The Depression of 1873

One reason for the Democratic resurgence was the depression of 1873 whose advent startled the nation. On September 18, 1872, Jay Cooke and Company failed. This powerful banking house, virtually without profit to itself, had served as the government's agent for floating bonds during the Civil War. Its stability was popularly unquestioned, but overinvestment in the Northern Pacific Railroad led to its collapse, followed by a general fall of security prices, and a panic so intense that September 19 was referred to as another "Black Friday," a prelude to a sharp, five-year depression. Speculation was a factor, but overinvestment in railroads and industry stimulated by easy credit was more basic. A reduction in European demands for agricultural products also was of significance.

During the depression at least three million of the nation's thirty-six million people were unemployed, thousands of companies failed, and commodity prices fell so low that many farmers were forced into tenancy and were attracted to reform movements. Despair and confusion engulfed millions before conditions began to improve.

As debtor America groped for a solution to its problems, many of the farmers of the West and South came to advocate an increase in the amount of money in circulation as a means of promoting inflation which promised to lessen the burden of debt and raise prices. On the other hand, many businessmen wanted a return to the single gold dollar, which they believed offered the only sound medium of exchange. Under these contrary pressures, the nation's political leaders failed to see the correlation between the monetary issue and economic development, and their legislation was dictated by the exigencies and pressures of the time.

In 1873, in a period when gold was underpriced compared with silver, Congress omitted provision in the Coinage Act for the continued minting of silver dollars. At the time, only gold dollars were circulating, and no protest was raised. Soon, however, the economic relation of the two metals reversed, and the inflation advocates as well as the silver producers, decrying silver demonetization as "the Crime of 1873," initiated a crusade for reversal of the action, but with little effect.

In the 1870s, however, the greatest monetary controversy centered on the status of greenbacks. Some of this war-issued paper had been retired but, after a slump in 1867, a portion was restored. In the First Legal Tender Case in 1870, a divided U.S. Supreme Court invalidated wartime laws which made greenbacks legal tender for payment of contracts negotiated before the laws' passage, but the next year, after President Grant appointed two new justices, the decision was reversed.

Resumption Act of 1875

After the depression of 1873 struck, the Treasury increased the quantity of greenbacks in circulation by $26 million, but when Congress in 1874 attempted to raise the amount to $400 million, Grant vetoed the bill. In both 1869 and 1874, the president recommended resumption of specie payments for greenbacks, and, spurred by the business community, Congress passed a Resumption Act in January, 1875, before the newly elected Democratic House came

to power. To conciliate the South and West (as well as to give the Treasury time to accumulate reserves), exchange of all legal tender paper at par for gold was delayed until January 1, 1879. In a concession to the inflationists, the number of national banks was enlarged, and, due to an increase in federal bond sales to accumulate gold, so were the number of banknotes. After an abortive effort to reduce the greenbacks in circulation to $300 million, the administration accepted a congressional act setting the amount at the quantity in circulation, $346,681,000. This number has remained constant, although the number of dollars in other currency has greatly fluctuated.

The business community generally was pleased with the compromise legislation and ascribed much of the nation's returning prosperity to it. The inflationists were not happy, however, and in 1876 a National Greenback convention, meeting in Indianapolis, nominated the pioneer ironmaker and founder of the Cooper Union, Peter Cooper, for president. Although Cooper received only 81,737 votes, two years later his supporters, augmented by laborers disgusted by reverses of the 1870s, created the Greenback Labor party. Eight hundred delegates from twenty-eight states attended its 1878 convention in Toledo, which, in addition to denouncing resumption, urged free coinage of silver, restrictions on the hours of labor, and a limitation of Chinese immigration. The party's candidates received over a million votes in 1878, and fourteen of its members were elected to Congress. Although in 1880 the party liberalized its platform to include women's suffrage, federal regulation of interstate commerce, and a graduated income tax, its high-water mark had passed. Returning prosperity and concern with other forms of inflation resulted in its 1880 presidential candidate, James B. Weaver, receiving only 308,578 votes, and its 1884 candidate, General Benjamin F. Butler, 175,370.

The Disputed Election of 1876

Discontent with the depression and the corruption of the Grant administration was so great that the president withdrew as a candidate for a third term, a serious disappointment to his ardent supporters, known as "Stalwarts," led by New York's Senator Roscoe Conkling. The balance of power in the Republican convention swung to the "Half-Breeds," self-confessed reformers who looked to Senator James G. Blaine for leadership. Blaine would have received the presidential nomination had he not recently been exposed as profiting from bond sales of the Little Rock and Fort Smith Railroad, a line which had received a federal land grant with his support. Therefore, on the seventh ballot the convention nominated another Half-Breed, Rutherford B. Hayes, a former Union general and three-time governor of Ohio, whose record was unquestionable. William A. Wheeler of New York was chosen as his running mate.

The Democrats, meeting shortly after the Republicans, chose Governor Samuel J. Tilden of New York, a sixty-two-year-old conservative corporation lawyer, as their presidential nominee. Tilden, as chairman of the Democratic State Committee, had defeated the Tweed Ring and aided in jailing its leading members, while as governor his actions resulted in tax reform and shattering of "the Canal Ring" corruptionists in state government. However, he had participated in rigging of the stock market and used court orders to confiscate James Parton's exposé of his activities in a book entitled *Manual for the Instruction of "Rings," Railroad and Political.* To counterbalance the hard-money Tilden, the inflationist Thomas A. Hendricks of Indiana was nominated for vice-president.

Spurred for the first time in twenty years by hopes of victory, the Democrats waged a spir-

Rutherford B. Hayes

ited campaign emphasizing Republican shortcomings, while their opponents revived the issue of the war and challenged Tilden's honesty. The election returns seemed to indicate Tilden had won; he had a 250,000 popular vote majority and had carried New York, New Jersey, Rhode Island, Connecticut, Indiana, Missouri, and the non-Radical South. It soon became apparent, however, that twenty electoral votes could be challenged, nineteen in three southern states which still had Republican governments, and if all these votes went to Hayes, he could win.

A crisis occurred when dual returns were submitted from Radical Louisiana, Florida, and South Carolina. No provision existed for settling disputed returns, as the Constitution provided only for their tabulation by a joint session of Congress. Since the vice-president was a Republican and the house speaker a Democrat, an impasse seemed inevitable. To avert this, in late January 1877, Congress established a fifteen-man Electoral Commission composed of five senators, five representatives, and five associate justices of the Supreme Court who were divided politically into seven Democrats, seven Republicans, and an independent, Justice David Davis. At the last minute Davis, who was elected to the Senate by the Illinois legislature, was forced to withdraw. No other independent justice was available, and Davis' replacement, the moderate Republican Justice Joseph P. Bradley, was pressured into voting with his fellow party members. By a strictly partisan eight-to-seven vote, all three southern states' electoral votes were declared to be Republican.

Apparently Republican officials in the three states threw out large numbers of Democratic votes to achieve this result, but this action was partially justified by the fact that the Democrats had frightened many blacks from the polls. In a genuinely free election, Hayes would probably have carried Louisiana and South Carolina, but due to the strength of the white man's movement and the smaller number of blacks in Florida, Tilden would likely have carried that state and the election. News of what many Democrats considered the grossest fraud stirred the country as did northern Democratic threats of a filibuster to prevent the vote count and the inauguration. Even more menacingly, rumors circulated that Democrats would converge on Washington and use force to prevent an injustice being perpetrated.

The Compromise of 1877

Serious national disruption was averted in 1877 when southern Democratic leaders agreed to compromise with the Republicans. Negotia-tions between them had been underway for some time before the report of the Electoral Commission and were facilitated by southern recognition that a Republican president could remove all federal troops without the difficulty a Democrat would encounter. Many of the southern Democratic leaders were also former Whigs, a number of whom had participated in Radical governments in the South. As they saw the effects of federal expenditures for internal improvements in the North, they were motivated by a desire to obtain similar benefits for their own enterprises and their own sections as well as the privilege of again holding federal office.

Through a series of informal contacts made with Hayes' approval, Republican leaders pledged to give the southerners what they wished including a cabinet position. In return, it was anticipated that southern Democrats would offer no objection to Hayes' election and would support a Republican, James A. Garfield, for speaker of the House. In working out the compromise, a great deal of aid was received from the powerful forces behind Thomas A. Scott, president of the Pennsylvania Railroad which hoped to obtain government funds for building the Texas and Pacific Railroad. Eventually, when doubts arose regarding commitment to the agreements, the Wormsley Hotel Conference of southern and Republican leaders was held, and the compromise was sustained.

As a result of the Compromise of 1877, Hayes assumed the presidency without difficulty, northern Democratic eruption being contained by southern coolness. Troops were removed from Florida before the inauguration, and Hayes recalled those in Louisiana and South Carolina after becoming president. He also appointed a former Confederate general, Senator David M. Key of Tennessee, as postmaster general and a number of other Democrats to lesser positions in the South.

Other aspects of the bargain were not fulfilled, however. Southern Democrats did not support Garfield for speaker, and, despite strong support from Hayes, the bill subsidizing the Texas and Pacific Railroad failed. Republican leaders frowned on the appointment of Democrats to office in the South and blocked the effort to do this to any degree until the era of Theodore Roosevelt. However, substantial federal monies were made available for river and harbor improvements, including opening the thirty-six-mile ship channel through Mobile Bay to the Gulf.

The Compromise of 1877 ended all federal efforts to reconstruct the South and established a truce between the sections which lasted longer than any previous one. It turned the fate of the freedmen over to native, white southerners whose fears and antagonisms had been aroused by a decade of false starts, threats, unfulfilled promises, and intimidation. Although it brought peace and a great degree of sectional harmony to the nation, it did so at a sacrifice of black rights and the economic interests of the more plebeian whites whose union with western agrarians had been impeded by a conservative coalition of former southern Whigs and eastern Republicans.

Selected Bibliography

The period is surveyed in Robert H. Jones, *Disrupted Decades, The Civil War and Reconstruction Years* (1972), and in James G. Randall and David Donald, *The Civil War and Reconstruction* (rev. ed., 1969). Excellent accounts of Reconstruction incorporating the latest syntheses are found in Kenneth M. Stampp, *The Era of Reconstruction, 1865–1877** (1965); John Hope Franklin, *Reconstruction: After the Civil War** (1961); David Donald, *The Politics of Reconstruction, 1863–1877** (1965); and Rembert W. Patrick, *The Reconstruction of the Nation** (1967). For a contrast in views on Radicalism and the role of the blacks see W. E. B. DuBois, *Black Reconstruction in America, 1860–1880** (1969), and E. M. Coulter, *The South During Reconstruction, 1865–1877** (1965).

Lincoln's Plan of Reconstruction* (1967) is treated in a work by William B. Hesseltine. George R. Bentley, *History of the Freedman's Bureau* (repr. of 1955 ed., 1970), contends it maneuvered blacks politically, but a different view emerges from William S. McFeeley, *Yankee Stepfather: General O. O. Howard and the Freedmen** (1970). Joseph B. James, *The Framing of the Fourteenth Amendment** (1965), shows the Radical use of it.

Eric L. McKitrick, *Andrew Johnson and Reconstruction** (1960); William R. Brock, *An American Crisis: Congress and Reconstruction, 1865–1867** (1963); and LaWanda and John H. Cox, *Politics, Principle, and Prejudice, 1865–1866** (1969), are critical of President Johnson. These works revise the earlier views of George F. Milton, *The Age of Hate: Andrew Johnson and the Radicals* (repr. of 1930 ed., 1965), and Howard K. Beale, *The Critical Years, A Study of Andrew Johnson and Reconstruction* (1958).

Black conditions in both the North and South are treated in C. Vann Woodward, *The Strange Career of Jim Crow** (2d rev. ed., 1966); Paul Lewinson, *Race, Class and Party* (repr. of 1932 ed., 1963); James M. McPherson, *The Struggle for Equality: Abolitionists and the Negro in the Civil War and Reconstruction** (1964); Robert Cruden, *The Negro in Reconstruction** (1969); and Gerald Sorin, *Abolitionism: A New Perspective** (1972). Peter Kolchin, *First Freedom: The Responses of Alabama's Blacks to Emancipation and Reconstruction* (1972), presents detailed accounts of the black struggle for independence in one state. Otis A. Singletary deals with *Negro Militia and Reconstruction** (1957). The earlier primacy ascribed by Beale and others to economics as a motivation for Radical Reconstruction is challenged by many authors including Robert Sharkey, *Money, Class and Party, An Economic Study of Civil War and Reconstruction** (1959).

Leonard D. White, *The Republican Era, 1869–1901; A Study in Administrative History** (1958), provides an understanding of Grant's self-chosen role as president. William B. Hesseltine, *Ulysses S. Grant,*

---

*Available in paperback

Politician (1957), is a full biography but useful insights may be obtained from Bruce Catton, *U.S. Grant and the American Military Tradition** (1954). The crass materialism of the times is seen in Matthew Josephson, *The Politicos, 1865–1896** (1938); Alexander B. Callow, Jr., *The Tweed Ring** (1966); and Allan Nevins, *Hamilton Fish: The Inner History of the Grant Administration** (2 vols., 1957). For additional coverage of foreign relations see Dexter Perkins, *The Monroe Doctrine, 1867–1907* (1937), and Goldwin A. Smith, *The Treaty of Washington, 1871, A Study in Imperial History* (repr. of 1941 ed., 1971). The important questions of money, finance, and depression are treated in Irwin Unger, *The Greenback Era: A Social and Political History of American Finance, 1865–1879** (1964), and Walter T. Nugent, *Money and American Society, 1865–1880* (1968). Much information on the Liberal Republican movement is in Glyndon G. Van Deusen, *Horace Greeley, Nineteenth-Century Crusader** (1953).

The return of the South is admirably presented in C. Vann Woodward, *Origins of the New South, 1877–1913** (1971), and Paul H. Buck, *The Road to Reunion, 1865–1900** (1937); the aftermath of the 1876 elections is found in Woodward, *Reunion and Reaction: The Compromise of 1877 and the End of Reconstruction** (1966).

Events in
Indian Life

1851	Fort Laramie Treaty
1864	Chivington's Massacre
1876	Battle of the Little Big Horn
1881	Publication of *A Century of Dishonor*
1884	Coercion begun to destroy tribal customs
1886	Surrender of Geronimo
1887	Dawes Act
1890	Oklahoma Territory created

Completion of Major
Transcontinental Railroads

1869	Union Pacific and Central Pacific
1883	Sante Fe Northern Pacific
1884	Southern Pacific
1893	Great Northern

Milestones in the
New South

1871	Birmingham founded
1890	Exclusion of black voters initiated by Mississippi
1895	Washington's "Atlanta Compromise" Address
1896	*Plessy* v. *Ferguson* decision
1902	Agitation begun for control of southern child labor
1907	Tennessee Coal Iron and Railroad Company absorbed by United States Steel
1910	South revealed to have a majority of nation's cotton spindles

14

The West and the South in the Gilded Age

Long-Range Developments

For Economics and Corporate Enterprise

The discovery and mining of large quantities of silver resulted in the crusade for the free coinage of silver in the 1890s.

The building of the transcontinental railroads enormously stimulated business growth and the American economy.

Railroad pressure to obtain federal subsidies served as a training ground for later governmental lobbying.

For the Westward Movement, Nationalism, and Expansion

The closing of the American frontier contributed to increased public interest in foreign affairs.

For Civil Liberties, Freedom, and Reform

Humanitarian attempts to apply white justice to the Indian resulted in a further degradation of Indian life, a condition reversed to a degree only in the 1930s.

The failure of the United States government to enforce the *Plessy* v. *Ferguson* requirement of "equal" facilities contributed to much social discontent and promoted the end of segregation.

Failure of whites to apply the "Atlanta Compromise" as Washington envisioned it resulted in increasing black repression until World War II.

The Farmers' Alliance movements and the Populist party projected many reforms that were achieved in the decades following their demise.

Extermination of the Indian

While reconstruction absorbed the interest of much of the nation, economic and social developments of great significance were initiated. One of these was the opening of large portions of the South and West to white settlement, which was completed by the late nineteenth century. In this process no development was more important than the subjugation of the Indian. By 1860 the remnants of the civilized tribes of the Southeast were living on Oklahoma reservations, but some 250,000 primarily nomadic tribesmen roamed the Great Plains from Texas to Canada and from central Kansas and Nebraska to the Rockies. They were among the world's finest horsemen, and most of these tribes depended on the region's millions of buffalo to sustain every aspect of life. This animal dominated their religion, their dances, their ornaments, and all their art forms.

In early contacts with the whites, including the 1840 wagon trains to California and Ore-gon, the Indians were generally friendly, but their attitude soon changed as their life style and even their existence was threatened by the increasing intrusion of whites. With the white man came susceptibility to alcohol and strange diseases, as well as the use of guns which the Indians found convenient, even though many warriors were able to deliver several arrows while a rifle was fired once. In 1851 the federal government, responding to public pressure, opened much of the West by convening a meeting near Fort Laramie of many tribal representatives. Each tribe, in return for white promises not to violate its lands, agreed in the Fort Laramie Treaty to limit its area of movement. However, the whites did not understand the Indian life style and were unwilling to allow large areas of land to remain in their hands. The only way they would tolerate the Indian was for him to adopt white ways and become a farmer, a conversion many Indians found impossible to make. Moreover, the notoriously corrupt Indian agents of the Department of the

Hunting the buffalo.

Interior, who often pillaged more food and clothing than they distributed to the Indian, encouraged white violation of the treaty, which occurred increasingly as settlers moved into western Kansas and Nebraska and rushed into the Colorado country to seek gold in 1859. In this case and innumerable others, the unsuspecting Indians were victimized by the whites who took advantage of their simple approach to life and unfamiliarity with legal niceties. Even then, the whites frequently failed to comply with most pro-white treaties, an action that seldom encountered opposition from even ethically sensitive individuals, most of whom regarded the destruction of the tribes as essential for progress.

White aggression brought Indian rebellion during the Civil War when troops could not be spared for the frontier, and white overreaction at times produced outrageous occurrences. Though flying the U.S. flag as a sign of peace, 450 Cheyenne were massacred by Colonel John M. Chivington at Sand Creek, Colorado, in November, 1864. Such vicious actions forced the complete surrender of the Cheyenne, Arapaho, and Comanche, who were then restricted to smaller areas. After the Indians were falsely accused of giving aid to the Confederacy, much of the civilized tribes' lands in the western portion of Indian Territory (later Oklahoma) was confiscated and used as reservations for southwestern Indians.

At the end of the Civil War an intense conflict erupted with the Sioux, the largest of the northern tribes, when in 1865 the government began to build a road along the Bozeman Trail from Cheyenne westward through the foothills of the Big Horn Mountains to the mouth of the Rosebud River in Montana Territory. This road traversed and impaired one of the Sioux's favorite hunting grounds but satisfied the miners' urgent demands for better transportation to Montana. In December, 1866, infuriated by the white invasion, Chief Red Cloud's warriors ambushed and killed eighty-

The Sioux chief, Sitting Bull.

two soldiers commanded by Captain W. J. Fetterman, who had disobeyed orders and moved aggressively against the Indians. The massacre was followed by Indian besiegement of the forts along the Bozeman Trial, and in 1868 the government agreed to abandon the road through the Indian country along with its attendant forts, one of a few white retreats before Indian aggression. But the pressure of the increasing number of whites grew and persuaded the Indians in 1868 at the Ft. Laramie council to accept confinement on reservations in the Black Hills region of Dakota territory in return for government payments and promises. Earlier, the southwestern Indians, meeting at Medicine Lodge Creek in 1867, agreed to confinement on reservations in the Indian Territory for the same reasons. In 1868 government agents also received agreements from the tribes in the Rocky Mountain country to move to reservations.

The new government policy forced abandonment of the traditional Indian way of life and ultimately succeeded because of the extinction of the buffalo on which the plains Indians had depended for most of life's necessities. Its removal, which proved to be an engaging sport for whites, left the starving Indians no alternative but to go to reservations. Thousands of buffalo were killed only for thrills, but, after 1871, their hides were marketed commercially, and by 1880 a large portion of the animals had been destroyed.

The Indians did not take docilely to the destruction of the buffalo nor the efforts made to convert Indians into second-class whites. Between 1868 and 1875 innumerable Indian violations of government policy occurred, and hundreds of pitched battles were fought between U.S. Army regulars and the constantly weakening tribesmen. In 1875, when subjugation seemed almost complete, the Sioux were outraged when the government gave permission for thousands of gold seekers to violate their Black Hills' reservation. In 1876, after they were joined in revolt by other northern tribes, three army units were sent against them. A segment of one of these, led by the flamboyant General George A. Custer, violated orders to block a retreat route and attacked an Indian force almost ten times its size. As a result, all 264 men were massacred at the Little Big Horn on June 25, 1876. The white reaction was intense, and with the coming of fall, the hard-pressed Indians surrendered and were forced back on the reservation. Chief Sitting Bull and some warriors escaped to Canada but returned in 1881. Generally the plains fighting was over, though the Apaches in the Southwest did not give up until 1886, when Chief Geronimo surrendered. As a result of their defeat, the Indians were reduced to a small portion of their previous numbers, their proud civilization was overshadowed, and they became objects of contempt and charity. On the reservations the Indians again found that the promises made to them were not carried out. Often the land they received bore little resemblance to that promised them with much of it being unfit for cultivation, while the Indian agents and the army's treachery continued unabated.

George A. Custer, center, in the Black Hills, 1874.

Popular Reaction

As the whites gained control of the West, humanitarians arose who deplored Indian treatment, and their efforts led to a change in government policy. Congress became aware of corruption in the Department of the Interior's Indian program and the inability of the independent Board of Indian Commissioners, established in 1869, to alter conditions. Under its tutelage, Congress accepted the belief that the Indians would become farmers and lose their tribal identity. In 1871 the government abandoned the custom of making treaties with the

Geronimo, the last Apache chief.

tribes, thus ending the policy of treating them as domestic nations, a procedure which had been validated by John Marshall's decision in *Cherokee Nation* v. *Georgia* and by several subsequent decisions.

The public owed some of its awakened consciousness of Indian mistreatment to the writings of Helen Hunt Jackson, daughter of an Amherst College professor, whose marriages to an army officer and a Colorado banker exposed her to Indian life. In addition to numerous other writings, she published *A Century of Dishonor* in 1881, which graphically depicted Indian mistreatment. This was followed in 1884 by *Ramona,* a novel which presented a romantic defense of Indian character and was written after Miss Jackson had served as a special commissioner investigating the Mission Indians in California.

The revised attitude toward the red man led to the passage of the Dawes Act in 1887, which, though enacted with the best of intentions, was disastrous in its results. Under it,

heads of Indian families received the use, under government trusteeship, of 160 acres of land, single adults and orphans 80 acres, and dependent children 40 acres. At the end of twenty-five years they received complete ownership of the land with the right to dispose of it as they pleased. Unfortunately, many Indians were induced to lease their lands at ridiculously low prices, and in 1906 the Burke Act gave the Secretary of the Interior authority to lessen the trusteeship period. Participants in the government program were granted citizenship, but the economic basis for communal living was removed. Full citizenship was not conferred on all Indians until 1924, and it was not until 1934, at a time when the nation began to concern itself with the wrongs of many groups, that the government confessed its error and began a successful effort to restore tribal life and lands.

Meanwhile the five civilized tribes, whose members had obtained full citizenship in 1901, had fared somewhat better. Beginning in 1889 they sold large portions of their lands to the federal government and great rushes to Oklahoma occurred periodically until 1895 as those lands were opened. The white Oklahoma Territory, carved from Indian holdings in the Indian Territory, was created in 1890 and had grown to 722,441 settlers by the time statehood was attained in 1907. Concurrently, the Indian Territory achieved a population of 691,-736 and sought unsuccessfully to be admitted to the Union as the State of Sequoyah. The Indian Territory was given half the delegates to the Oklahoma constitutional convention, a tribute to its adaptation to white ways and participation in the social and economic life of the area. Development of public and private schools, some of which were modeled after the famous Indian boarding school at Carlisle, Pennsylvania, were of great aid in attaining this success. Few other Indians had such a happy experience as those of Oklahoma, however. After 1884 coercion was used to destroy Indian religious practices and tribal customs. Under these conditions the Indians' lot worsened and their numbers declined. The Indian was not prepared to become a small, subsistent farmer and to function as an individual apart from the tribe.

The Mining Frontier

In addition to the availability of lands formerly held by Indians, the various gold and silver rushes that occurred periodically from the late 1850s to the 1870s were among the most propulsive forces leading to settlement of the West. Commercial companies had replaced the solitary prospector in California before William Green Russell, a Georgian who had prospected in California, discovered gold in the Colorado country in 1858. When news of this event reached Missouri in 1859, 50,000 men headed to the Pike's Peak region. Though some discoveries were made, most of the precious metals in the area were entombed in lodes or veins in the mountains and were only discovered and exploited later with the development of quartz mining, an expensive process in which machinery was used to bring a portion of the vein to the surface where by treatment the gold was removed from the minerals which encased it. Despite the failure of most prospectors to strike it rich, many remained as settlers. They organized and maintained an independent government before the U.S. established the Colorado Territory in 1861, but the great gold discoveries in Colorado came only after its admission to statehood in 1876.

Meanwhile a rush to the Nevada area, across the Sierras from the California fields, began in 1859 when two Irishmen, Patrick McLaughlin and Peter O'Riley, accidentally discovered silver. Thousands of Californians rushed to the Virginia City region where Henry Comstock had finagled his way into a partnership with McLaughlin and O'Riley. The three sold their interests to commercial miners who in 1873 discovered the Big Bonanza which, by extensive tunneling and deep mining of the quartz-enveloped vein, proved to be the world's richest discovery. By 1880 the Comstock Lode had yielded over $300 million, and Virginia City's millionaires had attained international notoriety. Although most of the capital they produced was exported to California, the rush to Nevada resulted in its being swept into the Union in the fall of 1864 to aid in Lincoln's reelection.

From the early 1860s until near the end of the decade, other rushes occurred to Idaho and Montana, but the inadequacy of transportation presented an impediment which discouraged would-be prospectors. The mining frontier moved from section to section as the "surface placers," those who searched for gold on the earth's surface, farmed the available finds. Alder Gulch in Montana produced some $30 million in gold in three years and, at one time, had 10,000 settlers. Its sheriff, Henry Plummer, organized a notorious band of robbers which intercepted many shipments before he and twenty-one others were executed by vigilantes in 1864. Both Idaho and Montana received territorial status in 1864, but many of the original settlers left before commercial companies began profitable mining operations in the 1870s.

The last great mining rush was to the Black Hills of Dakota between 1875 and 1877. After rumors of gold in the region were received, the army sent General George A. Custer to investigate. In a typical action, he exaggerated his findings, and, as a result, within months 15,000 prospectors moved into the main camps at Custer City and Deadwood. All the mining frontiers were characterized by lawlessness, drunkenness, open prostitution, excessive gambling, and crude conduct, but Dakota, which attracted "Wild Bill" Hickok, "Calamity Jane" Canary and other colorful figures, saw the ultimate in excesses. In a few years, however, the quieter forces of civilization began to assume the ascendancy, and the larger mining companies began exploitation of the gold and silver.

The various gold and silver rushes promoted western settlement and increased the available quantity of precious metals, especially silver. As silver became a cheaper metal, the pressure grew for a revision of government policy regarding its use as money, and the issue became a major one politically.

The Transcontinental Railroads

The completion of the transcontinental rail lines was basic to the settlement and development of the West. Almost all of them were built with substantial government subsidies, the only apparent alternative to government ownership, which would have been unacceptable to the public at the time.

When the Pacific Railway Act chartered the Union Pacific to build west from Omaha and the Central Pacific east from Sacramento in 1862, they were granted five alternate sections of land ten miles deep on each side of the track for each mile of railroad built, and the government agreed to extend loans amounting to $16,000 per mile in level country, $32,000 in the foothills, and $48,000 in the mountains. In 1864 the government loan was reduced to second mortgage status, which permitted the railroads to borrow from other lenders on first mortgages. Since the grants had proved inadequate for construction, the land allocation was also increased from ten to twenty sections per mile.*

Using Irish laborers extensively, the Crédit Mobilier, a construction company established to build the Union Pacific, moved its line rapidly across the plains. Meanwhile the Central Pacific headed by the "Big Four" of Sac-

ramento business—merchants Collis P. Huntington, Leland Stanford, Charles Crocker, and accountant Mark Hopkins—used Chinese laborers who by heroic efforts, including work in the midst of winter and the use of nitroglycerin to blast tunnels, eventually built 689 miles of line to the Union Pacific's 1,086. The Central Pacific too had a comparable construction company which probably stole and squandered more monies than the Crédit Mobilier. It was never investigated, however, partially because its records disappeared. After Congress passed a law requiring the Union and Central Pacific lines to join rather than parallel each other, the union was made at Promontory Point, north of Ogden, Utah, on May 10, 1869. The nation was bound by bands of rail, although poor construction soon necessitated rebuilding of much of the lines.

In the next decade and a half additional federal subsidies were given to three transcontinental lines, the Southern Pacific and the Santa Fe, which were south of the Union and Central Pacific, and the Northern Pacific to the north. In all, American railroads received over 130 million acres of government land of which at least 75 percent went to the four major transcontinental lines. Moreover, until 1887 when President Cleveland ended the practice, the alternate sections between railroad grants were withheld from sale to enable the railroads to sell their lands at profitable prices. Federal subsidization proved a wise policy since the government ultimately received higher prices for its western lands following the coming of the lines.

The southern-most transcontinental line, the Southern Pacific, was the project of Collis P. Huntington, who dreamed of uniting San Francisco with Los Angeles and New Orleans. By ability and bribery, he prevented Thomas A. Scott's Texas and Pacific from receiving the federal subsidy which had been a bargaining factor in the Compromise of 1877. Though blocked to the west, Scott's successor, Jay

---

*Lincoln chose five feet as the gauge for the transcontinental lines but was overruled by Congress which stipulated 4 feet 8½ inches, the standard British gauge which had also been the standard gauge of Roman chariot wheels.

The meeting of the locomotives Jupiter, Central Pacific, and No. 119, Union Pacific, at Promontory Point, Utah, 1869.

Gould, forced Huntington to give his railroad's shipments and passengers access to the coast over the Southern Pacific after the two lines met in El Paso in 1882. At that time the lines jointly offered a direct route from California to New Orleans, but in 1884 the Southern Pacific reached New Orleans with its own tracks.

The Santa Fe received a congressional grant of three million acres of Kansas land in 1863 and began construction from Kansas City to Los Angeles by a southwestern route. By 1872 the line reached Colorado and defeated the Denver and Rio Grande for control of Raton Pass which gave it access to Albuquerque. In

1880 it merged with the Atlantic and Pacific which had been chartered by Congress in 1866 with land grants of twenty sections per mile built in the states and forty in the territories. These subsidies financed Santa Fe construction west of Albuquerque, but when it reached the Needles and found the Southern Pacific blocking access to California, an agreement was reached permitting the Santa Fe to use its tracks in the state. Though the Santa Fe had reached the coast by 1883, it did so on Gould's terms since he had come to dominate the Southern Pacific.

The Northern Pacific, chartered by Congress

in 1864 to run from Lake Superior to Puget Sound, received the same generous land grant as the Atlantic and Pacific. Five hundred miles of line had been laid when the depression of 1873 ended construction, but in 1881 the German immigrant, Henry Villard, reorganized the company, which joined another line to reach Portland, Oregon, in 1883. Ten years later James J. Hill completed the Great Northern, a second route to the Northwest which ran even nearer the Canadian border. It received no government grants and was completed through Hill's genius in combining smaller lines and developing the country as the road was constructed. His wisdom enabled the Great Northern alone of the transcontinental lines to avoid bankruptcy in the depression of 1893.

In return for extensive support, the subsidized railroads gave the government reduced rates, which over the years repaid the grants received in terms of dollars. Also the stimulus to agriculture and business probably justified the aid given the lines and resulted in the government receiving higher prices for the land it sold. However, there was much criticism of the virtual land monopoly the railroads received in many areas, a condition which in conjunction with a number of other unfair practices earned much western contempt.

The Range Cattle Industry

One subsidiary benefit of the railroads was the development of the range cattle industry in the

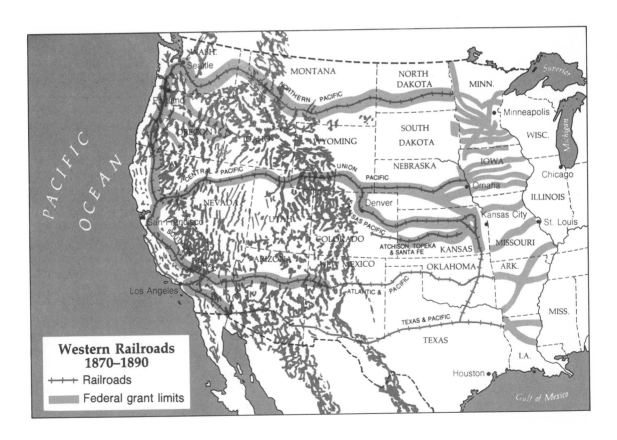

Western Railroads 1870–1890

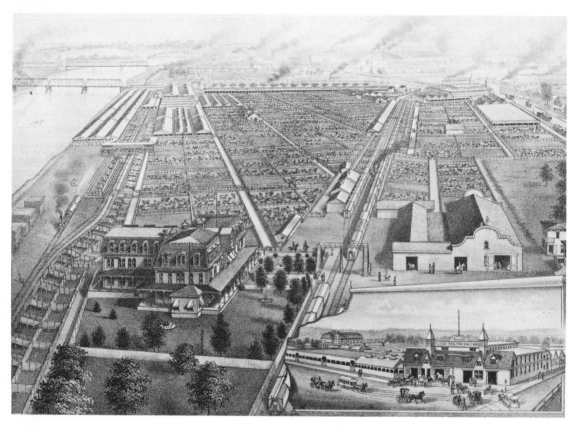

The stockyards in Kansas City, Kansas.

two decades following the Civil War. Stray cattle brought centuries before by the Spanish interbred with the animals of U.S. settlers until there were millions of Texas longhorns roaming the range between the Rio Grande and Nueces Rivers. These animals were vigorous, muscular creatures with an enormous capacity to thrive under adverse conditions. Eventually, when interbred with blooded bulls, they were to become ancestors of a number of the modern American breeds. Although edible, the meat of the longhorns was tough, but there was an Eastern market for it. Cattle valued at $3 or $4 a head in Texas were worth ten times as much in Kansas City. When Texas cattlemen gathered some 200,000 animals and drove

them over the Sedalia Trail to Sedalia on the Missouri Pacific Railroad for shipment east in 1866, the range cattle industry was born.

To avoid difficulty with irritated farmers, the Chisholm Trail, named for a widely known Scotch-Cherokee trader, was laid out, and the terminus for the cattle drives was moved west in 1867 to Abilene on the Kansas Pacific, the first of the great cow towns which mushroomed overnight. It was developed by Joseph G. McCoy, an Illinois livestock dealer, and was undisputed as a cattle center for five years. In 1872 much of the drive was diverted to Ellsworth, Kansas, when the Kansas Pacific reached that town, and Wichita on the Santa Fe. Some cattlemen preferred to drive their herds further north, and Ogallala, Nebraska, located 300 miles above Ellsworth on the Union Pacific, became a shipping center. After 1874, Dodge City, Kansas, which was on the Santa Fe and was the terminus of the Western Trail, also became a cow town although it never attained the trade volume of Abilene and Wichita.

Companies which were formed in the East and Europe to exploit the range cattle industry came to dominate the business by the early 1880s and rushed so many cattle onto the range that it became overcrowded. The coming of farmers contributed to this condition also by constantly reducing the area of open pasturage.

Over half the cattle that moved north over the various trails from Texas were not shipped directly east since, at times, buyers could not be found or prices were too low. Therefore millions of cattle were moved further north

Cattle Trails and Cattle Towns

where some were sold to the army and to Indian reservations. Many of those which moved over the Goodnight-Loving Trail after its development in 1866 were fattened and later shipped east or became the breeding stock for the states of that region.

Although remnants of the range cattle industry continued for a decade, the industry as such ended by 1887. By that time, the Chisholm Trail was practically closed by settlers, and overgrazing reduced profits. The severe winter of 1885–86 was followed by a summer drought and by the winter of 1886–87, which produced the greatest blizzard in Western history. Many of the companies dominating the industry were wiped out, and thereafter the producers chose to develop fenced ranches where selective breeding and better care of animals produced a better product.

One of the range cattle industry's most permanent contributions was the conception it gave the nation of the cowboy as a legendary western figure. Due to the hardships of the trail, the cowboy was usually a young man, frequently illiterate, and noted for his sparseness of speech. A surprising number were black, perhaps as many as 25 percent. Riding herd in the thick dust of the trail drive for stretches as long as thirty-six hours was a grueling life. Cowboys worked very hard, but at the end of the trail the cow towns offered every inducement to gain the $15 or $20 a month pay the cowboys received for their two or three months' endeavor. The bawdy houses, saloons, and professional gamblers were more of a menace than the romanticized gun battles portrayed today.

After the permanent end of the long drives, the cowboy remained prominent on the western ranch. His quaint clothing, including his spurs, high-heeled boots, gloves, and sombrero, was as functional as before, yet riding fence and doing the mundane work of the ranch lacked the color and thrill of life on the trail, and the earlier period of his history has remained the center of interest.

Settlement of the Great Plains

West of the 98th meridian the rainfall normally did not exceed twenty inches a year, and the prairie country was suitable primarily for ranching which required 2,000 acres for a successful operation, many times that needed for a farm. The Homestead Act and subsequent land laws did not recognize this fact and, through the subterfuge of speculators, the laws were used mainly to gain large tracts of land. The Timber Culture Act of 1873 permitted the acquisition of an additional 160 acres of land if trees were planted on one-fourth of them within four years. Of course, most of those who acquired land under the law never complied with its terms, nor did those who utilized the two succeeding laws. In 1877 the Desert Land Act permitted the acquiring of 640 acres at twenty-five cents an acre provided an intention was expressed to irrigate within three years, and, when irrigation was complete, the full title was obtained by paying an additional $1 an acre. Under the Timber and Stone Act of 1878, 160 acres of land unfit for cultivation could be bought for $2.50 an acre.

Utilizing the various laws, large quantities of lands were obtained by speculators while the average settler was forced to buy small holdings at higher prices from them or a railroad company. The plains also presented many other disadvantages including inadequate rainfall and absence of timber which made the use of split rail fences unthinkable. The wind blew constantly, drying everything that it touched and turning the skin of young women into that of old ladies. Plagues of grasshoppers periodically visited the region, devouring everything edible including curtains and clothes, while

rattlesnakes were a lurking menace to the unsuspecting. Tornadoes descended with heart-sickening frequency throughout the level country. The winters were long and cold, often bringing severe blizzards, while the wheat crops produced in summer were likely to be destroyed by hailstorms before harvest. The prairie sod itself was so tough that great effort was required to prepare the land for cultivation. No wonder disillusioned farmers held that the government under the Homestead Act was simply betting 160 acres of land that no one could endure the Great Plains for five years.

Many adversities had to be overcome, but the plains were settled with the aid of a series of unique adaptations and inventions. Until they had acquired enough money to import lumber for frame houses, the settlers lived in caves and, more frequently, sod houses built from three-foot blocks of earth and grass cut from the prairie. Usually structures of this type lasted six or seven years and were comfortable enough heatwise, but constantly crumbling dirt and water leaks which came during cloudbursts hardly made them pleasant. Buffalo chips and cow chips were burned for heat, but as time passed stoves which burned cornstalks and grass came into use. The perfection of barbed wire by Illinois' Joseph F. Glidden in 1874 permitted fencing of the plains, and in 1880 over 80 million pounds of the new wire were sold. Windmills, which used the plains' constant wind to raise water from a depth of 500 feet or more, were being widely manufactured and sold by 1880, although their cost was beyond the reach of the poorer farmers. The chilled-iron plow was developed by 1877, which permitted the rapid, effective cutting of the sod. New, hardy varieties of European winter wheat were introduced and machinery developed to process it. However, improved farm machinery, including planters and threshing machines, raised the cost of farming,

A western ranch house, 1888.

leading to an increased number of mortgage foreclosures and a higher tenancy rate after 1880. Serious droughts in 1879, 1880, 1889, and 1890 also contributed to the ruin of many families.

Despite hardships, the dreams of thousands led them to rush into available western lands, and their presence combined with a Republican search for votes led to statehood for Nebraska in 1867, Colorado in 1876, Montana, North Dakota, and South Dakota in 1889 (at the time of Washington's admission), and Wyoming and Idaho in 1890. Pressure was so great for lands in the Indian Territory that the government threw open two million acres in the Cherokee Outlet in 1889, after which thousands moved into the region, establishing instant cities, and the Oklahoma Territory was created in 1890.

The superintendent of the census in 1890 noted that no distinct frontier line could be drawn due to the infusion of settlers into previously unpeopled areas, and three years later the historian Fredrick Jackson Turner presented his important paper, "The Significance of the Frontier in American History." In it and other works produced throughout a distinguished career, Turner developed one of the most important interpretations of national life. He contended that initial American settlements were outposts of Europe, but that on the frontier the white man was transformed by his encounter with the wilderness. As a result, many of America's distinctive features, including democracy, arose. Free land offered a "safety valve" mitigating against European-type revolutions and providing an opportunity to re-create civilization and preserve individualism.

Turner overemphasized the frontier's influence, neglecting the significance of the philosophy brought with the settlers and overvaluing both the democracy present on the frontier and the economic opportunities available. Yet his work remains significant. The frontier was a phenomenon which placed a premium on what a man could do rather than on his ancestry or previous achievements. If not an actual site of refuge for many of the disgruntled, it was an intellectual haven whose romantic appeal was important, and its effect, as Turner demonstrated, was profound.

The Myth of the New South

While the West was being settled, heroic efforts were made to transform southern life. The ascendant political and social leaders who ended reconstruction, often described as the redeemers, envisioned a rejuvenated society that was industrial and urban in nature, an ideal which demanded a break with the past and emulation of northern developments. The transformation of southern thought was made easier by the material rewards the economic changes were to bring and an idealization of the past whose leaders were presented as advocates of change and progress.

Leading journals and newspapers throughout the South supported the crusade, sparked by chambers of commerce and other business organizations. None were more zealous or effective than the *Manufacturers' Record* of Baltimore, a leading voice for textile interests, and the *Atlanta Constitution,* edited by Henry W. Grady. In 1886, Grady delivered a celebrated address on "The New South" before the New England Society of New York. In it he gave an appealing rationale for unbridled industrial development throughout the region.

Devotees of the "New South" obtained state and local concessions, including tax remissions and gifts of land and capital, to promote industrialization, and in certain industries marked success was attained. After 1885 North Carolina's James Buchanan Duke came to dominate cigarette manufacturing when cigarette smoking became a fad of the period. In 1890 his company expanded into the monopolistic American Tobacco Company with eastern headquarters and financial connections.

Chattanooga emerged as an iron-producing center after the war but was quickly outdistanced by Birmingham, founded in 1871 at the crossing of two rail lines in the Alabama mineral belt. Under the patronage of the Louisville and Nashville Railroad and a coterie of able promoters, it led the South in a remarkable increase in mineral production. The Birmingham area was the only one on earth where iron ore, coal, and limestone—all the essential ingredients for pig iron and steel production—were in close proximity. By the turn of the century it was the nation's largest shipper of pig iron. In 1907 the United States Steel Corporation purchased the region's largest producer, the Tennessee Coal, Iron and Railroad Company, but the even greater developments expected did not materialize. The corporation chose to protect its eastern operations by refusing to allow Birmingham products their natural competitive advantage. At first, under the "Pittsburgh Plus" system, even local buyers had to pay freight from Pittsburgh plus the Pittsburgh price for products, although they were produced more cheaply in Alabama. After 1909 this system was replaced by the "Birmingham Differential," under which customers paid the Pittsburgh price, plus a differential of $3 a ton, plus freight from Birmingham. Although the Federal Trade Commission ordered abandonment of the system in 1924, ways were found to evade its ruling, and the practice was not ended until 1938.

Birmingham's development and that of much of the New South depended on an enormous increase in southern railroad mileage which more than doubled in the 1880s alone. The railroads not only permitted exploitation of mineral resources but also, by penetrating the forested regions, produced a flourishing lumber industry. Unfortunately much of the lumber was wastefully cut, creating additional drainage and erosion problems. Moreover, the railroads divided the nation into a number of rate zones. The zone east of the Mississippi and north of the Ohio, known as the "Official Territory," enjoyed lower rates, supposedly because of its heavier traffic. Nevertheless, raw materials transported out of the South and finished products coming into it were given lower rates than southern products shipped north. This system continued with Interstate Commerce Commission approval until the 1940s.

Obviously the hopes sustained by advocates of the New South met with many reversals. No aspect of its development was more disappointing than that of the cotton mills which many hoped would liberate rural communities and promote prosperity by bringing "the cotton mill to the cotton patch." The advantage of cheaper labor induced many New England mills to relocate in the four southern textile states, Georgia, Alabama, and the Carolinas, which had a majority of the nation's spindles after 1910. Yet the pay of laborers was miserably poor, and in 1900 one-fourth of the workers were under sixteen years of age. The Reverend Edgar Gardner Murphy, an Alabama minister, began agitation in 1902 which led to the formation of the National Child Labor Committee and eventually the removal of the younger children from the mills. However, the southern factories continued primarily to produce cheaper grades of goods and unfinished materials which were sent north for fabrication into salable items. Nonunionized labor and mills largely owned by nonregional interests did little to change the economic lot of the South.

Despite great quantitative increases in industrial production, the New South of the late nineteenth and early twentieth century fell even further behind in national production. Its industries were mainly of the less sophisticated type, and its industrial leaders were increasingly the agents of northern owners.

The Southern Black

Of all New South citizens, the black man suffered most. Leading northern intellectuals and publications openly professed his innate inferiority, which spurred southern militants to perfect and standardize repression. In 1891 railway car segregation was required in nine states, and all the former slaveholding states except Missouri did so by 1907. In 1896 the U.S. Supreme Court in the case of *Plessy* v. *Ferguson* validated "separate but equal" facilities, but the Court consistently failed to go beyond lower court decisions to test the provision of equality. Year by year, greater segregation was imposed; in 1910 Baltimore provided for residential area segregation, an action nine other cities followed by 1914.

Concurrently, blacks were forced out of many crafts and service industries, and in the 1890s, with the increase of poorer white power in government, disfranchisement swept the South. In 1890, Mississippi effectively excluded black voters by the imposition of a literacy test, residence requirements, and a poll tax. With some modification of technique, South Carolina followed suit in 1895, Louisiana in 1898, and the rest of the South by 1908.

As these events occurred, mob violence came to play an important role. Between 1889 and 1899, an average of 140 lynchings per year occurred in fourteen southern states, compared to about 30 in the rest of the nation. The yearly southern average declined to around 60 in the years from 1900 to 1929, but the average elsewhere in the nation was only about 4. Approximately 90 percent of twentieth-century southern victims were blacks.

Plagued by limited opportunity and repression, education seemed to many blacks to offer their one hope. In the late 1860s, the Massachusetts merchant-banker George Peabody established an endowment of $2 million to aid the South, but, although it supported a number of black educational projects, black education remained a wasteland. After 1882 the Slater Fund, endowed with a million dollars by the New England textile magnate John F. Slater, was devoted exclusively to promoting black education in the South, yet it diffused its limited gifts to so many schools that little was accomplished.

At this time Booker T. Washington, a man born as a Virginia slave, rose to eminence as a black leader. After graduating under the most adverse conditions from Hampton Institute, Washington, in 1881, opened a crude school in central Alabama which later developed into Tuskegee Institute. His institution combined vocational training with more formal studies and in the early 1890s won the support of leading northern philanthropists. In 1895 he earned national fame by an address delivered at the world's fair in Atlanta in which he proposed what has often been termed the "Atlanta Compromise." Washington's plan advocated that blacks forego political and social rights until

A laboratory at Tuskegee Institute, Alabama.

Booker T. Washington

attempted unsuccessfully to prevent black disfranchisement and to obtain court orders impeding segregation. In a posthumously published work, he held all thoughtful blacks knew segregation was an injustice which promoted unjust measures and widened the chasm between the races. Yet he advocated temporary acceptance of restrictions until blacks could develop a means of self-help. Some of his philosophy was based on a false evaluation of prevailing conditions, including the failure to assess the role of urban life, the declining significance of the farm, and the value of labor unions. Unwittingly, he contributed to conditions he hoped to destroy by temporarily accepting them. However, much of the blame for the failure of the Atlanta Compromise must be placed on the whites who modified the rules Washington had stipulated. Opportunity was closed to blacks by denying them the right to obtain an adequate education and to vote when they had the same qualifications as whites, conditions Washington never willingly accepted.

they attained the economic base which would enable them to command respect.

To many, Washington's philosophy seemed to offer a solution to the black problem, and they patronized vocational education of the Tuskegee type. Until his death in 1915, Washington was a national figure, serving as a principal patronage referee for the South under the Republican administrations and almost an arbiter on matters relative to black education and life. Some of the younger, more sensitive blacks objected to his views and, led by W.E.B. DuBois and others, were influential in founding the National Association for the Advancement of Colored People in 1909.

However, it should be noted, Washington

The Plight of the Farmer

Many black problems stemmed from the fact that most southern blacks were farmers, and the farmer everywhere had grave difficulties, especially in the South in the late nineteenth century. Improvements in transportation forced him to compete in a world market, while mechanization, notably in the North and West, increased initial outlays and reduced prices. The tariff and business trusts sustained and increased the price of goods he purchased, but the returns on what he sold declined.

Much of the farmer's difficulty was due to deflation, a characteristic of the period attributable in part to the small quantity of money placed in circulation. This increased only from $19.42 per capita in 1870 to $22.67 in 1890, during a period in which a rapidly developing, industrialized, urban economy needed much more available liquid capital. Interest rates remained high with the result that the proportion of farms under mortgage increased, as did the percentage of tenants. With a constantly growing debt, an economic situation in which added production usually brought lower prices, and a production unit too small to influence general conditions, the average farmer became increasingly disillusioned.

Monopoly of Railways

Slowly the nation's farmers identified the forces which they considered oppressive and began to attack them. The railroads, in particular, were indicted as unholy monopolies responsible for much agrarian misery and, though they were not solely responsible for the farmer's plight, their unfair practices left them vulnerable to attack. In many areas a single line enjoyed a monopoly and charged exorbitant rates on shipments from noncompetitive points. Small farmers often were billed at a higher rate than commercial shippers; rebates were also given to wholesalers but not to individual producers. In the West, where many grain elevators were railway owned, their fees were so high that farmers frequently risked ruin of their crops rather than use them.

Disgust with the railroads played a leading role in crystallizing agrarian discontent. The farmers made little allowance for the lines' problems, since their own survival was at stake, and their fear and disdain led most Americans to move toward cooperative action. Many, for whom the sanctity of private property was an article of faith, came to advocate government control of the railroads or even their nationalization.

The Formation of Protest Movements

As early as 1867 Oliver H. Kelley, a clerk in the Department of Agriculture in Washington, and six of his associates began an organization known as the National Grange of the Patrons of Husbandry, popularly called the Grange. Kelley, who was deeply distressed by the miserable lot of southern farmers, whom he encountered when President Johnson sent him to the South, sought to improve their condition by forming a secret organization which would unite the people for economic and social action. By 1875 the Grange had grown to over a million and a half members, principally in the South and West. It became the first of many secret societies in America to admit women without discrimination. Grangers founded many cooperatives which engaged in a wide variety of buying and selling, but eventually the lack of business experience resulted in the collapse of many cooperatives. Their failure and improved agricultural prices led to the decline of the Grange after 1878.

In addition to other activities, the Grange promoted the establishment of agricultural and mechanical colleges and opposed monopoly. It aided in the election of Granger partisans to state legislatures in the mid-West who enacted laws regulating warehouses, elevators, railroads, and other essential public facilities used by farmers. The Illinois Warehouse Act of 1867 was the first piece of Granger legislation, which was followed in 1871 by an Illinois law establishing a commission to fix maximum railroad and elevator rates. Similar legislation was enacted by 1874 in Minnesota, Iowa, and Wisconsin. In 1877 the U.S. Supreme Court dealt with eight cases arising under these laws. In *Munn* v. *Illinois,* which challenged Illinois' practice of setting maximum rates for grain storage, the Court asserted that regulation came within the scope of the state's police

An Illinois Grange meeting.

power and opposition should find redress at the polls, not in the courts. It denied the railroad any redress under the Fourteenth Amendment on the grounds that it was being denied property without due process. In *Peik* v. *Chicago and Northwestern Railway Company*, a Wisconsin case, the Court upheld state regulation of railroad rates, a decision that prompted reformers to seek additional state laws to govern railroad policies.

In less than a decade, however, the Supreme Court greatly weakened state railroad regulation, which in several instances had already proved ineffective. In the *Wabash* case (*Wabash, St. Louis and Pacific Railway Company* v. *Illinois*) in 1886, it invalidated a law designed to end the levying of a higher charge for a short

haul where there was no competing rail line than for a longer haul where there was competition (the long and short haul abuse). It held that the federal government had the exclusive right to regulate interstate commerce. As a result, the Interstate Commerce Act was passed in 1887 establishing the first of the federal regulatory commissions, but, for almost two decades, it lacked effective power. It could not set rates but could only ask courts to reduce rates that seemed too high, an action that was seldom taken.

The conservative approach of the courts hampered even the limited power enjoyed by the I.C.C. In the *Slaughterhouse Cases* of 1873, the Supreme Court, in a split decision, had held that the due process clause of the Fourteenth

Amendment was objective in nature, which in effect ruled that state actions which were in accordance with a written law were constitutional. Louisiana's grant of a monopoly was not changed even though it was challenged as violating the rights of U.S. citizens. The equal protection clause of the Fourteenth Amendment was limited almost exclusively to state laws which directly discriminated against blacks. In 1886 a change to a broader, more substantive interpretation of the Fourteenth Amendment was apparent in the case of *Santa Clara County* v. *Southern Pacific Railroad Company* when the Supreme Court accepted the contention that corporations were legal persons. The courts themselves were to examine state laws and actions taken under them to see if corporations were being deprived of property without due process. Rights were more than procedural; actions that were unreasonable or confiscatory were held to be violations of due process. Thus in 1890 in the *Minnesota Rate Case* (*Chicago, Milwaukee and St. Paul Railway Co.* v. *Minnesota*), the Supreme Court invalidated a Minnesota law giving rate-setting powers to a commission without right of appeal to the courts on the grounds that denial of access to the courts was evidence of deprivation of property without due process. The courts henceforth were concerned less with whether an action was in accordance with a state law than with the effects of the action.

Disenchantment with effective railroad regulation at both the state and federal levels and the inability of the farmers to obtain protection for their rights in other areas led to the Farmers' Alliance movements. The initial organization arose in Texas in 1875 as a group formed to advance farm interests. The Southern Alliance soon coalesced with a similar organization known as the Agricultural Wheel, and, under the stimulus of depressed conditions and the leadership of C. W. Macune, spread like wildfire, eventually gaining three million members. It sponsored more cooperatives than the Grange, established scores of local newspapers, and affiliated with a separate Colored Farmers' National Alliance.

The Northwestern Alliance which arose in the same period was important but never attained the numerical strength of the southern group, which in 1889 changed its name to the National Farmers' Alliance and Industrial Union. This action came after the powerful alliances of Kansas and the Dakotas had joined those of the South. The Northwestern Alliance was offended by the National Alliance's centralization and secrecy as well as its advocacy of the subtreasury system, under which the government would have established warehouses and made loans on crops up to 80 percent of their market value. The National Alliance, because of its southern base, also attempted to obtain its political ends by working within the Democratic party. Particularly after 1889, it ran Alliance candidates and sought to control the party in the individual states, thus avoiding the danger of splitting the white vote. A contrary policy was pursued by the Northwestern Alliance which entered politics with its own candidates.

Despite differences, however, the various alliances shared common antipathies and much the same program. In 1890 many alliancemen from the various organizations met in Ocala, Florida, and issued a platform including the subtreasury system, a federal income tax, the increase of currency to $50 per person, the abolition of national banks, the free coinage of silver at the ratio (to gold) of 16 to 1, the limitation of land ownership to American citizens, and a number of other liberal demands. By this action, the farmer was projected into politics in a most significant fashion. Much of the aggrieved West and South, whose immense problems had remained unsolved, began to fight as they had not previously done to attain a larger portion of the rewards industrial America had to offer.

Selected Bibliography

For general surveys of the West and South see Ray A. Billington, *Western Expansion: History of the American Frontier* (4th ed., 1974), and C. Vann Woodward, *Origins of the New South, 1877–1913** (1972). Billington, a disciple of Frederick Jackson Turner, evaluates the influence of the frontier in *America's Frontier Heritage** (1967).

William T. Hagan, *American Indians** (1961), is a general treatment of Indian developments. Norman Feder, *Two Hundred Years of North American Indian Art** (1972), demonstrates continued Indian creativity after white contact. M. Thomas Bailey, *Reconstruction in Indian Territory, A Story of Avarice, Discrimination, and Opportunism* (1972), follows the ordeal of the five civilized tribes. Paul I. Wellman presents *The Indian Wars of the West** (1971). Chester M. Oehler, *The Great Sioux Uprising* (1959), and Odie B. Faulk, *The Geronimo Campaign* (1969), deal with specific episodes. Indictments of government policies and pleas for Indian rights are contained in Alvin M. Josephy, Jr., *Red Power, The American Indians' Fight for Freedom** (1971).

Rodman W. Paul, *Mining Frontiers of the Far West, 1848–1880** (1967), deals with the entire region and relates the districts to each other. For more detail on specific areas see Grant H. Smith, *History of the Comstock Lode, 1850–1920* (1943); Merrill G. Burlingame, *The Montana Frontier* (1942); and Estelline Bennett, *Old Deadwood Days* (1935).

Western transportation is surveyed in Oscar O. Winther, *The Transportation Frontier: Trans-Mississippi West, 1865–1900** (1964), while Robert E. Riegel deals with *The Story of the Western Railroads, From 1852 Through the Reign of the Giants* (repr. of 1926 ed., 1964). Specific lines are treated in Robert W. Fogel, *The Union Pacific Railroad: A Case in Premature Enterprise* (1960); Richard C. Overton, *Burlington Route, A History of the Burlington Lines* (1965); and Lawrence L. Waters, *Steel Rails to Santa Fe* (1950).

The Range Cattle Industry, Ranching on the Great Plains from 1865 to 1925 (repr. of 1930 ed., 1969) is admirably presented in a work by Edward E. Dale as well as in Ernest S. Osgood, *The Day of the Cattleman** (1929), and Louis Pelzer, *The Cattlemen's Frontier, A Record of the Trans-Mississippi Cattle Industry from Oxen Trains to Pooling Companies, 1850–1890* (1936). Lewis Atherton, *The Cattle Kings* (1961), magnifies the role of ranchers rather than cowboys. Joe B. Frantz and Julian E. Choate, Jr., skillfully depict *The American Cowboy: The Myth and the Reality* (repr. of 1955 ed., 1968), while Philip Durham and Everett L. Jones deal with *The Negro Cowboys* (1965).

Gilbert C. Fite, *The Farmers' Frontier, 1865–1900** (1969) is a splendid survey of the settlement of the trans-Mississippi West. Walter P. Webb tells the story of the settlement of *The Great Plains** (1957) whose social

---

*Available in paperback.

conditions are picturesquely described in Everett Dick, *The Sod-House Frontier, 1854–1900* (1954). The influence of land policies is traced in Roy M. Robbins, *Our Landed Heritage: The Public Domain, 1776–1936** (1962).

In addition to Woodward's volume on the New South previously cited, see Paul M. Gaston, *The New South Creed: A Study in Southern Mythmaking* (1970); Raymond B. Nixon, *Henry W. Grady, Spokesman of the New South* (repr. of 1934 ed., 1969); and Broadus Mitchell and George Mitchell, *The Industrial Revolution in the South* (repr. of 1930 ed., 1970). The emergence of the common man and black repression can be studied in two leading states in Albert D. Kirwan, *Revolt of the Rednecks: Mississippi Politics, 1876–1925** (1964), and Francis B. Simkins, *Pitchfork Ben Tillman, South Carolinian** (1967).

On the ideology behind black repression see August Meier, *Negro Thought in America, 1880–1915: Racial Ideologies in the Age of Booker T. Washington** (1963). Louis R. Harlan, *Booker T. Washington: The Making of a Black Leader, 1856–1901* (1972), is the first volume of a projected definitive biography. Two interesting studies of Washington are Samuel R. Spencer, *Booker T. Washington and the Negro's Place in American Life** (1955), and Basil J. Mathews, *Booker T. Washington: Educator and Interracial Interpreter* (repr. of 1948 ed., 1969). The views of Washington's most potent critic are contained in Elliot M. Rudwick *W.E.B. DuBois: Propagandist of the Negro Protest** (1968). For accounts of Negro life and abandonment politically see Rayford W. Logan, *Betrayal of the Negro: From Rutherford B. Hayes to Woodrow Wilson* * (1965); Vincent P. DeSantis, *Republicans Face the Southern Question: The New Departure Years, 1877–1897* (1959); and Pete Daniel, *The Shadow of Slavery, Peonage in the South, 1901–1969* (1972).

The conditions provoking farmer discontents and attemps to change them are described in Fred Shannon, *The Farmer's Last Frontier, Agriculture, 1860–1897** (1945), and more limited studies include Russel B. Nye, *Midwestern Progressive Politics, 1870–1958* (rev. ed., 1963); Theodore Saloutos, *Farmer Movements in the South, 1865–1933** (1964); and Solon J. Buck, *The Agrarian Crusade* (1921) and *The Granger Movement: A Study of Agricultural Organization and Its Political, Economic and Social Manifestations, 1870–1880** (1963). Irwin Unger, *The Greenback Era: A Social and Political History of American Finance, 1865–1879** (1964), and Earl W. Hayter, *The Troubled Farmer, 1850–1900: Rural Adjustment to Industrialism* (1968), emphasize the conflict with an industrial society. George H. Miller, *Railroads and the Granger Laws* (1911), and Lee Benson, *Merchants, Farmers, and Railroads: Railroad Regulation and New York Politics, 1850–1887* (repr. of 1955 ed., 1969), trace the movement for railway control. For works on Populism see chapter 16.

Industrial Achievements

1872	Standard Oil Company incorporated
1876	Telephone perfected
1877	Phonograph invented
1879	Incandescent light bulb developed
1880s	73,000 miles of railroad built
	Supplanting of iron by steel for many industrial uses
1882	Commerical use of electricity inaugurated
1886	Uniform railroad track gauge established
1892	General Electric Company formed
1895	*U.S.* v. *E.C. Knight Company* decision
1901	United States Steel Corporation organized

Developments Affecting Labor

1866	Organization of National Labor Union
1868	Eight-hour day for government workers
1869	Knights of Labor formed
1881	Organization of American Federation of Labor
1886	Haymarket Riot
1892	Homestead strike
1894	Pullman strike
1908	*Danbury Hatters* case

15

The Triumphs
of an
Industrial Society

Long-Range Developments

For Economics and Corporate Enterprise

The consolidation of American industry and its resulting efficiency enabled it to attain world primacy by the mid-twentieth century.

The perfection of electricity, modern water and sewage systems, and other developments have permitted urbanization to continue to an unprecedented degree in the twentieth century.

For Democratic Government

Consolidation of business organizations and controls led to abuses which resulted in an increasing degree of governmental regulation.

For the Westward Movement, Nationalism, and Expansion

Pride in American artists and writers has grown and study of their works has in-creased in an attempt to understand "the American experience."

For Civil Liberties, Freedom, and Reform

Popular fear of immigration resulted in severe limitation on admissions in the 1920s.

Disgust with detestable urban living and working conditions was a powerful factor in the development of the Progressive Movement, the New Deal, the Fair Deal, and the Great Society.

Pragmatism has continued not only to influence education but also to justify changes in long-accepted social and ethical values.

The conservatism of the American Federation of Labor did much to dispel popular fears of labor unions and to prepare the way for prolabor laws and union victories.

The Expansion of the Railways

American industry grew at an unparalleled rate in the late nineteenth century and came to have an unprecedented influence on the nation's life. The value of manufactured products increased 400 percent between 1859 and 1899, but concurrently prices declined, making more goods and services available to the people than ever before. Tremendous outlays of capital were required for expansion, three-fourths of which came from Americans who plowed back their savings and earnings into industrial growth. These developments affected every aspect of national life, changing the very nature of American civilization.

The railroads, the most basic of all American industries and the pioneer big business, led the way in expansion and consolidation. An almost 600 percent increase in the nation's 35,000 miles of railway lines occurred between 1865 and 1900 with the greatest railroad building boom in history coming in the 1880s when 73,000 miles of track were laid.

As railways expanded, the great trunk lines came into being. The transcontinental lines were trunk lines from the beginning, but in the East and South the major systems were developed by railroad barons in the period after the Civil War. One of the first was "Commodore" Cornelius Vanderbilt, a New Yorker who dropped out of school at age eleven, acquired his own boat by the age of sixteen, and opened a freight and passenger service between New York and Staten Island. By the age of forty, he had become a millionaire through his successful steamboat operations on the Hudson River. In 1867 he organized the New York Central Railroad which by the mid-1870s had completed a network connecting the East with most midwestern cities. Meanwhile in 1874, Thomas A. Scott, who as Lincoln's assistant secretary of war rendered invaluable service by organizing railroad operations, became president of the Pennsylvania Railroad. Under his leadership, this pioneer holding company came to control or lease lines linking New York, Philadelphia, and Washington with the Midwest. The Baltimore and Ohio and the Erie systems also developed direct lines in the same general area. Unfortunately, Daniel Drew, Jay Gould, and Jim Fisk so watered the Erie's stock that the line became bankrupt in 1875 and was

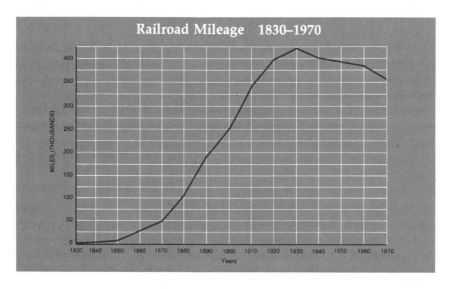

not successfully reorganized for almost two decades.

In the South, comparable developments took place, the most spectacular being the development of the Richmond and Danville Railroad. It absorbed twenty-six lines before becoming part of the Richmond Terminal Company, a system that before 1890 acquired 8,500 miles of track from Washington to New Orleans. Scores of smaller lines were built which were united in the 1890s. In addition to consolidating the Kansas Pacific with the Union Pacific, Jay Gould came to dominate many southwestern lines in the 1870s, including the Missouri Pacific and the Texas and Pacific.

The rapid growth and consolidation of rail lines brought transportation to many areas, improved services to others, and increased the value of lands everywhere. Advances came

The interior of a Pullman sleeping car.

through the introduction of innovations such as the Pullman sleeping car, the Westinghouse air brake, which eliminated the necessity of applying hand brakes on each car, the automatic coupler, the much stronger and smoother T-shaped steel rail, and the automatic block signal, which prevented many accidents. Under railroad tutelage, the country was divided into four standard time zones in 1883, and a uniform track gauge was adopted in 1886. Yet the railroad's successful expansion and improvement cost enormous sums of money, approximately a third of which came from abroad. In 1890 the railroads' income was over twice that of the federal government, but their debt was also several times as great.

Although a number of states, including some eastern ones, attempted to regulate the lines, they were largely ineffective, and unwarranted stock watering and other practices continued. Railroad speculation contributed heavily to the coming of the 1873 depression, after which the lines suffered many reverses, and, following the depression of 1893, even more were forced into bankruptcy.

As a result of the 1893 crisis, the nation's bankers assumed a dominant role in railroad reorganization and control. Most conspicuous was J. Pierpont Morgan, son of a wealthy Connecticut merchant and banker, who established his own New York banking firm in 1860. He won control of his first railway line from Gould and Fisk in 1869 and continued his interest afterwards, using capital obtained at home and from allied banking houses abroad. Morgan emphasized the need for order, centralized financial control, and consolidation to take the uncertainty out of business. He became an arbiter among American financial leaders and played a leading role in reorganizing the railroads. The House of Morgan created the Southern Railway System on the basis of the Richmond Terminal Company, and, among others, came to control the Baltimore and

J. Pierpont Morgan

duced through the Bessemer or open hearth process by removing most impurities and adding silicon, carbon and manganese. In 1873 only one ton of steel rails was rolled for every seven of iron, but by 1885 very few iron rails were used. Comparable conversions to steel occurred in other fields, greatly increasing the scope of its market.

The larger, more extensive steel plants required great expenditures of capital, and an intense competition developed between their owners after 1880. Out of the conflict Andrew Carnegie, who began his career as a poor Scottish immigrant, rose to dominance. In 1853, at eighteen years of age, he had become Thomas A. Scott's personal secretary at a time when Scott was general superintendent of the Penn-

Ohio, the Erie, and the Northern Pacific. Comparable if less extensive control was assumed by other bankers, and the railroads remained generally beyond public regulation. Most lines went through a period of unscrupulous control, though simultaneously profits were often increased and services improved.

The Advent of Steel

The new industrial America was as dependent on iron and coal as were the railroads. Fortunately, a rich supply of iron became available when the Lake Superior region's fields were opened in the 1870s, from which a million tons of ore were shipped in 1873. Additional ranges were opened yearly in Michigan and Minnesota, including the Menominee and the exceedingly rich Mesabi. Many of their ores were sent east over the Great Lakes to Pittsburgh, which remained the leader in iron production, although important new plants were constructed in Gary, Chicago, and Birmingham.

Slowly the railroads and other consumers were converted from iron to steel, a much harder, tougher, longer-wearing alloy pro-

Making Bessemer steel at a Pittsburgh plant.

sylvania Railroad. A shrewd young man, he carefully gleaned business information and made contacts which enabled him to become wealthy before leaving Scott in 1865. As an independent operator, he invested in iron and devoted himself exclusively to steel after 1872. Though he knew little of the technical aspects of the business, he was an excellent judge of men and employed the finest experts, whom he backed in introducing the latest production techniques. As a salesman he was incomparable, utilizing his personal relations with the nation's railroad executives to obtain orders. He also became a major defender of the acquisition of wealth, although he held the rich had a responsibility to use their resources to improve humanity.

Much of Carnegie's success came from his independence of the banking community, and

Andrew Carnegie

his company was run as a limited partnership with himself the majority owner. Financing came from profits which were conserved and often used advantageously for expansion during recessions. In competition, Carnegie was completely ruthless, employing rebates, ruinous price decreases, and other devices to force the opposition to the wall. By 1890 his company dominated steel production; its output increased almost tenfold between 1890 and 1900, and profits grew from $5.4 million to $40 million, of which Carnegie's share was $25 million. Though Carnegie swallowed much of the opposition, his efforts, like J. P. Morgan's, resulted in greater efficiency for his industry. Then, at the height of his success, Carnegie sold out in 1901, both to avoid newly emerging competition and to have the luxury of giving his wealth away.

John D. Rockefeller

Somewhat earlier than Carnegie, John D. Rockefeller applied the most ingenious techniques of business engineering to establish control of oil refining and distribution in the United States. In 1859, following Edwin L. Drake's drilling of the nation's first oil well at Titusville in western Pennsylvania, a brisk demand arose for kerosene as an illuminant for oil lamps. Rockefeller, a native of Richmond, New York, had grown up in Cleveland Ohio, where he became a merchant. In his mid-twenties he joined in establishing an oil refinery, which in 1872 was incorporated as the Standard Oil Company. It immediately cooperated with the Erie, New York Central, and Pennsylvania railroads to found the South Improvement Company in an effort to dominate the petroleum industry. The rail lines agreed that oil producers and refiners unaffiliated with the South Improvement Company would be charged twice the rate of affiliated interests; to achieve this result, uniform charges were made for everyone, but Standard Oil received rebates of half its freight charges. Moreover, the railroads gave the freight revenues in excess of that paid by Standard to the South Improvement Company and, of course, these drawbacks found their way into the Standard treasury. When news of this unfair operation became widespread, public opinion was incensed and the South Improvement Company was abandoned. Rockefeller, however, continued to extract rebates and drawbacks from the railroads for years. These practices aided Standard Oil in absorbing most of its competitors, and by 1879 it had 90 percent of the nation's refining business. This development occurred while oil consumption was increasing at an enormous rate, and it reached almost a million barrels yearly by 1900.

Rockefeller was a morally austere Baptist whose parsimony became famous. Much of his success was due to meticulous attention to details and the institution of every possible economy in his business. The same type of care was used in crushing the opposition, an action he felt to be morally imperative to overcome inefficiency. Control was obtained over pipelines constructed to carry oil and the opposition forced to surrender. The public was sold Standard kerosene at ridiculously low prices to bankrupt competing companies. Stores were subsidized to carry Standard oil and legislatures bribed to pass laws in its behalf.

Rockefeller became fabulously rich, his fortune reaching a billion dollars before his retirement in 1910, by which time his carefully gathered wealth had become the basis of the most extensive philanthropies in American history. Over $136 million was given to the General Education Board in the years after 1905, an endowment that did much to transform all types of American education. Many other millions as well were used for public health work both in the United States and

John D. Rockefeller

throughout the world, and, in addition to other philanthropies, the University of Chicago was endowed in 1892.

The Perfection of the Trust

Rockefeller insured his control over the oil industry by developing and perfecting a form of business organization known as the trust. The Standard Oil Corporation was chartered in Ohio, whose laws prohibited Ohio companies investing in corporations functioning in other states. Since Standard had assumed control of 90 percent of oil refining and distribution, some legal means had to be devised to exercise its control. This came in 1879 when nine trustees were chosen to administer Standard of Ohio and all the other companies under its control. Each company released its stock to the trustees, who, in return, gave the company's stockholders trust certificates.

The trust arrangement worked well, bringing unified control to the oil industry, and very soon trusts emerged in at least fifteen fields, including sugar, lead, whiskey, beef, and linseed oil. After the public became afraid of the new form of organization following an 1888 New York investigation of Standard Oil, Kansas enacted an antitrust law in 1889, as did fourteen other southern and western states by 1893. The Ohio Supreme Court held the Standard Oil trust to be illegal in 1892, but it was not dissolved until 1899. The Standard interests were then reorganized under a holding company form as the Standard Oil Company of New Jersey. Continued central direction was retained by obtaining a substantial portion of the subsidiary companies' stock until Standard's use of this organizational form was held illegal in 1911.

State antitrust laws proved ineffective since they could not regulate trusts dealing in interstate commerce. The demand for national action increased, although in most instances trusts improved the quality and lowered the prices of goods they controlled. The giant combinations frightened many people who felt they were destroying economic opportunity and individual enterprise. Therefore in 1890 Congress, under the leadership of Massachusetts' Senator George F. Hoar, overwhelmingly passed the Sherman Antitrust Law. In 1888 and 1889 Senator Sherman had introduced a measure which was much more comprehensive, but conservatives succeeded in largely rewriting the measure which was enacted. It made a long-standing common law principle federal law by declaring illegal every "contract, com-

bination, in the form of trust or otherwise, or conspiracy, in restraint of trade or commerce among the several states or with foreign nations."

The Sherman Antitrust Act was a sincere effort to end competition-restricting combinations, but the goal was not achieved. The act did not define its terms clearly nor indicate whether labor unions and railroads were covered by it. (In 1894 and 1897 the courts decided they were.) Its effects, however, were largely destroyed by the pro-trust attitudes of the courts. In 1895 in *U.S.* v. *E. C. Knight Company,* the Supreme Court held the sugar trust had not violated the law by acquiring additional companies which gave it control of 98 percent of the country's sugar refining. The Court drew a spurious distinction between manufacturing and commerce, holding the former affected the latter only indirectly. "Commerce succeeds to manufacturing," the majority opinion held, "and is not a part of it."

In 1897 in a case unquestionably involving transportation, the Supreme Court in a five-to-four decision outlawed an association of eighteen railroads which fixed transportation rates as a violation of the Sherman Act. It held in *U.S.* v. *Trans-Missouri Freight Association* that all combinations in restraint of trade were illegal, not just those which were in unreasonable restraint of trade, a doctrine which the Court later accepted. Despite this effective application of the Sherman Act, the judicial reasoning in the *Knight* decision prevented its effective use for a decade. Between 1890 and 1901 only eighteen suits were brought under the law, four of which were against labor unions. Meanwhile business consolidation continued at an accelerated pace, often attaining the same ends as true trusts without violating the letter of the law. A favorite device used in this way was the holding company, which held enough stock in a number of corporations to determine their policies and practices.

For many years the nation's largest holding company was the United States Steel Corporation, which was organized in 1901 by J. P. Morgan, Chicago's Judge Elbert H. Gary, and other financiers. It was the world's first billion-dollar corporation, whose capitalization at $1.4 billion was twice the current value of all its properties. Yet it controlled 60 percent of the nation's steel production, and shrewd management enabled it to absorb effectively the stock watering present in its creation. The government offered no opposition to its formation, and federal court decisions under Presidents Theodore Roosevelt and William Howard Taft only partially restrained holding companies.

Alexander Graham Bell and Thomas Alva Edison

By the turn of the century another holding company, the American Telephone and Telegraph Company, had come to dominate the nation's telephone system, and ultimately A.T.&T. became the nation's most widely owned business. Its success was based on the perfection of the telephone in 1876 by a twenty-nine-year-old Scottish immigrant, Alexander Graham Bell. This invention and the multiple telegraph came as a result of knowledge Bell gained while teaching the deaf in Boston. The Western Union Company refused to buy Bell's invention for $100,000, but soon recognized its mistake and hired a self-educated young inventor who had worked for the company as early as 1868, Thomas Alva Edison, to produce a device that would enable it to gain primacy in the field. Though Edison improved the transmitter, Western Union abandoned the fight, and Bell and his associates formed A.T.&T. By 1900 the country had approximately 800,000 telephones, which were transforming business and social life through instantaneous communication.

Meanwhile Edison continued his remarkable career, building a research facility at Menlo Park, New Jersey, in 1876, and in 1887 moving to larger quarters at Orange, New Jersey. In 1877 he invented the phonograph, followed by many other developments, including the storage battery, dictaphone, mimeograph, electric dynamo, and electric locomotive. His most important invention, made in 1879, was a durable incandescent electric light bulb, which made possible the establishment of commercial lighting companies, the first of which began service for select New York City customers in 1882.

Edison used direct current in his facilities, which limited transmission to approximately two miles, but George Westinghouse, originator of the railroad air brake, overcame this limitation by perfecting transformers which transmitted high-powered alternating currents and reduced them for use. He also bought the patent for an alternating current motor, which

Thomas Alva Edison with his first phonograph.

made his system feasible as a source of mechanical power.

The Westinghouse approach prevailed but had to share equipment manufacturing and transmission success with the General Electric Company, which had been formed in 1892 by the merger of Edison's operations with a major competitor. By the turn of the century electric light and power were radically altering American life, breaking the stranglehold of water and steam power and allowing plants to locate nearer markets and labor supplies. Although in 1899 electric motors still supplied less than 2 percent of the power in manufacturing, a new day had dawned industrially. At the same time city life became more tolerable and safer as electricity supplied lighting and transportation for more and more urban people.

Urbanization and Immigration

The rapid introduction of the electric streetcar in the 1890s accelerated the growth of cities, for the first time permitting people to live six or seven miles from their work. Industrialization, while not the sole impetus, was, of course, the major one in urban growth. Merchandising and commercial centers expanded their fields of economic endeavor, attracting millions of farmers, pressured by low income and debt, from rural America. In addition, immigrants settled primarily in the cities, where the greatest job opportunities existed. Between 1870 and 1900, the percentage of the population living in towns or cities with a population of 2,500 or more increased from approximately 25 to 40 percent. In 1860 only New York and Philadelphia had a population over 500,000, but at the turn of the century six cities exceeded that number. New York had grown to almost 3.5 million, Chicago 2.7 million, and Philadelphia 1.3 million.

Unanticipated city growth created new, unexpected problems and an instability of life for many people. Neighborhoods changed constantly, with the more affluent and better educated moving to the suburbs as immigrants took control of the least desirable, central city. Immigration doubled in the 1880s, and a shift in national origins began from Northern and

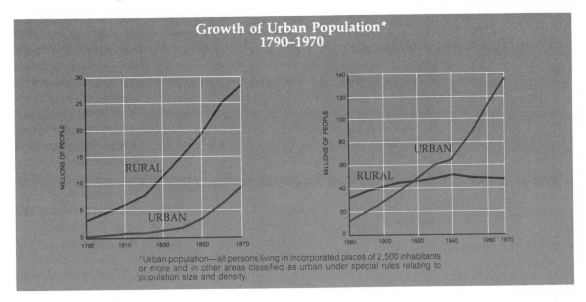

Growth of Urban Population*
1790–1970

*Urban population—all persons living in incorporated places of 2,500 inhabitants or more and in other areas classified as urban under special rules relating to population size and density.

Western to Southern and Eastern Europe. The Italians, Russians, Poles, Austrians, and other "new migrants" were usually Catholic or Jewish in religion and appeared to native Americans and earlier arrivals to be difficult to assimilate into American society. In reality, assimilation difficulties may have come primarily from the increased numbers of migrants; in only two years of the 1880s did the number drop below 400,000, and in 1903 and 1904 it exceeded 800,000. All-time peaks were hit in 1905, 1906, 1907, 1913, and 1914, in each of which over a million immigrants entered the country. After 1890 over 50 percent were new migrants, a proportion which increased in the following year and reached 74 percent in 1914.

Before 1880 most immigrants had been welcomed as workers, consumers, and even as bearers of some capital, but this attitude changed and strong antiforeign movements arose in the country which tried to impede the flow of migrants. Diverse groups comprised the movements including organized laborers, who feared the new arrivals as strikebreakers, and conservative businessmen, who associated anarchist leadership with European radicals. In 1887 the influential American Protective Association, a secret, primarily midwestern, anti-Catholic association, was formed, but it was unable to prevent President Grover Cleveland vetoing an 1897 act establishing a literacy test which would have excluded many of the new immigrants. President Taft successfully vetoed a similar law in 1913, but in 1917 Congress overrode Woodrow Wilson's veto and passed a measure the scholarly president contended tested opportunity rather than ability.

Before 1917 there was no effective exclusion except of Chinese and Japanese and certain classes of undesirables. In 1882 criminals, paupers, the insane, and other poor risks were excluded, while in 1901 and 1903 the list was expanded to include beggars, prostitutes, epi-leptics, anarchists, and polygamists. Although the Chinese were given the right to immigrate to the U.S. by the Burlingame Treaty of 1868, protests from the West coast in the 1870s and a peak migration of 160,000 in 1882 led to their exclusion by an act of Congress in that year. President Theodore Roosevelt attained the same result with Japanese immigration through the "Gentleman's Agreement" of 1908 (see p. 129).

Millions of immigrants peopled the city slums, many living in the compact "dumbbell" tenements erected after 1879, which had many interior rooms without access to air and light and completely inadequate water and sewage facilities. They became a breeding ground for disease, despondency, and despair, and the political precincts in which they were located gave city bosses the votes that enabled them to dominate municipal government. Though they milked the city through crooked franchises, overcharges for services, and purchase of inferior merchandise, the bosses also performed vital social services, often dispensing alms generously and enabling the immigrant and the poor to survive.

Disease and vice, however, could not be confined to the core city, and, frightened by their expansion, the suburbs took the lead in obtaining reforms. In the 1880s and 1890s streets were paved, sewage and water systems installed, and substantial citizens led in attaining needed changes in laws. Good government clubs arose in many cities, over two hundred of which were affiliated with the National Municipal League after it was organized in 1894. Strong emphasis was placed on making the mayor a responsible official and on obtaining effective codes in various municipal areas. At the turn of the century, Governor Theodore Roosevelt of New York appointed a State Tenement House Commission, whose exhaustive report resulted in sweeping revision of city ordinances and a state law whose impact led to comparable investigations and changes elsewhere.

In the 1880s extensive state laws regarding working conditions, many of which imposed restrictions in behalf of women and children, were passed with increasing frequency. A number were not effectively enforced, but those that were brought substantial results. Under the leadership of such crusaders as Florence Kelley, the head of the Consumers' League, and Samuel Gompers of the American Federation of Labor, child labor laws were enacted in the northern states. As a result the percentage of children under sixteen in the total northern labor force declined from 15.6 to 7.7 between 1880 and 1900. In the South, where laws were not passed until after 1900, the number of mill workers under sixteen remained constant at 25 percent.

The new social legislation received a mixed reaction by the courts which, acting under the Fourteenth Amendment's prohibition of deprivation of property without due process of law, invalidated many state laws regulating working conditions but sustained others. A pioneer Massachusetts law of 1874 restricting the hours of women and children was upheld as a proper exercise of the reserved police power, and in 1898 the U.S. Supreme Court in *Holden* v. *Hardy* held a Utah law setting maximum working hours in mining industries to be a reasonable use of the state's police power. It stated freedom of contract could legally be modified when inequalities existed in bargaining power. This decision aided in obtaining the passage of other state laws regularizing working conditions, but a number of these were struck down by the courts. The most crucial setback came in 1905 when the Supreme Court in *Lochner* v. *New York* first invalidated a state social welfare law. It held a New York act setting ten hours a day or sixty hours a week as maximum hours for bakers constituted unreasonable interference with freedom of contract guaranteed by

the Fourteenth Amendment and was an unjustifiable use of state police power. Justice Oliver W. Holmes, who recognized the inequality of workers and employers in the bargaining process, dissented in a notable opinion in which he urged judges not to confuse their own economic theories with the Constitution. In only three years, the Court took a contrary position when it was influenced by a brief of Louis D. Brandeis which utilized economic, sociological, and historical data. In *Muller* v. *Oregon*, it held an Oregon law setting a maximum ten-hour working day for women did not interfere with liberty of contract. This decision led to the enactment of many laws regulating working conditions, and in 1917 in *Bunting* v. *Oregon*, the Supreme Court upheld a ten-hour law which applied to both sexes. For the next two decades, however, many court decisions continued to pose major difficulties for governmental action.

Legal regulation of working and living conditions reflected changes in public opinion which came over a period of years. A significant force producing these modifications were the settlement houses which were modeled after London's famous Toynbee Hall. The first opened in 1886 on New York's Lower East Side, but the most famous were Jane Addams' Hull House, opened in 1889 in Chicago, and Lillian Wald's Henry Street Settlement founded in New York in 1893. By the turn of the century over fifty were operating in major cities and were not only rejuvenating entire neighborhoods but serving as training centers for cadres of young social workers who came to have substantial public influence. In magazines devoted to their cause, such as *Charities* and *The Survey*, they carried the results of their findings to the people. Prominent contemporary reformers, such as Alexander J. McKelway and Samuel Gompers, joined youngsters who later became national leaders, such as Frances Perkins and Harry Hopkins, in proclaiming that philanthropy was essential but inadequate. They held laws must be passed and, above all, effectively administered to correct the glaring abuses in American social life.

The Knights of Labor

In the late nineteenth century, some of the most incisive criticism of the American economy and attempts to change it came from representatives of labor, particularly union leaders. During the period, except in depressions, most workers had jobs, and, outside the southern textile field, there was a general decrease in hours worked until by the 1890s the workday was below ten hours for almost everyone. Very few, however, attained the eight-hour day which was first provided for government workers in 1868. Pay continued to be relatively low, averaging less than $10 a week in the 1890s, but the general deflation brought an increase in purchasing power for many. The American laborer, under the circumstances, remained loyal to capitalism and dreamed of advancing within the system to become something other than a laborer.

As skilled craftsmen lost status through mechanization and the disparity between the rich and the average worker increased, craft union membership became more attractive. In the period immediately after the Civil War, thirty national unions recruited approximately 300,000 members. Among these unions were the Railway Brotherhoods and the influential Molders' Union, whose president, William Sylvis, brought the various organizations together as the National Labor Union in 1866. Its leaders were idealists who envisioned the workers themselves becoming plant owners and opposed the use of strikes and other coercive techniques. After it failed to obtain an eight-hour day, the union concentrated its efforts on political changes. It provided the

nucleus for the organization of the National Labor Reform Party which nominated Judge David Davis for president in 1872, but his withdrawal led to the collapse of the party and the union.

The depression of 1873 resulted in the death of all but nine national craft unions at a time when workers most needed protection and leadership. Many businesses, severely pressed to survive, reduced wages, increased demands on workers and used a variety of techniques to destroy unions. After a secret organization of miners in eastern Pennsylvania known as the Molly Maguires encouraged labor violence and evidence was gathered against them by Pinkerton detectives, twenty-four members were convicted of law violations and ten hanged for murder. In 1877 a general railroad strike was suppressed by the use of federal troops after nine persons were killed at Martinsburg, West Virginia, and upwards of $10 million damage was inflicted at Pittsburgh.

As the effects of the 1873 depression ended, another national union, the Knights of Labor, rose to prominence. It originated as a secret order among Philadelphia garment workers in 1869, and the president for its first decade was Uriah S. Stephens. In 1879, secrecy was abandoned, and Stephens was succeeded by the equally visionary Terence V. Powderly, whose romantic nature is revealed in the title of his autobiography, *The Path I Trod.*

The Knights, like the earlier National Labor Union, were more concerned with basic reforms than immediate gains, yet the union was unique in that it was industrial in nature. All employed persons, including the unskilled, blacks, and women, were combined into one big organization. After successful strikes in 1884–85 against Jay Gould's railroad lines in the West, membership grew to 700,000 members in 1886. Following this, disaster struck after a foreman was dismissed at the Texas and Pacific Railroad shops in Marshall, Texas, sup-

A meeting of Molly Maguire men.

posedly for membership in the Knights of Labor, and shopmen throughout Gould's southwestern railroads prevented the movement of all trains except those carrying mail. Public opinion was sympathetic with the strikes until food and fuel shortages began to emerge. Under pressure, Powderly ordered the strike halted in the hope arbitration would vindicate the union's position, but Gould consistently refused. The strike was resumed but lost in early May, 1886.

At the time of Gould's triumph, general strikes for the eight-hour day were begun in a number of cities despite Powderly's opposition. They drew their greatest support in Chicago, but even there they soon collapsed. Among the most zealous supporters of the strikes were a small group of anarchists affiliated with the "Black International," or, more properly, the International Working People's Association which had been formed at Pittsburgh in 1883. Believing that labor could never obtain justice until society was reorganized, they attempted to use trade unions to destroy prevailing institutions. They found their opportunity for agitation when trouble emerged on May 3, 1886, near the McCormick Harvester Company where a labor stoppage, which had begun before the general strike, continued. When police attempted to disperse demonstrators at the McCormick factory, four men were killed and several others wounded. Anarchists and labor leaders called a protest meeting the following day, May 4, 1886, for

Haymarket Square in Randolph Street. As it progressed, the authorities decided the speeches were too revolutionary and ordered the police to break up the meeting. A bomb was thrown as they did so which killed seven men and wounded seventy others. In hysteria, anarchists in the area were rounded up and tried; seven were sentenced to death and one to prison. Four were executed in November, 1887, and one of the condemned men committed suicide. The three others were pardoned by Illinois' liberal Governor John P. Altgeld in 1893. Unfortunately, the Knights of Labor were unjustly blamed for the Haymarket Riot and never recovered from the stigma.

The American Federation of Labor

A far happier fate was experienced by the American Federation of Labor, the first true labor union, which was founded as the Federation of Organized Trades and Labor Unions of the U.S. and Canada in 1881 by Samuel Gompers and others, and reorganized under its

Samuel Gompers

present name in 1886. An English-born Jew who immigrated to the United States as a teenager, Gompers became president of the Cigarmakers' Union in 1877 and, abandoning his early visionary outlook, concentrated on concrete gains for workers. The A. F. of L. sponsored autonomous trade unions for skilled workers in the various crafts and sought through the use of the strike and other coercive practices to obtain better hours, wages, and working conditions. From 1886 until his death in 1924, with the exception of one year, Gompers served as the union's head. Under his statesmanlike leadership, the A. F. of L. avoided commitment to any political party but used its influence to aid those candidates advancing its goals.

The A.F. of L. securely organized large numbers of skilled workers and made notable gains, especially after the end of the depression of 1893. Even though the National Association of Manufacturers, which was organized in 1895, undertook an anti-union campaign, by 1904 the A.F. of L. claimed over 1.6 million members.

Despite these impressive gains, only 10 percent of America's industrial workers were unionized at the turn of the century, and notable failures occurred in efforts to organize certain industries, including iron and steel. By 1892 the A.F. of L.'s strongest union, the Amalgamated Association of Iron and Steel Workers, had organized approximately 25 percent of the workers in its field, establishing locals in a number of Carnegie plants. In that year, however, Henry Clay Frick, chairman of the Carnegie Company, decided to make the Homestead, Pennsylvania, plant a nonunion facility. After wages were reduced 18 percent, negotiations ended; the plant was fenced in, and the workers struck. A turning point in the strike came when 300 Pinkerton detectives, who were often used as strikebreakers, were fired upon by the workers as they attempted to move into the

Workers fired on 300 Pinkerton detectives, who arrived by barges at the Homestead steel plant.

plant, and seven men were killed. Soon afterward, the aroused public was further incensed when Frick was shot and stabbed by an anarchist. Under these conditions, strikebreakers and the 8,000-man state militia broke the strike, and the steel industry remained unorganized until the 1930s.

Direct federal intervention occurred in 1894 when an injunction was used to end the Pullman strike, an action which inaugurated an era of increased anti-union activity by the national government. When George Pullman reduced wages but not the costs of housing and company services at his paternalistically run Pullman Palace Car Works near Chicago, the American Railway Union called a strike. This independent union, headed by Eugene V. Debs, had some Pullman workers as members and was a competitor of the A.F. of L.-affiliated Railway Brotherhoods. During the strike, it refused to handle Pullman cars on trains, and the railway owners would not allow the trains to run without them.

The strike was broken when President Cleveland's attorney general, Richard Olney, obtained an injunction ordering an end to the strike and, over the protest of Governor Altgeld of Illinois, sent two thousand troops to Chicago. Debs, who was cited for contempt for violating the injunction, requested the Supreme Court to issue a writ of habeas corpus which it declined to do. In its decision in *In re Debs,* however, it justified the issuance of the injunction as a means of preventing obstruction of interstate commerce and the flow of the mails, a broader basis than reliance on the Sherman Act. Debs was sentenced to jail for six months and while imprisoned converted himself to socialism by extensive reading. In 1900 and four elections afterwards, he ran as the Socialist party's candidate for president.

Eugene V. Debs

Between 1901 and 1928 at least 116 federal injunctions were applied for in labor disputes, a number of which were granted, but many applications ended strikes before a decree could be issued. Ironically, the Sherman Antitrust Act came to be used effectively during these years not to destroy trustlike organizations but to break strikes. The first instance of this came in 1908 in the *Danbury Hatters Case* (*Loewe* v. *Lawlor*) in which a secondary boycott was held to constitute a conspiracy in restraint of trade. The Court held individual union members were responsible to the extent of their property for losses suffered as a result of the interstate boycott of a producer's goods. As a result most of the Danbury strikers were financially destroyed.

Earlier in 1908, the Supreme Court, taking a narrow view of the commerce clause, had invalidated a national attempt to protect the rights of individual workers to join unions. The Erdman Act of 1898, which provided for mediation of railroad labor disputes, also prohibited interstate railroads from requiring workers to agree they would not join a labor union. (Contracts containing this stipulation were known as "yellow-dog" contracts.) In *Adair* v. *United States* the Supreme Court held this feature of the Erdman Act unreasonably violated an individual's freedom of contract and property rights guaranteed by the Fifth Amendment and that union membership was not subject to regulation as interstate commerce. Federal decisions of this type and an even larger number of state court decisions seriously affected the growth and functioning of unions and the well-being of many workingmen.

The Impact of Religion

By the 1880s the poor living and working conditions of many employees promoted move-

ments in organized religion which ultimately led to reform. This development was paradoxical since the church and synagogue tended to be among the most conservative forces in American life and were greatly concerned with their own internal problems. The new immigration enormously increased the number of Roman Catholics and Jews in the country, but, due to their greater numbers and hierarchical organization, the Catholic influence was far more significant. Catholic population alone doubled between 1870 and 1900, when it reached 10 million. From 1850 to 1900 approximately 4 million Catholics left Ireland, most of them for the United States, where they came to control the electorate in the nation's largest cities and to wield enormous political influence.

Amazingly little Catholic concern was exhibited for social reform, although the church established innumerable agencies and houses to minister to the needs of the people. Part of the responsibility for the failure to seek reform lay with reactionary papal views on social questions which found expression in Pope Pius IX's *Syllabus of Errors.* The situation began to change in the 1880s when America's second Cardinal, the popular James Gibbons, urged the church to reevaluate its attitude toward organized labor and social change generally. In 1891 Pope Leo XIII sanctioned this view in a new encyclical, *Rerum novarum,* and slowly Catholic reformers began to emerge.

Much of Protestantism was equally oblivious to social needs, and for it the late nineteenth century was an era of personal evangelism in which Dwight L. Moody, a Chicago Y.M.C.A. worker turned revivalist, was most outstanding. He spoke to millions of people at home and abroad, and among other achievements led college students to form the Student Volunteer Movement. Revivalism of the Moody type, which emphasized personal reform and disregarded social issues, was responsible for much of the vigorous growth of American Protestantism. Thousands of people were also attracted by the vigorous clerical attacks on the teachings of Charles Darwin, whose theories were not widely known in America until some time after their publication. Because of Darwinism, furious controversies arose within the churches as to whether or not the Bible should be understood literally. Those contending it should were called Fundamentalists and remained influential until the mid-twentieth century. Their attacks may have led to intimidation of teachers in both public and church schools but probably increased interest in religion. Yet in the core city the traditional denominations tended to become less attractive to the poor, who increasingly turned to the Salvation Army, which was imported from England in 1880, or to various holiness sects.

Christian Science was an interesting new religious movement whose appeal was to the more affluent classes rather than the poor. It was founded as the Christian Scientists Association in 1876 and chartered in 1879 as The Church of Christ, Scientist by followers of Mary Baker Eddy, who studied and practiced mental healing for years and personally experienced a miraculous recovery from a serious injury. Her book *Science and Health with Key to the Scriptures,* first published in 1875, sold over 400,000 copies before her death in 1910 and has continued to attract many converts.

Christian Science's influence, though interesting, was limited, and the greatest impact of the church in dealing with social issues came with the development of the "Social Gospel" in the major denominations. Its inception dates from the 1880s when a number of Protestant ministers began to preach that Christ came to transform not only the individual but society as well. They advocated a variety of reforms, and the left wing of the movement became Christian socialists. Among the most influen-

Mary Baker Eddy

tial advocates of the new approach was the Congregationalist Washington Gladden, who in 1886 published *Applied Christianity* in which he strongly defended labor unions and urged stringent public laws regulating living and working conditions. Another leader, R. Heber Newton, a New York Episcopal priest, championed cooperation as an alternative to competition and popularized many socialistic doctrines from England among American Episcopalians. Although the Social Gospel movement had attained wide influence by the time Walter Rauschenbusch, a Baptist minister, published *Christianity and the Social Crisis* in 1907, his indictment of the industrial revolution and unbridled capitalism infused a moral fervor in the activities of many reformers.

The church, though divided on the question, had at last come to advocate change in this world as a response to God's will.

Educational Changes

Among all the reforms proposed, the one that received most widespread support was the effort to provide universal education, which many embraced as a panacea for all of society's ills. As public support increased and the economy advanced between 1870 and 1900, enrollment in public schools more than doubled while expenditures tripled. By the turn of the century over $200 million a year was expended on public education, and outside the South laws requiring compulsory primary education were in effect. Concurrently, curriculum was revised to include instruction in the sciences and manual arts, and the high school was becoming an integral part of most school systems, increasing from approximately 100 in 1860 to 6,000 in 1900. As a result of these changes, illiteracy nationally decreased from 17 percent in 1880 to less than 11 percent in 1900.

Educational progress in the South was much less than elsewhere, and in 1900, of 217 counties in the nation in which 20 percent of white men were illiterate, 212 were in the South. The percentage of southern illiteracy was as great at the turn of the century as it had been in 1850. This condition was due in great measure to the rural nature of the South, the coexistence of two school systems due to segregation, the region's greater percentage of school-age children, and southern poverty. Private philanthropy from outside the region created the Peabody Fund in 1867 and the Slater Fund in 1882 which funded improvements in many local systems, but little general progress was made. The need was so great that many could see no solution without federal aid, but opportunities were lost to obtain it when Congress

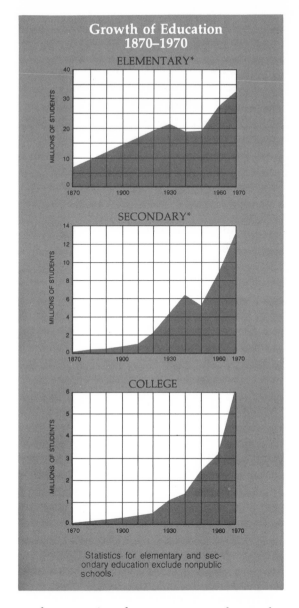

Growth of Education 1870–1970

ELEMENTARY*

SECONDARY*

COLLEGE

Statistics for elementary and secondary education exclude nonpublic schools.

on four occasions between 1883 and 1890 defeated the Blair Bill, which over a period of years would have distributed to the states on the basis of their illiteracy $105 million for educational use.

Southern educational advances came after 1900 through a cooperative effort of local leaders and northern philanthropists, who, working through the Southern Education Board and annual Conferences for Education in the South, mounted a religious-type crusade in behalf of the schools. In five years the southern states increased their educational appropriations by $14 million, and the value of universal education was generally accepted. However, even greater advances in other regions kept the South lagging behind the nation's educational progress.

The increasing literacy of the American people resulted in the support of mass educational enterprises such as the Chautauqua movement which after 1874 brought thousands of lecturers to platforms across the country. Simultaneously, public libraries grew at a rapid pace, numbering over 9,000 by 1900. Many of those established after 1881 received their buildings as gifts from Andrew Carnegie, whose only stipulation when making his grants was that municipalities adequately finance the libraries by annual tax appropriations.

Meanwhile readable literature for mass purchase became much easier to obtain, especially in magazine form, and the number of magazines published in the United States increased 700 percent in the last third of the century. Some of the newer ones, such as *McClure's* and *Cosmopolitan,* monthlies which sold for ten cents, attained popular appeal by publishing lighter materials, but they also contained much fiction and many excellent articles written by leading authors. The *Arena,* the *Review of Reviews,* the *Forum,* and some other magazines came to equal the best English reviews in content and greatly influenced public opinion.

Even more influential was the newspaper, whose circulation grew rapidly at the close of the century. The invention of linotype in 1885 facilitated the mechanics of publishing but also increased publishers' investments. The day of personal journalism largely passed as syndicated material and feature stories became more important, while advertising replaced subscriptions as the main source of support.

A new type of newspaper emerged in 1883 when Joseph Pulitzer made radical changes at the *New York World.* Combining sensationalism with first-class reporting and crusades for local improvements, he raised circulation from 15,000 in 1883 to over a million by 1900. His accomplishments did not pass unnoticed and other newspapers followed his techniques, most notably, after 1895, William Randolph Hearst's *New York Journal.*

Unlike innovations in contemporary journalism, many of the late nineteenth-century changes in higher education were substantial improvements. Between 1880 and 1900 the number of colleges increased by 50 percent to 500 while their number of students increased by at least 300 percent. Many southern and western schools became coeducational, and the curriculum was broadened by the infusion of new subjects. Harvard's President Charles W. Eliot led in the institution of the elective system which permitted student choice of subjects

William Randolph Hearst

to be taken. After 1918 it was recognized that the system had been carried too far and a core of basic subjects came generally to be required of freshman and sophomores, but, in the earlier years, the elective system provided much needed flexibility and freedom.

In 1876 another major change was introduced in education when the Johns Hopkins University was established in Baltimore and named for the Baltimore merchant who in 1873 left $7 million to be divided between the projected university and a hospital which was also to bear his name. From the first, Johns Hopkins concentrated on graduate education and introduction of the German system of graduate studies in the United States. Emphasis was placed on original research, the seminar method of instruction as well as the granting of the Ph.D. degree after intensive study in one field and the production of an exhaustive work of original scholarship. Other universities such as Harvard, Yale, and Chicago followed Johns Hopkins' lead and soon became nationally acclaimed graduate centers.

Intellectual Critics
of the System

Despite their increasing importance, the colleges and universities had not come to have the influence in American life which they have today. Therefore the most notable critics of the period usually were not professors.

Henry George, one of these critics, had been a printer and newspaperman before publishing his major work, *Progress and Poverty,* in 1879. In it he contended that labor was the source of all wealth, and capital was unjustly acquired by withholding land until adjacent development inordinately increased its price. To prevent this injustice, he recommended a single tax on land as the basis of government's support. George's theories found sympathetic advocates around the world, including David Lloyd George in Great Britain, who utilized them in a controversy leading to parliamentary reform in 1911. Henry George also ran well as a candidate for mayor of New York in 1886, though he was defeated by the ironmaker, Abraham Hewitt, who had the support of the Catholic church.

In 1888 another critic, Edward Bellamy, published a utopian vision of a socialist state in *Looking Backward, 2000–1887,* which indicated competition as a force leading to misery and universal monopoly. When this occurred, Bellamy held, peaceful, evolutionary nationalization would take place. As a result of his novel, Nationalist clubs arose, but their members usually abandoned them for more practical political organizations.

Lester Frank Ward, government geologist and paleontologist who did not accept a professorship of sociology until he was sixty-five, converted Darwinism into a force for reform. Unlike William Graham Sumner and other advocates of laissez faire, he held society was subject to forces other than evolutionary determinism. Progress came through the use of intelligence in social planning, a procedure essential even to insure the survival of the fittest. Without government regulations, he contended, unfair and partial men would rig the game. Ward's *Dynamic Sociology,* published in 1883, was followed by four other major works which did much to establish sociology as a distinct discipline and to challenge the prevailing Social Darwinism, the belief that those who attained power and prestige were naturally superior and deserved their position.

In some ways an even more potent challenge to the system was levied by Thorstein B. Veblen, a conventional academician, who earned a Ph.D. in economics at Yale and taught at the University of Chicago, Stanford, Missouri, and the New School for Social Research. In his later works, Veblen was highly critical of unbridled capitalism's ability to avoid recurrent crises. To prevent these, he envisioned a system of planned production and distribution which would end capitalism's evils and excesses. Veblen's major fame, however, stemmed from his first book, *The Theory of the Leisure Class,* published in 1899. In this analysis of middle-class values, he held "conspicuous consumption," the self-conscious, demonstrative use of goods and resources, had become a means of attaining social status and a primary factor in economic life. Veblen held the attributes that distinguished the business class were those which had formerly been associated with the barbarian while those of the industrial classes, in which he included technicians and engineers who retained an instinct for work, were characterized by social concern more than lust for wealth. Obviously the morals of supposedly Christian America were based on principles other than selfless service.

Collectively the works of George, Bellamy, Ward, Veblen, and others formed an intellectual challenge to prevailing American thought. They not only revealed fundamental weaknesses in the nation's social structure but also suggested alterations which could be made in it.

The New Men of Letters and the Arts

The tendency to face conditions and portray them as they were resulted in the emergence of realism in the arts in the 1880s, a challenge to romanticism which, in literature, first appeared in the early postwar works of "local color" writers. The father of this type work was Bret Harte, a native of Albany, New York, who moved to California at fifteen and spent the next few years teaching, mining, and typesetting. In 1868 he became editor of *The Overland Monthly* and wrote for it "The Luck of Roaring Camp" followed in 1869 by "The Outcasts of Poker Flat," his most famous stories on the

rough aspects of western life. He returned East in 1870 where he wrote almost exclusively for the *Atlantic Monthly* for fifteen years, contributing many local color stories whose quality did not equal those of his earlier works.

Another local colorist, Joel Chandler Harris, a quiet, shy man who spent most of his career writing for Savannah and Atlanta newspapers, first published his "Uncle Remus" stories in the *Atlanta Constitution* before they appeared in book form in 1880. His skillful use of dialect and incorporation of folk tales presented the southern black man in a different manner from his previous portrayal. Uncle Remus was a sage, lovable character whose unique world of animals became a part of Americana.

Another southerner, George Washington Cable of New Orleans, produced almost twenty novels throughout a long career. Some, such as *The Grandissimes,* dealt with racial conflict in Louisiana and presented sympathetically the problem of miscegenation. However, Cable's most famous work was one of his earliest, a series of short stories known as *Old Creole Days.* Though his books were largely responsible for the revival of New Orleans' French Quarter, he was unpopular with many Creoles because he did not enhance their romantic image, and his criticism of repressive racial policy offended them and many other southerners. By 1884 he had abandoned the South for Connecticut, ostensibly to be nearer his publishers and lecture circuit but probably because of popular opposition to his criticism.

Cable's works became so well known that he joined the most renowned of the realistic writers, Samuel L. Clemens, or, to use his pen name, Mark Twain, in a successful reading tour. Born and reared in frontier Missouri, Twain enlisted in the Confederate army in 1861 but soon abandoned it for the turbulent life in Virginia City, Nevada. There he began to write humorous, satirical stories, and in 1865 he became famous for "The Celebrated

Jumping Frog of Calaveras County." By this time the ever-dissatisfied Twain had moved to California, and, soon after the war, he toured Europe and the Near East, from which emerged his widely acclaimed *The Innocents Abroad* in 1869. In the next two decades Twain became an American institution. His greatest works—*The Adventures of Tom Sawyer, Life on the Mississippi,* and *The Adventures of Huckleberry Finn*—depict life as it was, not as the American Victorians felt it should be. Humor was endemic in them but also a perceptive criticism of a society whose noblest characters, such as Nigger Jim, were held in inferior positions.

Other local colorists who produced significant works included the Indiana-born Joaquin Miller who was taken as a child to Oregon and wrote such colorful, vigorous selections as "Song of the Sierras" and "Song of the Sunlands." Another Indianian, Edward Eggleston, vividly depicted local life and customs in his novels, the most famous of which was *The Hoosier Schoolmaster.* Virginia life and the Old South were romantically portrayed by Thomas Nelson Page in both novels and short stories including *Meh Lady, Marse Chan',* and *Two Little Confederates.* The repressed lives of New Englanders were effectively presented by Mary

Tom and Huck in the treasure cave, a wood engraving from the first edition of The Adventures of Tom Sawyer, *1876, by Mark Twain.*

Eleanor Williams in such short stories as "A New England Nun" and novels such as *Pembroke.*

Local color was only one feature of postwar letters, and some would contend the primary literary figure was William Dean Howells, an Ohio newspaper man who became a realistic novelist, America's most acclaimed literary critic, and a major advocate of such realistic writers as Twain, Frank Norris, Stephen Crane, Hamlin Garland, and others. After writing a campaign biography of Lincoln, Howells was appointed U.S. Consul in Venice (1861–65) and returned in 1866 to work for the *Atlantic Monthly,* serving as editor-in-chief from 1871 to 1881. In 1872 he began publication of a score of novels which were quite different from earlier romantic works. As a result of the Haymarket Riot, Howells developed a deep interest in social questions. In *A Hazard of New Fortune* (1890), he presented many of capitalistic America's ills through the treatment of a disruptive strike; in it the squalor and misery of the city were seen in sharp contrast to the life of the rich. *A Traveler from Altruria,* published four years later, projected a utopian society where the inequities were corrected.

While in New England, Howells became a close friend of Henry James, a novelist who like himself and Twain was a celebrated realist. James was the son of a distinguished theologian and the brother of William James, the psychologist. After initial schooling in France, he entered the Harvard Law School in 1862, but, soon turning to letters, moved easily in the most polite British literary circles and in 1876 settled permanently in London. Though he yearned to see American literary genius recognized abroad, his own works were only partially American oriented. Often, as in *The American,* his concern was with the conflict in American and European culture. He wrote primarily about and for the upper classes, yet his penetrating analysis of individuals, as in *The*

Bostonians (1886), and his dedication to his craft have earned his works an increasing appreciation.

The average man who probably never heard of Howells and James was likely to be a fan of Horatio Alger. A Massachusetts native and graduate of Harvard College and the Harvard Divinity School, Alger served for two years as pastor of the Unitarian church in Brewster, Massachusetts, before moving to New York as a writer. He wrote widely for newspapers and periodicals, but over a thirty-five year period produced approximately seventy juvenile novels, including the *Ragged Dick, Tattered Tom* and *Luck and Pluck* series. His never-failing plot portrayed a rags-to-riches drama in which virtue led to material success. The millions who grew up on his works and read them after reaching adulthood were influenced in forming their concepts of what America should be by his moralizing.

Developments comparable to those in writing characterized late nineteenth-century painting, and, though America produced few artists comparable to Europe's best, it did have some outstanding craftsmen. Winslow Homer of Boston began as a magazine illustrator, a craft he abandoned after moving to Maine in 1882. There and on excursions to the Caribbean, he produced vividly colored, originally designed marine pieces. His water colors, in particular, have been acclaimed as outstanding. George Inness was virtually self-taught, although he studied in Italy and France before settling in Medfield, Massachusetts, Montclair, New Jersey, and New York City to do most of his work. As a landscapist, his paintings, including *Sunset in the Woods* and *March Breezes,* were increasingly lyrical and subjective, using color patterns to achieve lightness and airiness. Childe Hassam, a native Bostonian, was both an etcher and impressionistic painter whose landscapes, figures, and sea paintings were distinguished by their color and luministic qualities. *Summer Sea* and *The Church at Old Lyme* are among his most highly regarded works.

American realism reached its height in the works of Thomas Eakins, a native Philadelphian who spent his career there except for four years' study in Europe. At the Jefferson Medical College, he mastered presentation of the human figure, and study of the French and Spanish masters helped him depict strength and character in such works as *The Swimming Hole, The Gross Clinic,* and *The Thinker.*

The mysticism of Albert Ryder, who spent most of his life as a New York recluse, has come to be highly valued since his death in 1917. By the use of luminous color and, at times, weird forms and masses, he produced works with a poetic quality, among the most acclaimed being *Macbeth and the Witches* and *The Flying Dutchman.*

In addition to Homer, Eakins, and Ryder, the United States was the birthplace of James A. McNeill Whistler, whose portrait of his mother is among the most famous of paintings, and Mary Cassatt, an able impressionist. However, both spent their careers abroad and were truly European artists.

At home, Americans distinguished themselves in art forms other than painting. In sculpture, craftsmanship and style improved as the Irish-born Augustus Saint-Gaudens, Daniel Chester French, and George Gray Barnard drew heavily on Italian Renaissance models. In architecture, the jigsaw styles of the earlier postwar years changed to more appealing designs. Henry Hobson Richardson, a native Louisianian who studied at Harvard and abroad, abandoned the Victorian Gothic and introduced a Romanesque revival whose excellent use of mass, space, and line was a decided improvement. The Chicago World's Fair in 1893 sparked a classical revival of appealing Greek, Roman, and Renaissance forms. Richard M. Hunt, who was trained in Paris, im-

"The Shaw Monument" by Augustus Saint-Gaudens.

proved and refined the style of the "Brownstone-front house," an adaptation of the French Renaissance style which utilized mansard roofs, lavish ornamentation, coupled columns, and large cornices. He designed numerous homes for American millionaires who wanted mansions that looked as if they might belong to a French nobleman.

While these art forms were being utilized, America gave the world a unique architectural development, the skyscraper, a primary example of form following function. Its earliest development came in 1884 when William LeBaron Jenny used cast iron columns and wrought iron beams to produce Chicago's Home Insurance Building. Following this, Louis H. Sullivan, realizing the potential of the new materials and the feasibility of high-rise construction with the advent of the elevator, perfected the design in a number of major structures.

Though the late nineteenth and early twentieth century was not a great age of art in America, it was an interesting period in which competent, even outstanding artists arose in the various media. The prevailing forms were successfully challenged, and increasing wealth permitted greater private and collective support of the arts.

Pragmatism

Experimentation and innovation were not limited to the arts, and in developing the philosophy of pragmatism the United States made a contribution as original as the skyscraper. Charles Sanden Pierce, a philosopher and scientist who for thirty years was a staff member of the U.S. Coast Survey and lecturer at Harvard and elsewhere, may have been its originator. There was no question, however, that its popularizer was William James, who abandoned a Harvard professorship in medicine for one in philosophy. Pragmatism, as James presented it, held purported truths could be tested by their practical consequences, and thus truth was relative, changing with each circumstance and individual. Pragmatism rejected determinism and exalted the individual, holding the world should be accepted as a place of change, an outlook which encouraged reformers to believe it could be channeled into desirable forms.

Pragmatism was for most an optimistic philosophy, but for many, accustomed to a world of eternal verities, it produced uncertainty and doubt. Its most immediate impact came in the field of education where the work of John Dewey and his disciples proved to be significant. Dewey, a Vermont native, received his Ph.D. in 1884 from the Johns Hopkins University, and, after teaching philosophy at Michigan, Minnesota, and the University of Chicago, became director of Chicago's School of Education. While there, he founded the Laboratory School in 1896 and published the influential *The School and Society.* In 1904 he joined the faculty of Columbia University, where for almost three decades he led the movement for "progressive education" in the United States.

Dewey's pragmatism demanded that education be child-centered; curriculum and teaching methods should be flexible and all instruction based on what the child knew. Some of Dewey's followers carried an attack on the established disciplines to the extreme, but even the most conservative educators were affected by the progressive revolution which spread across the land in the twentieth century.

Pragmatism was only another of the swift and pervasive changes that came to industrial America. Collectively they resulted in the greatest transformation in the manner of living, thinking, and producing that the country had yet seen. However, the manner of life was to be even more radically altered as its tempo increased in the twentieth century.

Selected Bibliography

Industrial developments and their effects are surveyed in Edward C. Kirkland, *Industry Comes of Age: Business, Labor and Public Policy, 1860–1897** (1967). Additional information is in Samuel P. Hays, *The Response to Industrialism* * (1957); Thomas C. Cochran and William Miller, *The Age of Enterprise: A Social History of Industrial America** (1968); section III of Cochran's new *Business in American Life: A History* (1972); and the older but detailed Ida M. Tarbell, *The Nationalizing of Business, 1878–1898** (1971).

Railroad expansion may be followed in John F. Stover, *American Railroads** (1961) and *Railroads of the South, 1865–1900* (1955); George R. Taylor and Irene D. Neu, *The American Railroad Network, 1861–1890* (1956), and Thomas C. Cochran, *Railroad Leaders, 1845–1890: The Business Mind in Action* (repr. of 1953 ed., 1966). Especially useful are Edward G. Campbell, *The Reorganization of the American Railroad System, 1893–1900* (repr. of 1938 ed., 1969) and biographies of financial leaders including Frederick L. Allen, *The Great Pierpont Morgan** (1965), and Julius Grodinsky, *Jay Gould: His Business Career, 1867–1872* (1957).

The significance of new inventions and modern techniques in industry are shown in John W. Oliver, *History of American Technology* (1956). Developments in major industries and lives of their leaders are included in Joseph F. Wall, *Andrew Carnegie* (1970); Allan Nevin's flattering *Study in Power: John D. Rockefeller, Industrialist and Philanthropist* (2 vols., 1953); and Matthew Josephson, *Edison** (1963). Edward C. Kirkland, *Dream and Thought in the Business Community, 1860–1900** (1964), and Richard Hofstadter, *Social Darwinism in American Thought** (rev. ed., 1955), reveal the thinking and social attitudes of business leaders and society. Gilman M. Ostrander, *American Civilization in the First Machine Age: 1890–1940** (1972), analyzes the new industrial society's effect on national character.

Blake McKelvey, *The Urbanization of America, 1860–1915* (1963), is a good survey. More details for the late nineteenth century are found in Arthur M. Schlesinger, *The Rise of the City, 1878–1898** (1971), and Alexander B. Callow, Jr., ed., *American Urban History: An Interpretive Reader with Commentaries* (2d ed., 1973). Vincent Scully, *American Architecture and Urbanism: A Historical Essay** (1969), is a fascinating account of urbanism's effect on one aspect of cultural life.

Immigration is treated in Carl Wittke, *We Who Built America* (rev. ed., 1964), and Marcus L. Hansen, *The Immigrant in American History** (1964). The trauma suffered by the "new immigrants" is shown in Oscar Handlin, *The Uprooted** (2d ed., 1973); Peter Roberts, *The New Immigration: A Study of the Industrial and Social Life of Southeastern Europeans in America* (repr. of

---

*Available in paperback.

1912 ed., 1970); and John Higham, *Strangers in the Land: Patterns of American Nativism, 1860–1925** (1963).

Philip Taft, *Organized Labor in American History* (1964), surveys labor developments. More detailed information on the Knights of Labor is in Norman J. Ware, *The Labor Movement in the United States, 1860–1895, A Study in Democracy** (repr. of 1929 ed., 1959). On the A.F. of L. see Philip Taft, *The A.F. of L. in the Time of Gompers* (repr. of 1957 ed., 1969), and Bernard Mandel, *Samuel Gompers: A Biography* (1963). The failure of socialism in the labor movement is treated in William M. Dick, *Labor and Socialism in America, The Gompers Era* (1972). Two major strikes are the subject of Leon Wolff, *Lockout: The Story of the Homestead Strike of 1892: A Study of Violence, Unionism and the Carnegie Steel Empire* (1965), and Almont Lindsey, *The Pullman Strike** (1943). The courts' attitude toward unions, strikes, and social legislation are reviewed in Loren P. Beth, *The Development of the American Constitution* (1971).

Religious developments are surveyed in William W. Sweet, *The Story of Religion in America** (rev. ed., 1970) and *Revivalism in America** (1965), and in Clifton E. Olmstead, *History of Religion in the United States* (1960). John T. Ellis, *American Catholicism** (2d ed., 1969); Lyman P. Powell, *Mary Baker Eddy, A Life Size Portrait* (Christian Science 1950); Henry F. May, *Protestant Churches and Industrial America** (1963); and Charles H. Hopkins, *The Rise of the Social Gospel in American Protestantism, 1865–1915** (1940), deal with specific groups and movements. James F. Findlay, Jr., *Dwight L. Moody, American Evangelist: 1837–1899* (1969), is a biography of the era's leading evangelist.

For changes in formal education see Ellwood P. Cubberley, *Public Education in the United States: A Study and Interpretation of American Educational History* (1934); H.G. Good, *A History of American Education* (1956); and Horace M. Bond, *The Education of the Negro in the American Social Order* (rev. ed., 1965). Charles W. Dabney, *Universal Education in the South* (2 vols., repr. of 1936 ed., 1969), deals with the southern renaissance. *The Development and Scope of Higher Education in the United States* (1952) is treated in a work by Richard Hofstadter and C. De Witt Hardy and in Laurence R. Veysey, *The Emergence of the American University** (1970). Joseph E. Gould gives a history of *The Chautauqua Movement, An Episode in the Continuing American Revolution* (1961). Frank L. Mott, *A History of American Magazines,* Vol. 3, 1865–1885, Vol. 4, 1885–1905, (1938, 1957) and *American Journalism* (3rd. ed., 1962), presents trends in the magazine and newspaper fields.

American thought is analyzed in Henry S. Commager, *The American Mind, An Interpretation of American Thought and Character Since the 1880's** (1950); Ralph Gabriel, *The Course of American Democratic Thought,* (2d ed., 1956); and Merle Curti, *The Growth of American Thought* (3rd ed., 1964). Useful studies of individual critics include Charles A. Barker, *Henry George* (1955); Sylvia E. Bowman, *The Year 2000, A Critical Biography of Edward Bellamy* (1958); Samuel Chugerman, *Lester F. Ward, The American Aristotle; A Summary and Interpretation of His Sociology* (1939); and David Riesman, *Thorstein Veblen, A Critical Interpretation* (1960).

Literary developments are presented in Robert E. Spiller, *The Cycle of American Literature** (1967); Van Wyck Brooks, *The Confident Years, 1885–1915* (1960); and J.B. Hubbell, *The South in American Literature 1607–1900* (1954). Illuminating studies of major figures include Arlin Turner, *George W. Cable, A Biography** (1966); Dixon Wecter, *Sam Clemens of Hannibal** (1952); Everett Carter, *Howells and the Age of Realism* (1966); and Ralph B. Perry, *The Thought and Character of William James: Brief Version* (1948). Edgar P. Richardson, *Painting in America: From 1502 to the Present** (1965), and Lorado Taft, *The History of American Sculpture* (1930), describe fine arts changes. John Szarkowski, *The Idea of Louis Sullivan* (1956), is informative on the development of the skyscraper.

Pragmatism may be studied in Joseph Blau, *Men and Movements of American Philosophy* (1952); Sidney Hook, *John Dewey, An Intellectual Portrait* (1939); George R. Geiger, *John Dewey in Perspective* (1958); and Lawrence A. Cremin, *The Transformation of the School: Progressivism in American Education, 1876–1957** (1961).

Conservative Politics

1878	Democrats capture both houses of Congress
	Bland-Allison Act
1881	Stalwarts defeated in Senate
	Garfield assassinated
1883	Pendleton Act
	Steel naval vessels authorized
1886	Presidential Succession Act
	Tenure of Office Act repealed
1887	Electoral Count Act
	Dependent Pension Bill vetoed
	Cleveland's "State of the Union" Address
1890	Dependent Pension Act
	Republican humiliation in congressional elections
	McKinley Tariff
	Sherman Silver Purchase Act
1892	Populist challenge in national and state elections
1893	Repeal of the Sherman Silver Purchase Act
1894	Wilson-Gorman Tariff
1894–95	Struggle to save the gold standard
1896	Defeat of William Jennings Bryan and "Free Silver"

16

Conservatism Triumphant 1876-1900

Long-Range Developments

For Economics and Corporate Enterprise

The tariff, which was made a party issue in 1887, remained a highly controversial political subject until after 1934, when the president was authorized to negotiate reciprocal trade agreements.

Cleveland's low tariff stand embedded the policy among the canons of the twentieth-century Democratic party.

For Democratic Government

Contempt and disdain for American politics of the late nineteenth century influenced twentieth-century political attitudes.

The Populist movement evoked fears that were used to aid in the defeat of William Jen-

nings Bryan not only in 1896 but also in 1900 and 1908.

*For Civil Liberties, Freedom,
and Reform*

Civil service reform initiated under the Pendleton Act, though at times subject to reverses, has continued to the present.

The Lodge Bill's arousal of southern fears may have been in part responsible for concessions to the South by early twentieth-century presidents on racial issues.

Cleveland's conservatism and McKinley's prolabor attitude prepared the way for Theodore Roosevelt's progressive administration.

Late Nineteenth-Century Politics

The last quarter of the nineteenth century was far from a stellar era in American politics though partisanship was intense. Few issues of significance divided the parties which were motivated primarily by a desire for the spoils of office. Both major parties were quite conservative in their attitudes which forced many advocates of even moderate reform into transitory third-party movements. Nationally, the Republicans and Democrats were almost evenly balanced, with the swing of a small number of voters in such critical states as New York and Indiana determining presidential elections. In most elections a president was chosen who had not received a majority of the popular vote, and more often than not the Democrats controlled the House of Representatives and the Republicans the Senate. Under such conditions, local issues and personal considerations received an emphasis of undue proportion.

During most of the period, the presidency suffered its lowest status in American history, in part due to the dominance of Congress under Johnson and the decay of the presidential

Office seekers in the lobby of the White House, awaiting an interview with President Hayes.

image under Grant. The presidents themselves contributed to the situation, since on most issues they acquiesced in legislative dominance. After Grant, no president served two consecutive terms before 1900, and before McKinley none had his party in control of both the House and Senate for more than two years. To obtain any desired legislation, congressmen had to be cultivated, and many responded only to the commands of city and state political machines. Accordingly, the spoils of office were crassly used as a bargaining medium with a corresponding decay in the quality of the civil service.

The Hayes Administration

Like most of the late nineteenth-century presidents, Rutherford B. Hayes, a war hero and three-time governor of Ohio, was an admirable person who courageously espoused some excellent policies but lacked the political capacity to achieve his goals. He angered his party's spoilsmen by choosing an independent cabinet including Carl Schurz, an advocate of civil service reform, for secretary of the interior. Hayes also promised a complete reform in the appointing process and protection of officeholders from political pressures. These intentions were not carried out, although in a celebrated struggle the president wrested control of the New York Customs House from protégés of New York's Stalwart Senators Roscoe Conkling and Thomas Platt. He removed Chester A. Arthur as collector of the port and persisted until the Senate confirmed his successor.

Presidential authority received a badly needed boost when Hayes thwarted Democratic efforts to modify existing laws by adding riders to appropriation bills. By this means, the Democrats, who controlled both houses of Congress after the 1878 elections, attempted to nullify the president's authority to use federal

troops in congressional elections. By seven votes, the president foiled the Democratic effort and sustained the independence of the executive branch; however, he did not use force to protect black rights in the South. Although deploring unjust treatment, he would do nothing to destroy the Compromise of 1877.

In his personal life, the always cheerful but austere Hayes became more reserved after becoming president, and his refusal to serve any alcoholic beverages at state functions did nothing to endear him to most professional politicians. Moreover, he became increasingly willing to assert his views but proved unwilling to do battle for them.

In economic matters, there was no disparity between the president's policies and actions since both were uniformly conservative. In the general railroad strike of 1877, he acceded to the request of four governors and furnished troops to restore order, an action which ended the strike and served as an unwholesome precedent for decades. In money matters, no man was more devoted to the sound, gold dollar than Hayes, who did not realize that deflation contributed greatly to the misery of the masses. Many congressmen from the South and West openly embraced an inflationist policy based on the free coinage of silver at the ratio of 16 to 1, and in both 1876 and 1877 the House passed a measure authored by Representative Richard "Silver Dick" Bland of Missouri providing for this. The Senate killed the first bill but modified and passed the second, the Bland-Allison Bill, which was enacted in 1878 over Hayes' veto. It stipulated the U.S. Treasury would buy no less than $2 million nor more than $4 million of silver each month to be converted into standard dollars. Though Hayes disliked the Bland-Allison Act, it did not have the effects he feared since unlimited purchase and coinage of silver was prevented and the inflationary effects severely restricted. The Treasury purchased the minimum quantity of silver and always exchanged silver coin and notes for gold at par. With the return of prosperity in 1879, pressure for free coinage slackened until the mid–1880s when a faltering economy revived interest in it.

Economic improvement and the president's evident honesty and integrity won him increasing respect in his final days in office, yet no movement arose to have him rescind a pledge not to seek reelection. The professional politicians wanted a more formidable candidate and the reformers a more zealous advocate.

Hancock's Defeat

At the 1880 Republican convention a battle developed between the Stalwarts, who for two years had been grooming Grant for a third term, and the Half-Breeds, who wished to nominate Blaine. After thirty-five ballots the forces of Treasury Secretary John Sherman, a poor-running third candidate, coalesced with those of Blaine and on the thirty-sixth ballot nominated Ohio's James A. Garfield, Sherman's campaign manager and leader of the stop-Grant forces. Though a dark horse in the convention, Garfield had served in Congress since 1863, where he had attained prestige second only to that of Blaine. To appease the Stalwarts, Chester A. Arthur, who had been removed by Hayes as collector of the port of New York, was nominated for vice-president.

The Democrats averted some indictments on the patriotism issue by nominating a Union general and Gettysburg hero, Pennsylvania's Winfield Scott Hancock, for president and William H. English of Indiana for vice-president. There was little difference in the party platforms, but Hancock voiced, perhaps unwittingly, a profound truth regarding the tariff which may have cost him the election. He asserted that the tariff was "a local issue," and,

in the sense that it was the result of thousands of compromises in congressional logrolling deals, he was precisely correct. But many manufacturers and workers who felt their jobs depended on protection did not appreciate his wisdom and supported his opponent. Returning prosperity also aided the Republicans, who waged the most effective campaigns in the decisive states. Garfield won the election when he carried Indiana and New York by 7,000 and 20,000 votes, although nationally his plurality was less then 10,000.

Garfield Bests Conkling

Though Garfield was a compromise candidate for the presidency, he found neutrality impossible in the rigid contests between factions of

Winfield Scott Hancock

his party. He paid his debt to the Half-Breeds by appointing Blaine secretary of state and, under his persuasive guidance, by replacing the collector of the port of New York with William H. Robertson, an action which challenged Stalwart control of all New York's patronage. Despite tremendous pressure, the president stood his ground and after two months obtained Robertson's confirmation.

After defeat in the Senate, both Stalwart Senators Conkling and Platt resigned and returned to Albany, confident their hands would be strengthened through reelection. They were keenly disappointed, however, for even though Vice-President Arthur personally interceded, the New York legislature refused to reelect them. The episode ended Conkling's political career, temporarily impeded Platt's,

discredited the Stalwarts, and enhanced the power of the presidency.

Garfield's presidential career thus began with great promise but was tragically ended before the nature of his administration became apparent. On July 2, 1881, Charles J. Guiteau, a mentally deranged office seeker, shot him in the Washington railroad station. As he did so, he was heard to gloat that he was a Stalwart and now Arthur was president. After weeks of pain, Garfield died on September 19. Guiteau was later convicted of murder and executed.

Arthur's Administration

The dapper Arthur, who had been a successful abolitionist lawyer, assumed the presidency under a cloud of distrust, but he conducted himself so circumspectly that he earned the enmity of both Republican factions. Soon after he assumed office, the Half-Breeds and Independents left the cabinet, and the Stalwarts were favored in patronage matters. However, prosecution was continued of those Stalwarts who had stolen over $4 million from the Post Office Department through fraudulent "Star Route" contracts, and Conkling and other Stalwart leaders did not control the administration's patronage.

As time elapsed President Arthur proved to be surprisingly independent, and he pursued enlightened policies in several areas; one of these was the tariff which, due to its high rates, produced a surplus each year from 1875 to 1893. The excess revenue was used to reduce rapidly the national debt, a policy which contributed to the general deflation and was also a constant stimulus for raids on the Treasury. To correct the inequitable condition, Arthur vetoed a number of pork-barrel laws and in 1882 obtained the appointment of a nine-man tariff commission. Its study revealed that the high wartime rates, though lowered in 1872,

James A. Garfield

Chester A. Arthur

had been restored in 1875. The commission recommended a general reduction in rates which would reduce income by 20 percent. Though the president gave the measure strong support, he did not exert the executive leadership required for its enactment. Therefore the Tariff of 1883 lowered rates by only 5 percent and in no way reversed the protectionist principle.

Arthur's promotion of civil service reform was more successful and was spurred not only by Garfield's assassination but also by the organization of the National Civil Service Reform League in 1881 and by the Democratic capture of the House of Representatives in 1882. In 1883 the Congress passed the Pendleton Act, which was sponsored by Ohio's Democratic Senator George H. Pendleton but drafted by the secretary of the National Civil Service Reform League, Dorman B. Eaton. It provided for the appointment of a three-man commission to frame and administer competitive examinations which provided a merit basis for appointing classified employees to office. Initially the act applied only to customs and post offices with more than fifty employees, and only 15 percent of federal employees were placed on the classified list; since the president was authorized to add others, the percentage rose to 40 by 1900. Arthur cooperated fully in the passage and implementation of the law, selecting the author of the act as the commission's head.

The president, partially motivated by a desire to dispose of surplus revenue, also pursued an enlightened naval policy in an effort to update the antiquated, wooden-vessel U.S. Navy which in 1881 had declined to twelfth in rank among the world's fleets. After a naval advisory board in 1881 recommended the building of steel cruisers, Arthur pressed Congress for action and in 1883 obtained authorization for the construction of three vessels. The movement initiated by Arthur continued in the next administration, and by 1889 twenty-two steel ships had been built or authorized. Navy Secretary William C. Whitney, in particular, stimulated American industry in insisting that it furnish the heavy ship plates and large naval guns for new craft. Progress continued through the 1890s, and by 1900 the American navy was the third largest in the world and smaller only than that of Great Britain and Germany.

Although Arthur had not proved to be an outstanding leader as president, he had advocated honest, forward-looking policies incongruent with his background whose partial achievement was of great benefit to the nation. In most eras his record would have earned him a nomination for the presidency in 1884, but he had alienated so many Republicans that he was never seriously considered.

Grover Cleveland's Election

In 1884 the Republicans nominated the most popular personality in their party, James G. Blaine, for president and Illinois' John A. Logan for vice-president. Blaine's selection offended a small but significant independent segment of the party which regarded him as a corruptionist and an enemy of civil service reforms. These men, including George William Curtis, who had headed an abortive Civil Service Commission under Grant, and the old Liberal Republican leaders, Carl Schurz and E. L. Godkin, broke with their party and as independent "Mugwumps" supported the Democrats.

The Democrats nominated Grover Cleveland, governor of pivotal New York, for president and Thomas A. Hendricks from equally crucial Indiana for vice-president. Cleveland was largely a self-made man who had risen from district attorney of Erie County, New York, in 1863, to sheriff in 1869, mayor of Buffalo in 1881, and governor in 1882. In his rise to power, Cleveland mastered grass-roots politics, and it was said that he had spoken in every Democratic saloon in Erie County. His reputation for integrity and fair play enabled him to overcome the stigma of having purchased a substitute during the Civil War when, instead of enlisting, he had stayed home and cared for his widowed mother and sisters.

As New York's chief executive, Cleveland displayed the qualities which enabled him to characterize himself as "an ugly, honest man." He defied Tammany Hall but also vetoed bills to reduce fares to five cents on New York City's elevated railways, owned by Jay Gould, and to restrict streetcar conductors to a twelve-hour day. These vetoes required courage, but they also revealed his very conservative outlook on social and economic questions.

Grover Cleveland

As Cleveland's conservatism would suggest, there was no fundamental difference in the attitudes of the two major parties or their candidates in 1884, and the campaign became a bitter personal contest. The Democrats renewed the charges which had first emerged in 1876 that Blaine as house speaker had used his political influence to aid the Little Rock and Fort Smith Railroad, in which he had a personal interest, and contended the Mulligan letters proved his guilt. These letters, written by Blaine to a Boston businessman, Warren Fisher, Jr., between 1864 and 1876, were described to a congressional committee in 1876 by James Mulligan, a Fisher employee who had them in his possession. Blaine immediately obtained them and defended his conduct by explaining portions of them to the House. When eventually published in 1884, however, the letters were effectively used against him as a presidential candidate by the Democrats. The Republicans countered by attacking Cleveland's war record and his relationship with a widow which supposedly resulted in the birth of a child. Forthrightly the bachelor Cleveland acknowledged the child could be his.

Trivial incidents in late October may have given Cleveland the 1,149 votes by which he carried New York and the election. Weary after a day of campaigning, Blaine was greeted by a clergy group whose spokesman, the Reverend Samuel D. Burchard, referred to the Democratic party as that of "Rum, Romanism and Rebellion." Blaine may not have noticed the remark, but his failure to renounce it offended many Catholics, even though his own sister was a nun. The same evening Blaine dined with a number of the country's wealthiest men, including the popular villain, Gould, and stories of this event offended additional voters when magnified out of proportion by the Democratic press. The Mugwump defection was a factor also in New York, but it may have been countered by Tammany's lukewarm support of Cleveland.

The election was a cliff-hanger in which Cleveland emerged with 219 electoral votes to Blaine's 182. Due to its closeness, two minor third parties played an unusually significant role. The National Greenback Labor Party's candidates, Benjamin F. Butler and A. M. West, polled 175,370 votes, and the Prohibitionist candidates, John P. St. John and William Daniel, 150,369 of which 25,000 were in New York state. For the first time since 1861, the

nation had a Democratic president, but the Senate retained a Republican majority and the House a reduced Democratic one.

In November, 1885, soon after the new administration came to power, Vice-President Hendricks died leaving the Republican president pro-tem of the Senate, under the terms of the Presidential Succession Act of 1792, next in line for the presidency should Cleveland become unable to serve. To alter this condition, the Presidential Succession Act of 1886 was enacted in January of that year and remained in operation until 1947. It provided in case of the inability of both the president and vice-president, the heads of the executive departments in order of the creation of their offices should succeed to the duties of the president. In January, 1887, an Electoral Count Act was passed to avoid the possibility of another disputed election such as that of 1876. It specified the electoral returns of each state certified by the state in accordance with its laws would be accepted by Congress. Should the state be unable to decide the proper returns, Congress could do so provided both houses concurred in the decision. If disagreement arose between the houses, the state returns certified by its governor would be counted. These much-needed reforms removed possible inappropriate political impediments in the operation of the national government and were welcomed by Cleveland.

Cleveland Loses the G. A. R.

Cleveland's rugged independence lost none of its potency after he became president, and his deficiencies stemmed primarily from inadequate social and economic attitudes, not personal zeal. He demonstrated typical Cleveland stamina when he refused to consult the Senate regarding removals and suspensions, feeling that they were the exclusive prerogative of the president. His strength impressed the Congress, and, after he clearly defined his views in a message sent to the Senate in March, 1886, the Tenure of Office Act was repealed.

The president's courage approached political foolhardiness in his dealing with veterans, however. By 1885 the strongest veterans' group, the Grand Army of the Republic (G. A. R.), had grown in membership to a half million and had become an extremely effective pressure group which, in many areas, functioned almost as a wing of the Republican party. Under G. A. R. prodding, thousands of private pension bills had been forced through Congress and signed by previous presidents. Cleveland was incensed as an increasing number were passed, feeling many were fraudulent. He began to investigate individual cases and to veto those which seemed unwarranted. Even though he vetoed only 228 pension bills out of a total of 1,871, and annual pension expenditures rose from $56 million in 1885 to $80 million in 1888, Cleveland's action evoked the contempt of the G. A. R..

The G. A. R.'s rage was increased in 1887 when the president vetoed the Dependent Pension Bill, which provided pensions for all honorably discharged veterans with ninety days or more service who were unable to do a full day's manual labor. Cleveland was apparently not opposed to universal pensions but felt not enough time had elapsed to make this policy justifiable. At the time, he believed that pensioning those without service-connected disabilities was a fraud on the government, and his veto was sustained.

Three months later, the president unconsciously offended the G. A. R. again when he approved a War Department order returning Confederate battle flags to the South. Senator John Sherman appropriately appraised the action when he observed that it was "the President's recognition of a lost cause," but Corporal James Tanner, a G. A. R. leader, reportedly exclaimed, "May God palsy the hand that wrote that order." Emotionalism ran high,

and charges of disloyalty were levied against the Democratic party and Cleveland. A week after its issue, the president revoked the order, and the flags were not returned until 1905 during the administraton of Theodore Roosevelt.

State of the Union Message, 1887

On the tariff question, Cleveland assumed a clear position which polarized the leadership of the major parties. Before 1887 ambiguity existed as to the parties' attitudes on the tariff, and a minority of congressional Democrats from protectionist districts provided the votes which enabled Republicans to prevent meaningful downward revision. Meanwhile many Mugwumps and intellectuals joined southern and western Democrats in protesting that the high rates were maintaining high prices in protected industries, discriminating against nonprotected producers including farmers, and were reducing the amount of money in circulation through forced debt reductions. The president and others came to feel that "the tariff was the mother of trusts" and that action must be taken.

At last, in 1887, Cleveland decided to devote his entire annual message to the tariff, pointing out its injustices and demanding substantial revision downward. This decision was made with typical Cleveland independency and without consulting party leaders even though he was warned by some astute political advisers that his action would cost him reelection.

In response to Cleveland's leadership, the House passed a bill, sponsored by Texas' Representative Roger Q. Mills, which placed a number of raw materials on the free list and provided a reduction in rates on lumber, woolens, and finished goods of approximately 7 percent. Northerners protested the changes were sectionally oriented to the South and

West, and the Republican-controlled Senate defeated the measure. The issue was left for popular consideration in the 1888 elections.

Benjamin Harrison's Election

The Republicans chose Benjamin Harrison, a grandson of former President William Henry Harrison and a resident of Indiana, as their presidential candidate. He had risen to colonel's rank in the Civil War and served in the Senate from 1881 to 1887, where he opposed Cleveland's pension policy and advocated civil service reform. Levi P. Morton, a prominent New York banker, was his running mate.

The Democrats renominated Cleveland on a lower tariff platform but removed some of the effectiveness of the issue by choosing a na-

Benjamin Harrison

tional committee chairman and vice-presidential candidate, Allen G. Thurman, who were protectionists. The tariff was important in the campaign, enabling the Republicans to raise large sums of money from industrialists and wage a most effective campaign in critical states, especially Indiana and New York. The issue was probably not decisive, however, since the Democrats made gains in a number of protectionist districts and carried industrialized Connecticut and New Jersey.

Harrison's extremely close victory came through more efficient organization and the use of corruption induced by the large quantity of available funds. Near the end of the campaign, Republican connivance also produced an incident which influenced Irish votes. A California Republican using the pseudonym Charles F. Murchison wrote the British Minister in Washington, Sir Lionel Sackville-West, stating he was a British-born, naturalized American and asked which candidate would best promote good relations between the two countries he loved. Sackville-West fell for the trap, indicating Cleveland was the man who should be supported. Though Cleveland asked his recall the day the story broke, the damage had been done. In the election Cleveland received almost 100,000 more popular votes than his opponent, but Harrison gleaned 233 electoral votes to Cleveland's 168.

Harrison's Mid-Term Defeat

In 1889, for the first time in fourteen years, the Republicans controlled both houses of Congress and the presidency. The margin was close, however, and in 1890, when Thomas B. Reed was chosen House speaker, he felt the use of unprecedented measures was necessary to control the chamber. Refusing to permit traditional delaying measures, he counted all those visible as present even though they wished to be recorded as absent to prevent the gathering of a quorum. Such action was highly unpopular with the opposition and earned the speaker the title "Czar Reed."

Republican control of Congress did not inspire President Harrison to offer vigorous leadership, however. Though an ardent "waver of the bloody shirt," he did nothing in 1890 to expedite passage of the Force Bill (or Lodge Bill). The measure, which provided for national supervision of federal elections to protect black voters in the South, cleared the House but was defeated in the Senate. He was equally weak in his civil service policy, although he had often spoken as an advocate of reform in this area. He did launch Theodore Roosevelt on a six-year career as a member of the Civil Service Commission in 1889, but, when crucial aid was needed, he failed to support him in achieving reforms.

No such failures occurred in efforts to increase pensions and raise the tariff. Upon assuming office, Harrison appointed Corporal James Tanner as Commissioner of Pensions, who, when he took command, supposedly declared, "God help the surplus." Though Tanner served only six months, he added numerous applicants to the pension rolls, and, with his approval in June, 1890, Congress passed and the president approved the Dependent Pension Act, a measure similar to the bill earlier vetoed by Cleveland. It not only provided pensions for all veterans but also grants for their minor children, dependent parents, and widows who had to work for subsistence. Under the Harrison administration, annual expenditures for pensions soared from $90 million to $157 million, and the number of pensioners reached a peak of 970,000 in 1893.

Harrison was also pleased by Congress' enactment of the McKinley Tariff in June, 1890. Since river, harbor, and other grants did not adequately deplete the surplus, Representative William McKinley, a twelve-year House veteran from Ohio and a tariff expert, was chosen chairman of the Ways and Means Committee to deal with the situation. The measure he fathered raised the average rate to 49.5 percent, making many duties prohibitive. Additional surgery was also done on the surplus by placing sugar on the free list, which pleased the sugar trust, and paying a two cents per pound subsidy to domestic producers. At the instigation of Secretary of State James G. Blaine, a reciprocal trade feature was included which empowered the president to impose specific rates on free list goods provided the nations producing them refused to grant comparable advantages to U.S. products. It was hoped especially that the availability of reciprocity would promote trade with Latin America. Though its results were disappointing, it was a precedent which proved useful in the twentieth century.

To obtain passage of the McKinley Tariff, concessions had to be made to the silver-oriented western congressmen whose number had been augmented by the addition of the new states of North Dakota, South Dakota, Montana, and Washington in 1889 and Wyoming and Idaho in 1890. The concern of lawmakers from silver-producing states increased as the decline continued in the price of silver, which on the free market stood at a ratio of 20 to 1 to gold in 1890. The Senate actually passed a free coinage of silver bill in June, 1890, which would have permitted the unlimited coinage of silver into dollars with a weight sixteen times the weight of gold in the gold dollar. Prompted by this crisis, Republican leaders agreed to replace the Bland-Allison Act with the Sherman Silver Purchase Act which was passed by a straight party vote but contained some negative features disliked by inflationists. It provided the government would buy 4.5 million ounces of silver each month, approximately all the domestic production, paying for it with legal tender notes redeemable in gold or silver at the Treasury's choice.

Though the Sherman Silver Purchase Act was initally a boon to the silver producers, it did not achieve the inflation America wanted. Under the Bland-Allison Act, as the quantity of silver increased and the price declined, more dollars could be issued on the basis of the minimum $2 million of silver which must be purchased monthly. By pegging purchases to a specific quantity of silver, the cheaper silver became, the less the 4.5 million ounces purchased under the Sherman Silver Purchase Act would cost and the fewer treasury notes would be issued. Had the minimum purchases under the Bland-Allison Act been made in 1894, 41 percent more money would have been put in circulation than was done under the Sherman Silver Purchase Act. The Treasury also controlled the inflationary effects of the purchases by electing to redeem the silver notes exclusively in gold. While not appeasing the free silverites, the act weakened the gold reserve, and for this reason aroused fear among conservatives.

By the fall of 1890 much of the electorate was disillusioned with the Harrison administration for a number of reasons. It was indicted for extravagance, particularly because the 51st Congress was the first to appropriate a billion dollars, while the tariff was castigated as the exploiter of the masses and the cause of high prices. Democrats in some doubtful states subsidized peddlers to tell their customers that unreasonable prices were due to the Republican duty increases. As a result of widespread disillusionment, in the 1890 elections the Republican membership in the House was reduced from 166 to 88 with a corresponding Democratic increase. The administration and the party in power had received one of the most pointed reprimands in American history.

The Populist Challenge

The continuing agricultural depression and labor distress resulted in the formation of the People's Party in 1892. Fourteen hundred delegates representing the various Alliances, the declining Knights of Labor, the Grange, the Greenbackers, and other protest organizations met in Cincinnati in May, 1891, and called for the organization of a new political party. The formal organization occurred at a February, 1892, meeting in St. Louis attended by eight hundred delegates who, in turn, called a national convention to meet in Omaha in July, 1892.

The Omaha convention was a revival-type gathering which incorporated the basic Alliance principles into the most comprehensive reform platform yet presented by an American political party. Nothing was omitted; included

Ignatius Donnelly

were free coinage of silver at the 16 to 1 ratio, the subtreasury, expansion of the currency, government ownership of the railroads, direct election of senators, and many other reforms, most of which were to be attained in the following decades. Ignatius Donnelly of Minnesota, who in an 1891 novel, *Caesar's Column,* had presented a horrid picture of America under oligarchical control, was a major architect of the platform. His sense of burning indignation expressed the zeal and determination of the delegates who returned home to lead the crusade.

Unfortunately, the Alliances' greatest leader, North Carolina's Leonidas L. Polk, son of the Confederate Bishop-General, died before the Omaha convention. Therefore former Union General James B. Weaver of Iowa, the Greenback presidential candidate in 1880, was nominated for president and former Confederate General James G. Field of Virginia for vice-president.

In many ways the Populist excursion was an interesting and admirable one. Its colorful and stimulating leaders including Donnelly, Representative "Sockless Jerry" Simpson, Mrs. Mary Elizabeth Lease of Kansas, who advised farmers "to raise less corn and more hell," and many others who spoke in an idiom the people understood. Their very effectiveness in communication enabled the opposition unjustly to portray the party as a radical instrument which would destroy the American way of life. This accusation more than any other limited the party's success in creating a new political synthesis uniting labor and agricultural interests on a nonsectional, nonracial basis. In 1892 its presidential candidate obtained 1,027,329 popular votes, approximately one-fifth that of each of the major parties. Although ten Populist representatives and five senators were also chosen, the number did not adequately reflect the political disenchantment with the older

parties. The congressional victories came primarily in the western states, which were excessively concerned with silver, and did not augur well for the party's ultimate success. However, the party's achievements shook the opposition, forcing it to begin serious consideration of issues which had been avoided, and, at the state level, a number of legislatures passed to Populist control, which increased the leverage of the reformers.

Populism in the South

Populism suffered from an inability to attract a great deal of labor support but its major failure was the refusal of the average southern Allianceman to abandon the Democratic party. This was a surprising development since as early as 1890 eight southern legislatures passed under Alliance control and four Alliance-backed governors were elected, including Benjamin Tillman in South Carolina and James S. Hogg in Texas. These victories were triumphs of the common man and resulted in many local reforms including the more equitable levying of taxes, establishment of new schools and colleges, increased control of the fertilizer trust, and penitentiary reform. A number of Alliance-supported congressman were also chosen in the South in 1890, but only one, Thomas E. Watson of Georgia, refused to cooperate with the regular Democratic organization. Initially Watson and other avowed southern Populists maintained a truly biracial appeal and organization, but they were defeated in subsequent elections and became more racist in attitude than the more conservative Democrats.

In some southern states such as Alabama, Alliancemen were too disenchanted with the reactionism of the regular Democratic party to support its nominees. Due to fear of possible black control should the Democratic party be split, they supported "Jeffersonian Democratic" candidates who contended they were the nominees of the "true Democratic" party. In 1892 the Jeffersonian Democrats' candidate for governor of Alabama, Reuben F. Kolb, was probably fraudulently defeated by the regular Democrats' use of Black Belt votes.

The small Populist parties in the South frequently coalesced with the Republicans since hatred of Democratic fraud was more potent than ideology. In North Carolina the coalition captured control of the state government in 1894 and elected a United States senator. Such success was not attained elsewhere in the South, but as economic conditions worsened many regular Democrats were increasingly converted to Populist principles, especially on monetary matters. By 1896 the South was ready to aid in revising the attitude of the national party on silver and in its movement to the left.

Cleveland's Reelection

The candidates of the major parties in 1892 were predetermined and nominated without difficulty. Harrison was chosen without enthusiasm by the Republicans, and *New York Tribune* editor, Whitelaw Reid, was nominated for vice-president. The Democrats tapped Cleveland with much more enthusiasm and designated Illinois' Adlai E. Stevenson, grandfather of the 1952 and 1956 Democratic presidential nominee, as his running mate.

The two major candidates offered the voters little choice. Though the Democratic platform declared that only a tariff for revenue was constitutional, Cleveland, sobered by four years as a successful New York attorney, did not press the issue. Instead, he strongly defended the gold standard which aided him in gaining the support of eastern leaders. On the other hand,

Harrison was hurt by the unpopularity of the McKinley Tariff and labor unrest, including a bloody strike in Idaho's silver mines and the Homestead debacle in Pennsylvania (see pp. 68–69).

When the election returns were in, Cleveland had attained the most solid victory in two decades. He won over 360,000 more popular votes than Harrison, carrying New York, Indiana, Illinois, and California and obtaining 277 electoral votes to 145. His second administration with Democrats in control of both houses of Congress was inaugurated with confidence, but the depression which had already begun placed it in a vulnerable position.

Cleveland Defends the Gold Standard

The United States had been moving toward its most severe depression for months before Cleveland reassumed office. Much of agriculture had been depressed for years, and business generally began to be affected following the failure of Britain's Baring Brothers banking house in November, 1890. Its collapse led British investors to sell American securities and drain gold from the United States. In late February, 1893, the failure of the Philadelphia and Reading Railroad resulted in unprecedented stock trading. In May and June stock prices crashed, and concerned investors began to convert government bonds into gold. By December, 1893, the government's gold reserve had declined to $80 million, well below the $100 million considered safe.

Cleveland incorrectly believed the Sherman Silver Purchase Act was primarily responsible for the depression, reasoning that the silver certificates issued under the law placed a constant drain on gold reserves and destroyed business confidence. This explanation was naïve, neglecting a multiplicity of causes for any complex economic development, but the president insisted on calling a special congressional session to repeal the act. By using great pressure, Cleveland obtained his wishes by votes of 239 to 108 and 48 to 37 in the House and Senate. In doing so, however, he permanently alienated much of his party in the South and West.

Much to Cleveland's disappointment, repeal of the Sherman Silver Purchase Act did not end the depression. Bankruptcies, including a number of leading railroads, continued unabated; unemployment grew to affect millions; and the drain on gold increased. When the reserves fell to approximately $60 million in January, 1894, the president ordered the first of four bond sales to meet the crisis. The first two had little permanent effect, since bankers withdrew gold to purchase bonds. In desperation, when the reserve reached $41 million in January, 1895, the president turned to J. Pierpont Morgan who with August Belmont and other associates purchased a $65 million bond issue. By obtaining from Europe half of the 3.5 million ounces of gold furnished the government, the bankers aided in preserving the gold standard. Although another bond sale was necessary, the menace was never as great again. Cleveland's action endeared him to conservative businessmen, but many farmers and laborers, who saw no improvement in their condition, were convinced he had sacrificed their interests. Wages continued to be cut, unsuccessful strikes were staged, and the Pullman strike was broken by the use of troops, all of which promoted a despondency that gripped millions.

As the depression reached its depth in 1894, jobless men across the country formed "armies" commanded by "generals" and sought to obtain government action in their behalf. The most famous was that commanded by a wealthy Ohio Populist, Jacob S. Coxey, who advocated a national public works program to be financed by federal issue of $500 million in legal tender notes. To gain a hearing for his scheme which hopefully would provide both employment and inflation, Coxey staged a march on Washington that brought some five hundred people to the capital. It and a score of similar marches were ended when the police arrested their leaders.

The Wilson-Gorman Tariff

Cleveland's one progressive stand during the depression and his second administration was an effort to lower the tariff. Under his prompting, a commendable bill emerged from the House, but in the Senate 600 amendments were added before the Wilson-Gorman Bill was passed in 1894. Although it lowered average rates approximately 10 percent (to 39.9 percent), Cleveland was so disappointed he allowed the measure to become law without his signature. He felt a great opportunity had been missed to cripple the unholy combinations which charged exorbitant prices for their products and contributed much to the nation's economic misery.

The Wilson-Gorman Tariff's one redeeming feature was a tax of 2 percent on incomes over $4,000, included primarily to lure the votes of Populists. In 1895 the Supreme Court by six-to-two and five-to-four decisions in the cases of *Pollock* v. *Farmers' Loan and Trust Company* invalidated the tax, holding it was a direct tax which under the Constitution must be apportioned among the states on the basis of population. Its decision was a reversal of that in *Springer* v. *United States* (1881) which upheld the Civil War income tax. The Court's opinion was as conservative as that of the president and led many people to resolve that national leadership must be changed.

Democrats Nominate Bryan

Disenchantment with Cleveland's policies and the depression cost the Democrats more than half their House seats in the 1894 elections, and many victorious Democrats in the South and West were openly anti-Cleveland. Senator Ben Tillman of South Carolina, who pledged to go to Washington and "prod" Cleveland with a pitchfork "in his old fat ribs," was only the most vulgar of a numerous band. The situation intensified in 1895 and 1896, and a majority of House Democrats signed an "Appeal of the Silver Democrats," drafted by Representatives Richard Bland and William Jennings Bryan, advocating immediate institution of free silver coinage. Subsidies by western silver producers permitted the holding of a number of southern and western free silver conventions and the distribution of a great deal of literature including "Professor" William H. "Coin" Harvey's effective pamphlet, *Coin's Financial School.* Though deficient in economic theory, it thoroughly castigated the "gold bugs" as the cause of hard times and suffering.

The outcome of the Democratic convention was predetermined except for its candidates since by 1896 the entire party organization in the South and West had passed into free silver hands. Over strong opposition of the Cleveland forces and guided by Governor John P. Altgeld, a platform was adopted urging free coinage of silver at the 16 to 1 ratio, promising effective railroad regulation, and condemning the use of injunctions in labor disputes, the national banking system, the Supreme Court's invalidation of the income tax, the protective tariff, and trusts.

For once a convention speech was influential in the selection of a presidential candidate. Representative Richard Bland had a number of supporters, but when the thirty-six-year-old William Jennings Bryan spoke on the platform's silver plank, he swept the convention off its feet. Using an agrarian approach whose antecedents were deeply entrenched in United States history, he asserted rural America sustained the nation's life. Should the cities be destroyed, they could be revived, but if America's farmers were maimed, grass would soon grow in the streets of every city. After "exposing" the conspiracy of the conservative business classes, in a marvelous simile, he proclaimed, "You shall not crucify mankind upon a cross of gold."

Bryan, who was nominated on the fifth ballot, was a native of Salem, Illinois. After graduating from Illinois College and Chicago's Union Law School, he moved to Lincoln, Nebraska, where at twenty-seven he became active in politics. He was elected to Congress in 1890 and 1892, and after defeat in 1894 became editor of the *Omaha World-Herald.* For two years before his nomination in 1896, he traveled widely, speaking for free silver and, in effect, preparing for his great convention oration. In many ways, Bryan was a simple, honest man who did not adequately appreciate the complexities of modern life. Yet he was sincerely sympathetic to reform and had the youth and dedication to mount a crusade to bring overdue changes in the system. Arthur Sewall, a conservative Maine banker opposed to the gold standard, was chosen to run with him.

Almost a month before the Democratic convention the Republicans had nominated Ohio's William McKinley on the first ballot at their convention, and Garrett A. Hobart of New Jersey was chosen as the vice-presidential candidate. Following extensive service in the Civil War during which he rose to the rank of major, McKinley practiced law in Canton, Ohio, and served six terms in Congress where he became a tariff expert. His sponsorship of the 1890 tariff, however, cost him reelection, but in 1891 and 1893 he was elected governor of Ohio. McKinley was not only a kindly, gen-

William Jennings Bryan

McKinley, Hanna was a moderate in politics and had a prolabor attitude. At the Republican convention, he allowed eastern conservatives

William McKinley

erous man but also was far from being a reactionary. He had moderate views on free silver, having voted for both the Bland-Allison and Sherman Silver Purchase Acts, and was a friend of labor, more than once having defended union leaders in the courts when most lawyers would not take their cases.

McKinley's rise to the governorship and the presidency was engineered by his close friend and alter-ego, Mark Hanna. A native Ohioan also, Hanna had become wealthy through diverse investment in coal, iron, and banking. Before he retired in 1894 to promote McKinley, he had become the principal owner of Cleveland's street railways and sole owner of its opera house and the *Cleveland Herald.* Like to force his acceptance of the gold standard which led Senator Henry M. Teller of Colorado and some other silver Republicans to bolt and support the Democrats. The Republican platform also endorsed the protective tariff and a vigorous foreign policy.

Democratic choice of a free-silverite on a free-silver platform left the surprised Populists in a dilemma. Many southern Populists especially distrusted Bryan's ability to obtain action on most Populist demands and feared merger with conservative southern Democrats. However, western leaders feared a split in the free-silver vote would bring defeat and engineered the convention's acceptance of Bryan. This occurred after Nebraska's Senator William V. Allen incorrectly told the convention that the Democrats would withdraw Sewall as a vice-presidential candidate and replace him with Tom Watson.

Although the Populists removed one candidate, the gold Democrats interjected another in the race. Sickened by "radical" capture of their party, they nominated Illinois' John M. Palmer and Kentucky's Simon B. Buckner for the nation's highest offices on a gold standard platform.

The Campaign of 1896

Though he had limited resources, Bryan mounted the first modern presidential campaign. Traveling incessantly, he spoke in twenty-nine states to five million Americans, many of whom would remember the experience for life. He was well received as he not only indicted the nation's monetary policy but also the need for government action in many other fields. His position and appeal forced the most intense debate on real issues that the nation had seen for decades.

Meanwhile, McKinley received numerous visiting delegations on the front porch of his Ohio home. Hanna planned excursions of party leaders and the faithful from across the land to Canton, and they left deeply impressed with their candidate.

Nationally the Republicans unjustly portrayed Bryan as a wild radical whose triumph would bring the end to free, capitalistic America. Much of industrial America contributed handsomely to the Republican campaign fund, which enabled Hanna to carry his message to every corner of the land. Some employers applied pressure to their workers, informing them that should Bryan be elected they need not return to work. Much of this effort was unnecessary, since many workers feared the effects of a lower tariff on their jobs and of free silver on their wages' purchasing power. Bryan's failure to capture the labor vote was instrumental in his defeat.

In the election Bryan carried the South, the plains and mountain states, but McKinley swept the East and Midwest and had almost 600,000 more popular votes than his opponent; the electoral vote stood 271 to 176. The farmers' vote was divided, with McKinley carrying such states as North Dakota, Minnesota, and Iowa. Obviously the class crisis many had predicted had not materialized, and, despite Hanna's propaganda, McKinley had been elected as a unifier and harmonizer, a role for which he was well fitted.

McKinley's Administration

The realistic, considerate McKinley won the confidence of a large cross section of America, an achievement made easier by returning prosperity and the president's innate ability as a politician. He deliberately delayed consideration of the silver question until developing conditions largely removed its critical nature. Due to gold discoveries in Australia, Alaska, and South Africa and development of a new

Mark Hanna administers "That Deadly Dope" for the McKinley campaign in a cartoon which appeared in the Washington Post, *April 2, 1896.*

method to exploit low-grade ores, the quantity of gold increased, removing much of the advantage of free silver. Meanwhile, improved business conditions, increased European demands for agricultural products, and the economic stimulation connected with the Spanish-American War brought economic relief. The quantity of paper money national banks could issue was also increased to 100 instead of 90 percent of their federal bond holdings. By 1899, when McKinley recom-

mended the formal adoption of the gold standard, the issue had become dated. Congress, by a purely party vote, complied with his request in 1900.

Though the president later began to question the value of a protective tariff to a highly industrialized nation, he called a special session of Congress shortly after his inauguration to deal with import duties. With Republicans firmly in control of both houses, the Dingley Tariff was enacted, which pushed rates to a new high. However, general prosperity made the measure less repugnant to many than it would otherwise have been.

By 1900 the nation was more unified than it had been in the previous century. Though conservatism appeared to be in the saddle, the national administration was controlled by moderate men who were at least amenable to some changes. At the state and local level, grass-roots reform movements were well under way and gave every indication that they would grow and influence national developments, while, concurrently, a new interest had arisen in foreign affairs which led the United States to assume a position as a world power.

Selected Bibliography

Late nineteenth-century politics are surveyed in H. Wayne Morgan, *From Hayes to McKinley: National Party Politics, 1877–1896* (1969), and in Ray Ginger, *Age of Excess, The U.S. from 1877 to 1914** (1965). Matthew Josephson, *The Politicos, 1865–1896** (1963), is a stern indictment whose overdrawn pictures are corrected by John A. Garraty, *The New Commonwealth, 1877–1890** (1968), and Harold U. Faulkner's fine study of the 1890s, *Politics, Reform and Expansion, 1890–1900** (1959). Leonard D. White, *The Republican Era, 1869–1901, A Study in Administrative History** (1965), is an effective analysis.

Kenneth E. Davison, *The Presidency of Rutherford B. Hayes* (1972), does much to enhance the reputation of Hayes' administration. Robert D. Marcus, *Grand Old Party: Political Structure in the Gilded Age, 1880–1896* (1971), studies Republican campaigns and conditions in five elections. A. Bower Sageser has analyzed *The First Two Decades of the Pendleton Act, A Study of Civil Service Reform* (1935). Though old, Edward Stanwood, *American Tariff Controversies in the Nineteenth Century* (2 vols. repr. of 1903 ed., 1967), provides indispensable information on that troubled issue.

Allan Nevins, *Grover Cleveland: A Study in Courage* (1932), and Horace S. Merrill, *Bourbon Leader: Grover Cleveland and the Democratic Party** (1957), reveal the strengths and weaknesses of his leadership. The Mugwumps are treated in Richard Hofstadter, *Anti-Intellectualism in American Life** (1963). Almont Lindsey, *The Pullman Strike, The Story of a Unique Experiment and of a Great Labor Upheaval** (1943), does justice to that major crisis. David S. Muzzey, *James G. Blaine, A Political Idol of Other Days* (1963); W. A. Robinson, *Thomas B. Reed, Parliamentarian* (1930); and Harry J. Sievers, *Benjamin Harrison, Hoosier President: the White House and After* (1968), assess Republican leaders.

The monetary question is treated in Allen Weinstein, *Prelude to Populism, Origins of the Silver Issue, 1867–1878* (1970), and D. R. Dewey, *Financial History of the United States* (rev. ed., 1936). An understanding of Populism still begins with John D. Hicks, *The Populist Revolt: A History of the Farmers' Alliance and Peoples' Party** (1961). Richard Hofstadter, *The Age of Reform: From Bryan to F.D.R.** (1955), indicts Populism for simplistic solutions and anti-Semitism, a view refuted by Norman Pollack, *The Populist Response to Industrial America** (1966), and Walter T. Nugent, *The Tolerant Populists: Kansas Populism and Nativism* (1963). Effective studies of the movement's effect in the West and South are in Russell B. Nye, *Midwestern Progressive Politics, . . . 1870–1958* (1965); H. S. Merrill, *Bourbon Democracy of the Middle West, 1865–1896** (1969); Richard J. Jensen, *The Winning of the*

*Available in paperback.

Midwest, Social and Political Conflict, 1888–1896 (1971); and C. Vann Woodward, *Origins of the New South, 1877–1913** (1971).

J. Rogers Hollingsworth, *The Whirligig of Politics, The Democracy of Cleveland and Bryan* (1963), traces the divided mind of the nation through a study of the Democratic party. The election of 1896 is treated in Paul W. Glad, *McKinley, Bryan and the People** (1964), and Robert F. Durden, *The Climax of Populism: The Election of 1896** (1965). Paolo E. Coletta, *William Jennings Bryan* (3 vols., 1964–1969), supersedes earlier biographies. Margaret K. Leech, *In the Days of McKinley* (1959), and H. Wayne Morgan, *William McKinley and His America* (1963), cover the politics of the times and portray McKinley as an effective leader, an image also presented in Wilfred E. Binkley, *American Political Parties* (3rd. rev. ed., 1958).

United States
Foreign
Intervention

1889	Samoa
1893	Hawaii
1895	Venezuela
1898	The Philippines, Cuba, Wake Island, and Puerto Rico
1903	Panama
1905	Dominican Republic
1906	Cuba
1912	Nicaragua
1915	Dominican Republic

Major Diplomatic Events
in which the
United States Participated

1889	Inter-American Conference
1895–99	Venezuelan Boundary Arbitration
1898	Treaty of Paris
1899	First "Open Door" notes
	First Hague Conference
1900	Second "Open Door" notes
1905	Portsmouth Conference
1906	Algeciras Conference
1907	Second Hague Conference
1908	Root-Takahira Agreement

17

A New Imperalism

Long-Range Developments

For Economics and Corporate Enterprise

American dependence on overseas markets has continued to increase in the twentieth century.

The completion of the Panama Canal has been a boon to American commerce but has necessitated foreign and military policies designed to protect the vital lifeline.

For Democratic Government

United States discrimination in its immigration policy against the proud Japanese increased the tensions between the two nations.

For the Westward Movement, Nationalism, and Expansion

British capitulation on the Venezuelan boundary dispute promoted closer Anglo-American cooperation which has continued until this time.

United States participation in the Spanish-American War and its intervention in Latin American countries have contributed to the increased anti-Americanism of that region.

The Spanish-American War and territory gained from it greatly promoted American interest in foreign affairs and stimulated imperialist forces in the United States.

Acquisition of Hawaii and the Philippines made the United States a Pacific power and was in part responsible for its involvement in World War II, the Korean War, and the Vietnam War.

The American agreement with the new state of Panama regarding the isthmian canal has proved a troublous source of controversy in recent years.

The New American Attitude

For two decades after the Civil War, concern with foreign affairs languished in the United States, despite the increased prestige it enjoyed as a major power. The nation's energies were absorbed in conquering the West and industrializing the East and South, and, as Secretary of State Seward, President Grant, and other expansionists learned, the public was apathetic to imperial gains.

Slowly changes occurred that ushered in a new attitude toward expansion, including industrial growth which produced a surplus of manufactured goods needing markets abroad. By 1898 the country was exporting more industrial goods than it imported; total exports had tripled since 1870. While most business leaders did not advocate the establishment of colonies, they came to welcome economic penetration of other regions, although in America, as in contemporary England, a diverse segment of society, including many intellectuals, remained opposed to expansion as undemocratic and unworthy of national tradition. However, a larger, more effective group, motivated by many factors, embraced the new imperialism. A number of Social Darwinists accepted the expansion and dominance of America's superior civilization as inevitable. Some intellectuals espoused a new racism which found the roots of Anglo-American culture in its Germanic origin and believed particular nations were composed of inferior peoples. John Burgess, John Fiske, and even Woodrow Wilson were among the historians who propounded this view. Contemporary Protestant theologians, backed by the personal witness of many missionaries, saw the hand of God in the expansion process. The Reverend Josiah Strong, writing in *Our Country* (1885), contended the Anglo-Saxon race had become "the depository" of the highest Christian civilization, "first, a pure, spiritual Christianity, and, sec-

ond, civil liberty." Without question, he believed its international predominance would be the will of God.

Superpatriots, including Theodore Roosevelt and Massachusetts Congressman Henry Cabot Lodge, found expansion to be a testing of the nation's mettle. An expanded U.S. Navy became the goal of many vigorous partisans who read and utilized the writings of Captain Alfred T. Mahan, firmly believing national greatness depended on the development of sea power and the acquisition of territories.

Secretary of State Blaine

The new outward thrust of America found expression in the policies of James G. Blaine as secretary of state. A conscious disciple of Henry Clay, he dreamed of closer relations with Latin America which would end the unfavorable U. S. balance of trade with the region and result in U.S. economic penetration and the acquisition of naval bases as well as the site for an isthmian canal. In his brief tenure as secretary of state under Garfield, Blaine called an inter-American conference which was not held. In 1888 the invitations were reissued by President Cleveland and Secretary of State Thomas F. Bayard, but Blaine returned to office as Harrison's secretary of state in time to preside over the meeting. Delegates from all Latin American states except Santo Domingo attended, but efforts to lower tariffs and establish procedures for arbitrating disputes failed. However, an organization later known as the Pan-American Union was formed, which provided for the exchange of cultural and commercial information.

In a series of diplomatic events, Blaine exhibited a new militancy in foreign affairs which destroyed much of the goodwill obtained in Latin America. After the New Orleans police chief was slain in 1890, reportedly

James G. Blaine

by Mafia forces, a mob lynched eleven persons, three of whom were Italians. Though the Italian government withdrew its minister to the United States, Blaine refused to intervene, asserting the crime was a subject of state rather than federal concern. Eventually President Harrison ended the episode by apologizing in his annual message and recommending a $25,-000 indemnity.

In another incident, war was almost precipitated with Chile, a nation Blaine disliked because of its close economic relations with Great Britain. In 1891, when the President of Chile attempted to become a dictator, a revolt oc-

curred and a rebel steamer, the *Itata,* tried to take arms purchased in the United States to the revolutionists. Fearful of becoming embroiled in an internal dispute, the United States detained the vessel in San Diego. The *Itata* managed to escape, however, and was joined by a rebel cruiser, ostensibly to defend it against an American vessel which was in hot pursuit. Many expected an armed clash, but the *Itata* reached Chile safely. Once there, the rebels surrendered the ship to the United States, but it was ultimately returned when a U.S. court held the vessel had been improperly detained. In October, 1891, while feeling was still running high over the *Itata* affair, some 120 unarmed sailors from the U.S.S. *Baltimore* were given shore leave in Valpariso. A riot occurred, supposedly after a Chilean spat in an American's face. Two were killed and seventeen injured by the mob which some contended was aided by the police. After the Chilean foreign minister sent a denunciatory cablegram to Harrison, the president threatened to sever diplomatic relations and virtually demanded war. Hostilities were averted when Chile retracted its charges, apologized, and paid a $75,000 indemnity.

Blaine also displayed a marked anti-British attitude which delighted the Irish element of his party. In diplomatic notes whose effect was mainly confined to American public opinion, he protested the 1850 Clayton-Bulwer Treaty requirement of joint U.S.-British construction of an isthmian canal. In another area, he precipitated a crisis with Britain over its violation of American rights by purported killing of seals just beyond the three-mile limit of the Pribilof Islands (which had been acquired with Alaska). As early as 1886, U.S. revenue cutters had begun seizing Canadian sealers, and, after assuming office in 1889, Blaine, who held that the wholesale killing of seals was basically immoral, contended that since the seals bred in U.S. territory they were subject to American protection even beyond coastal waters. Eventually, in 1893, an arbitration board decided against the United States, and in 1898 $473,151 damages were paid to Britain. The arbiters, however, prohibited the catching of pelagic seals within a sixty-mile zone around the Pribilof Islands during certain months of the year. The agreement did not work since the months chosen were not the proper ones to protect the young seals. The situation was resolved only in 1911 when concern over the diminishing herds led the United States, Great Britain, Russia, and Japan to sign an effective Pelagic Sealing Agreement. It outlawed pelagic sealing north of the 30th parallel, gave the United States a monopoly of the catch, and allocated a portion of the profits to Great Britain and France for their withdrawal.

In one area, Samoa, Blaine's influence had a moderating effect. Since 1878 the United States had used Samoa's excellent Pago Pago harbor, but a British-German agreement, by which Britain accepted German control in return for German recognition of British mandates elsewhere, threatened to shut out the United States. Conflict was averted at Apia Harbor in March, 1889, when a hurricane destroyed all the German and two American vessels. At a conference the following month in Berlin, the autonomy of Samoa was recognized, and, for the first time, the United States joined in a protectorate arrangement, in this case with Britain and Germany. Ten years later the islands were partitioned between Germany and the United States.

Cleveland's Venezuelan Policy

Grover Cleveland's administration was much less imperialistic than that of Harrison, yet when a boundary dispute between Venezuela and British Guiana became intense in 1895 the president assumed a Blaine-like position. He may have been partially motivated by a desire to find a popular issue for the administration, but his action was typical of Cleveland when aroused.

The Venezuelan boundary dispute had been smoldering since 1814 when the British assumed control from the Dutch in Guiana. In 1887 Venezuela severed diplomatic relations with Britain and asked the United States to arbitrate, but the British refused to agree to the proposal. In 1894 Cleveland, who was distrustful of Britain, received Congress' approval to renew the arbitration offer, but it was again refused. The discovery of gold in the disputed area, Venezuelan propaganda in the United States, and the new militancy of American opinion led Cleveland to take action. Without consulting Venezuela, Secretary of State Richard Olney demanded that Britain allow the U.S. to arbitrate; to fail to do so would be considered a violation of the Monroe Doctrine. Olney flamboyantly asserted, "Today the United States is practically sovereign on this continent, and its fiat is law upon the subjects to which it confines its interposition."

The British government waited four months before replying that the Monroe Doctrine was not applicable to the dispute and refusing arbitration. Infuriated, in December, 1895, Cleveland submitted the correspondence to Congress and recommended a commission be appointed to decide the boundary. If subsequently Britain should attempt to take territory the commission held was not British, the president declared the United States would use the necessary means to prevent aggression.

The British were shocked but reevaluated their position in light of their contest with Germany and their isolation in Europe. They not only agreed to arbitration but also furnished data to aid in the task. When the awards were made in 1899, the British received much of what they claimed; however, Venezuela ob-

The Venezuelan Boundary Settlement 1899

Area in dispute between Venezuela and Great Britain

CARRIBEAN SEA

Orinoco River

VENEZUELA

FINAL SETTLEMENT

BRITISH GUIANA

DUTCH GUIANA

BRAZIL

tained the mouth of the Orinoco River. More significantly, British-United States relations improved, and, when the Spanish-American War came, Britain alone among the major European powers was sympathetic to the United States.

The Tariff

Concern with the internal affairs of other countries was precipitated by the United States' tariff policy which promoted revolutions in Hawaii and Cuba, but President Cleveland steered the United States away from involvement in both countries. American capital had come to control Hawaiian sugar plantations, and after 1875 sugar was admitted duty free to the United States in return for a Hawaiian promise not to grant any territory to another foreign state. Sugar production increased rapidly, and in 1887 the planters obtained control of the government by forcing the Hawaiian king to accept a liberal constitution.

Stable, profitable Hawaiian conditions changed after the McKinley Tariff placed sugar on the free list but provided a bounty to U.S. producers. The Hawaiian planters began to incur large deficits, and when the king died in

1891 his successor, Queen Liliuokalani, attempted to restore absolute rule. As a result, the American residents of the islands led by Sanford B. Dole, the pineapple king, planned a revolt. With the aid of the United States minister, John L. Stevens, who imported 150 marines from the U.S.S. *Boston* to intimidate the natives, the queen was overthrown in January, 1893. A new provisional government was formed, which Stevens recognized, and a commission was sent to Washington to arrange for annexation and with it access to the U.S. sugar bounty.

By the time an annexation treaty reached the Senate, however, Cleveland had returned to power. Questioning the situation, he sent former Georgia Congressman James H. Blount to investigate, and, after receiving his report, dispatched a new minister to Hawaii with orders to restore Queen Liliuokalani. President Dole of the provisional government refused to yield power, and Cleveland was not willing to use force to overthrow him. However, he withdrew the annexation treaty and denounced the means by which the revolt had taken place. Yet, following the proclamation of the Hawaiian republic on July 4, 1894, the president formally extended recognition. Annexation was approved by the 1896 Republican platform and was obtained by joint resolution of Congress in July, 1898. Fear of Japanese interest in the islands was a factor, but more significant was the increased desire for eastern bases promoted by the Spanish-American War.

Another tariff, the Wilson-Gorman Tariff of 1894, helped revive a major rebellion in Spanish Cuba in 1895. It increased by 40 percent the U.S. duties on Cuban sugar and intensified the effects of the 1893 depression in the island. The suffering Cubans, who were chafing under the inefficiency and corruption of Spanish rule, conducted widespread destruction of American-owned sugar plantations and mills in an effort to involve the United States. Congress, sympathetic with the Cuban struggle for freedom, adopted a resolution urging the president to grant belligerent status to the rebels, but Cleveland refused to act. As the situation intensified, however, McKinley's administration assumed a different attitude.

Initiation of War with Spain

The policies pursued by General Valeriano Weyler, called "the Butcher" by pro-rebel American newspapers, who was sent by Spain to suppress the Cuban revolt, did much to arouse U.S. opposition. Confronted by the mass destruction being committed by the rebels, he herded large segments of the people into reconcentration camps in the belief that this was the only means of removing the widespread aid the rebels were receiving. In the camps lack of proper hygiene, in particular, led to much suffering and innumerable deaths. Over a two-year period more than 10 percent of the Cuban population died as a result of this and other Spanish policies.

These events furnished grist for the mill of the United States "yellow press," a name given to sensational newspapers because of their cheap, yellow newsprint. Hearst's *New York Journal,* Pulitzer's *New York World,* and other newspapers to a lesser extent dispatched reporters and artists to Cuba who, by exaggerated stories and sketches, converted the American people to intervention. Many Protestant publications began to present Cuba as a moral responsibility where Christianity demanded rectification. Concurrently, naval expansionists and some imperialists contended that national honor required intervention, and also that control of Cuba furnished the key to the entire Caribbean.

In general, the American business community opposed involvement, and where overseas affairs were concerned a number preferred to concentrate on Chinese investments and development. As usual, any element which would interject instability, including the prospect of higher taxes, was distrusted by business, especially after the depression began to recede in 1897. Many feared American property in Cuba would be lost during an all-out conflict, but the drift to intervention continued despite American reservations and Spanish efforts to prevent it. The American Federation of Labor, patriotic organizations, and many Protestant leaders favored war. Moreover, the government in Madrid was caught in a dilemma which forced it to temper its concessions to remain in power. However, a more liberal ministry made a number of conciliatory moves in October, 1897, including the recall of General Weyler, a lightening of the reconcentration camp policy, the release of U.S. nationals, and the grant to Cuba of a degree of self-government, but McKinley's proposal of Cuban autonomy was not granted. These actions did not please either side in Cuba, and the struggle continued since the rebels would accept nothing less than complete independence.

Two events in February, 1898, precipitated a U.S.-Spanish crisis. The first came on February 9 when Hearst published a letter in the *New York Journal* from the Spanish minister to the United States, Dupuy de Lôme, which had been stolen from the Havana post office. In it he characterized President McKinley as a weakling "who tries to leave a door open behind himself while keeping on good terms with the jingoes of his own party." Though de Lôme quickly resigned, the attack on McKinley angered even his political opponents.

Six days after the appearance of the de Lôme letter, a second crisis developed when the new U.S. battleship *Maine* was sunk in Havana harbor by an explosion which killed 260 officers and men. The *Maine* had been ordered to Cuban waters following loyalist riots upon the

The first photograph of the wreckage of the **Maine** *in Havana harbor.*

dismissal of Weyler. Soon after the explosion, a naval investigation indicated it was caused by an external mine but did not place responsibility for its planting. On the other hand, the yellow press ascribed the explosion to Spanish agents, and the public generally accepted its verdict. All indications are that this conclusion was incorrect since the last thing Spain wanted was a war with the United States. It was far more likely that the mine was planted by rebels who wished to provoke a Spanish-American war.

Before receiving this information, McKinley bowed to the pressure of public opinion, including that of William Jennings Bryan, and began work on a war message presented to Congress April 11. Information regarding Spain's concessions was included but not emphasized, and Congress scarcely noted them. On April 20, 1898, by a vote of 311 to 6 in the House and 42 to 35 in the Senate, the independence of Cuba was recognized, withdrawal of Spanish forces was demanded, and the president was authorized to use the armed forces to

carry out this policy. By the unanimously adopted Teller Amendment, the Senate renounced any intention of gaining Cuban territory, although, as Teller pointed out, his amendment did not preclude the taking of territory elsewhere. Spain declared war on the United States on April 24, 1898, and the United States reciprocated the following day. A sense of honor, frustration with a "cesspool" on the American doorstep, and imperial ambition had led a reluctant president and business community to accept war.

Victory at Manila Bay

When war began, the new United States Navy with 26,000 officers and men and a number of new steel vessels was in excellent condition. Without the knowledge of the navy secretary, on February 25, 1898, Assistant Secretary Theodore Roosevelt, with McKinley's approval, had secretly cabled Commodore

George Dewey at Hong Kong to move against Manila should hostilities begin.

When Dewey learned war had been declared, he promptly moved his four cruisers and two gunboats to the Philippines, entering Manila Bay on the evening of April 30. Early the following morning his force began the first of five passes against ten inferior Spanish cruisers and gunboats. All the Spanish vessels were destroyed and 381 men killed. The American craft were undamaged; no men were killed, though eight were wounded.

The victory at Manila Bay brought an outpouring of national joy and a new interest in the Far East. Dewey did not have manpower to occupy the city and had to content himself with imposing a blockade. At last, large numbers of troops arrived in late July, and, assisted by Filipino guerrillas, they assaulted and took

the city on August 13, after operations in the Caribbean were completed.

Success in the Philippines offered a new challenge to imperialists who became intensely interested in the possibilities the islands offered for trade and political influence. Their control became a major question at the peace conference and in American politics during the next few years.

The Battle for Cuba

The army was far less prepared for war than the navy, and, when hostilities began, it numbered only 28,000 men, most of whose training and equipment had been designed for Indian duty on the plains. Congress authorized an increase of the regular army to 60,000 and the

The battle of Manila Bay.

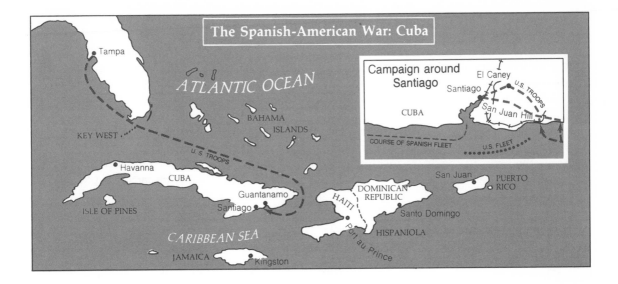

The Spanish-American War: Cuba

Campaign around Santiago

addition of 200,000 volunteers. These added numbers posed monumental problems for the inefficiently run organization in attempting to plan the necessary invasion of Cuba. General William R. Shafter, a veteran of the Civil War, was placed in command of the operations, but he was so infirm that he had to be carried from place to place on a litter—an appropriate symbol of the army's entire endeavor.

As the U.S. Army began to bestir itself, a Spanish fleet of four decrepit cruisers and four destroyers commanded by Admiral Pascual Cervera succeeded in crossing the Atlantic. Before its arrival in Cuban waters, Admiral William T. Sampson blockaded the northern coast of Cuba, but Commodore Winfield S. Schley's delay in blockading the southern coast enabled Cervera's force to enter Santiago harbor. Ten days later, the navy located the Spanish ships and bottled them up.

Meanwhile, in the midst of chaos, an American expeditionary force of 17,000 men gathered at Tampa, Florida, for the Cuban invasion. Tampa, which was served by a single track rail line, was difficult to reach, and there was an inadequate number of ships to move the men

and materials. Some of the most determined action of the war occurred when units, such as the Rough Riders commanded by Colonel Leonard Wood and Lieutenant Colonel Theodore Roosevelt, commandeered transport space in Tampa harbor. After agonizing delays, the force sailed on June 14.

Cervera's sanctuary in Santiago made it the principal target for the American invasion. The U.S. forces began disembarking just east of the city on June 22 and commenced a march to Santiago on June 30. The total Spanish forces in Cuba outnumbered the Americans more than ten-to-one, but they were so disorganized and poorly led that only 13,000 were mustered to meet the invaders.

American strategy called for the capture of San Juan Hill, the heights commanding Santiago, followed by seizure of the city. Determined Spanish opposition was met on July 1, and it took much of the day for 7,000 U.S. troops to take the heavily fortified village of El Caney. At San Juan Hill, the United States sustained over 1,500 casualties, but the horseless Rough Riders charged up the hill under the daring leadership of Theodore Roosevelt, whose courage captured the popular fancy; however, American losses could have been lightened by careful planning.

With Santiago in American hands, Cervera attempted a futile escape rather than surrender, and on July 3, he steamed out of the harbor, pursued by five American battleships and two cruisers. In the ensuing battle, over which Sampson and Schley feuded for years as to who was the hero, all the Spanish ships were destroyed within four hours. Only two Ameri-

cans were killed, while 474 Spaniards were killed or wounded. The following day, American forces occupied Wake Island in the Pacific, and on July 16 the Spanish in Cuba formally surrendered. On July 25 another expeditionary force under General Nelson A. Miles took Puerto Rico virtually without resistance.

While victory was being attained, the U.S. Army, clad in woolens designed for the West, fell prey to disease which killed 5,462 men compared to 379 lost in battle. Typhoid fever

Teddy Roosevelt (center) and the Rough Riders on San Juan Hill.

flourished in the unsanitary Cuban camps, as did malaria and yellow fever, and food poisoning was endemic, due in part to canned beef to which preservatives had been added and which the men called "embalmed beef." Some people, fearing contagion, hesitated to bring the troops home, but Roosevelt, among others, pressured national leaders to do so at once. In the late summer they were returned to a quarantined area of Long Island, where, now clad in summer fatigues, many continued to suffer for weeks.

Despite incompetent direction, the Spanish-American War was a popular conflict. Its brevity and small number of casualties made it a painless war for the average American, whose sense of pride was inflated by the tangible evidence it produced of American superiority.

The Peace of Paris

In August, 1898, the Spanish, who had opened formal negotiations through the French ambassador to the United States, signed a protocol ending hostilities and calling for a peace conference in Paris and agreeing to abandon Cuba. They agreed to cede Puerto Rico and an island in the Marianas (Guam) to the United States. It was also stipulated the United States would occupy Manila until the peace conference made a disposition of the Philippines.

In the ensuing weeks, the American people were torn by a debate on the nation's role as an imperialist power. Strong forces, including the navy advocates and expansionists, such as Lodge and Roosevelt, demanded the Philippines' annexation. Surprisingly, much of the business community, which formerly had opposed such action, was now staunchly for it. It envisioned great economic advantages including use of the Philippines as a base for expansion of trade with China.

The imperialists did not win easily. A diverse segment of Americans including many in the academic world, such as Harvard President Charles Eliot, union leaders such as Samuel Gompers, and a number of literary figures including Mark Twain became active in the Anti-Imperialist League. It challenged annexation as an undemocratic action which would lead to serious entanglement in the Far East. The League's arguments were used by some Republican congressmen and an even larger number of Democrats.

President McKinley had no difficulty rationalizing his action in sending a pro-annexation commission to Paris with orders to take the Philippines. He confided to a church convention that in response to prayer he could see it was not God's will to allow the islands to founder without guidance or fall prey to a vicious foreign power. Instead, it was America's duty "to educate the Filipinos, and uplift and civilize and Christianize them. ..." Yet McKinley's conscience was sufficiently troubled that he agreed to pay Spain $20 million as compensation.

Despite McKinley's attitude, there was serious doubt that the Senate would ratify the Paris Treaty. Surprisingly, aid in attaining this accomplishment came from William Jennings Bryan, who, though strongly opposed to Philippine acquisition, refused to use his influence to defeat the treaty. He held approval was tolerable as a means of bringing peace and the overall question of expansion should be decided at the next election. Bryan obviously hoped to obtain a winning issue for the 1900 presidential campaign and could not foresee that by that time few people would be concerned with the question.

As the Senate prepared to vote on the treaty, news arrived that the Filipinos were revolting against U.S. control, a report which may have provided the margin of victory for the treaty. On February 6, 1899, by a vote of 57 to 27, the

Senate narrowly approved America's imperialistic venture.

Problems in the Philippines and the Caribbean

The new American empire, especially the Philippines, soon confronted the nation with serious problems. Early in the Spanish-American War, Emilio Aguinaldo, a rebel Filipino leader, had been allowed to return home where he aided in leading an insurrection against Spanish rule. On June 12, 1898, he proclaimed a provisional Filipino government under the assumption that victory would lead to independence.

News of the Treaty of Paris was received with consternation in the Philippines, and Aguinaldo immediately called on the people to maintain their independence. A month later, on February 4, 1899, armed revolt erupted against American rule. In response, the U.S. dispatched four times the number of troops used in Cuba to the Philippines. With a force of 70,000 men, superior equipment and organization, they defeated an equally large Filipino force by the end of the year.

The greatest difficulty in the Philippines had only begun, however, since the natives resorted to guerrilla warfare, which tried the very soul of the American army. The stealthy Filipinos, practicing excellent psychological warfare, even slipped into military camps without detection and murdered selected individuals. Provoked to the extreme, the army responded by torturing the captives to obtain confessions. Thousands were herded into concentration camps whose conditions approximated those of prewar Cuba. Much of the strength of the insurrection was broken when Aguinaldo was captured in March, 1901, but warfare continued until mid-1902.

Emilio Aguinaldo

To appraise the situation, McKinley appointed a Philippine Commission in early 1899 which recommended the United States rule the islands until the people were prepared for self-government. The following year, he drafted William Howard Taft, a circuit judge and dean of the University of Cincinnati Law School, to head a second commission. The kindly, jovial, 350-pound Taft had sincere empathy with the Filipinos. In 1901 he began three years' service as the first civilian governor of the islands and instituted many reforms including limited self-government, which quieted much of the opposition.

Ties between the Philippines and the United States grew with each passing year, and the economy of the islands came to be closely related to the mother country with trade in sugar becoming especially significant. Public improvements were undertaken with U.S. patronage, and even the school system came to be modeled on that of the United States. Yet the average Filipino, despising American tutelage and patronage, longed for independence.

The Philippines were not alone in providing difficulties for the United States since new relationships in the Caribbean also furnished many problems. Puerto Rico was a poor country with many difficulties which required heavy outlays of U.S. funds. In 1900 the Foraker Act reestablished civil government with the president appointing a governor-general and the upper house of the legislature. It also applied the Dingley Tariff to Puerto Rico, establishing duties of 15 percent of authorized levies. By amazing ingenuity in reasoning, the Supreme Court declared in two *Insular Cases* (1901)—*De Lima* v. *Bidwell* and *Dooley* v. *United States*—that Puerto Rico was no longer a foreign state and that duties could not be imposed on goods imported from Puerto Rico without the action of Congress and that goods shipped to Puerto Rico were duty free. However, in *Downes* v. *Bidwell* (also 1901), the Court held that while Puerto Rico was not a foreign state, it was "unincorporated" territory to which constitutional privileges and citizenship did not automatically extend, but Congress could extend such privileges as it chose. On these grounds, the tariff features of the Foraker Act were sustained. In 1903 in *Hawaii* v. *Mankichi* the Court held fundamental features of the Constitution bound Congress in dealing with all territories but that it was not inhibited by constitutional restrictions in dealing with procedural rights in unincorporated territories. A complete compilation of fundamental and procedural rights was never drawn up by the Court, however. Eventually Puerto Ricans were made U.S. citizens in 1917, but an independence movement remained strong on the island.

In Cuba, a military government under Colonel Leonard Wood instituted effective physical changes and for the first time freed the area of yellow fever. Much to the world's surprise, the United States withdrew in 1902, but only after it had dictated terms permitting it to intervene and granting it special advantages. These terms, which were stipulated by Congress in the Platt Amendment to an army appropriation bill and included in the Cuban constitution, provided Cuba would not impair its independence by treaties with foreign powers; the Cuban government would not amass debts it could not pay; the U.S. had the right to intervene to maintain independence or law and order; and Cuba would sell or lease the U.S. lands for naval or coaling stations. The required concessions, of course, ultimately aroused much anti-U.S. feeling in Cuba and elsewhere in Latin America.

The Open Door

Increased American interest in the Far East led to alarm at the economic partitioning of China which came after its defeat by Japan in 1895. United States business interests were fearful that their small but growing Chinese trade might be destroyed, and imperialists resented exclusion of their country from any area. A number of missionary-oriented churches, which feared their work would be impeded, joined newspapers and magazines, partly seduced by British free trade propaganda, in demanding action.

Responding to public pressure, Secretary of State John Hay, whose long public career had begun as President Lincoln's assistant private secretary, attempted to protect American interests without joining in the economic division of China. However, the original instigation of a policy providing equal commercial opportunities in China came from a British citizen who had worked in the Chinese customs service, Alfred E. Hippisley. In August, 1899, Hippisley prepared a draft of his proposal for W. W. Rockhill, private adviser on Far Eastern Affairs to Secretary Hay. Rockhill revised Hippisley's suggestions, which then became the basis of Hay's action. On September 6, 1899, he sent notes to the major powers asking them to guarantee in their Chinse spheres that they would not discriminate against other countries in levying railroad charges and harbor dues, that the Chinese government would be allowed its tariff, and that no interference would be made with treaty ports or vested interests. This agreement would provide an "Open Door" in China which the United States had been seeking for decades.

John Hay

Only Italy, which had no Chinese sphere of influence, accepted Hay's recommendations unconditionally. Russia refused while Britain, France, Germany, and Japan made acceptance contingent upon approval by the other powers. Yet Hay, concluding none would publicly call his hand, announced on March 20, 1900, that the powers had unanimously accepted the Open Door policy.

Though highly valued in America at the time, the Open Door policy probably had little intrinsic significance, and even Hay conceded that the United States would not back its ideals with troops. However, when the nationalistic Boxers attempted to expel all foreigners from China in 1900, the United States furnished 2,500 men to the 18,000-man force which rescued the foreigners besieged in Peking.*

Fearful that the rebellion would result in the complete subjugation of China, in July, 1900, Hay circulated a note to the major powers again, this time without asking for a reply. In it he asserted that the U.S. Open Door policy included all of China, not merely the spheres of influence, and stated Chinese territorial and administrative integrity must be preserved. No one openly disagreed with Hay, and China retained a government of its own, though foreign powers had privileges normally not enjoyed in sovereign states. Without a Chinese political sphere, however, U.S. trade did not develop as Hay and others had hoped. The reason for preservation of even limited control by the Chinese government was probably the balance maintained among the European powers rather than American idealism or diplomatic skill.

The United States' increasing concern with foreign affairs was also demonstrated when delegates were sent to the First Hague Confer-

*The United States received $24.5 million in indemnity but remitted much of it, which the Chinese government used to support Chinese students in American colleges.

ence in 1899 which was called by Czar Nicholas II of Russia to find means of averting war, to attempt disarmament, and to place limits on the methods of warfare. Little was accomplished by representatives of the twenty-six nations attending except the establishment of a Permanent Court of International Arbitration. Much effectiveness was denied the tribunal by excluding questions involving national honor, and, at United States instigation, exemption of issues arising under the Monroe Doctrine. However, the United States gave strong support to the court and had the distinction of bringing the first case before it for adjudication.

McKinley and Roosevelt's Victory

Prosperity and a victorious war earned McKinley renomination without opposition in 1900, while a mass movement arose to draft Theodore Roosevelt, who had been elected governor of New York in 1898, as vice-president. This drive was engineered in part by the state's Republican boss, Thomas Platt, who wished to get the independent, unpredictable Roosevelt out of New York. At first Roosevelt proclaimed his unavailability, but his every action and monumental ego led to his unanimous choice. In addition to its candidates, the Republican party based its appeal to the country on a platform which solidly supported the gold standard, an isthmian canal, and McKinley's foreign policy. The Democrats renominated Bryan and Cleveland's former vice-president, Adlai E. Stevenson, and Bryan dictated a platform which severely indicted U.S. imperialism but advocated free silver, though the issue was now dead.

The 1900 campaign was similar to that of 1896, and Bryan traveled thousands of miles seeking to arouse the people on the expansion question. When it engendered little enthusiasm, he talked increasingly about monopoly and the abuses of business. McKinley, conducting another "front porch" campaign, emphasized the nation's prosperity and well-being. Republicans everywhere indicted Bryan as a madman whose election would reverse recent national gains.

The voters, fearful of changes which Bryan might bring, reelected McKinley by a greater margin than in 1896. He received almost a million more popular votes than Bryan and 292 to 155 electoral votes.

On September 6, 1901, six months after his second inauguration, McKinley was shot by an anarchist, Leon Czolgosz, while attending a reception at the Pan-American Exposition in Buffalo. He died eight days later, and Vice-President Theodore Roosevelt, the man Hanna had stigmatized as a "damned cowboy," assumed the presidency.

Roosevelt's Policy in Panama

At forty-two Roosevelt became the youngest president in American history. Though born into a wealthy family, he had many adversities to overcome and had conquered physical weakness, through a strenuous exercise program, and despair, following the death of his wife and his mother, through hard work. Two years on a North Dakota ranch had brought him inspiration and insight into American life which aided in his writing of the multi-volume *The Winning of the West* and increased his diverse tastes in evaluating men and events. Though often frustrated, Roosevelt was always energetic and determined, characteristics that qualified him to serve ably as federal Civil Service commissioner, 1889–1895; president of

President McKinley's funeral.

New York's Board of Police Commissioners, 1895–1897; and assistant secretary of the navy, 1897–1898. Of course his Spanish-American war record and achievements as governor of New York resulted in his nomination as vice-president.

Roosevelt knew many critics found him rash and impulsive, and therefore as president he attempted to quiet the opposition by retaining McKinley's cabinet and pledging to continue his policies. He proved to be a splendid chief executive, knowing which issues to avoid and serving as an able synthesizer of opinion. Al-

though he professed to believe in the old West African proverb, "Speak softly and carry a big stick [and] you will go far," it was impossible for Roosevelt ever to speak softly, but his zeal proved irresistible to most Americans.

In foreign affairs, Roosevelt implemented the policy of national expansion and intervention which he had long advocated. One of his principal concerns was obtaining an isthmian canal to unite the territories gained in the Caribbean and the Pacific, a need which the nation's newspapers had dramatized for two months in 1898 by chartering the movement around the Horn of the U.S.S. *Oregon* from California to Cuba. Negotiations had been underway for some time with Great Britain to obtain modification of the Clayton-Bulwer treaty so that the United States could have exclusive control of a canal. The First Hay-Pauncefote Treaty, which provided this, was rejected by the British government in March, 1901. Increasing European tensions, however, led it to accept substantially the same terms in a Second Hay-Pauncefote Treaty in November, 1901, but one important addition provided the canal was to be open to all nations' shipping on equal terms.

Two years before the Senate ratified the Second Hay-Pauncefote Treaty, in December, 1901, the Walker Commission had been appointed to report on the best route for a canal. Some contended a sea-level route through Nicaragua was best though it was four times longer than a fifty-mile route across Panama, which was a province of Colombia. Ferdinand de Lesseps, the builder of the Suez Canal, had attempted a second miracle in Panama, but the adverse terrain and tropical illnesses led his company into bankruptcy. Its successor, the New Panama Canal Company, did little better, but it demanded $109 million for its holdings and its franchise which was to expire in September, 1904.

In November, 1901, the Walker Commission reported that the Panama route was a superior one but, because of the New Panama Canal Company's excessive demands, recommended the Nicaraguan route, a conclusion two earlier commissions had also reached. Confronted by the loss of its only potential buyer, the New Panama Canal Company, now under control of American interests, lowered its price to $40 million, and its two major representatives, the New York lawyer William N. Cromwell and its engineer, Philippe Bunau-Varilla, began an effective campaign to influence the U.S. government. In January, 1902, the Walker Commission reversed itself and recommended construction in Panama after Bunau-Varilla cleverly aroused fears of volcanoes in Nicaragua, distributing postage stamps showing the eruption of a dormant crater. In June, 1902, Congress, acceding to his pressure, established the Isthmian Canal Commission and authorized it to build a Panama Canal, provided the New Panama Canal Company's property and rights could be purchased for $40 million and Colombia would grant a permanent right of way.

Roosevelt, now fully committed to construction in Panama, urged Colombia to agree, and, in January, 1903, the Hay-Herran Treaty was negotiated with Colombia's representative in Washington. Under it a ninety-nine-year lease was obtained to a six-mile area across Panama for $10 million and an annual payment of $250,000. Colombia's government, which felt it should receive at least $25 million, rejected the treaty since it did not see why the New Panama Canal Company should obtain four times its grant, primarily for a franchise which would expire in slightly over a year.

Roosevelt, who regarded all Latin Americans with contempt and was conscious of the need for action to assure his reelection, was infuriated by Colombia's action. Though he considered seizing Panama, he decided against such a movement and encouraged the Panamanians to establish their independence. The isolated province, which had long desired freedom and frequently revolted, was aroused by agents of the New Panama Canal Company who used visions of an economy transformed through American development to provoke revolution in November, 1903. Acting under an 1846 treaty with Colombia's predecessor state by which it guaranteed free transit across the isthmus, the United States used the U.S.S. *Nashville* to prevent Colombia from landing troops to quell the revolt. On the third day after the rebellion began, Roosevelt recognized the new state of Panama and a week later received Bunau-Varilla as its minister. By the Hay-Bunau-Varilla Treaty of November 18, 1903, Panama granted the United States a ten-mile strip of territory on the terms formerly rejected by Colombia.

In 1904 construction was begun on the canal, during which engineering and sanitation miracles were effected by the forces under Colonel George W. Goethals and Colonel William Crawford Gorgas, the physician who freed Cuba of the mosquito. The locks were ready for the canal's official opening on August 15, 1914.

Roosevelt consistently defended his policy in Panama, holding that he had a "mandate from civilization" for his actions. He asserted that a lesser man would have held fruitless congressional hearings, but from the highest motives he had "made the dirt fly."

Though the canal was sorely needed, the manner in which it came into being brought much discredit to the United States throughout

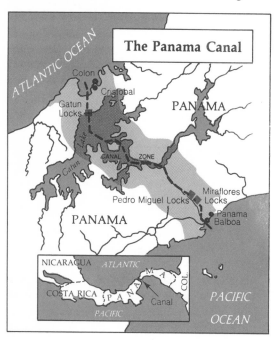

The Panama Canal

Latin America, but as long as Roosevelt lived no action could be taken that would reflect on his motives. In 1921, after his death and in a period when American interests wanted to play a leading role in developing Colombia's oil resources, the United States paid Colombia $25 million, and Colombia then recognized Panama's independence.

The Roosevelt Corollary

Roosevelt's activist foreign policy led to intervention in other Latin American states and the declaration of a new philosophy regarding them. Some states tended to contract foreign debts beyond their ability to pay, which resulted in constant threats of European intervention. After Venezuela's dictator, Cipriano Castro, defaulted on his debts, Roosevelt proclaimed the U.S. did not wish to protect any state against punishment for misconduct, "provided that punishment does not take the form of acquisition of territory by any non-American power." In late 1902 Great Britain, Germany, and Italy blockaded Venezuela, and Venezuela asked the United States to obtain arbitration. Germany not only refused to agree but also bombarded a port and sank some Venezuelan craft, after which Roosevelt sternly protested, and arbitration took place.

The Venezuelan episode primed Roosevelt for more direct action in the Dominican Republic. When its revenues were jeopardized by political developments in 1903, Belgium proposed the United States join in running the country. The United States refused, but, when it seemed the European powers would intervene, Roosevelt inserted a policy statement in his 1904 annual message which came to be called the Roosevelt Corollary to the Monroe Doctrine.

The Roosevelt Corollary asserted that the United States had the right to intervene in

President Roosevelt at the controls of an American steam shovel during the construction of the Panama Canal.

Western Hemisphere states to prevent interference from states outside the hemisphere. It held, "Chronic wrongdoing, or . . . impotence . . . may in America, as elsewhere, ultimately require intervention by some civilized nation. . . ." In the Western Hemisphere, due to adherence to the Monroe Doctrine, that power would be the United States. Under the new philosophy, an agreement was reached with the Dominican Republic in 1905, and, despite Senate refusal to approve the arrangement, for two years the United States administered the state's customs service and debt management. When revolt erupted in Cuba in 1906, marines were landed at the invitation of the Cuban president and remained for three years. These events were preludes to similar developments in the following decade.

Roosevelt's high-handed, independent policy in Latin America fostered strong anti-United States attitudes. It converted the Monroe Doctrine from a shield against foreign domination into an excuse for what many Latins believed was unwarranted American imperialism.

The president displayed a similar militancy when a dispute arose with Britain over the Alaskan Panhandle. After the 1896 gold rush to the Klondike, the Canadians claimed the boundary line should be measured from the promontories rather than the heads of bays and inlets which would have given the British control of the major harbors. When arbitration of the dispute was proposed, Roosevelt at first refused, but in 1903 he submitted to it while implying he would not abide by a decision denying the United States its just claims. The commission was composed of three British and three American delegates. When it met, Lord Alverstone, the Lord Chief Justice of England, sided with the United States and additional difficulties were averted.

The Western Hemisphere Intrudes in the East

Although Roosevelt was quick to evoke the Monroe Doctrine to keep European powers out of Western Hemisphere affairs, he was not reluctant to intrude in the East. In 1904 he responded to American public opinion by suggesting a Second Hague Peace Conference which, due to the Russo-Japanese War, could not be held until 1907. The United States was an active participant and tried in vain to have a world court established. It did succeed in having the European powers renounce the use of force for collecting debts in the Western Hemisphere and aided in the establishment of rules protecting neutral rights and prohibiting barbarous wartime practices.

In 1904–5 the Russo-Japanese War, which delayed the meeting of the Second Hague Conference, caused the United States much concern. Lacking military strength in the Far East, the U.S. attempted by diplomacy to establish an acceptable balance of power there and to protect the Open Door policy which Roosevelt feared Russia would defy if it obtained Manchuria. Accounts of Russian despotism had destroyed much of the goodwill it had enjoyed in the United States, while Japan, which was rapidly becoming westernized, was greatly admired. The world was startled by Japanese victories, but, severely strained by the effort, Japan asked Roosevelt to arrange mediation. Japan also assured the president it would maintain the Open Door in Manchuria and restore it to China. Roosevelt, fearful that the balance of power might be upset in the East, invited both sides to negotiate at the navy yard in Portsmouth, New Hampshire. Before the negotiations were concluded, Secretary of War William Howard Taft, as the president's representative, negotiated the Taft-Katsura executive agreement with the Japanese premier which gave Japan a free hand in Korea and pledged it would not expand in the Philippines. This understanding led Japan to establish a protectorate over Korea in December, 1905. Though the agreement was realistic and improved Japanese-American relations, it was clearly a violation of Open Door principles.

The Portsmouth Conference won Roosevelt his desires in the East and the Nobel Peace

Prize in 1906 but did not endear the United States to either Russia or Japan. Russia lost more than it would have liked, and Japan gained less. Japan improved its position in Manchuria by obtaining Port Arthur and the South Manchurian Railroad, but it did not receive a desired indemnity and only half of Sakhalin Island. The Japanese government was able to place popular blame on Roosevelt, although its allegations were primarily for domestic, political reasons.

Roosevelt's penchant for world affairs was not satiated by involvement in the Far East and resulted in United States participation in a major conference dealing with a dispute between the two major European alliances. For several years France had been obtaining recognition by major powers of its control in Morocco in return for French acceptance of their influence elsewhere in Africa. In 1905 the German Kaiser, William II, visited Morocco and, reflecting his country's opposition to French expansion, proclaimed his support of Moroccan independence. This action precipitated a crisis, and the Kaiser asked Roosevelt to obtain French participation in an international conference on the question. Fearing a major war, Roosevelt not only obtained a conference at Alegeciras, Spain, in 1906, but also sent two American delegates. When the German position was rejected at the conference and an agreement was reached permitting French and Spanish control of the Moroccan police, Roosevelt pressed Germany to accept it. The U.S. Senate approved the settlement but ironically stipulated its action did not depart from the traditional policy of U.S. noninvolvement in European affairs.

Fundamentally, Roosevelt's participation at Algeciras and in other aspects of world affairs was a realistic appraisal of the United States' new position as a major power. His moralizing and sanctimonious invocation of the Monroe Doctrine could be questioned, but his evaluation of the role of the country in power politics could not. The United States could no longer isolate itself from important world events.

Japanese-American Irritations

Even domestic politics created conditions leading to foreign difficulties for the United States, a fact proven in 1906 when the federal nature of American government produced conditions which led to a worsening of Japanese-American relations. Though the Japanese had voluntarily limited immigration to the United States in 1900, the flow of laborers continued via Hawaii, Canada, and Mexico, while a stiffening opposition arose to their presence. In 1905 a Japanese and Korean Exclusion League was formed on the West Coast, where approximately 70,000 Japanese immigrants had settled.

A crisis in Japanese-American relations came when the San Francisco schools reopened following the devastating earthquake and fire of 1906, and the school board ordered the segregation of Oriental children. The proud Japanese strongly protested this action was a violation of an 1894 treaty guaranteeing free entry into each country. President Roosevelt sympathized with Japanese sensitivity but also understood the Californians' fear of unrestricted immigration. With masterful artistry, he invited the entire San Francisco school board to Washington in February, 1907, where he persuaded them to rescind their segragation order by promising that the government would restrict Japanese immigration. Concurrently, an exchange of notes was begun with Japan which resulted in what was called the "Gentlemen's Agreement." In it the Japanese promised not to issue passports to laborers whose ultimate destination was the United States and agreed the United States could exclude immigrants whose passports were issued for travel to other countries.

The Japanese immigration crisis led to increased concern with the "yellow peril" in the United States, which was a figment of the American imagination. It was used by the administration to obtain increased naval appropriations, and Roosevelt, fearful that Japan might regard American concessions as weakness, decided to send the navy around the world, with a stop in Japan. Over strong congressional opposition, the president ordered the fleet, which was now second only to Britain's, to depart in December, 1907.

Anxiety existed as to the reception the navy would receive in Japan, but this proved unfounded when the Japanese gave the sailors a warm welcome. This cordiality prepared the way for the signing of the Root-Takahira Agreement in 1908 by which both powers agreed to maintain the *status quo* in the Pacific, to respect each other's territorial possessions, to uphold the Open Door policy, and to maintain China's territorial integrity. Through conciliation and firmness, both of which he believed essential, Roosevelt not only resolved the Japanese-American crisis but also improved the relationship between the two countries. Later, in 1913, the California legislature, over presidential protests, severely limited the right of Japanese to own or lease land in the state by denying these privileges to persons ineligible for citizenship. The admission to citizenship had been limited by the Naturalization Act of 1790 to free white persons, but in 1870 the right was also extended to aliens of African descent. During the nineteenth century, Orientals were naturalized, but, as their number increased, some courts and states held they were ineligible since they were neither white nor black. Chinese were excluded by the Chinese Exclusion Act of 1882. No federal law was passed regarding other Eastern nationals, but

the Supreme Court sustained the opinion of the courts which held that Orientals could not be naturalized. The ineligibility of Japanese was confirmed in the case of *Ozawa* v. *U.S.* (1922), Hindus in *U.S.* v. *Thind* (1923), and Filipinos in *Toyota* v. *U.S.* (1925).

Dollar Diplomacy

Roosevelt's successor, William Howard Taft, who was less concerned with foreign immigration to the United States than with export of American capital, attempted to expand American influence and earn profits by what he termed "dollar diplomacy." Believing investment rather than political control backed by armed force was the modern, capitalistic means of national penetration and expansion, Taft persuaded American bankers to invest in China and, by pressure, obtained their admission to a consortium of the major powers being formed to operate the Manchurian railroads. Britain and France acquiesced, since they had their own spheres of influence and did not wish to arouse Japanese anger. The scheme folded when Japan and Russia, fearful of U.S. efforts to preserve China, carved out spheres of influence of their own, and their protests also led to the collapse of other U.S. efforts to obtain investment in China. Roosevelt, who had high regard for Japanese power, felt Taft had sorely blundered.

In the Caribbean the story was quite different. Secretary of State Philander C. Knox obtained an agreement in June, 1911, with Nicaragua's new government which gave the United States the right to manage its debts should it default. In less than a month, when Nicaragua failed to meet a British loan, a group of New York bankers assumed control of the country's finances. However, the Senate rejected the Nicaraguan agreement and a similar one with Honduras. Moreover, the unpopularity of the arrangement led to a revolt in Nicaragua in 1912 and, in response to the request of the British and several other European governments as well as that of Nicaragua, the United States sent troops which remained until 1933.

Taft's dollar diplomacy was far from an economic failure, since millions of American dollars were invested in the Caribbean area. The largest concentration of funds was in Cuba but sizable sums were placed elsewhere; the United Fruit Company invested so heavily in the Central American states that they were often called the "banana republics." Substantial profits were obtained and American influence expanded, but, unfortunately, economic and political instability were so widespread in the region that Taft's liberal successor, Woodrow Wilson, felt impelled to dispatch additional troops to Latin America. United States forces were kept in Haiti from 1915 to 1933 and in the Dominican Republic from 1916 until 1924. (Financial control was maintained in both countries until 1941.)

Obviously, dollar diplomacy did little to develop the indigenous characteristics of the people of Latin America. In essence it was a form of imperialism which sought to avoid the use of armed force but resorted to it when necessary to protect investments. It was related to the concept of the Open Door in China and the Roosevelt Corollary, all of which reflected a new American interest in international affairs but were also egocentric and isolationist. While the United States occasionally dabbled in European and Asiatic affairs, it was fundamentally concerned with being allowed to expand the influence of American civilization without interference. It assumed that the United States was innately superior and other people exposed to American values would seek to emulate them. Those who opposed should be dealt with as renegades and obstructionists.

The limited economic and cultural gains of dollar diplomacy were largely confined to Latin America where the strength of Japan and the major European powers was weak. In the long run it aroused much national feeling and resulted in intense anti-Americanism. By 1913 the United States had greatly matured as an economic and military power, although it still had much to learn politically before it could most effectively use its strength in dealing with other nations.

Selected Bibliography

The origins and flowering of late nineteenth-century imperialism is surveyed in Foster R. Dulles, *Prelude to World Power: American Diplomatic History, 1860–1900** (1971), and Walter LaFeber, *The New Empire: An Interpretation of American Expansion, 1860–1898** (1963). On all developments relative to Latin America see Samuel F. Bemis, *The Latin American Policy of the United States** (1967).

The Foreign Policy of James G. Blaine (1965) is covered in a work by Alice F. Tyler. G. R. Dulebohn deals with *Principles of Foreign Policy under the Cleveland Administrations* (1941), which should be supplemented by Allan Nevins, *Grover Cleveland: A Study in Courage* (1932). Expansion and annexation of Hawaii are covered by Sylvester K. Stevens, *American Expansion in Hawaii, 1842–1898* (repr. of 1945 ed., 1968), and William A. Russ, Jr., *The Hawaiian Revolution, 1893–1894* (1959) and *The Hawaiian Republic, 1894–1898, and Its Struggle to Win Annexation* (1961).

The imperialism of the 1890s is treated by Ernest R. May, *Imperial Democracy** (1973). The coming of the Spanish-American War is analyzed in May's work and in Howard W. Morgan, *America's Road to Empire: The War with Spain and Overseas Expansion** (1965), which are less condemnatory than Walter Millis, *The Martial Spirit* (1965), and Julius W. Pratt, *Expansionists of 1898, The Acquisition of Hawaii and the Spanish Islands** (1964). For the military and naval aspects of the war in addition to Millis' work see Frank Freidel, *The Splendid Little War** (1958), and Harold and Margaret Sprout, *The Rise of American Naval Power, 1776–1918* (1966). Opposition to expansion is the subject of Robert L. Beisner, *Twelve Against Empire: The Anti-Imperialists, 1898–1900** (1968).

The problems posed by colonies are revealed in Julius W. Pratt, *America's Colonial Experiment* (1964). The Philippines struggle is presented in Leon Wolff, *The Little Brown Brother* (1961). Tyler Dennett, *John Hay, From Poetry to Politics* (1963), is useful on the Open Door policy, but on all Far Eastern developments see also Dennett's *Americans in Eastern Asia: A Critical Study of the United States' Policy in the Far East in the Nineteenth Century* (1963), and A. Whitney Griswold, *The Far Eastern Policy of the United States** (1962).

Roosevelt's foreign policy is the subject of Howard K. Beale, *Theodore Roosevelt and the Rise of America to World Power** (1956), while Foster R. Dulles surveys foreign policy generally in *America's Rise to World Power, 1898–1954** (1955). Dwight C. Miner, *The Fight for the Panama Route* (1966), presents the details of that episode. The troubled relations with Japan are analyzed by Thomas A. Bailey, *Theodore Roosevelt and the Japanese-American Crisis* (1964), and C. E. Neu, *An Uncertain Friendship: Theodore Roosevelt and Japan, 1906–1909* (1967). Dexter Perkins treats *The United States and the Caribbean* (rev. ed., 1965) as does D. G. Munro, *Intervention and Dollar Diplomacy in the Caribbean, 1900–1921* (1964).

---

*Available in paperback.

132

Major National Progressive Legislation

1902	Newlands Act
1903	Elkins Act
1906	Hepburn Act
	Pure Food and Drug Act
	Meat Inspection Act
1910	Mann-Elkins Act
1913	Underwood-Simmons Tariff
	Federal Reserve Act
1914	Smith-Lever Act
	Federal Trade Commission Act
	Clayton Antitrust Act
1915	LaFollette Seaman's Act
1916	Bankhead Good Roads Act
	Federal Farm Loan Act
	Warehouse Act
	Keating-Owen Child Labor Act
	Adamson Act
1917	Smith-Hughes Act

18

The Progressive Era

Long-Range Developments

For Economics and Corporate Enterprise

Progressive failure to control adequately corporate organizations has resulted in later efforts to achieve this goal.

Increased Progressive usage of regulatory agencies has continued, and their importance has become so great that they have been called a "fourth branch of government."

For Democratic Government

President William Howard Taft's legalistic attitude toward reform was accepted by the regulatory agencies and the administrations of the 1920s.

For Civil Liberties, Freedom, and Reform

A number of the social workers and intellectuals who supported Progressive reforms became leaders of the New Deal in the 1930s. Some contemporary columnists and television commentators have attained a reputation and influence comparable to the muckrakers.

The use of federal police powers, in its infancy in the Progressive Era, has continued to increase and become the basis for much national action.

The federal income tax has grown to be a major revenue source for government and a principal means of using governmental power in the redistribution of wealth.

Progressive sponsorship of federal job segregation and inertia in defense of minority rights led to popular disapproval and later growth of the civil rights movements and a reversal of the federal policy.

Progressivism

In the imperialist era from the late 1890s until the First World War, reformist attitudes and policies produced the Progressive Movement which arose from a diversity of sources and motives and gave a distinct tenor to the period. Many of the reformers' demands, such as those for an effective civil service and the control of prostitution and vice, were not new, but the changes were sought in new ways and with a great new zeal.

Progressives were shocked by the conditions they unearthed—the low level of wages, the absence of employers' liability for injuries, the opposition of union labor to wages and hour legislation, child labor, the deplorable living conditions in the ghetto, and the availability to the average city dweller of only the poorest education and medical care. But, like the enlightened *philosophes* of the eighteenth century, the Progressives had a profound belief in their ability to effect change. A number, like the prohibitionists, were so dedicated to their goals that they were willing to impose their wills on reluctant people for what they believed was the common good.

Some Progressives were motivated by strong evangelical impulses emanating from the Social Gospel, while for others the influence of latent Puritanism was much more subtle. The Populist experience of the 1890s had awakened many to the desirability of government action to remedy the chaos and injustice of an industrialized, urban society. Many former Populists emerged as supporters of Progressive causes, yet the leadership and psyche of the movement were different. The Populist crusade had been rural based, rural oriented, and had within it segments of bitter militancy. Progressivism was urban in nature; its leaders were the attorneys, editors, writers, and businessmen who were the establishment, although many of them were first-generation urbanites who pre-

sented their appeal in terms clearly understood by their rural brethren. Undoubtedly many were frightened by the rise of trusts and national unions which concentrated power among very few people. In seeking to reestablish competition, they were fighting to secure their positions in society, and, if possible, return to a more personalized era in American life.

Though some of their critics tried to style the Progressives as radicals, they were far from it. Most believed strongly in the capitalist system, and they were concerned with its perfection and the availability of opportunity for all. Their ethics and morals were conventional but far more sensitive than those of their opponents who accepted the abuses Progressives tried to correct.

The Role of Critics and Reformers

Political and social reform never occur in a vacuum but come only when the public conscience is aroused. For decades writers, editors, ministers, and others had been portraying faults in the American system, and, as previously seen, such critics as Henry George, Edward Bellamy, and Thorstein Veblen had presented challenges and ideas for reform to the nation's intellectuals. In the 1880s, Jane Addams and other social workers opened settlement houses which began to deal directly with urgent social needs. From these settlements emerged a constant stream of young social workers who created a cadre of significant reformers.

To translate the programs of the social reformers into political pressure, mass-oriented propaganda campaigns had to be developed. This came at the turn of the century when popular writers emerged who could dramatize the evils which existed and effectively portray the results of reform. President Roosevelt described some of the more sensational exposé writers for such magazines as *McClures, Everybody's,* and *Cosmopolitan* as "Muckrakers" because they reminded him of the character in *Pilgrim's Progress* who could never look up but only down at the muck. He intended the term to be applied only to those who wrote for personal gain alone or produced filth for filth's sake since he approved of most of the writers who were exposing what was wrong with America, but the characterization came to be applied to the entire group. In addition to the magazines which emphasized muckraking, some more conservative publications such as *The Forum* and, after 1900, the *World's Work* also carried articles revealing the injustices perpetrated by the trusts, the need for increased support of education, and the results of reform administrations in certain cities and states.

Collectively the magazine articles primed a generation of Americans to a new awareness of national faults and possible alleviations of them. Lincoln Steffens, whose *Autobiography* remains one of the best windows on the Progressive mind, shocked many by his reports on "The Shame of the Cities." Ida Tarbell, who became a respected historian, initially gained fame for her serialized history of the Standard Oil Company. Ray Stannard Baker, among many other features, followed "the color line," presenting the plight of the black man, a revelation to most Americans. David G. Phillips challenged the integrity of Congress in "The Treason of the Senate." Their writings and that of many others increased magazine circulation and public concern.

Many serialized articles were later published as books, although some important exposés were initially published in book form. Milford Howard caught the attention of church-oriented people when he published *If Christ Came to Congress,* while Theodore Dreiser brought home to others the effects of poverty

in such novels as *Sister Carrie, The Financier,* and *The Titan.* Frank Norris, who lacked Dreiser's artistry, left no doubt of the evil use of corporate power in such novels as *The Octopus,* which dealt with the Southern Pacific Railroad, and *The Pit,* a castigation of dealers in wheat futures.

The most successful of all the novelists was the socialist Upton Sinclair who in 1906 published *The Jungle,* which was designed to show the misery, especially of immigrant laborers, in the Chicago packing houses. However, the public interest was captured by the filth he vividly portrayed in the meat-packing industry where rodents were ground up in the sausage and sawdust was scooped up at the end of the day and added to meat products. President Roosevelt proclaimed *The Jungle* had made America a nation of vegetarians, and its readers paid increased attention to the exposés of Dr. Harvey W. Wiley, chief chemist of the Department of Agriculture, who was concerned with the sale of poisonous drugs.

In keeping with the trend of the times, many organizations formed to promote change issued literature of their own. Among the most effective were the National Municipal League, which presented a program for urban improvement; the Consumers' League, which sponsored uniform state legislation on a number of subjects; and the National Child Labor Committee, whose efforts were instrumental in obtaining a national child labor law in 1916. The law attempted to end the evil by using the commerce clause to exclude the products of factories employing children under fourteen. Though invalidated in 1918, the child labor law aided greatly in raising state standards.

Within a few years, the popular writers and reform organizations wrought a change in the American outlook which began to recognize and support the need for political action to correct abuses. Laissez faire, if not abandoned, was at least questioned, and even conservative politicians felt the need to give lip service to reform.

Reform at the
Local and State Level

The grass-roots demand for reform first found political expression at the local level, where widespread corruption and inefficiency contributed to urban problems. In New York City, Tammany Hall was temporarily overthrown in 1894, and in 1895 the Municipal Voters League initiated a nonpartisan campaign in Chicago against the city council which had succumbed to the bribery of the utilities mogul, Charles T. Yerkes. By 1897 it had gained control of the council and elected Carter Harrison as mayor. The same year Samuel M. "Golden Rule" Jones was successful in Toledo, inaugurating a significant reform administration.

In 1901 Tom L. Johnson, a street railway operator and steel manufacturer who had been converted to free trade and Henry George's single tax philosophy, was elected mayor of Cleveland. In the following eight years he obtained just taxation of corporations and utilities and a three-cent trolley fare. In Minneapolis, San Francisco, St. Louis, New York City, Detroit, and elsewhere similar if less effective reformers came into office. All sought to eliminate graft and bring efficiency to government, and, in varying degrees, they succeeded in reforming the basis for taxation, regulating public utilities, and expanding the variety of services offered the poorer classes.

Disenchantment with corruption under the mayor-alderman system, in which the legislative branch of city government was elected by wards, led to the adoption of two alternate systems. Following a hurricane and tidal wave, Galveston, Texas, established a commission system in 1903 under which all five commissioners were chosen by the entire electorate and had both legislative and executive powers. Many reformers felt this concentration of responsibility was an improvement, and a number of medium-sized cities adopted it in the next few decades. Staunton, Virginia, changed the plan by having the policy-making commissioners hire a city manager as the executive, and, after the adoption of this modification by Dayton, Ohio, in 1913, other smaller cities followed suit. Impressive results were shown in many of the cities adopting the newer government forms, but these probably were more attributable to the reform spirit than to the changes in political mechanics.

Unfortunately, local reform was often stymied by state intervention, since most local governments were under rigid state control. In 1900 only California, Minnesota, Mississippi, and Washington granted home rule to their cities, and only eight other states had joined them by 1914. Therefore much of the struggle for reform had to be taken to the state level. In the South, several farmer-supported radicals, including Governor Benjamin Tillman of South Carolina and Governor James S. Hogg of Texas, came to power in the 1890s and introduced reforms bearing similarities to those of the later Progressives. Their struggles against corporations and for better education prepared the way for later reformers.

Wisconsin's Robert M. La Follette, one of the most successful of all Progressive governors, drew heavily on rural support and created a machine of his own. "Fighting Bob's" program, implemented after he assumed office in 1901, became known as the "Wisconsin Idea" and served as a model for Progressives everywhere. It included the use of technical experts from the University of Wisconsin as public consultants, the direct primary, which destroyed much of the bosses' control, civil service reform, increased taxation of corporations, an effective railroad commission, a state income tax, a conservation program, and limitations on lobbying.

Many of these reforms were adopted by other Progressive governors including Iowa's Albert B. Cummins and Arkansas' Jeff Davis, who also came to power in 1901, William S. U'Ren, the father of the initiative, by which legislation can be proposed by a certain number of citizens and adopted through a popular vote, who was elected in Oregon in 1902, and Charles Evans Hughes, who reformed the insurance industry following his 1906 election in New York. Braxton Bragg Comer, who was elected in Alabama in 1906, and Hiram W. Johnson, elected in California in 1910, obtained effective railroad regulation. By 1910 Progressives had also come to power in Colorado, Georgia, Kansas, Minnesota, and Mississippi. The ultimate in Progressive reform came during Woodrow Wilson's tenure as governor of New Jersey from 1911 to 1913. He obtained adequate support for public education, partially through just taxation of corporations. Utilities, common carriers, and corporations were at last regulated and many social services established, including medical and dental clinics for school children. Clearly his achievements and those of other Progressive governors indicated that a mass desire for reform existed on which federal changes could be based.

Roosevelt Assumes the Presidency

Theodore Roosevelt, who assumed the presidency in September, 1901, introduced Progressivism into the national government. Although the Supreme Court had rendered many conservative decisions, it had also sustained a number of state regulatory laws, and many Progressives, both in and out of government, acted on the assumption that there was a federal police

Robert M. La Follette

power which would permit national intervention to protect national citizens. In 1903 the Court sanctioned the concept of federal police power in the case of *Champion* v. *Ames,* upholding a federal law prohibiting the dissemination of lottery tickets through the mails on the grounds that the commerce power included the right to prohibit as well as regulate.

This interventionist view coincided with that of the dynamic Roosevelt whose activism and impetuosity often shocked conservatives. However, he was no radical, and, as his previous public service demonstrated, he was notably nondoctrinaire. His reform impulses stemmed from moral convictions and were attempts to correct wrongs in concrete situations. In almost every instance, he approached political problems with a pragmatic attitude and was less concerned with the manner in which correction came than in the result achieved.

Partially because of his down-to-earth approach, Roosevelt was a superb politician who chose to avoid divisive issues such as the tariff where little prospect for positive change existed. He deliberately cultivated a cross section of his party, winning many of the conservatives to his side well before the election of 1904. In addition, he sought to appeal to all Americans and, like McKinley before him, became a synthesizer and unifier who, when victory required it, could suppress his personal feelings to achieve his ends.

Roosevelt's intense interest in all sorts of people and situations led to decided opinions on many subjects. He articulated these successfully in a moralistic language most people could understand. Though at times guilty of oversimplification, he was frequently willing to consider alternatives to his own proposed solutions. He would experiment, even gamble, if there was a chance to obtain results. Although some people were offended by Roosevelt's maverick nature, most Americans were captivated by his zest for life, his excursions into the unconventional, and to them, to use one of his own favorite terms, he was a "bully" good guy.

The president, who characterized his admin-

istration as seeking a "square deal" for all Americans, had an opportunity to demonstrate his commitment to this goal when a nationwide anthracite coal strike was called in May, 1902. After gaining a 10 percent wage increase in 1900, the United Mine Workers of America, led by their president, John Mitchell, renewed negotiations in the fall of 1901, seeking an additional 20 percent raise, the eight-hour day, and union recognition. The operators refused, dragging the contest on for months in the hope public opinion would force union capitulation. Their spokesman, George F. Baer, angered the public and Roosevelt by anti-union state-

John Mitchell

ments, contending that labor could best "be protected and cared for, not by the labor agitators, but by the Christian men to whom God in His infinite wisdom has given the control of the property interests of the country."

In October, as the national situation worsened, Roosevelt summoned both sides to a White House meeting at which management representatives refused even to speak to the union men and were most apprehensive that the companies might be coerced into recognizing the union. They urged the government to break the strike by obtaining an injunction under the Sherman Antitrust Act. After the meeting, Roosevelt, referring to Mitchell, declared that there had been only one gentleman in the room, and he was not the president of the United States.

As the crisis deepened, Roosevelt proposed an impartial tribunal mediate the dispute. When the operators refused this plan, he threatened to use federal troops, not as strikebreakers, but to operate the mines. Under this threat and pressure from J. P. Morgan, the coal companies agreed to arbitration provided no union man was on the arbitration board. Roosevelt cheerfully agreed but promptly appointed the head of the Brotherhood of Railway Conductors to the board, listing him as an "eminent sociologist." The board awarded the miners a nine-hour day and a 10 percent raise but not union recognition. At the same time, it recommended an increase in coal prices which covered the higher wages. The principal gain scored in the conflict did not go to the miners, the union, or the companies but to the president, whose image as a bold, impartial leader was enhanced.

Trust-Busting
Is Initiated

The president's attitude toward big business reflected his matter-of-fact political approach. He assumed large-scale business organization had come to stay and could only be eliminated at a sacrifice of efficiency no one wished to make. He did not believe competition could be restored to make industries self-regulating. Instead, he felt government would have to intervene when the public interest was abused, but, when it was not, even the largest operations should be unmolested. He also knew many businessmen preferred national regulation to that of forty-five different states and saw it as a means of ending unjust competition from inferior goods.

After Congress failed to enact legislation regulating corporate abuses, as Roosevelt recommended in his first annual messages, the president ordered the attorney general to sue the Northern Securities Company for violating the Sherman Antitrust Act. The Northern Securities Company was a holding company created when an impasse was reached by the forces of J. P. Morgan and James J. Hill, who controlled the Northern Pacific and Great Northern Railroads, and E. H. Harriman and John D. Rockefeller, who ran the Union Pacific and Southern Pacific. A fierce struggle arose over control of the Chicago, Burlington and Quincy which was needed to give the other lines access to Chicago. When the Morgan-Hill forces purchased the controlling interest in the Chicago, Burlington and Quincy, the Harriman-Rockefeller associates attempted to gain control of the Northern Pacific by purchasing its common stock from every available source. As a result, a share of Northern Pacific stock soared to $1,000 before the demand collapsed in 1901. Prompted by fear of excesses such as this incident, Morgan promoted a compromise by which the lines agreed to pool their resources into the Northern Securities Company and virtually dominate the railroads of the Northwest. When the government challenged the Northern Securities Company in court, it argued that no wrong had been committed since no law or charter provision prohibited the purchase of one company by another. In reply the government contended that if the Northern Securities Company was not a violation of the Sherman Act then nothing could prevent the consolidation of all railroads under one giant company. The president used his suit as the basis for a popular antitrust appeal in which he pledged strict executive vigilance in applying the antitrust laws. In 1904 the Supreme Court ordered the dissolution of the Northern Securities Company, and the president was hailed as a public hero.

In all, Roosevelt prosecuted some forty combinations for violating the antitrust laws, and he was popularly proclaimed a "trustbuster." In 1905 he obtained dissolution of the beef trust when, by unanimous decision in *Swift and Co.* v. *United States,* the Supreme Court propounded a "stream of commerce" concept which recognized certain local business agreements were part of interstate commerce and subject to federal control. Some of the more important antitrust decisions in Roosevelt-initiated cases came after he left office, however. One of these decisions, that against the Standard Oil Company, was given in 1911 and reflected Roosevelt's philosophy in declaring that only unreasonable restraint of trade required government action. The same year the American Tobacco Company was also ordered to reorganize due to another Roosevelt-initiated suit.

More trust-type organizations were created during the Progressive era than were dissolved, and, as in the case of Standard Oil, formal dissolution was often replaced by less formal but equally effective arrangements between subsidiary companies. These events did not trouble Roosevelt, who often used informal means in obtaining acceptable corporation behavior. He led Congress to establish a Department of Commerce and Labor in 1903 whose Bureau of Corporations aided in keeping business in line by its investigations and publications. In 1903 also federal antitrust prosecutions were ad-

vanced by enactment of the Expedition Act which, upon request of the attorney general, gave such suits precedence in the circuit courts. In 1905, in return for cooperation with the Bureau of Corporations, Roosevelt agreed to allow U.S. Steel to correct any wrongdoings instead of initiating a suit. Two years later, when J. P. Morgan convinced him that the failure of the Tennessee Coal, Iron and Railroad Company would worsen the panic of 1907, he promised not to prosecute U.S. Steel when it acquired T.C.I. By this means, U.S. Steel safely obtained at bargain prices an enormous amount of coal and iron reserves as well as some excellent plants.

Roosevelt's realistic business philosophy brought positive results. The more flagrant corporate abuses were corrected, often without litigation, and in such a manner that business confidence was sustained and increased. By actions in this as in other areas, Roosevelt won friends in all segments of society and promoted unity and cooperation.

Roosevelt's Reelection

As the presidential elections of 1904 approached, it became apparent that Roosevelt's vigorous personality and leadership would be the primary issue, and every indication pointed to his easy reelection. With great political ability, he had succeeded in transferring the Progressive image to his party while retaining at least the public support of many "Old Guard" leaders, such as Speaker Joseph Cannon and Senator Nelson Aldrich. When Senator Mark Hanna died in February, 1904, his only possible conservative rival was removed.

Despite his political strength, Roosevelt was nervous and exerted every effort to be "elected in his own right." Pensions for Union veterans were liberalized and placed strictly on an age basis. A false Democratic charge was refuted that the president was blackmailing Wall Street for contributions, after which the Republican campaign manager appealed directly to corporations and obtained almost three-fourths of the $2,195,000 expended by his party in the campaign.

The Democrats, conscious of Roosevelt's liberal image and Bryan's two defeats, turned to the right and nominated a wealthy, conservative New Yorker, Judge Alton B. Parker, for president, and a railway executive, Henry G. Davis of West Virginia, for vice-president. An unsuccessful effort was made to capture the vote of business leaders in the East by having Parker telegraph his support of the gold standard to the convention and assail Roosevelt as an arbitrary leader whose victory endangered the nation. Conservatives generally found the acceptance of Bryan's party a difficult matter, however, and the nation's general prosperity contributed to Roosevelt's appeal. Personally, Parker appeared dull and unattractive in comparison to Teddy.

In the election the president and his "standpat" vice-presidential candidate, Indiana's Senator Charles W. Fairchild, won a smashing victory, polling 7.6 million popular votes, 2.5 million more than Parker and Davis. By carrying some normally Democratic border states, the Republicans won 336 electoral votes to the Democrats' 140. In the elation of election night Roosevelt made a pledge which he later regretted, declaring, "Under no circumstances will I be a candidate for or accept another nomination."

Following the election, a New York legislative committee, whose chief counsel was Charles Evans Hughes, investigated abuses in the insurance industry including the large amounts of money insurance companies contributed to the 1904 campaigns. As a result, the state outlawed such gifts, an action followed in 1907 by congressional prohibition of campaign contributions by national banks and other cor-

Theodore Roosevelt delivering his inaugural address, 1905.

porations chartered under congressional authority as well as corporate contributions in campaigns leading to the choice of presidential electors, members of the House of Representatives, or state legislators who would ultimately elect U.S. senators. In 1910, 1911, and 1912 laws were passed requiring political committees operating in more than two states to publish their campaign expenditures and congressional candidates to file statements of expenditures.

Railway Regulation

Roosevelt's reelection encouraged him to seek far-reaching reforms, and, when Congress reconvened in December, 1904, he turned immediately to railroad regulation. Earlier, in 1903, with the cooperation of many railroads, the president had been instrumental in obtaining enactment of the Elkins Act, which sought to end rebates by making receiving as well as granting them a federal offense; the railroads were also prohibited from deviating in any fashion from their published rates. Unfortunately, the Supreme Court destroyed much of the act's effectiveness by restricting the Interstate Commerce Commission's power.

In a new approach to the problem which encountered stiff railroad opposition, Roosevelt proposed the ICC be given authority to set rates upon the complaint of the public. Spurred by the aroused Progressive governors and infuriated shippers, he applied great pressure in 1905 and 1906 for the passage of the Hepburn Bill, although many conservatives, who regarded price fixing as a God-given right of business, encouraged their congressmen to resist. Senator Aldrich and other opponents in the upper chamber attempted to embarrass the president by allowing the uncouth Democratic Senator Benjamin Tillman to manage the bill, and they were able to obtain provision for railroad appeal of ICC rates to the courts and to prevent the commission from setting physical valuations of railroads as a basis for its calculations. Roosevelt fought back vigorously and brought a number of congressmen into line by threatening a downward tariff revision.

With all its flaws, the Hepburn Act, which became law in June, 1906, enabled the federal government for the first time to regulate the railroads with some effectiveness. It increased the ICC from five to seven members and empowered it to set rates and uniform accounting methods. A weakness existed in that railroads could increase rates without permission and were required to lower them only within a month of the ICC ruling, yet its orders were made binding unless reversed by a court. For the first time, oil pipelines, ferries, bridges, terminal facilities, and express and sleeping car companies were made subject to its jurisdiction. A commodity clause prohibited the lines

from carrying goods, such as coal, which they had produced themselves except for their own use. Roosevelt was delighted with the new law, and, shrewd politician that he was, felt that the possibility of court reversal of ICC rates would have a positive result by making business more amenable to the type of federal regulation the nation must have.

Despite the gains attained, court decisions negated some of the regulatory features of the Elkins and Hepburn Acts. Although Judge Kenesaw Mountain Landis found the Standard Oil Company guilty of rebating and fined it $29,240,000 in 1907, the verdict was reversed by a court of appeals. In 1909 the commodity clause was seriously weakened when the Supreme Court held no evasion existed if, before transporting goods they had produced, the railroads offered them for sale. These decisions paved the way for additional railroad legislation in 1910.

Meat Inspection and Pure Food and Drug Acts

As his second administration progressed, Roosevelt moved without hesitancy into other areas where government had not previously intervened. Enactment of an employers' liability act for railroad workers was obtained in 1906, and, though invalidated by the Supreme Court, a similar act in 1908 was sustained. The president seriously considered supporting a national child labor law sponsored by Senator Albert Beveridge, but when the National Child Labor Committee split over whether it should endorse the bill, administration support was switched to enactment of legislation providing for an exhaustive study of the working conditions of women and children. Two appropriations of $150,000 each permitted the marshaling of invaluable information and led in 1912 to the establishment of the Children's Bureau in the Department of Commerce and Labor.

Under Roosevelt's leadership, the government also began to regulate the processing and sale of meat, food, and drugs in 1906. For some time Dr. Harvey W. Wiley of the Department of Agriculture had been exposing the adulteration of food and drugs, even performing experiments on himself to show their effects. The muckraking magazines, especially *Collier's,* ably promoted his work, but it was not until the publication of Upton Sinclair's *The Jungle* that the public and the president became aroused. A federal investigation of the meatpacking industry in Chicago revealed deplorable conditions while, concurrently, opposition to federal regulation was muted by the packers' awareness that improved conditions would expand the export market.

In June, 1906, the Meat Inspection Act was passed which required the maintenance of sanitary conditions in packing establishments and provided for federal inspection of all facilities preparing meats for interstate shipment. To conciliate the packers, however, the president agreed to have the government, not the firms, pay inspection costs.

The Pure Food and Drug Act, which was passed at the same time, prohibited the manufacture, sale, or shipment in interstate commerce of falsely labeled or adulterated food or drugs, and an amendment in 1911 outlawed misleading labeling of medicines. The skull and crossbones became a common sight in American medicine chests, and the people at last had an opportunity to know what they were buying. Unfortunately, many producers chose to use formulas and scientific names which meant nothing to the average man, and the use of small print made labels too hard to read. These factors and unregulated fraudulent advertising resulted in increased sales of many foods and medicines which did not merit consumption.

Conservation

Although the passage of a number of needed laws was largely attributable to Roosevelt, perhaps his greatest contribution as president was the popularization of reform—the conversion of what had often been considered radical schemes to moral imperatives which just men could scarcely afford to oppose. In no area was he more effective than in conservation, which was not surprising since Roosevelt was a sportsman and naturalist who wished to prevent the destruction of nature's equilibrium by profit-seeking men. As president he resolved to do something in this vital area.

Surveying the nation's timber resources, Roosevelt found that only one-fourth of the country's primitive forests remained unscathed and most of them were in private hands. Some 45 million acres had been preserved under the Forest Reserve Act of 1891, which authorized the president to close timber areas and establish national parks, but this was not nearly as much as the country's earnest conservationists desired. Roosevelt was privy to their ideas, especially through the influence of Gifford Pinchot, head of the Forestry Service in the Department of Agriculture and a member of the president's "Tennis Cabinet" to which he often turned for advice. Prompted by the conservationists, he obtained passage of the Newlands Act of 1902, which allocated proceeds from federal land sales in sixteen western states to construct and maintain irrigation projects. More significantly, he began withdrawal of some 125 million acres of forest lands and 25 million acres containing coal and other mineral deposits, water power sites, and oil reserves. Simultaneously, widespread intrusion of lumbermen and cattlemen on federal lands was ended.

The reaction of the vested interest groups to the new federal conservation policy was quick and intense. In 1907, led by western grazing interests, they held a protest meeting in Denver and obtained a rider on an Agriculture Department appropriation bill which repealed the Forest Reserve Act of 1891. Though Roosevelt felt he had to sign the measure to continue department operations, he delayed long enough to place seventeen million additional acres of land in federal reserves.

Congressional reversals convinced the president that the people must be educated to protect their resources, and in 1908 he convened the Conference of Governors at the White House to consider conservation. Forty-four chief executives, as well as many other national leaders and experts, attended the meeting which gave the conservation movement a great impetus and led to the creation of conservation commissions in most of the states.

Roosevelt's appeal to the state and local levels was fortunate since Congress proved to be hostile to additional immediate reforms. It did authorize the creation of a Commission on Country Life in 1908, which by national action sought to improve living conditions in the rural areas and reverse the exodus to the cities. However, when the commission submitted extensive reports which advocated a reorganization of the basis for rural life through such programs as federal subsidies for education and transportation, no funds were appropriated for its publication.

Incorrectly, much of the business community blamed Roosevelt-initiated changes for the brief panic of 1907 and aided in defeating his proposals to improve the capitalistic system. The one exception was the Aldrich-Vreeland Act which was passed in 1908 with the aid of conservatives who realized an inadequate monetary system had contributed to the

1907 panic. It provided some temporary elasticity in the currency and established a commission headed by Senator Nelson W. Aldrich to study banking and currency systems of the United States and Europe and report on needed U.S. reforms. However, the president met only rebuffs in seeking approval of the commission's recommendations during his last year in office. He also unsuccessfully advocated federal income and inheritance taxes, federal incorporation and control of interstate business, and federal intervention in labor disputes.

Part of the reason for Roosevelt's defeats could be attributed to his distinctive style and general attitude which frightened conservatives as much as his proposals. They were especially concerned when he criticized the courts for invalidating a worker's compensation act and when he attacked the "malefactors of great wealth" who opposed change. Though the conservatives temporarily prevailed on many questions, the reforms advocated by Roosevelt were the wave of the future and were worthy of the nation's first Progressive president.

Taft's Election

Roosevelt's 1904 pledge not to run again precluded his acceptance of renomination, though he felt many reforms remained to be achieved and that he could be renominated without difficulty. Instead of running, he had to content himself with the selection of the Republican nominee. His first choice was Elihu Root, who had served the administration brilliantly as secretary of war and then secretary of state, but Roosevelt recognized that the Progressive Midwest would not accept a noncrusading, eastern corporation lawyer. As second best, the president drafted Secretary of War William Howard Taft.

Taft, as a cabinet member, governor of the Philippines, and judge, had been an able administrator, but he had little experience in the rough and tumble political game. He was intelligent, gentle, good-natured, and, as Roosevelt knew from the support he gave the administration's programs, he was genuinely committed to the well-being of the masses. What the president did not discern was that he also had a legalistic temperament and a marked ability to offend even those with whom he agreed. Taft was chosen specifically to advance Roosevelt's achievements, and the party platform pledged stricter antitrust legislation, an enlarged conservation program, and tariff revision.

The Democrats, chagrined by the poor showing of an eastern conservative candidate in 1904, turned to William Jennings Bryan for a third time. More liberal than ever, he not only assailed the tariff and trusts but pledged an end to the unfair use of injunctions in labor disputes. However, he showed admirable restraint when Taft, as Republican candidates before him, indicted him as a demagogue whose victory would endanger the nation.

Though Taft was an easy winner, Bryan ran considerably better than Parker had in 1904, carrying four additional states in the West and South and receiving 162 electoral votes to Taft's 321. Both houses of Congress remained Republican but with a marked increase in Progressive membership, especially from the Midwest.

Taft's Achievements

Taft continued to advocate Roosevelt-type reforms, and his administration inaugurated policies and obtained the enactment of laws which

William Howard Taft with his sons in 1909. Robert Taft, on the right, later became a leading U.S. senator.

substantially advanced Progressivism. Unfortunately, Taft alienated many liberals and found himself regarded as the leader of the reactionaries.

The president, who was a poor politician, tried unsuccessfully to continue Roosevelt's policy of conciliating all segments of the party. Roosevelt had difficulty with the experiment during his last years in office, and it broke down in less adept hands. Taft made every effort to appease the conservatives, or the "Old Guard" as their enemies called them, who were led by Speaker Joseph Cannon and Senator Nelson W. Aldrich. In temperament, if not in program, he was perhaps closer to them, and in time he found himself cast as their ally, though they never fully accepted him.

As president, one of Taft's first actions was to summon a special session of Congress to deal with the delicate tariff issue. Immediately after its convocation, he alienated many western Progressives by refusing support of their effort to overturn the dictatorial role of the speaker of the House. The president was influenced in his decision by Speaker Cannon's promise, in return for Taft's aid, to support his legislative program. The revolt was contained, primarily due to southern and New York Democrats reneging, but Taft lost much of his image as a liberal.

Following the dispute over the speakership, the "Old Guard" in the Senate betrayed the president on the tariff issue. The administration's bill, presented by Representative Sereno E. Payne, contained substantial revisions downward, especially on steel and iron products, and established an inheritance tax, ranging from 1 to 5 percent, partial free trade with the Philippines, and a tariff commission to study rates. Progressives were generally pleased even though Democratic efforts to include an income tax amendment failed. The Payne Bill cleared the House in good order, but in the Senate, where Aldrich's Finance Committee was in charge, 847 amendments were added which actually increased the average ad valorem duty over 2 percent to about 38 percent, and, in addition, the inheritance tax was dropped.

In disgust, a number of midwestern Republicans, including Robert La Follette of Wisconsin, Albert B. Cummins of Iowa, and Albert J. Beveridge of Indiana, attacked the proposed Payne-Aldrich tariff. They joined the Democrats in obtaining a 2 percent tax on corporate incomes, agreement for approval of an income tax amendment, and revision downward of a number of rates. The bill as it emerged from conference committee still had an average rate of 37 percent and continued unbroken the protectionist principle desired by eastern industrialists.

Taft did not like the Payne-Aldrich tariff but felt he would avoid a tragic split in the party by signing it, although the opposite result was obtained. The Progressives incorrectly believed he had sold out to the vested interests, and their split was widened when Taft, who undertook a 13,000-mile speaking tour to allay criticism, defended the measure. At Winona, Minnesota, he was reported by newsmen to have said that the Payne-Aldrich tariff was the best ever passed by the Republican party and therefore the country's best. His quotation was taken out of context since the president's remark had actually been an apt description of the new system of tariff administration. Many felt the president's assertion revealed he was either a charlatan or a fool, a misapprehension he did not correct by clearly expressing his reservations about the tariff. His position was in decided contrast to Cleveland's reluctant acceptance of the Wilson-Gorman Act of 1894.

The furor over the tariff had not subsided before a more personalized controversy arose over conservation, a dispute in which both sides were equally conscientious but neither looked charitably at the other. The disagreement was especially unfortunate since Taft was a sincere friend of conservation who obtained legislation to withdraw millions of acres containing mineral deposits in Montana and Wyoming and water power sites in many regions. Both he and Secretary of the Interior Richard A. Ballinger were legal minded, however. Not only did they proceed cautiously in withdrawing lands, but Ballinger reopened to the public some lands he felt had been illegally taken.

The most celebrated conservation controversy was initiated when Gifford Pinchot confronted the president with the reports of Louis R. Glavis, an investigator for the Field Division of the Interior Department, that charged Ballinger had unjustly upheld the improper claims of a Morgan-Guggenheim syndicate to government coal lands in Alaska. Upon investigation, Taft concluded Ballinger had acted properly and authorized him to fire Glavis. This action gave the conservationists a martyr whom Pinchot defended in magazine articles and a letter to the Senate. Reluctantly, Taft fired Pinchot in January, 1910, although he knew his action would anger Roosevelt. A joint congressional committee soon began an extensive inquiry and by majority vote exonerated Ballinger of any impropriety. Yet Glavis' counsel, the brilliant Louis D. Brandeis, directed questions to Ballinger which revealed he did not share the conservationists' zeal for withholding lands from private use. Though he remained in the cabinet for fourteen months after Pinchot's removal, Ballinger was a constant source of controversy which widened the rift between Taft and the Progressives.

The final break between the administration and the Progressive rebels, whom the press labeled "insurgents," came when the president did not support them in dethroning the speaker of the House in 1910. Liberal House Republicans, led by Nebraska's George W. Norris, joined Democrats in taking from the speaker the right to appoint and serve on the Rules Committee, whose special orders channeled the course of legislation. The following year, the speaker also lost the important privilege of appointing members of all standing committees. By removing the speaker's dictatorial control, the Progressives hoped to obtain enactment of previously blocked bills as well as a democratization of the House. Taft privately fumed at the young radicals, whose rashness he did not understand. Though he shared some of their frustration with Speaker Cannon, he began to deprive the insurgents of patronage and to deny that they were good Republicans. Instead he supported the conservatives who came to be called "standpatters." (The name arose from an 1899 statement of Mark Hanna's in which he asserted that all the Republican party need do to win the next election was to "stand pat.") Despite presidential opposition, the insurgent forces gained strength in the 1910 elections, while other Republicans lost, and the Democrats captured control of the House with 228 members to the Republicans' 161.

Other controversies arose between Taft and the Progressives, amazingly enough regarding issues on which they both took liberal positions. After the Supreme Court weakened the commodity clause of the Hepburn Act and Progressives increased their complaints about the railroads' ability to impose increases before the Interstate Commerce Commission could act, Taft pressed for a new law giving the ICC extensive rate-making powers with the result that the Mann-Elkins Act was passed in 1910. Much credit for its enactment was due to Democratic support obtained by a commitment to admit Arizona and New Mexico to statehood. While the Mann-Elkins Bill was under consideration, Progressives attacked its provisions permitting competing lines to consolidate and providing a Commerce Court to hear appeals from ICC rulings. They feared the

Commerce Court would take control of the railroads away from the ICC and the Supreme Court and place it in the president's hands. Insurgent Republicans joined Democrats to add amendments, and the resulting bill, which was more to their liking, was passed in 1910. The law greatly strengthened government regulation since the ICC was authorized to suspend general rate increases for ten months pending an investigation and to use its own initiative in revising rates. The ICC's authority was also extended to include telegraph, telephone, cable, and wireless operations, but it was not authorized to establish the physical valuation of company property; this reform was obtained in 1913 during Taft's last days in office, at approximately the same time Congress abolished the Commerce Court.

The administration obtained little more Progressive support in dealing with big business than with the common carriers, even though it initiated almost twice the number of antitrust cases as its predecessor. In part this failure was due to offense given Roosevelt's partisans when suits were instituted against United States Steel and International Harvester, both of whose activities Roosevelt did not consider "an unreasonable restraint of trade." In the U.S. Steel case a question arose regarding the company's acquisition of the Tennessee Coal, Iron and Railroad Company, which Roosevelt had sanctioned, and, when the Supreme Court ruled against the government, many felt Teddy had been vindicated.

On other questions, Taft had quite liberal attitudes but his incapacity as a political leader prevented him from using them to gain support. He personally favored the Sixteenth Amendment, submitted to the states in 1909, which permitted the levying of a federal income tax, and the Seventeenth Amendment, submitted in 1912, which required direct election of U.S. senators. Yet he did not publicly endorse them, a failure leading to his castiga-

tion by some Progressives. Both were adopted in 1913, the same year that labor won an increased voice in the executive branch when the Department of Commerce and Labor were separated into two departments. In 1911 many Democrats joined Taft supporters in Congress to obtain approval of an enlightened reciprocal trade agreement with Canada. A number of western insurgents demurred, feeling the measure sacrificed western farm products, which were placed on the free list, to benefit eastern manufacturers. The measure never became operative since the Canadian government which sponsored it fell, due to fear that the agreement would lead to U.S. annexation. Apparently there was no way Taft could win, a reality that led many Progressive Republicans to become completely disillusioned with the administration.

The Disruption of the Republican Party

Progressives were delighted in June, 1910 when, after a lengthy absence in Africa and Europe, Roosevelt returned to the United States where he was hailed as a conquering hero and bombarded by requests for support from both factions of the Republican party. Initially he tried to remain neutral, but the effort was doomed from the beginning. After being offended by the administration's refusal to use him as a New York peacemaker, he began a speaking tour in the summer of 1910 which attracted strong Progressive support. At Osawatomie, Kansas, in August he startled many conservatives by his address on the "New Nationalism," a synthesis of his political views containing many concepts he had previously advocated and new ideas drawn from Herbert Croly's book, *The Promise of American Life,* published in 1909. Renouncing the free market as a means of economic control and chastising the judiciary for placing property rights above human rights, he proposed the president become the leader of a vigorous central government which would bring economic and social change. Among other reforms, he urged income and inheritance taxes, expanded conservation programs, child labor legislation, the direct primary, a lower tariff, and more effective federal regulation of corporations.

In January, 1911, the National Progressive League was formed which was dedicated to the prevention of Taft's renomination. For a year it devoted much effort to promoting the candidacy of Senator Robert M. La Follette, a man for whom Roosevelt had little regard. Meanwhile, in November, 1911, Roosevelt began openly to attack the administration. Most of the insurgents preferred him to La Follette, considering him their true leader and the man most likely to win if nominated. After an exhausted La Follette lost control of himself and delivered a two-hour tirade against the nation's newspapers in February, 1912, Roosevelt announced his candidacy.

In the ensuing months, the struggle between the Taft and Roosevelt forces became bitter. Roosevelt captured 281 primary delegates to 71 for Taft, although in states where the party regulars were in control Taft gained most of the support. Before the convention's credentials committee, the Roosevelt forces challenged many of the Taft delegates but lost all except nineteen contests. Later, in an appeal to the entire convention, 72 delegates were challenged, but, when the disputed delegates were allowed to vote on their own cases, the Taft men won. Under orders from Roosevelt, his partisans abstained from voting in the choice of a presidential candidate, and Taft received a first ballot nomination. His incumbent vice-president, James S. Sherman of New York, was also chosen to run again.

Following his convention defeat, Roosevelt advised those delegates devoted to him to return home and ascertain the will of the people. Almost two months later, they met in a National Progressive convention studded with the nation's leading intellectuals, social workers, and some outstanding industrialists. They adopted a platform which included every Progressive demand including workers' compensation, the eight-hour day, child labor legislation, minimum wages for women, the initiative, referendum, and recall, and establishment of regulatory agencies to control industry and the tariff. Roosevelt and California's Hiram Johnson were nominated as the party's candidates, and, after Roosevelt declared he felt as fit as a "Bull Moose," the third party received a new popular name.

Meanwhile the Democrats had concluded their intraparty struggle which resulted in the nomination of Woodrow Wilson. Colonel George Harvey, the conservative publisher of *Harper's Weekly*, proposed him as a candidate while he was still president of Princeton, a position he lost rather than sacrifice his plans to democratize student life and emphasize scholarship. Harvey initiated a campaign in his behalf after Wilson was elected governor of New Jersey, but within three months the movement collapsed. Before becoming governor, Wilson had appeared to be a "safe" state's righter who detested Bryan as a dangerous radical, but, once in office, he outmaneuvered Jim Smith, head of the New Jersey Democratic machine, and enacted a most comprehensive Progressive program. Immediately his desirability as a presidential candidate became apparent.

Meanwhile another campaign to promote Wilson's nomination, initiated in 1910 by a number of southerners living in New York, began to obtain results. Walter McCorkle and William F. McCombs, successful New York lawyers, and Walter Hines Page, the editor of the *World's Work*, formulated a publicity program and a national speaking tour for Wilson in the spring of 1911. They were soon joined by two other men who were to be important in the campaign and the years ahead, Colonel Edward M. House and William Gibbs McAdoo. House, the promoter and confidante of four Texas governors, was a shrewd political judge and an adviser in whom Wilson came to place great confidence, while McAdoo, a southerner responsible for the tunnels under the Hudson River, became an able campaign strategist. Their efforts were instrumental in obtaining almost one-fourth of the convention's delegates for Wilson. However, Speaker Champ Clark, an old-line politician from Missouri, attained a majority of the delegates during the early balloting but did not have the two-thirds necessary for nomination.

Bryan, who played an important role in the convention, was influential in obtaining a liberal platform which pledged a lower tariff, vigorous antitrust laws, and a revision of banking and currency laws. The third day he introduced a resolution stating the convention was opposed to the nomination of anyone "under obligation to J. Pierpont Morgan, Thomas F. Ryan, August Belmont, or any other member of the privilege-hunting and favor seeking class. . . ." Though watered down before adoption, the resolution was a challenge to the established eastern financial interests. On the fourteenth ballot, after the Tammany-dominated New York delegation switched to Clark, Bryan threw his support to Wilson, an action that was significant but not crucial.

The Wilson managers utilized Bryan's actions in every possible way and pursued an effective strategy which led to victory. Early in the convention, they reached an agreement with the managers of Representative Oscar W. Underwood, the chairman of the House Ways and Means Committee, who had about half the southern votes. Together the Wilson and Underwood forces withstood the Clark onslaught, and a slow attrition set in on the front runner's strength. On the forty-second ballot Illinois

switched to Wilson, giving him a majority, and he was nominated on the forty-sixth.

The postconvention campaign was marked by personal attacks of Roosevelt and Taft on each other and a serious debate between Roosevelt and Wilson. With verve, Roosevelt urged the adoption of his Hamiltonian "New Nationalism" as the only adequate means to deal with the nation's complex society. Wilson, whose most important campaign adviser was Louis D. Brandeis, called for a "New Freedom" under which competition would be restored as a means of bringing self-regulation to business and industry. In Wilson's opinion, Roosevelt's plans would create a plutocracy which would not only control workers but also the government itself. As a recent convert to Progressivism, Wilson advocated a solution which time was to prove inadequate, yet its emphasis on old-fashioned liberalism, state's rights, and local control appealed greatly to the average rural and small-town, middle-class American.

Wilson won by holding the support of the Progressive Democrats as well as southerners and the urban ethnic groups which traditionally supported his party. Though he obtained only 42 percent of the popular vote, he gleaned 435 electoral votes to 88 for Roosevelt and 8 for Taft. There was no doubt Progressivism was ascendant since Wilson and Roosevelt jointly obtained 10.4 million votes to Taft's 3.5 million. Also Eugene V. Debs, the Socialist candidate who advocated even more extensive revision of the system, received almost a million votes. Clearly the time was ripe for reform.

Wilson's Concept of the Presidency

No American president has assumed office with better preparation than Wilson. In his published Ph.D. dissertation, *Congressional*

Woodrow Wilson with his wife and daughters.

Government, which had gone through numerous editions, he portrayed the need for strong executive leadership. At one time he had felt the presidential system, with its fixed terms for the president and congressmen and division of powers, should be abandoned for a British-type parliamentary system. He had modified this view, but he still believed the president must be more than an administrator. The success of the system demanded that much legislation originate with the president, who would use his effectiveness as a party leader and his leverage on Congress to see that it was enacted.

Wilson, who was concerned with much more than the mechanics of presidential leadership, had a profound moral concern which dominated his responses to many situations. Though his knowledge was deep and broad, in his decision making the question of "rightness" was always paramount which, at times, resulted in overzealousness in action and the imputation of unworthy motives to admirable men. However, on most issues, at least during his earlier presidential years, Wilson maintained an unusual balance and charitableness which commanded the respect of his opponents, and, above all, he excelled in articulation and communication. He was the last and one of the few American presidents to write his own state papers, which were models of clarity and style and were punctuated with phrases which etched themselves on the public mind. But it was in the spoken word that Wilson reached the ultimate in effectiveness. Few could hear him speak boldly on a major issue and forthrightly propose a course of action without becoming an enthusiastic supporter or a dedicated opponent.

The New Freedom

The new president had scant affection for professional politicians but carefully balanced his new cabinet with men of ability from various sections of the party. Bryan was made secretary of state, and, though he troubled Wilson at times by urging appointments for "deserving Democrats," he shared much of his pacifism and idealism. Texas Representative Albert S. Burleson, a favorite with party regulars, became postmaster general, and McAdoo, who was in close contact with numerous Progressives and businessmen, became secretary of the treasury. Many outside the official family played important roles, since Wilson con-

tinued his academic penchant for getting expert advice from a variety of sources. Colonel House became virtually his alter ego, while others who were more distant gave explicit advice which was always welcomed if not heeded. Among these was Walter Hines Page, who was appointed ambassador to Great Britain, although Wilson had slated him to be secretary of the interior before objections arose to a southerner administering the pension system. It was Page who suggested that Wilson abandon a system in use since Jefferson's presidency and address Congress in person.

In April, 1913, the president convened Congress in special session and eloquently pled for a revision of the tariff. This action was to be the first part of his program which he called the "New Freedom," the freeing of the individual by removing unfair advantages, restoring competition, and enabling enlightened self-interest to arise in business. Within a month the bill Representative Underwood introduced passed the House. It lowered average rates to approximately 29 percent, placing trust-manufactured goods on the free list as well as most raw materials and many food and clothing items. Under the new Sixteenth Amendment, an income tax, which ran up to 3 percent on personal and corporate incomes over $100,000, was included. To obtain approval in the Senate, where the Democratic majority was small, Wilson had to apply all the political pressure at his command, including a public indictment of lobbyists. Aided by La Follette and other Progressive Republicans, the administration coerced senators into revealing their personal property holdings in tariff-related industries. As a result, the Simmons tariff bill reduced the Underwood rates by an additional 4 percent, and the maximum income tax rate was raised to 6 percent. All Democratic senators, except the two from Louisiana who were concerned with sugar, voted with the administration. The resulting Underwood-Simmons Tariff was a solid reform victory. At the time it could not be foreseen that war in Europe would prevent its effects being widespread and that the measure would be replaced by a higher tariff in 1921.

Even before the passage of the tariff, the president began to press Congress for banking and currency reform. Few denied the need for greater elasticity in the nation's money supply and the inappropriateness of continuing reliance on a system that directly related it to the national debt. Many recognized that the safest, wisest policy was to establish reserve banks which would issue currency based, at least in part, on commercial paper, the collateral for loans private banks had made, but the means to achieve this reform remained a moot point. The National Monetary Commission, headed by Senator Aldrich, recommended the establishment of a central banking system controlled by private bankers. This proposal was politically unacceptable to many Progressives, whose fears were heightened in 1913 by the report of a special congressional committee headed by Louisiana's Representative Arsène Pujo which held a money trust run by bankers dominated numerous insurance, railroad, utility, and manufacturing companies.

Many conservative Democrats shared the views of Representative Carter Glass of Virginia, chairman of the House Committee on Banking and Currency, whose committee produced a conservative bill providing for up to twenty privately controlled reserve banks which would operate independently. However, Bryan, McAdoo, and other Progressives strongly protested and were supported by Brandeis. As a result a compromise was reached known as the Glass-Owen or Federal Reserve Bill in which the Progressives attained three of their major demands: a national board was established with governing power over the entire system; bankers were excluded from membership on this board; and the currency to be issued by the Federal Reserve Banks was

made an obligation of the United States. The newly created Federal Reserve notes were to be issued by the various Federal Reserve Banks on the basis of commercial paper and agricultural paper, the collateral borrowers had placed with member banks of the system to receive loans. For this service, the Federal Reserve Banks charged a rediscount rate, comparable to interest paid by individuals, which the national board was empowered to raise or lower. Yet the conservatives were appeased also; instead of a central bank, twelve regional banks were established which were owned by the member banks and until 1935 were largely controlled by their own boards of directors, who were primarily bankers. All national banks were required to join the system, while state banks could do so if they wished. Members were required to deposit 6 percent of their reserves in their Reserve Bank, thus removing them from speculation. Despite a requirement of a 40 percent gold reserve against outstanding Federal Reserve notes, a means was provided for greatly increasing or decreasing the amount of money in circulation or, to use a banker's term, obtain greater currency elasticity. The volume of Federal Reserve notes could be altered by the Federal Reserve Banks changing the gold reserve requirements in times of emergency, by buying and selling government bonds, and by changing the rediscount rate charged member banks on commercial and agricultural paper.

Though some Progressives like La Follette were disappointed that the Federal Reserve system was not exclusively under national control, its enactment was in harmony with the New Freedom philosophy. While retaining much private and regional control, it provided a means of mobilizing the nation's banking reserves and attaining flexibility in the quantity of money in circulation.

In January, 1914, Wilson again appeared before Congress to ask for action in an area in which the New Freedom felt reform was essential—antitrust legislation. The administration's policy, typified by the Clayton Antitrust Bill in the House, initially sought to spell out illegal action under the Sherman Act, but many Progressives felt this task was an impossibility and that the law would not regulate the financial giants which had come into being. They were joined in their criticism by organized labor, which was disgusted when the measure did not exempt it from antitrust prosecutions, and business leaders, who feared it would stifle legitimate growth.

By April, 1914, the president was in a dilemma and turned to Brandeis for rescue with the result that the provisions of the Clayton Act were weakened before its passage. A number of practices were forbidden, such as purchase of stock by one corporation in that of another, but only when such action lessened competition. Moreover, the act declared neither labor unions nor farm organizations were per se to be held illegal combinations in restraint of trade. Though Samuel Gompers declared this exemption a "Magna Carta" for labor, in actuality it was not. Courts had previously held labor unions as such were not illegal but had frequently held their actions to be, an attitude they continued to maintain.

Instead of increasing antitrust suits and defining illegal acts, the administration, for the first time, turned to a Roosevelt-type policy. In the Federal Trade Commission Act, it outlawed unfair trade practices in general and established a powerful quasi-legislative, executive, judicial commission with authority to move against any guilty person or corporation. The Clayton Act provided the body of law which the Federal Trade Commission attempted to enforce through its hearings, investigations, and "cease and desist orders," which only the federal courts had the power to impede.

Enactment through strong administration pressure of the Federal Trade Commission Act was the first indication Wilson would consider altering his New Freedom philosophy and use centralized control to obtain social and economic reform. At the time, he was apparently unaware of the significance of his action. In 1914 he reverted to his earlier attitude and blocked a bill establishing long-range rural credits and a national child labor bill, contending they were class legislation. Moreover, with the enactment of the antitrust laws, he, with pardonable pride, held the New Freedom had succeeded in destroying the system of privilege which had thrived with government acquiescence. Within two years, however, the president was to continue the policy first accepted with the Federal Trade Commission Act and in some ways was to "out Roosevelt Roosevelt."

Wilson's 1916 Conversion

In the 1914 elections, before Wilson's conversion to more vigorous national controls, the Democrats lost congressional seats but retained control of both houses of Congress. However, the Progressive Democratic candidates in the South and West did very well and increased their influence in the government and the party. The import of this development was not lost on the president, although he gave few indications in 1915 that his basic attitude toward government was changing. He did support the La Follette Seaman's Act, which gave much needed protection to merchant seamen, but only after the State Department was given time to rework the nation's treaties with foreign powers whose seamen under the new law were released from their slave-like labor contracts when they called at American ports.

Wilson's change of attitude came in 1916 and was partially attributable to political pressure. The Progressive party had begun to disintegrate in 1914, and by early 1916 it was clear Roosevelt would return to the Republican party. It was also apparent to many knowledgeable observers that unless Wilson could obtain much of the former Progressive vote the Democrats would be defeated. Coupled with this realization was the president's awareness that the New Freedom philosophy had proved inadequate to deal with many complex problems.

An indication that the president's attitude was changing came when he announced his choice of Brandeis to fill a vacancy on the United States Supreme Court, and, after a bitter fight, Brandeis was confirmed. Legislatively the president first revealed his new attitude by supporting a rural credit bill which he had previously opposed, and, after a struggle of several months, the Federal Farm Loan Act was passed, which established twelve Federal Land Banks. They lent money to cooperative farm-loan associations composed of farmers who wished to borrow on their lands while the Warehouse Act provided loans on the basis of crops deposited as collateral, the realization of the Populist subtreasury ideal. Thus the federal government supplied the deficiencies private capital could not furnish and made sorely needed credit available to farmers.

As the presidential contest developed, it became apparent that Progressives regarded the passage of a federal workmen's compensation act and a national child labor bill as crucial. Wilson strongly supported both measures, even going to the President's Room at the Capitol to urge approval of the Keating-Owen Child Labor Bill, and both bills were enacted. For the first time the Workman's Compensation Act provided liability coverage for federal employees, and the Keating-Owen Child Labor Act excluded from interstate commerce the products of factories where children under fourteen were employed and those with laborers under sixteen working more than eight hours a day or at night, as well as products of mines and quarries with workers under six-

teen.* The child labor law was especially significant since it used the federal authority over commerce to dictate how industries should be run.

In other actions, the president aided in obtaining passage of the Bankhead Good Roads Act, which allocated millions of dollars to aid the states in road building, and the Smith-Hughes Act, which furnished support for agricultural and vocational education. Both laws provided matching funds to the states, a procedure the administration had first used in 1914 in the Smith-Lever Act which appropriated funds to support agricultural extension work in every rural county in the nation. In 1916 when the railroad unions threatened a nationwide strike to obtain the eight-hour day, Wilson tried to persuade the companies to grant it. Failing in his efforts, he obtained passage of the Adamson Act, which gave the unions what they wished. Wilson's actions made it clear to all discerning observers before the close of the 1916 presidential campaign that he had accepted much of the New Nationalism.

Racial Attitudes

Contrary to the position assumed in other areas, Wilson, like many contemporary liberals, became less progressive in racial attitudes and policy as time passed. Among the intellectuals, there was an increasing acceptance of the Anglo-Saxon myth, and there was strong support from all Progressive segments for restrictions on immigration. Spurred by the American Federation of Labor, Congress passed a bill in 1915 requiring all immigrants to pass a literacy test. It was vetoed by Wilson who strongly believed in Anglo-Saxon superi-

---

*This law was invalidated by the Supreme Court in 1918 and a similar measure, passed in 1919, in 1922.

ority but felt the bill was primarily a test of opportunity, not native ability; a similar measure was passed over his veto in 1917.

In past administrations, both Presidents Roosevelt and Taft displayed an inconsistent attitude toward blacks, but their overall policies were unfavorable. Roosevelt offended southern opinion by having Booker T. Washington to dinner at the White House, and, when criticized, he declared he would have him to dine whenever he pleased, but he never chose to have him again. He appointed a black collector of the port of Charleston and closed the post office at Indianola, Mississippi, when whites demonstrated against a black postmistress. Yet in a fervent desire to break the Democratic "Solid South," Roosevelt came generally to support the "Lily White" Republicans of the region rather than the integrated "Blacks and Tans." On two southern tours in 1905, he not only advocated industrial training as a solution for the racial problem but also praised racial purity as a basis for national greatness. In 1906 he gave dishonorable discharges to 160 black soldiers who were implicated by flimsy circumstantial evidence of conducting a riot in Brownsville, Texas.

Under the circumstances, it was not surprising that the Republican platform in 1908 failed, for the first time since their enactment, to call for enforcement of the Reconstruction amendments. In office, Taft reduced the number of black officeholders and initiated the first moves toward segregation in government agencies. This was followed in 1912 by Roosevelt's increased efforts to gain southern electoral votes by excluding black southern delegates from the Progressive party convention.

Disillusioned by Republican abandonment, blacks gave Wilson, the Democratic presidential nominee, unprecedented support in 1912. Yet he too accepted the Booker T. Washington educational philosophy and made a sharp distinction between the masses of both races. Under the leadership of Postmaster General Burleson and Navy Secretary Josephus Daniels, Wilson discreetly but consistently segregated the Post Office and Treasury departments. By 1914 the Bureau of Printing and Engraving was included, and a photograph began to be required of all job applicants. Militant protests from the National Association for the Advancement of Colored People, the black press, and such liberals as Oswald G. Villard, publisher of the *New York Evening Post,* helped contain the movement. However, nationally as well as locally, there continued to be general Progressive apathy toward the rights of racial minorities.

Progressivism, like all movements, had its weaknesses, but they were far outnumbered by its strengths. With zeal and courage, the movement aroused large segments of America, especially from the economically and socially established middle classes, to undertake a variety of reforms which were primarily designed to help the industrious poor rise into the middle class. Changes were induced, although not as many or as completely as the more dedicated wished. By 1916, when the movement was largely burned out and its strength diverted to foreign affairs, much of the laissez faire concept which had dominated American government had been modified, and the grosser inequities of the nation's industrial society had at least been catalogued and publicly indicted.

Selected Bibliography

Motivations for progressivism are suggested in Richard Hofstadter, *The Age of Reform, From Bryan to F.D.R.** (1955); Gabriel Kolko, *The Triumph of Conservatism: A Reinterpretation of American History, 1900–1916** (1967); Robert H. Wiebe, *Businessmen and Reform, A Study of the Progressive Movement** (1968); and Eric F. Goldman, *Rendezvous with Destiny: A History of Modern American Reform** (abr. & rev. ed., 1956). Two excellent studies survey the period with emphasis on politics: George E. Mowry, *The Era of Theodore Roosevelt, 1900–1912** (1958), and Arthur S. Link, *Woodrow Wilson and the Progressive Era, 1910–1917** (1954). Social and economic conditions are reviewed in Harold U. Faulkner, *The Quest for Social Justice, 1898–1914** (repr. of 1931 ed., 1971) and *The Decline of Laissez Faire, 1897–1917* (1968).

The role of critics and reformers may be studied in Henry May, *The End of American Innocence: A Study of the First Years of Our Own Time, 1912–1917** (1964); Louis Filler, *Crusaders for American Liberalism* (1964); David Chalmers, *The Social and Political Ideas of the Muckrakers** (fac. ed., 1964); Allen F. Davis, *Spearheads for Reform, The Social Settlements and the Progressive Movement, 1890–1914** (1967); Hugh C. Bailey, *Liberalism in the New South, Southern Social Reformers and the Progressive Movement* (1969); and the classic *Autobiography of Lincoln Steffens** (2 vols., 1968).

Reform at the state level is presented in Hoyt L. Warner, *Progressivism in Ohio, 1897–1917* (1964); George E. Mowry, *California Progressives** (1963); Robert S. Maxwell, *LaFollette and the Rise of the Progressives in Wisconsin* (1973); C. Vann Woodward, *Origins of the New South, 1877–1913** (1971); Blake McKelvey, *The Urbanization of America, 1860–1915* (1963); Zane L. Miller, *Boss Cox's Cincinnati: Urban Politics in the Progressive Era** (1968); and Melvin G. Holli, *Reform in Detroit, Hazen S. Pingree and Urban Politics* (1969). Stanley P. Caine, *The Myth of a Progressive Reform: Railroad Regulation in Wisconsin, 1903–1910* (1970), depicts La Follette as an inept leader.

Roosevelt's career is analyzed in William H. Harbaugh, *Power and Responsibility, The Life and Times of Theodore Roosevelt* (1961), and J. M. Blum, *The Republican Roosevelt** (1962), as well as the older critical Henry F. Pringle, *Theodore Roosevelt, A Biography** (1956). George E. Mowry, *Theodore Roosevelt and the Progressive Movement** (1960), shows the critical relation of each to the other.

Various aspects of progressive reform are detailed and evaluated in Gabriel Kolko, *Railroads and Regulation, 1877–1916** (1970); Samuel P. Hays, *Conservatism and the Gospel of Efficiency, The Progressive Conservation Movement, 1890–1920** (1969); and the more complete M. N. McGeary,

---

*Available in paperback.

Gifford Pinchot: Forrester-Politician (1960), and Oscar E. Anderson, *The Health of a Nation: Harvey W. Wiley and the Fight for Pure Food* (1958).

Henry F. Pringle, *Life and Times of William Howard Taft* (2 vols., repr. of 1939 ed., 1964), is a detailed biography. Taft's presidency is evaluated in Mowry's *Theodore Roosevelt and the Progressive Movement* and in studies of the administration's difficulties, including James Penick, Jr., *Progressive Politics and Conservation: The Ballinger-Pinchot Affair* (1968), and Kenneth Hechler, *Insurgency: Personalities and Policies of the Taft Era* (repr. of 1940 ed., 1970). Amos R. Pinchot, *A History of the Progressive Party, 1912–1916* (1958) is an account by one of its leaders.

Arthur S. Link's multivolume *Wilson* (Vol. 1–5, 1947–1965) is a definitive biography covering his life and political leadership to 1917. Its first volume, *Wilson: Road to the White House** (1947), has an excellent account of the 1912 election. Other volumes are *Wilson: The New Freedom* (1956); *Wilson: Struggle for Neutrality, 1914–1915* (1960); *Wilson: Confusions and Crisis, 1915–1916* (1964); and *Wilson: Campaigns for Progressivism and Peace, 1916–1917* (1965). The most adequate complete life of Wilson is A. C. Walworth, *Woodrow Wilson* (2 vols., 1958), while J. M. Blum, *Woodrow Wilson and the Politics of Morality** (1956), has illuminating observations.

Progressive racist attitudes and policies may be studied in August Meier, *Negro Thought in America, 1880–1915: Racial Ideologies in the Age of Booker T. Washington** (1963); Ann J. Lane, *The Brownsville Affair: National Crisis and Black Reaction** (1971); and Charles F. Kellogg, *NAACP, A History of the National Association for the Advancement of Colored People, I, 1909–1920* (1967). The influence of increasingly hostile white attitudes is seen in Allan H. Spear, *Black Chicago, The Making of a Negro Ghetto, 1890–1920** (1969).

Drift of the United States into War

1915   German blockade of British Isles

Sinking of the *Lusitania*

Exposure of Dr. Heinrich Albert's papers

Arabic Pledge

1916   German announcement of impending attacks on armed enemy merchantmen

Sinking of the *Sussex*

Sussex Pledge

1917   German reinstitution of unrestricted submarine warfare

Zimmermann note

Arming of the United States merchant vessels

United States declaration of war

United States Senate Rejection of the Versailles Treaty

1919   Lodge "Round Robin"

Wilson speaking tour

Rejection of Forty-Five Amendments and Four Reservations of Lodge Committee

Wilson's stroke

Treaty rejected with and without reservations

1920   Treaty defeated with reservations

19

Idealistic Foreign Policy

Long-Range Developments

For the Westward Movement, Nationalism, and Expansion

The dispatching of troops to Nicaragua, the Dominican Republic, and Haiti increased the United States' commitment to intervention in Latin America, a policy later reversed by Presidents Herbert Hoover and Franklin D. Roosevelt.

Unsuccessful United States attempts to mediate the European war and the idealism of President Woodrow Wilson's state papers contributed to the international image of the United States as an impartial major power.

Some of the congressional opponents of war remained to become leaders of the isolationist forces in the 1930s.

The effectiveness of American military forces stimulated much national pride which veterans organizations utilized in the next two decades to obtain benefits for their members.

Wilson's role at the Versailles Conference in the establishment of new states and in obtaining self-determination of peoples earned the United States the respect of much of the world.

Wilson's peace plans, though defeated in the United States by Senate rejection of the Versailles Treaty, remained a blueprint for permanent peace which is still venerated by many liberals.

Postwar revelations of the secret agreements among the major powers other than the United States and the power struggle at the peace conferences promoted disgust and isolationism in the United States.

U.S. Recognition Policy

When Woodrow Wilson assumed office, many Americans were highly concerned with domestic problems and clung to the belief that the United States could avoid entanglement in European affairs despite the nation's emergence as an industrial and colonial power. President Wilson's acceptance of this philosophy did not prevent him from initiating a new departure in foreign policy. Since the administration of Thomas Jefferson, the United States had recognized *de facto* governments, i.e., those in actual control of countries. Wilson reversed this tradition, choosing to recognize only those he considered to be *de jure* governments, i.e., those who ruled by right. This new policy symbolized Wilson's entire approach to foreign affairs which was predicated on a sincere dedication to justice and peace, but in pursuing these goals he at times took actions which had an opposite effect.

Though their idiom was different, Wilson and Secretary of State Bryan shared many attitudes toward foreign affairs and cooperatively developed a number of significant policies. They readily agreed to remove U.S. support of a financial consortium to build railroads in China for fear of infringing on the Open Door policy and to recognize the newly created Republic of China. The president supported Bryan in obtaining arbitration treaties with thirty countries, including Great Britain and France, although recent secretaries of state had encountered difficulties in gaining Senate approval of such treaties. Bryan averted this barrier by simply having the powers agree to postpone hostilities and halt armament increases for a year (a "cooling-off" period) while the commission investigated. Though later critics sneered, the agreements were operable in cases where mutual self-interest prevailed and represented an honest attempt to avert war.

Equal commitment to principle was demonstrated after the British government protested exemption of American coastal shipping from Panama Canal tolls. Upon reflection, Wilson decided that this U.S. action was a violation of the Hay-Pauncefote Treaty, and, throughout the first six months of 1914, he urged Congress to rescind the exception. In a personal address he pled, "I shall not know how to deal with other matters of even greater delicacy and nearer consequence if you do not grant it to me in ungrudging measure." Congress heeded his request.

A less statesmanlike policy toward Japan was pursued by the president, who may have been partially influenced by racist attitudes. Though he opposed exclusion of Japanese by name from owning land in California, he connived in efforts which had the same effect, and aliens ineligible to become citizens were excluded from the privilege. When Japan prepared for war, the president used the utmost effort in diplomatic notes to avert conflict.

Another serious diplomatic exchange occurred in 1915 when the Japanese presented the Twenty-One Demands to China which, if accepted, would have greatly compromised Chinese sovereignty and seriously violated the Open Door policy. Backed by Great Britain, the United States persuaded Japan to modify these, and China preserved a degree of independence.

The saddest departure from Wilson's high-toned liberalism occurred in Latin America where economic and fiscal incompetence spawned continual troubles. Though Wilson's intentions were sincere, instability, fear of European involvement, a need to safeguard the isthmian passage, and diplomatic incompetence led to increased American intervention. Secretary Bryan proposed a plan for U.S. assumption of the debts of the smaller states, which Wilson rejected as too radical. Confronted by essentially the same problems as his predecessors, Wilson continued their policy of using the U.S. military forces to maintain law and order. Troops were kept in Nicaragua and a treaty was negotiated providing an option on a canal route for $3 million. Forces were sent to the Dominican Republic and Haiti to end anarchy, and the Danish West Indies, whose name was changed to the Virgin Islands, were purchased for $25 million to avoid their potential use by Germany. When Wilson tried to use cooperative inter-American efforts to stabilize the region, Chile and Argentina blocked the action, and American imperialism grew, even though the government was not jingoistic (belligerent).

The Conflict with Mexico

Serious involvement in Mexico occurred when Wilson refused to recognize a new despotic Mexican regime. In 1911 Porfirio Díaz, a long-time dictator friendly to foreign interests, was overthrown, and Francisco Madero, a visionary reformer, succeeded him. In turn Madero was murdered by Victoriano Huerta, the full-blooded Indian leader of the army. Wilson would not recognize the regime of such an "unspeakable" man, and, attempting to mediate, he encountered the opposition of all Mexican political segments, a recurring Latin American reaction to outside interference whose import the administration did not adequately assess.

After Huerta deposed most of the Chamber of Deputies in October, 1913, Wilson tried to engineer his overthrow. In February, 1914, he removed the arms embargo imposed by Taft and began shipment of goods to the Mexican constitutionalists. Soon afterwards, in April, 1914, the temporary arrest of U.S. sailors at

Pancho Villa with his troops.

Tampico was used as an excuse for American seizure of Vera Cruz.* The Mexicans were outraged, and liberals in the United States protested, which led Wilson to accept mediation by Argentina, Brazil, and Chile. The mediation sessions at Niagara Falls ended shortly before Huerta's abdication on July 15 and the rise to power of Venustiano Carranza. Carranza's representatives asked the U.S. to withhold any intervention, and Wilson agreed provided there were no wholesale confiscations or executions.

All might have been well if Carranza's ablest general, Francisco (Pancho) Villa, had not begun an insurrection. Acting on Wilson's advice, a convention of revolutionary leaders was held which elected Villa head of a provisional government. He proved to be ignorant and incompetent, however, and by April, 1915, was forced to retreat into northern Mexico. From there he tried to provoke U.S. intervention by conducting raids against United States citizens, eighteen of whom were killed at Santa Ysabel, Mexico, in January, 1916, and nineteen when Columbus, New Mexico, was burned in March, 1916.

Meanwhile Wilson had recognized Carranza's government and, deeply involved with Germany over submarine warfare, had become fearful of German attempts to provoke a Mexican war. In March, 1916, after the Mexican government had failed to protect U.S. citizens, with Carranza's reluctant consent, General John J. Pershing was sent to Mexico with an expeditionary force of 6,000 men to pursue Villa. When Villa retreated further to the south it looked as if the United States would become an occupying power. Carranza protested bitterly, but most of the U.S. National Guard was ordered to the Mexican border. Though ten-

sion became intense after a skirmish between the opposing forces at Carrizal in which each sustained casualties, agreement was reached in July, 1916, to appoint a Joint High Commission to resolve the difficulties. Although four months of sessions provided a relief period, no agreements were reached, partially because the U.S. insisted upon the right to pursue bandits who crossed its borders, but by January, 1917, the U.S. chose to withdraw due to the crisis with Germany and increased Mexican stability. Soon afterwards, in March, 1917, Wilson recognized Carranza's newly formed constitutional government.

Wilson's Mexican policy, while sorely trying and at times almost leading to full-scale war, was not a failure. It prevented European intervention, aided in Huerta's overthrow, and did not allow conservative U.S. forces to undo needed economic and social changes in Mexico. Its greatest failure was an increase in anti-

General John J. Pershing leads his forces in pursuit of Pancho Villa.

*The American naval commander had demanded a twenty-one gun salute in addition to an apology. The Mexicans refused the latter unless a U.S. vessel returned the salute.

U.S. feeling in Mexico, a consequence Wilson never intended.

The War in Europe

Shortly after difficulties began with Mexico, the American people were stunned in August, 1914, when war erupted in Europe. In recent years an intense contest had emerged between Europe's two alliance systems: the Triple Alliance consisting of Germany, Austro-Hungary, and Italy, and the Triple Entente composed of Great Britain, France, and Russia. Although neither side wished war, rivalry for advantage contributed to a series of incidents and minor conflicts which constantly threatened the peace. At last, in June, 1914, when Archduke

Francis Ferdinand, the heir to the Austro-Hungarian throne, was assassinated in Bosnia, a crisis was precipitated which led to World War I. Austro-Hungary blamed the tragedy on a conspiracy arising in Serbia, a close Russian ally, and demanded the right to go into Serbia to capture and punish the criminals. When Serbia refused, a series of military responses proved the Alliance systems were working only too well and led to war. Italy alone of the major alliance participants failed to respond and in 1915 entered the war on the side of Britain, France, and Russia—the Allied Powers.

Immediately after war began in Europe, President Wilson issued a neutrality declaration consistent with American tradition, which drew almost universal support. He declared the nation must be "neutral in fact as well as in

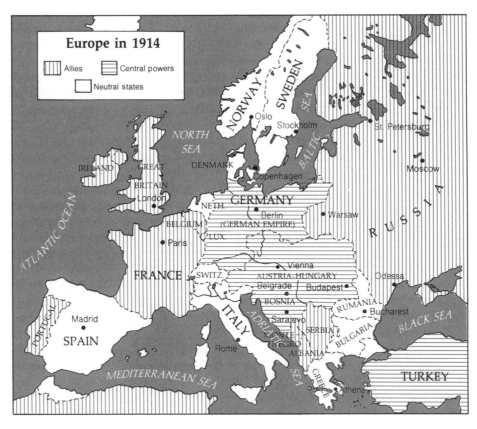

name. . . . We must be neutral in thought as well as in act. . . ." This demand was difficult to fulfill since one out of three Americans was either foreign-born or had a parent that was foreign-born.

Wilson sincerely desired to keep the United States out of the conflict and, if possible, to bring it to an end. He unsuccessfully attempted to mediate the dispute on three occasions, the first of which came when Colonel Edward M. House was sent to Europe in January, 1915, to contact leaders of Great Britain and Germany. The British agreed to consider peace, but German unwillingness to discuss Belgian freedom led to an impasse. (Much to the horror of the American people, Germany had chosen to seek a quick victory in 1914 by striking through Belgium at a comparatively poorly fortified section of France. In doing so, it violated a solemn agreement dating from 1839 which guaranteed Belgian independence and inflicted intense suffering on a valiant people.) A year later, convinced that only an end to hostilities would insure American rights, the president again sent House for talks with both sides. The British government was pressured by the promise that if it cooperated and failure ensued "probably the United States would leave the Conference as a belligerent on the side of the Allies. . . ." However, when the German government began attacks on armed merchantmen in February, 1916, the peace movement received a severe setback.

Though the president became increasingly sympathetic with the Allied cause, in late 1916 he made a last desperate effort to mediate. Before his plans could materialize, the Germans, who distrusted Wilson and had no intention of considering mediation attempts, called a peace conference without his involvement. Though the president explained to the Senate that the peace he envisioned was one without victory, Germany spurned all his efforts and pursued policies which made mediation impossible.

America's own policy, enunciated through Secretary of State Bryan in 1914, disapproved of even private loans to the warring powers as possible violations of neutrality, although internal pressure soon forced a modification of this attitude. Initially the war caused a notable drop in exports from the United States and such extensive stock sales by Europeans that the New York Stock Exchange was closed for over four months. As European conditions clarified, however, there was an enormous demand for American goods. Due to the effectiveness of the British navy, only the Allied powers could transport large quantities of American exports, and these could be paid for only by denuding the Allies of gold. In the early spring of 1915, Bryan agreed to the first of many private loans extended the Allies—a $50 million loan to France by J. P. Morgan's company. Ultimately over $2 billion in private loans were made, most of which were backed by American securities. The United States thus became a principal Allied arsenal playing an important role in war operations.

Wilson's Concept of Neutral Rights

Both the Allied and Central Powers* notably violated Wilson's high-toned view of neutral rights, the success of which depended on the warring nation's acceptance. Wilson based his views on the 1909 Declaration of London, the maritime code formulated under the sponsorship of the Second Hague Conference. Among other things, it distinguished between absolute, conditional, and noncontraband goods, allowing the latter to move even through a "true blockade." Great Britain, of course, had not accepted the conference's decisions be-

---

*Germany, Austro-Hungary, Bulgaria, and Turkey.

cause it would have destroyed the effects of much of its naval strength.

As the war progressed, Wilson protested British addition of conditional and noncontraband goods to the absolute contraband list. By April, 1916, the British ceased making any distinctions, partially because the United States did not threaten war to demand respect for its neutral rights. Americans were also aroused by the British practice of taking vessels into port for search, British use of the American flag to escape German submarine attacks, the censorship of American mail, and the publication, in July, 1916, of a "blacklist" of firms in neutral countries, including over eighty in the United States, believed to be trading with the Central Powers.

Under such provocation, it is amazing that relations between the United States and Great Britain did not become more strained. Part of the explanation lay in Wilson's anglophilism and his increasing belief that an Allied victory was essential. This view was promoted by U.S. Ambassador Walter Hines Page in London, who tempered American protests and left the impression that they were primarily for domestic political consumption. Moreover, British interference with American trade, while irritating, did not prove a financial liability. For example, after listing cotton as contraband, the British proposed buying the total American cotton crop. Seized goods were paid for, and the value of goods exported to the Allied countries increased 400 percent between 1914 and 1916. At the same time, exports to the Central Powers decreased to less than 1 percent of their former value. Both conviction and profit prompted the president to pursue the course he did. These motives were reinforced by the increasingly anti-German popular opinion, much of which was due to the Belgian invasion, German submarine warfare, and the German attempts to sabotage war industries in the United States.

Germany protested against the American sale of war materials to the Allies and predicated any concessions on the U.S. forcing Britain to respect American neutral rights. It contended British use of mines was illegal and that the submarine was a new weapon unbound by traditional rules of war; the submarine challenge proved to be the most difficult problem.

As the British noose tightened, the German government, in February, 1915, placed the British Isles under submarine blockade, stating that all enemy merchant vessels in the area would be sunk and that it might not "always be possible to save crews and passengers." Count Johann von Bernstorff, the German ambassador to the United States, who was conscious of U.S. public opinion and wished to avoid an American war, assured the U.S. that Germany would try to avoid violence to neutral vessels "in so far as they are recognizable." The question became critical when the British refused to lift their blockade on food and raw materials, and the Germans began to sink unarmed British passenger liners in the blockaded area.

Secretary Bryan sympathized with the German contention that the United States should warn its citizens not to travel on belligerent merchant ships, a policy he felt would balance concessions to the British and prevent the British from using passengers as a shield to transport contraband. From the beginning, however, Wilson insisted that Germany be held strictly accountable for its action. In the spring of 1915, several incidents occurred involving American neutral rights, including the death of an American citizen aboard the torpedoed British steamer *Falaba,* a German airplane attack on the American freighter *Cushing,* and the damaging of the American tanker *Gulflight* by a German torpedo. A major crisis occurred May 7, 1915, when the Cunard liner *Lusitania,* which carried much contraband

The Lusitania.

including 4,500 cases of ammunition, was sunk off the Irish coast with the loss of 128 American lives. Wilson protested in three notes, the second of which was so stern that Bryan resigned rather than sign it. He was succeeded by the more zealous Robert Lansing, former counselor of the State Department.

Wilson insisted that, before attacking, submarines must warn liners and provide for the safety of their passengers and crew; his third *Lusitania* note implied the U.S. might resort to war to defend its neutral rights. When the *Arabic,* a British liner, was sunk on August 19, 1915, with two American deaths, Ambassador Bernstorff pledged, "Liners will not be sunk by our submarines without warning and without safety of the lives of noncombatants, provided that the liners do not try to escape or offer resistance."

The president felt his policy had been vindicated by the "*Arabic* Pledge," although relations with Germany remained strained. Contributing to the malaise was a mistake made by Dr. Heinrich F. Albert, a German

agent, who in July, 1915, left a briefcase filled with papers on an elevated train in New York which revealed the extent of Germany's unneutral conduct and its effort to impede American aid to the Allies. Of far greater significance was an announcement by the German government in February, 1916, that its submarines would sink armed enemy merchantmen without warning. Wilson strongly protested but was confronted by a revolt in Congress. Frightened by the prospect of the United States being drawn into a war merely to secure American citizens' rights to travel on armed merchantmen, a number of congressmen supported the Gore-McLemore Resolutions, which would have denied Americans passports to sail on belligerent ships. The resolutions were defeated only when Wilson made a vote against them a test of party loyalty.

In March, 1916, shortly after the defeat of the Gore-McLemore Resolutions, a German submarine torpedoed a French packet, the *Sussex,* with the injury of several Americans. Three weeks later, the president delivered an ultimatum stating if Germany did not abandon its submarine warfare against passenger and merchant vessels the United States would sever diplomatic relations, a step then usually leading to war. The Germans, realizing that they did not have enough submarines for a tight blockade, submitted to the president's demands May 4, 1916, upon the condition that the U.S. force the Allies to respect "the rules of international law." Germany stated it was "prepared to do its utmost to confine the operations of war for the rest of its duration to the fighting forces of the belligerents." Merchantmen henceforth would not be sunk without warning, and provision would be made to aid crew members unless ships resisted or tried to escape. Wilson accepted this *"Sussex* Pledge" but refused to accept the German conditions attached to it.

Wilson's Reelection

The increasing likelihood of American participation in the war provoked a tempestuous domestic political controversy. Many people, especially in the East, felt the administration was not adequately defending U.S. rights and, following the example of former President Roosevelt, demanded a more vigorous policy. On the other hand, thousands, including many Irish-Americans and German-Americans, joined Bryan and the Hearst press in demanding restrictions on American travel as well as sale of munitions to the Allies. The president moved reluctantly to rearm the nation, and in November, 1915, submitted a program to Congress greatly increasing the army's size and substituting a 400,000-man volunteer reserve force for the National Guard, which many considered ineffective.

Wilson's proposals unleashed a spirited debate which shook the nation and the Demo-

cratic party. Many Progressives felt a preparedness program would end reform and was a prelude to war. Led by the House majority leader, Claude Kitchens of North Carolina, they assailed the proposals of the president, who in early 1916 turned to the country for support. Secretary of War Lindley M. Garrison was forced to resign and was replaced by the Cleveland Progressive, Newton D. Baker. At last in June, 1916, by exerting great pressure and modifying his requests, Wilson obtained passage of an army reorganization bill which improved the nation's military strength. Though the National Guard was retained, provisions were made for its modernization and integration into the total defense organization, while the regular army was increased in size to almost 230,000 men. Despite this, unwarranted commitments to neutrality and inertia prevented adequate expansion and equipment of the army. In naval matters less difficulty was encountered, and the Congress provided for an acceleration in the building schedule the president had projected, including the completion of four additional battleships, four cruisers, and lesser craft. To finance the new army and navy, income tax rates were doubled and taxes were levied on munitions manufacturers and estates. The energy of America was beginning to be diverted to defense and foreign affairs, but enough Progressivism remained to see that the added taxes were placed primarily on the well-to-do.

By the time of the Democratic convention, the major schisms in the party had been healed, in part because the president had accepted major changes in plans for army expansion and had averted war in handling the *Sussex* crisis. Though easily renominated, he failed in his attempt to commit the party to ardent support of preparedness. Instead the convention exalted Wilson for keeping the country out of war, a theme that became the major appeal of the Democratic campaign.

The Republicans, meeting in Chicago, passed over Roosevelt, who was an ardent advocate of a stern policy against Germany, choosing instead the former Progressive governor of New York and a current Supreme Court associate justice, Charles Evans Hughes. In the campaign Hughes attempted to retain support of the isolationist Midwest and the pro-German element as well as the pro-Allied East by playing down a discussion of neutrality while firmly indicting Wilson's Mexican policy. Since his criticism of Wilson's domestic reforms proved ineffective, he appeared to many to be a bumbling campaigner. In California he committed a cardinal error when, complying with the wishes of conservative leaders, he did not meet with Governor Hiram Johnson, even when they were in the same hotel. This blunder may have cost him the election since if he had carried California he would have won. Johnson, who was a candidate for the Senate, carried the state by 300,000 votes and Hughes, without his support, lost it by 4,000.

On election night, as the returns came in, it appeared Hughes had won since he swept the larger eastern states as well as Illinois, Indiana, and Michigan. However, Wilson, who received the unstinted support of organized labor and many farmers, carried the South and most of the states west of the Mississippi. Moreover, his victory was made possible by attracting the votes of many who in 1912 had supported the Progressive or Socialist parties. The response to the peace appeal in the West, where many women voted, may also have been significant. In the East, loss of the larger states was due in part to the Irish vote which detested what it considered to be the administration's pro-British policy.

The Coming of War

Wilson was scarcely reinaugurated before the onset of war. Following the *Sussex* Pledge, relations improved with Germany but deteriorated with Britain as it imposed tighter controls on neutral shipping, even demanding full compliance with admiralty rules to obtain coal in British ports. However, Germany knowingly scuttled improvements in American relations in early 1917 by refusing to modify its war aims and to allow United States participation in peace talks. On January 31, 1917, it announced that unrestricted submarine warfare would be resumed on February 1. The German government was gambling that the submarine (or U-boat) would defeat the Allies before America's war entry could make a significant difference.

As a result of resumption of unrestricted submarine warfare, the United States severed diplomatic relations with Germany on February 3, 1917. Initially Wilson refused to arm American merchant ships, but he changed his mind in late February, when the Zimmerman note from the German foreign secretary to his minister in Mexico was intercepted by the British. It proposed Mexico become a German ally in a war against the United States and, after its successful completion, that Mexico would receive the American Southwest. Moreover, Mexico was urged to bring Japan into the conflict against the United States. Though a small group of senators prevented enactment of Wilson's proposed legislation to arm merchant vessels, in early March, 1917, the president ordered them armed and called a special session of Congress.

Before Congress convened on April 2, 1917, German submarines sank several American vessels, which resulted in a rapid rise in popular indignation, in part because many first realized that between August, 1914, and April, 1917, 209 Americans had been killed on the high seas and 28 on U.S. vessels. For the first time, large segments of the South and West came to favor war. Appearing before Congress, Wilson urged a declaration of war, predicating it on the false belief that the Allied powers shared America's war aims and were motivated by a desire to promote the freedom of peoples rather than to obtain economic and territorial gains. He stigmatized the German government as an aggressor and depicted America's motive for entry on a higher plane than a mere desire to protect neutral rights, asserting the American people would fight

> for the things which we have always carried nearest our hearts—for democracy, for the right of those who submit to authority to have a voice in their own Governments, for the rights and liberties of small nations, for a universal dominion of right by such a concert of free peoples as shall bring peace and safety to all nations and make the world itself at last free.

A small but determined group of Progressives, including Senators Robert La Follette and George Norris, opposed the war resolution, yet the measure was passed by a vote of 82 to 6 in the Senate and 373 to 50 in the House. The United States had embarked on a crusade to make the world "safe for democracy."

Internal Mobilization

The mobilization of the nation's economy, a new experience for the unregimented American people, was essential if the United States were to play a vital role in the war. In 1916 a Council of National Defense composed of six cabinet officers had been created to direct the government's defense planning but their recommendations were to be based on the opinions of a seven-man Advisory Commission. After the coming of the war, a condition approaching chaos developed as new and expanded independent agencies arose. In July, 1917, the War Industries Board was created by the Council of National Defense to become the

czar for a temporary planned economy, and its work led to notable achievements in production and distribution. Bernard M. Baruch, assistant to the board's chairman and a highly successful New York broker, became its chairman in March, 1918, and most effectively dictated what materials manufacturers could use, what they would manufacture, and the price of raw materials. The War Finance Corporation, endowed with a $500 million revolving fund, aided in production by underwriting needed industrial expansion. The United States Shipping Board, directed after July, 1817, by Edward N. Hurley, chairman of the Federal Trade Commission, bought, leased, and built large numbers of vessels which kept the lifeline to Europe open. When private management of the railroads proved inadequate, Secretary of the Treasury William Gibbs McAdoo resigned to become director general of the railroads, which were operated on a noncompetitive basis after December 26, 1917.

Bernard M. Baruch

The threat of serious shortages of food and fuel led to the passage of the Lever Act in August, 1917, which authorized the president to assume wide control over the production and distribution of food and fuel as well as fix the price of wheat, coal, coke, and other commodities. The act also prohibited the use of foodstuffs to manufacture "distilled spirits for beverage purposes" and forbade their importation. Herbert Hoover was made food administrator and Harry A. Garfield, president of Williams College, became fuel administrator. Rationing was avoided by inaugurating "meatless," "heatless," and "sweetless" days, making "Hooverizing" a familiar national term. Congress in May, 1918, also passed the Overman Act giving the president ultimate authority to administer the government in the most expeditious fashion to promote the war effort. Until six months after its end, he was empowered to create new agencies and consolidate and change existing ones.

Support for the entire war effort was promoted by the Committee on Public Information established in April, 1917, and headed by the vigorous free-lance journalist, George Creel. Modern advertising techniques were utilized to mold public opinion including the use of thousands of "Four-Minute Men," speakers who addressed every conceivable type of group to obtain public support.

Popular fervor was relied upon to sell government bonds in four Liberty Loan drives conducted during the war and a Victory Loan drive afterwards. Two-thirds of the $33.5 billion cost of the war was added to the national debt, but over $10 billion was raised in additional taxes. American Progressives, some of whom blamed the business community for the nation's entry into the war, scored a victory in having most of the new taxes placed on excess profits, estates, and higher incomes. A maximum rate of 77 percent was levied on the high-est incomes, and excess profit taxes went as high as 60 percent.

One of the more deplorable aspects of the war was the most severe curtailment of civil liberties in the nation's history. Frightened by German efforts at sabotage, which were popularly overdrawn, Congress passed a series of laws, the most notable of which was the Espionage Act of June, 1917, and its amendment, the Sedition Act of May, 1918. Severe penalties were established for aiding the enemy; any expression which brought the government, the Constitution, the military forces, or the flag into disrepute was made illegal, and the postmaster general was authorized to exclude such materials from the mails. Over 1,500 persons were arrested for disloyal utterances, most of whom were socialists and other radicals who opposed the war on ideological grounds. Among those arrested was Eugene V. Debs, who served thirty-two months of a ten-year sentence for ascribing the war to capitalism. In addition, many German-American and Irish-American newspapers were barred from the mails, and the Industrial Workers of the World, a radical, violence-prone labor union which was strongest on the West Coast, was largely destroyed when its officers were removed by federal trials and state officials imprisoned many of its members. As these developments reveal, despite its commitment to liberal ideals, the Wilson administration did not resist popular pressure, and its civil liberties record forms one of the darker aspects of the war years.

As would be expected, the government's wartime infringement on civil rights was challenged in the courts which sustained its action. In 1919 the Supreme Court in the case of *Schenck* v. *United States* upheld by unanimous decision the conviction of a Pennsylvania German who had published pamphlets attacking conscription and the war. Justice Oliver Wendell Holmes, speaking for the Court, formulated the important "clear and present danger doctrine" which acknowledged the freedoms ordinarily guaranteed by the Constitution were not absolute and "the character of every act depends on the circumstance." Schenck's pamphlets were held to promote resistance to the draft, an action which constituted a genuine threat to the nation's existence. In a subsequent case, *Abrams* v. *United States* (1919), the Supreme Court upheld the Sedition Act and the conviction of a pamphleteer who had criticized an American expeditionary force to Siberia. In this case, however, Justice Holmes dissented, seeing no true threat to the nation in the man's activities.

American Military Contributions

The solid American support of the war effort at home enabled the nation to play a vital role in Allied victory. The Germans mistakenly calculated that the United States entry into the war would make no critical difference, and, in an intense campaign, submarine warfare was reinstituted with a vengeance. In 1917 less than half the tonnage sunk was replaced by total Allied construction, a loss which if unchecked could have led to Allied defeat. Steps were taken to rectify the situation when Secretary Josephus Daniels and other United States Navy leaders pressured the British into the use of the convoy system, which helped reduce losses to one-fourth their former amount by late 1917. American pressure also led to the mining of the sea between Scotland and Norway, a project begun in March, 1918, but uncompleted at the time of the armistice. Although the production of American vessels did not progress as well as other aspects of the war program, plans for a number of larger craft were abandoned in favor of smaller vessels useful in antisubmarine operations. As time passed, the American navy played a vital role in destroying the submarine's threat of strangulation and in transporting approximately half the troops sent to Europe as well as most of the supplies and equipment for these men.

German U-boat captured after the U.S. entered the war.

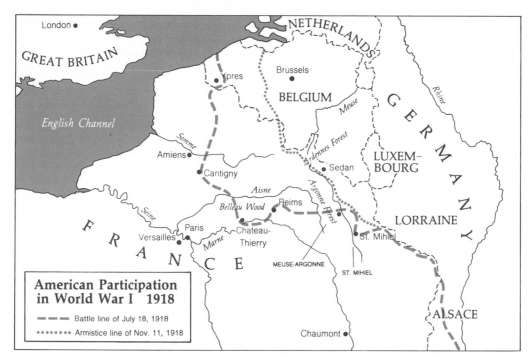

American Participation
in World War I   1918

- - - - Battle line of July 18, 1918
· · · · · · Armistice line of Nov. 11, 1918

The expanded American army had to be constructed from a small nucleus and was of necessity slow in getting large numbers of men to France. However, it played a critical role in Allied victory since the Germans' greatest offensive began in March, 1918, at a time when

American gun crew during the battle of Belleau Wood.

Allied forces were weakened and exhausted. In all, over 1,970,000 men went overseas in the American Expeditionary Forces. Their commander, General John J. Pershing, insisted that they be given distinct sectors of the front and retain their identity. In June, 1918, they contained the stubborn German offensive in the Château-Thierry sector of France and, clearing the Belleau Wood area, pushed the enemy across the Marne River. When the Germans countered with their last major drive, over 85,000 Americans joined the French to contain it, and in July and early August the "Marne bulge" between Rheims and Soissons was hammered flat.

In August, Pershing at last was able to take command of an army of his own and with 550,000 men assumed control of the St. Mihiel region located in the south near the Lorraine border. Destroying the German salient or bulge within three days, he wished to drive across the German border toward Metz but instead

Ferdinand Foch

was ordered by Marshal Ferdinand Foch, the Allied commander in chief, to move to the northwest and dislodge the Germans from the strategic area between Verdun and Sedan. This great Meuse-Argonne campaign lasted until the armistice, which came with Sedan still untaken, but it had cleared vital southern areas essential to victory. Especially significant was the U.S. severance of the Mézierès-Metz rail line which deprived the Germans of any chance to supply their forces. Although American casualties were only one-tenth those of the French or Russians, the presence of American troops came at the right time to insure Allied victory.

Wilson's Fourteen Points

From the beginning of the war, liberals in Europe and the United States had hoped that it

Armistice Day in Paris.

would result in a peace which would remove inequities, permit self-determination of peoples, end the arms race, open trade between countries, and avert future conflicts. In the spring of 1915, the League to Enforce Peace, which espoused these goals, was organized in the United States, and a year later Wilson publicly advocated many of its ideals, incorporating them into the 1916 Democratic platform. In January, 1917, he reiterated them in his "Peace without Victory" speech to the Senate.

Once the United States entered the war, Wilson learned the full extent of the secret treaties by which the Allies had committed themselves to postwar divisions and compensations. By this time, the U.S. entry could not be used as a bargaining lever to obtain renunciation of unjust and unwise commitments, and, to avert possible interference with the war effort, Wilson postponed demands for Allied concessions until after the coming of peace.

Meanwhile in March, 1917, the czarist government of Russia was overthrown, and the following November, the Communist Revolution occurred. After coming to power, the Reds immediately began negotiations which led to a humiliating peace with Germany in March, 1918, and the Communists threatened to publish the secret Allied agreements as proof of the decadent motives behind the war. To counter-act these charges and to direct the Allies on a more constructive path, Wilson in January, 1918, presented his blueprint for peace to Congress in the famous "Fourteen Points."

Wilson's grand design captured the imagination of liberals both at home and abroad, although eight of his fourteen points dealt with quite specific territorial questions. His proposals called for open diplomacy, complete freedom of the seas, removal of trade barriers, disarmament, and a just settlement of colonial claims. Self-determination for all peoples was to be sought and partially implemented by German evacuation of Russia, France, and Belgium and the restoration of Alsace-Lorraine to France; the Italian border was to be rerun on a national basis; the peoples of Austria-Hungary and Turkey were to receive autonomy; Serbia, Rumania, and Montenegro were to be evacuated and reestablished. An independent Poland with access to the sea was to be created. Lastly, and of great importance, "a general association of nations" was to "be formed under specific covenants for the purpose of affording mutual guarantees of political independence and territorial integrity to great and small states alike." This projection which became the basis for the League of Nations occupied a central position in Wilson's thought. By mutual cooperation of nations, he hoped freedom could be assured to all peoples and they could be guaranteed the maximum opportunity for self-realization. At last, he dreamed man could establish a means for continual readjustments between nations whose results would be infinitely preferable to a settlement imposed by a conference of international leaders.

Liberals in many countries hailed Wilson's Fourteen Points as a master plan for a just and lasting peace. Their enunciation of the rights of all peoples to self-determination and their plea for impartiality in the peace settlement were reiterated in the president's "Four Principles"

address to Congress on February 11, 1918, his "Four Ends" speech at Washington's tomb on July 4, and his "Four Ends" address delivered at New York's Metropolitan Opera House on September 27. Therefore it is not surprising that when Germany surrendered it did so on the basis of Wilson's Fourteen Points. Allied leaders did not hesitate to use them when convenient, but when peace negotiations began they revealed the extent of their opposition to them.

Wilson at the Peace Conference

Wilson took the unprecedented step for an American president of heading the delegation to the Paris Peace Conference. Before it opened in January, 1919, he visited London and Rome, where, as in Paris, he was hailed as a deliverer. In January, 1919, he was still associated in the popular mind not only with victory but also with the realization of each country's individual war aims. Yet, at the peace conference, Wilson's ideals soon began to meet rebuffs from the other Allied powers. The open con-

The Big Four. Left to right: Orlando, Lloyd George, Clemenceau, and Wilson in their meeting room in President Wilson's Paris home, May 27, 1919.

ference which he had sought quickly proved to be unworkable, and major decisions were referred to the Council of Ten, composed of the heads of states and the secretaries of state from the United States, Great Britain, France, Italy, and Japan. Even then most power rested with the Big Four—Wilson, Lloyd George of Great Britain, the octogenarian Clemenceau of France, and Orlando of Italy—who replaced the Council of Ten in March.

In four months of deliberation, Wilson was plagued by the nationalistic ambitions of Great Britain, France, Italy, and Japan, many of which conflicted with the Fourteen Points. By reasoning, arguing, and threatening to leave the Conference permanently, he was able to attain a surprising portion of his goals, though there were notable failures. France was obsessed with fear of Germany and wished to create buffer states on its western border. Instead, the west bank of the Rhine was demilitarized and placed under a fifteen-year Allied occupation; Great Britain and the United States also joined France in a mutual defense pact against Germany, and provision was made for permanent limitation of the size of the German army and navy. While Germany was not dismembered, the mines of the rich Saar Basin were given to France as reparation for German destruction of French mines, and the region was placed under international control for fifteen years.

On many questions Wilson was forced to compromise. While he could not obtain absolutely impartial adjustment of colonial claims, he prevented outright annexation of the German colonies by the Allies. They became League of Nations mandates administered by Great Britain, the British dominions, and Japan, a tacit recognition that the old-style colonialism was dead.

Far more effective realization of the self-determination of peoples came in the establishment of the new states of Yugoslavia and Czechoslovakia and the reestablishment of Poland with a corridor to the sea. Wilson was influential in preventing Polish acquisition of non-Polish territory and obtaining access to the sea for Yugoslavia through the Fiume region, an area coveted by Italy. There were notable cases where national will was violated, however, including that of many Austrians, Hungarians, and Bulgarians, whose states were punitively restricted in size. Yet never before had national feelings played such an important role in redrawing the map of Europe.

Wilson's greatest failures were probably unavoidable. Britain refused to consider implementing freedom of the seas, which in peacetime had little significance. The creation of new nations imposed additional trade barriers in the absence of a new attitude toward economic development. Disarmament was impossible in the absence of international machinery to enforce the peace, but Wilson hoped it would come through the League of Nations. In fact, he found many aspects of the proposed peace acceptable only because it contained provisions for the League.

Among the most notable failures of the Fourteen Points was the requirement that Germany assume liability for all the war losses of the Allied governments and peoples. In 1921 a Reparations Commission set the German debt at approximately $33 billion which was to be repaid in kind, i.e., industrial goods, vessels, and livestock; the long-range effects of this policy were devastating since they contributed to inflation and depression in Germany and economic difficulties throughout Europe.

Equally unwise was the action concerning Russia to whom the Fourteen Points had promised evacuation "and an unhampered opportunity to determine her own political development and national policy." Fear of Communism was so great that France wished troops sent in to destroy the Bolsheviks, but, instead, Lloyd George and Wilson tried to arrange a compromise between the Red and White leaders. When this failed, a secret mission was sent to Moscow which returned with a Communist offer to sign an armistice, come to the conference, and repay Russia's debts in return for troop withdrawals and diplomatic recognition. Popular reaction in the West prevented acceptance, while Allied support of an inadequate nature continued for the Anti-Bolsheviks. Recognizing the failure of the policy, Wilson, who had dispatched American troops to Murmansk and Siberia after Russia came to terms with Germany, began withdrawing them in May, 1919. Yet intervention produced serious alienation from the West. Russia, which was unrepresented at the peace conference, was not included in the League of Nations, and Eastern Europe, of necessity, was largely ignored.

U.S. Rejection of the Treaty

The unthinkable occurred when the United States Senate refused to accept the Peace of Versailles, the treaty signed with Germany,* because the Covenant of the League of Nations was incorporated in it. Genuine misgivings existed about the League, particularly Article X, which some feared could lead to the imposition of trade restrictions and boycotts without congressional approval because in it the League members pledged not only to respect but also to preserve "the territorial integrity and political independence" of all League nations. Leadership opposing it came from four Democratic and fourteen Republican senators, including such Progressives as Hiram Johnson, William E. Borah, and Robert M. La Follette, who were dedicated isolationists so completely opposed

*The same action applied to the treaties negotiated with the three states which joined Germany in making war on the Allies, Austro-Hungary, Bulgaria, and Turkey.

to the League that they were known as "irreconcilables." Throughout the country, their position was supported by many German, Irish, and Italian elements who were deeply disappointed by the treaty's provisions.

A substantial majority of Americans seemed to favor both the League and the treaty. A number of Republican senators, including Henry Cabot Lodge, chairman of the Foreign Relations Committee, held they would approve it but only if "strong reservations" were added; Lodge's purpose seemed to be to defeat the treaty. The proposed changes, however, would not have substantially altered the League, and the Allies were willing to accept them without an additional conference; the former British foreign secretary, Sir Edward Grey, even came to Washington to plead for their acceptance.

Lodge's opposition to the League had much to do with the treaty's rejection. He and Wilson, both of whom considered themselves "the scholar in politics," were personal enemies, and he was offended by Wilson's failure to use the Senate in formulating his peace policy and in negotiating the treaty. Lodge had serious doubts about the League, but he was also under pressure to produce a solution that would keep his party together even though it was seriously split on the question of League membership. He insisted on reading the treaty word for word before his committee and holding weeks of public hearings, actions which gave the opposition time to crystallize. After the Senate in September, 1919, rejected forty-five amendments and four reservations proposed by the Lodge Committee, the real battle came on acceptance of fourteen committee-proposed reservations.

However, the principal actor in the whole drama involving the League membership was Wilson, not Lodge. The president's miscalculations and mistakes began in the elections of 1918 when he interjected foreign affairs into

Henry Cabot Lodge

politics. Instead of supporting individual candidates, he gave a blanket endorsement to Democrats and stated the return of a Republican majority would be interpreted abroad as a repudiation of his leadership. The war-weary voters, who were disgusted with prohibition and inflation, did not adequately respond to the president's appeal, and the Republicans obtained control of both houses. Unwittingly, the president's action turned the election into a vote which seemed to repudiate his foreign policy.

Instead of heeding this caution, Wilson pressed ahead as if nothing had happened. In choosing the five-man peace commission to go to Paris, he ignored the Congress, realizing Lodge would be an essential appointee from the Senate. Only one Republican, Henry White, a knowledgeable diplomat but a man largely removed from political life, was in-

cluded. Worse still, the president in indiscreet remarks taunted the Congress. The situation was intensified when, in the midst of the peace conference, Wilson returned home for a brief working visit during which he was questioned pointedly by Republican congressional critics. On March 2, 1919, Lodge introduced a "Round Robin," signed by thirty-seven Republican senators and two senators-elect, which rejected the League in its existing form and opposed further consideration of it until after the peace settlement. Two days later, the measure was read in the Senate, and Wilson, speaking at New York's Metropolitan Opera House, declared that the League would be so entwined with the peace treaty that the two could not be separated. He apparently could not believe that Congress would refuse the entire treaty, although the votes of thirty-nine senators were more than enough to do so. In Paris, the president obtained modifications in the League to meet some congressional criticism, including recognition of the Monroe Doctrine, exclusion of internal affairs from its purview, and provision for withdrawal. Where the Lodge reservations were concerned, however, he was absolutely unyielding.

Ironically, two-thirds of the Senate probably wanted League membership, a reflection of public opinion since two-thirds of the state legislatures and governors had publicly endorsed American affiliation. To muster a national campaign to pressure the Senate, the president delivered thirty-seven addresses in September, 1919, which met with increasing public approval. After speaking in Pueblo, Colorado, on September 25, he was near collapse and was forced to return to Washington. On October 2 he suffered a stroke which incapacitated him for weeks and left his left side partially paralyzed. In the interim the Senate approved fourteen reservations to the Treaty of Versailles, twelve of which originated with Lodge and did not fundamentally change the

President Wilson delivering his League of Nations address in Boston.

League; most required congressional approval for U.S. compliance with specific League demands. When Wilson refused to accept the reservations, the Senate, which was composed of forty-nine Republicans and forty-seven Democrats, rejected the treaty with reservations thirty-nine to fifty-five with Wilson Democrats and "irreconcilables" voting against it; the treaty was then rejected without reservations fifty-three to thirty-eight. Public pressure would not let the issue die, and in February, 1920, the Senate reconsidered its action. Wilson, whose health had improved, applied great pressure to defeat the treaty with reservations, whose number had been increased to fifteen by Democratic insertion of one supporting freedom for Ireland. The president was not able to prevent twenty-one Democrats joining twenty-eight Republicans in voting for the treaty with reservations, but their forty-nine votes were less than the two-thirds needed for victory. Twenty-three Democrats, following Wilson's counsel, joined with 12 Republican "irreconcilables" to kill the treaty permanently. To formally end hostilities, in May, 1920, Congress repealed the war resolutions and accepted all benefits accruing under the Versailles Treaty.

Although he was dedicated to the League, Wilson's stubbornness was instrumental in keeping the United States out of it. His physical weariness and illness undoubtedly contributed to loss of political finesse and miscalculation as to the results of his action. As early as January, 1920, however, he foresaw defeat in the Senate but felt ultimate victory would come by making the 1920 elections a "great and solemn referendum" on the League. In attempting to do this, he again misjudged the political temper of the times.

The Election of 1920

In spite of the failure to obtain American membership in the League of Nations, the Wilson administration in its last years attained substantial Progressive political achievements at home. Included among them were the Revenue Act of 1919 which increased taxation on larger incomes and corporations; the Transportation Act of 1920 (the Esch-Cummins Act) which, in addition to returning the railroads to private management, gave the Interstate Commerce Commission absolute control over railway rates and sale of railway securities; and the General Leasing Act which withdrew vast oil reserves from public exploitation while permitting careful leasing of certain mineral and oil deposits. The Water Power Act established the Federal Power Commission to license and operate dams and power plants on public domain waterways. Though largely ineffective at first, it marked the beginning of federal control of the electric power industry. In 1919 the requisite number of states approved the Eighteenth Amendment establishing prohibition, and Congress submitted the Nineteenth Amendment to the states in June, 1919, which, upon its approval in August, 1920, removed discrimination against women voting.

Although liberal policies were pursued, the last years of the Wilson administration were also characterized by frustration. Demobilization occurred rapidly and with little planning, government contracts were abruptly canceled, and three million people were unemployed during early 1919. Suffering was not acute, however, and by the summer of 1919 the crisis was over. Militant inflation, which had resulted in almost a 200 percent rise in the price of manufactured goods since 1913, continued unabated. This condition sparked an unprecedented wave of successful strikes which enabled labor to gain additional real wages and shorter hours. However, the greatest strike of all, that of the A.F. of L. against U.S. Steel in September, 1919, was broken in early 1920 by the use of both state and federal troops to prevent picketing and by the company's successful propaganda campaign which cost the workers public goodwill.

While these events were occurring, a major "Red Scare" and wave of repression engulfed the nation. Communist success in Russia, reestablishment of the Internationale which sought to spread the revolution, and acts of violence in the United States contributed to the reaction. Many incorrectly assumed strikes were Communist inspired, and fear increased as acts of violence plagued the nation. A plot to assassinate a number of public officials, including cabinet members and governors, was revealed in April, 1919, and a bomb was sent to the home of Georgia Senator Thomas W. Hardwick, whose maid was permanently injured in the explosion. Sixteen other bombs were discovered in the New York post office addressed to government and business leaders. Attorney General A. Mitchell Palmer was the most prominent among a number of persons in several cities whose homes were bombed, and, as late as September, 1920, an explosion in front of J.P. Morgan and Co. in New York took thirty-eight lives.

Popular hysteria overreacted against the dangers which existed. A majority of the states passed laws forbidding seditious expressions, and a national campaign to suppress radicalism infringed on the civil rights of many Americans. Although Attorney General Palmer failed to obtain enactment of a law to punish the incitement of sedition, using the full forces of the F.B.I. he had 4,000 Americans, most of whom were non-Communists, arrested and detained, while 556 aliens alleged to be Communists were deported. The remaining members of the International Workers of the World were harrassed, and five New York legislators were denied their seats simply because they were socialists. Clearly a wave of reaction was nationally present, but it largely subsided before the end of Wilson's term as the good sense of the American people prevailed.

Treatment of blacks furnished one of the most reprehensible postwar conditions which was not alleviated. In 1919 alone some twenty-five race riots occurred, including a frightful encounter in Chicago which left thirty-eight dead and hundreds injured. Many of these conflicts took place in northern cities where a stream of black migrants from the South had come to fill the more menial jobs as European immigration declined during the war years. Blacks furnished low-wage competition for white workers, and their different manners and life style sustained by a ghetto existence made them the objects of contempt and scorn. Although white liberals were alarmed, little progress was made by the National Association for the Advancement of Colored People and other groups in efforts to obtain relief. Tragically, a number of disillusioned blacks came to support Marcus W. Garvey's Universal Negro Improvement Association which fraudulently solicited funds to reestablish a black empire in Africa.

In the midst of these confused conditions, the election of 1920 occurred. Wilson hoped to be drafted for a third term, but Democratic leaders wisely judged his health precluded such action. The convention struggled through forty-four ballots during most of which the principal contenders were former Treasury Secretary William G. McAdoo, who was handicapped by being Wilson's son-in-law, and the Red-baiting Attorney General Palmer. After the thirty-ninth ballot, the McAdoo forces began to shift to Governor James Cox of Ohio, the most attractive of the "favorite sons" and a man acceptable to the big-city bosses. After his selection, he chose Assistant Secretary of the Navy Franklin D. Roosevelt as his running mate. The Democratic platform urged League membership but stipulated opposition would not be offered to noncrippling reservations. It also advocated independence for the Philippines, statehood for Puerto Rico, lower taxation, and economy in government.

Earlier the Republicans had experienced a similar deadlock through four ballots at their Chicago convention. General Leonard Wood, a protégé of Theodore Roosevelt who had attracted much of his following, and former Illinois Governor Frank O. Lowden stymied each other. Fearing a display of party disunity and the nomination of an independent-minded candidate, a potent group of party leaders, principally U.S. senators, met for hours in Room 404 of the Blackstone Hotel. They chose Ohio's Warren G. Harding, a handsome, small-town newspaper publisher who was completing his first term in the Senate, as their nominee. Harding perfectly fitted their needs: he had voted for the League with the Lodge reservations, was a strict party man, was nonintellectual and nonideological, and would take orders. His running mate was Governor Calvin Coolidge of Massachusetts, who had obtained national fame by breaking the Boston police strikes of 1919. The platform denounced Wilson's League of Nations but equivocated by promising to work "for agreement among the nations to preserve the peace of the world" without compromising national independence. It also advocated membership in the World Court, a higher tariff, reduced taxes, and limitations on immigration.

Wilson's efforts to make the election a "solemn referendum" on the League failed. Many eastern Republicans voted for Harding in the belief that his election was the way to obtain

Warren G. Harding

membership, and for a large number of voters the League was at best a secondary consideration. Those disgusted with high taxes, suppression of civil liberties, the punitive nature of the peace treaty with Germany, Anglo-American cooperation, and government use of force in strike breaking found Harding's proposal of a return to "normalcy" and promotion of "Americanism" most appealing. Farmers whose incomes were cut by depression prices could not be expected to vote for the status quo, nor could many German-Americans, Irish-Americans, blacks, or victims of Attorney General Palmer's repression. As a result, the combination of dissidents with normal Republican voters gave Harding a smashing victory, enabling him to carry every state outside the South as well as Oklahoma and Tennessee.

In defeat, Wilson's idealistic foreign policy came to have an almost religious appeal to many Americans, and its author, in his few years of remaining life, became more a prophet than ever. From his home on "S" Street in Washington, he continued to agitate for full United States participation in international affairs. Many of the world's renowned made pilgrimages to see him, and as death approached in early 1924 hundreds knelt in the street before his home. In defeat, the Wilson concept of internationalism and liberalism in foreign affairs became a potent part of the American heritage.

Selected Bibliography

The most adequate treatment is found in Arthur S. Link, *Wilson* (5 vols. to date, 1947–1965), whose volumes are cited in the previous chapter. An overview of Wilson's policies is found in N. Gordan Levin, Jr., *Woodrow Wilson and World Politics: America's Response to War and Revolution* * (1970); Sidney Bell, *Righteous Conquest: Woodrow Wilson and the Evolution of the New Diplomacy* (1972); and Link's *Wilson the Diplomatist: A Look at His Major Foreign Policies* * (1965).

Wilson's relations with Japan are well presented in Roy W. Curry, *Woodrow Wilson and Far Eastern Policy, 1913–1921* (1968). James F. Rippy, *The United States and Mexico* (rev. ed., 1931), recounts the struggle between the two countries. R. E. Quirk, *An Affair of Honor: Woodrow Wilson and the Occupation of Veracruz* * (1967), provides additional insight while Robert F. Smith, *The United States and Revolutionary Nationalism in Mexico, 1916–1932* (1972), deals with the reactions of private U.S. groups as well as the government. Larry D. Hill, *Emissaries to a Revolution, Woodrow Wilson's Executive Agents in Mexico* (1973), reveals one method the U.S. used to aid in overthrowing the Huerta regime.

Works critical of Wilson's neutralist policies in relation to the European war include John M. Blum, *Woodrow Wilson and the Politics of Morality* * (1962); Walter Millis, *The Road to War, America, 1914–1918* (repr. of 1935 ed., 1970); and Charles C. Tansill, *America Goes to War* (1963). More favorable are the well researched Ernest R. May, *The World War and American Isolation, 1914–1917* * (1966); Daniel M. Smith, *The Great Departure: The United States and World War I, 1914–1920* * (1965); and the older Charles Seymour, *American Neutrality, 1914–1917: Essays on the Causes of American Intervention in the World War* (repr. of 1953 ed., 1967). Specific problems are analyzed in Barbara W. Tuchman, *The Zimmermann Telegram* (1966), and submarine warfare in Samuel R. Spencer, Jr., *Decision for War, 1917* * (2d ed., 1968). The important role of the U.S. ambassador to Great Britain is detailed in Ross Gregory, *Walter Hines Page, Ambassador to the Court of St. James's* (1970).

Internal developments during the war are presented in Frederic L. Paxson, *American Democracy and the World War* (3 vols., 1936–1948), and Preston W. Slosson, *The Great Crusade and After, 1914–1928* * (1971). Margaret L. Coit, *Mr. Baruch* (1957), is an interesting study of a key domestic figure. Horace G. Peterson and Gilbert C. Fite, *Opponents of War, 1917–1918* * (1968), and Harry N. Scheiber, *The Wilson Administration and Civil Liberties, 1917–1921* (1960), deal with the restrictions on civil rights.

The military and naval aspects of the war are well portrayed in Edward M. Coffman, *The War to End All Wars: The American Military Experience in*

---

*Available in paperback.

World War I (1968); Paxson's previously cited *American Democracy and the World War;* briefly in Harvey A. DeWeerd, *President Wilson Fights His War; World War I and the American Intervention* (1968); and in Donald W. Mitchell, *History of the Modern American Navy from 1883 through Pearl Harbor* (1946).

Wilson and the peace settlement may be studied in Thomas A. Bailey, *Woodrow Wilson and the Lost Peace** (1963); Seth P. Tillman, *Anglo-American Relations at the Paris Peace Conference of 1919* (1961); and Robert Lansing, *The Peace Negotiations: A Personal Narrative* (repr. of 1921 ed., 1969). The mood of America and Wilson's mistakes leading to U.S. rejection of the Versailles settlement are considered in Thomas A. Bailey, *Woodrow Wilson and the Great Betrayal** (1963); Seward W. Livermore, *Woodrow Wilson and the War Congress** (1968); and Selig Adler, *The Isolationist Impulse, Its Twentieth Century Reaction** (1957). The actions and motives of Wilson's major opponents are presented in John A. Garraty, *Henry Cabot Lodge: A Biography* (1953).

Robert K. Murray, *Red Scare: A Study in National Hysteria, 1919–1920** (1964), and Arthur I. Waskow, *From Race Riot to Sit-In, 1919 and the 1960's* (1966), present aspects of postwar reaction. Wesley M. Bagby, *The Road to Normalcy: The Presidential Campaign and Election of 1920** (1962), is a useful study. For works on prohibition, Harding, and related topics see chapter 20.

The Twenties

1920	Volstead Act became operative
	Radio station KDKA established
1921–22	Washington Naval Conference
1923	Death of President Harding
	Agricultural Credits Act
1924	National Origins Act
1925	Scopes trial
1927	Lindbergh's transatlantic flight
	Geneva Naval Disarmament Conference
1928	Pact of Paris
1929	Hemingway's *A Farewell to Arms*
	Faulkner's *The Sound and the Fury*
	Agricultural Marketing Act
	Panic on Wall Street
1930	Clark Memorandum issued
	Hawley-Smoot Tariff
1932	Reconstruction Finance Corporation established
	Glass-Steagall Act
	Norris-La Guardia Act
	Veterans march on Washington
	Election of Franklin D. Roosevelt
1933	Twenty-first Amendment

20

The Twenties

Long-Range Developments

For Economics and Corporate Enterprise

Wilson Dam and the federal facilities on the Tennessee River were fully developed by the government after 1933.

Union labor's defeats in the 1920s combined with the plight of many workers to produce an ideal situation for union expansion in the 1930s.

The role of the automobile, the movies, and the radio in America has continued to grow, lessening the restraints of time, place, and ignorance.

For the Westward Movement, Nationalism, and Expansion

Compromise agreements with Mexico and the Clark Memorandum prepared the way for Franklin D. Roosevelt's Good Neighbor Policy.

Failure of the United States to cancel the Allied debts contributed to European economic and political instability from which depression and later war arose.

For Civil Liberties, Freedom, and Reform

The attitudes which led to support of the Ku Klux Klan and nativism also increased the restrictions imposed on blacks in many regions until reversed by countertrends during World War II.

The increased freedom and opportunities for women available in the 1920s stimulated additional desires.

President Herbert Hoover's unprecedented efforts to combat the depression laid the foundation for even greater government innovations under the New Deal.

A Decade of
Progress and Regression

The liberal political, economic, and social sentiment which characterized much of twentieth-century America did not die with World War I or the retirement of Woodrow Wilson from the presidency. A large portion of the Congress continued to be motivated by Progressive ideals as did many state governments, especially in rural areas where the farmer's dismal economic condition was a powerful force throughout the 1920s. The average man continued to revise his attitude toward the legitimate role of government. Abetting him was a significant group of social workers who portrayed the distress of American citizens and the opportunities afforded by public and private cooperative action.

No segment of opinion was unaffected by the nation's new attitudes, but much controversy developed over their implementation. Powerful reactionary currents existed, at times ironically in the same individuals and groups who were liberals on some questions. Moreover, liberal forces were severely disrupted and not infrequently made impotent by divisions on such questions as prohibition and religion. In addition, the nation's presidents did not furnish the leadership necessary to attain reforms of the first magnitude. Harding, Coolidge, and Hoover each shared an exaggerated respect for congressional initiative in the legislative process, and Harding and Coolidge especially were naïve regarding the economy's operation and its ability to regulate itself.

The Harding Scandals

Much of the reactionary image of the twenties stemmed from the popular disgust with President Warren G. Harding which emerged after his death from a heart attack in August, 1923,

in San Francisco. The convivial Harding brought some outstanding men into his cabinet including Charles Evans Hughes as secretary of state, the Pittsburgh aluminum scion Andrew W. Mellon as secretary of the treasury, and the respected Iowa editor Henry C. Wallace as secretary of agriculture. But he also surrounded himself with cronies, primarily from Ohio, who did not merit the trust placed in them. They were excellent as bourbon-drinking, poker-playing buddies but lacked the morals and ethics necessary for their positions. They included Attorney General Harry M. Daugherty, whose friend, Jesse Smith, procured "protection" from the Justice Department for tax and prohibition evaders and obtained return of German property to its former owners by the Alien Property Custodian. When he committed suicide in Daugherty's apartment, the scandal broke. Veterans' Bureau Chief Charles R. Forbes filched at least a quarter of a million dollars before Harding allowed him to resign and escape to Europe early in 1923. After his return, he was tried and received a two-year sentence in 1925. Secretary of the Interior Albert B. Fall, after having the president transfer naval oil reserve lands to his department, leased Teapot Dome in Wyoming to Harry F. Sinclair's company, for which he received over $300,000 in bonds and cash from Sinclair, and Elks Hill in California to Edward L. Doheny in return for a $100,000 "loan." The government was not able to obtain court reversal of the leases until 1927. Eventually Sinclair and Fall received sentences for their offenses, and Fall became the first cabinet officer to go to prison. Daugherty was tried but not convicted after he refused to testify on the grounds that he could not betray his relationship with former President Harding.

Harding's lack of judgment and ethical sense merited the contempt heaped upon him but, on occasion, he exhibited courage and leadership. Amazingly, he pardoned the Socialist party leader, Eugene V. Debs, who had served several years in federal prison for his opposition to World War I. The president used his influence with industry leaders to obtain an eight-hour day for steel workers in 1922, the same year he vetoed a veteran's bonus bill, which had become a pet project of the American Legion. Under Secretary Hughes' leadership, as will be shown later, significant strides were made in ending the international naval race and restoring stability among the major powers.

Despite these limited achievements, Harding's administration was characterized by a lack of leadership and unfriendliness toward the disunited reform forces in Congress and the nation. Its major weakness was not corruption but unawareness and unconcern with major national problems.

Coolidge Becomes President

When Calvin Coolidge assumed the presidency, he restored the average American's faith in his government, an achievement of great significance for the nation. Appropriately, he was at his father's Vermont home when news arrived of Harding's death, and the oath of office was administered by his father, who was a justice of the peace, by lamplight, since his home had not yet obtained electricity. The new president commanded the respect of the people, in part because he chose two eminent, unimpeachable attorneys, one of whom was the future Supreme Court Justice Owen J. Roberts, to prosecute those charged with defrauding the government. When evidence led to the removal of Attorney General Daugherty, he was replaced by a former Columbia University law dean, Harlan Fiske Stone. In 1925 Coolidge appointed him to the Supreme Court, where he became famous for his liberal dissents on questions involving social issues.

While Coolidge's personal integrity was unquestioned, he accepted the American business philosophy with as much enthusiasm as Harding. By the 1920s the grosser forms of competition had ended, although a few large companies in the various fields often battled vigorously for their share of the enterprise. Concerned with profits and growth, business leaders sought to bring order and regularity to all aspects of company operation, often at the expense of the social effects of company policy. When Coolidge declared, "the Business of America is business," he reflected an admiration and awe which enabled "honest" business leaders to exert enormous control over every aspect of government and society. The president's laconic nature and his terse, matter-of-fact expression seemed perfectly attuned to the age of the machine, where the engineer and the efficiency expert were more important than old-time politicians. Only time would reveal that what many admired were techniques

Calvin Coolidge and his family.

whose value depended entirely on the purpose for which they were used.

Coolidge's Reelection

Coolidge's widespread popularity easily led to his renomination in 1924, although a potentially strong opponent emerged as early as 1922 when Henry Ford's advertising department began to promote Ford for the presidency. Ford's highly effective production and sales methods had earned him a national following, even though he was in many ways an ignorant man notorious for his anti-Semitic views. His withdrawal from the campaign may have come as the result of an attempt to gain control of government facilities in the Tennessee Valley.

During the war the federal government had built two large nitrate plants on the Tennessee River in north Alabama and almost completed Wilson Dam at Muscle Shoals. Ford proposed to buy the plants and lease the dam at ridiculously low prices, and, after Coolidge announced his support of private ownership, Ford withdrew his candidacy, declaring his support of the president. Largely due to the efforts of Nebraska's Senator George W. Norris, Ford's purchase plans were defeated. In 1928 and 1931 Norris and a progressive coalition obtained congressional acts for government operation and expansion of the Tennessee Valley facilities, but they were vetoed by Presidents Coolidge and Hoover.

In the 1924 campaign the Democrats offered little opposition to Coolidge since the party was torn apart by the internal contest between urban, wet, anti-Klan, anti-League partisans and their opponents. Former Treasury Secretary William G. McAdoo, who was supported by many former Bryan men, had been an early pre-convention leader, but his service as Edward L. Doheny's attorney cost him much Progressive backing. Nevertheless, he came to the convention with strong southern and western support. New York's Governor Alfred E. Smith, who had the backing of the party organization in the East and Midwest, rose to challenge him, although his Roman Catholic faith cost him much support. The Klan also became a major issue, but by a vote of 543-3/20 to 542-3/20 the convention refused to condemn it in the party platform. For an unbelievable 103 ballots the party displayed and deepened its division before the convention nominated John W. Davis, a conservative New York lawyer, for president, and William Jennings Bryan's brother, Charles, for vice-president.

The Democrats' failure to present an effective alternative to Coolidge led a number of former 1912 Progressives, farm leaders, socialists, and others to nominate the sixty-nine-year-old Senator Robert La Follette for president and Montana's Democratic Senator Burton K. Wheeler for vice-president. The name "Progressive Party" was again revived, and a platform adopted demanding railroad nationalization, public ownership of utilities, the end of the use of injunctions in labor disputes, and direct nomination and election of the president. La Follette campaigned vigorously, and the Republicans concentrated their attention on him, although Coolidge largely sat out the campaign. Despite declining A.F. of L. support and an increase in farm prices, La Follette obtained 4,822,856 popular votes and carried Wisconsin. Coolidge was overwhelmingly reelected, receiving 15,725,016 votes to Davis' 8,385,586. Democratic party dissension and failure to choose a strong leader cost it an opportunity to truly challenge the administration.

Isolationism Prevails

As in domestic affairs, the foreign policy of the 1920s was characterized by a common approach throughout the three administrations. In each there was concern with foreign affairs but, due to domestic politics, acceptance of a largely isolationist role. Peace societies flourished, and devout, sincere men such as Senator William E. Borah earnestly promoted the peace cause and American disarmament and disentanglement.

In 1921 and 1922 opponents of a new naval race with Great Britain and Japan led the Senate in approving a resolution urging the nation to call a naval disarmament conference. Since this proposal coincided with British desires, the conference was held with the participation of nine powers—Britain, Japan, China, France, Italy, Belgium, the Netherlands, Portugal, and the United States. Significant agreements were reached, including a Five Power Naval Treaty in which, for the first time, major powers agreed to disarmament. Hughes' suggestion that the United States scrap ships totaling 845,000 tons and that Great Britain abandon 583,000 tons and Japan 480,000 tons was accepted. In addition, his plans for a ten-year moratorium on construction of capital ships (those over 10,000 tons displacement or having larger than 8-inch caliber guns) and for the establishment of a fixed ratio among the powers were adopted. Great Britain and the United States were restricted to 525,000 tons, Japan to 315,000, and France and Italy to 175,000 each. Provision was made to replace vessels that were twenty or more years old, but replacement craft were limited to 35,000 tons and 16-inch guns as maximums.

By treaty all nine powers agreed to maintain the Open Door in China and to respect the independence and sovereignty of that state. Since 1902 Japan and Great Britain had been allied, a factor which forced the United States to predicate its naval policy upon a possible conflict with the two countries. Therefore the United States zealously promoted a Four Power Treaty by which the United States, Great Britain, Japan, and France agreed to mutual respect of their Far Eastern possessions and to confer if disputes arose or a nontreaty power menaced the peace. In a Five Power Pact which was part of the naval limitations treaty, the major powers agreed to construct no new facilities in the Pacific, a great boon to Japanese control. Had the United States chosen to expand its facilities, a loophole was available since Hawaii was exempted from the general limitations restriction. In other agreements, Japan promised to restore the Shantung peninsula to China and evacuate the areas of Siberia occupied by it; the Lansing-Ishii agreement of 1917, by which the United States recognized Japan had special interests in China, was abrogated, and Japan confirmed U.S. cable rights on the island of Yap.

The Washington Naval Conference ended a dangerous naval race for a decade and obtained paper parity with the British for the United States Navy. However, the American isolationist spirit destroyed many of its potential benefits. No provisions were written into the agreements to make sure they were enforced, as the continued foreign control in China revealed. Congress refused to appropriate funds to build a navy comparable to the British, and, even with a smaller number of ships, the Japanese were able to dominate the Pacific. Improved relations with Japan were dissipated in 1924 when all Japanese were excluded from immigration to the United States. By this one unwise action, Congress destroyed much of the goodwill the State Department had gained over a three-year period.

Rivalry in the construction of battleships and aircraft carriers was ended by the Washington Naval Conference, but as early as 1924 Great Britain began construction of five heavy cruisers; the Japanese promptly followed suit, and Congress authorized the building of eight such craft. By 1927 a new naval race was under way, and President Coolidge called a Geneva conference to deal with it. The sessions stalled when France and Italy refused to attend and the U.S. and Britain could not agree on a ratio for light cruisers. Public opinion in the English-speaking countries continued to press for action, and, after the coming to power in 1929 of the new Labour government in Britain, the 1930 London conference was held. A ratio of 10:10:6 for heavy cruisers and 10:10:7 for light cruisers for the United States, Great Britain, and Japan was agreed upon, and closely related tonnage figures were established for destroyers and other craft. France, worried by fascist control in Italy, refused to become a party to the treaty without an Anglo-American agreement to protect its security, and isolationist America would not consider this action. The British insisted on an escalator clause, permitting construction if national security were threatened, an exception which destroyed much of the effectiveness of the treaty. However, the United States chose to disregard rearmament taking place elsewhere and allowed the American navy to decline in strength.

Other indexes of withdrawal from world affairs were also present. Every president from Wilson to Franklin Roosevelt advocated membership in the World Court, an international tribunal to which disputes were referred and on which a number of American jurists served. Congress steadfastly refused to take this action for fear of compromising American independence, but the United States could not abandon all responsibilities of a major power. Therefore, it sent unofficial observers to the League of Nations and increasingly participated in the activities of many of its agencies.

Nonintervention policies were partially responsible for one solid gain in foreign affairs, improved relations with Latin America. Secretary of State Hughes, aided by Sumner Welles who served as chief of the State Department's Latin American Affairs Division, sought to undo the intervention of the previous two

decades. American forces were withdrawn from the Dominican Republic and Nicaragua. Though General Alvaro Obregón, who came to power in Mexico in 1920, threatened all American investments, Hughes extended recognition and obtained return of payment for U.S. holdings acquired before 1917. In 1924 Plutarcho Elias Calles and his radical followers came to power, and conditions worsened. Coolidge, instead of pursuing a sword-rattling policy, sent a partner of Morgan and Company, Dwight Morrow, as ambassador in 1927, and a compromise settlement was reached regarding oil lands.

Diplomatic expression was given to the revised government policy by the Clark Memorandum framed and released by the State Department in 1930. In it, the Roosevelt Corollary to the Monroe Doctrine was repudiated, and the right to keep Eastern hemispheric nations from intervening in the West was held to carry no justification for U.S. intervention. Though never officially proclaimed by the president, the Clark Memorandum prepared the way for Franklin Roosevelt's "Good Neighbor Policy."

The resolution of the war debts unfortunately did not have a satisfactory end. The U.S. lent the Allied governments $7 billion during the war and $3.25 billion soon thereafter, loans which the Europeans strongly contended should be canceled since most of the money had been spent for war supplies in the United States. They also held that there was a direct correlation between German repayment of its reparations bill, at first levied at $33 billion, and loan repayment by the Allies. The United States refused to concede either point, but when the German economy faltered the United States aided in preventing its collapse. Charles G. Dawes and Owen D. Young, the president of General Electric, served on an international committee in 1924 which lowered the annual reparations payments due from Germany and arranged for a $200 million loan from American bankers. In 1929 Young headed another committee which reduced the German debt to $8.032 billion payable over a fifty-eight year period at 5.5 percent interest. This sum was roughly equivalent to the Allied war debt owed the United States, and the plan provided that should the Allied debt be scaled down proportionate reductions would be made in Germany's obligations. In the final analysis, the Allied governments repaid the United States little more than they received from Germany, and it would have been much wiser for the U.S. to have canceled the war debt.

Coolidge's isolationist attitude was shared by many of the "peace forces" in the United States whose pressure, combined with French desires to quiet American fears of rearmament led to the Kellogg-Briand Pact in 1928. When the French foreign minister, Aristide Briand, proposed the two countries outlaw war in their relations with each other, Secretary of State Frank B. Kellogg, Hughes' successor, suggested other powers join in the agreement. Kellogg felt this procedure would remove intimations of a Franco-American alliance. In August, 1928, every major nation except Russia signed the Pact of Paris renouncing war "as an instrument of national policy in their relations with each other." Unfortunately, no enforcement machinery was provided nor was defensive war repudiated.

Resurgent Nativism and Anti-Intellectualism

Not all American opinion of the 1920s was charitable or kind. A virulent streak of nationalism spread throughout the country, promoted by disillusionment with the war's results and Europe's contempt for America's

new status. Expressions of nationalism varied from harmless chest thumping to membership in the Ku Klux Klan.

The modern Klan arose in 1915, when a Georgia teacher and lay minister, William J. Simmons, saw the opportunity to recruit native, white, American Protestants in an organization that would protect the old values from allegedly conspiratorial elements. A few thousand members were recruited by 1920, after which the group experienced phenomenal growth due to the efforts of two organizational experts. In the deep South the Klan attracted members who feared the war's effect on black subserviency, but elsewhere anti-Catholicism was apparently the organization's greatest appeal. In the Midwest, Indiana became the most completely Klan-dominated state in the nation until the moral depravity of its officials led to public revulsion. Ohio, Texas, Oklahoma, and Arkansas had strong Klan influences in their government as, surprisingly enough, did

A Ku Klux Klan initiation.

Oregon and California, two of the nation's most progressive states.

The Klan's appeal is difficult to understand. Its recruits were often sincere, decent members of the middle class, especially in the smaller towns and cities, who were seeking to prevent changes in their life styles. The Klan identified villains, provided action, and afforded drama and ritual for the lonely and bored. It was closely allied with various Protestant churches which it supported, at times with robed attendance at services. A personal zeal was evoked when local klaverns, as the chapters were called, conducted raids on bawdy houses and bootlegging facilities. By 1925 the Klan probably had five million members, but in the next few years the attrition was great as Klansmen became frightened by the violence and injustice perpetrated by the order. Though there were periodic revivals in local areas, the Klan's menace nationally had passed.

The nativist spirit which supported the Klan was partially responsible for the severe restriction placed on immigration, although the labor unions' desire to end the competition of cheap labor was also a factor. The movement for restriction encountered little of the moral and ethical opposition one would expect. Many intellectuals were influenced by the social workers' contention that exclusion of Eastern and Southern Europeans was necessary to solve urban problems. Therefore, in 1921 Congress limited immigration from outside the Western Hemisphere to 3 percent of each nation's people in the United States in 1910, and, though President Wilson vetoed the law, it was repassed and signed by Harding.

Under the new law, from July, 1921, to June, 1922, immigration declined to 309,556, a reduction of over 60 percent in one year. Restrictionists were not satisfied, however, and in 1924 obtained enactment of the National Origins Act. It excluded Orientals and limited

non-Western hemispheric immigration to 2 percent of the foreign-born population from each country in the United States in 1890, when there were fewer Eastern and Southern Europeans present than in 1910. More significantly, the act provided that in 1927 immigration would be restricted to an annual rate of 150,000 and quotas would be established for each country based on its total contribution to the peopling of the nation. This specification was impossible to determine with accuracy, and, due to the difficulty of the calculations, the new quotas were not imposed until 1929. Of course, they were highly favorable to the British and Germans and unfavorable to the Italians, Russians, and others whose migration had come mainly in the previous fifty years. The groups discriminated against indicted the law as a manifestation of racism and prejudice.

The anti-evolution crusade was another effort to save the nation from pollution. Its leaders were religious conservatives called Fundamentalists, a name stemming from belief in certain "fundamentals" including the acceptance of the Bible as literal truth. Many of them were frightened by concepts they did not understand, particularly the teaching of Darwinian evolution which they feared would destroy the church and society. As early as 1921, William Jennings Bryan warned that God must not be taken out of the schools, and he soon converted his monthly magazine, *The Commoner,* into a Fundamentalist organ. He also addressed various groups, including state legislatures, pleading for laws to forbid the teaching of evolution.

The Fundamentalist campaign reached major proportions especially in the South where it led to serious disputes in a number of churches, especially the Baptist and Presbyterian. In twenty states anti-evolution measures designed primarily to prevent or limit the teaching of Darwin's theory in state-supported schools were introduced, and spirited campaigns were conducted to obtain the laws Fundamentalists believed divinely ordained. However, approval of the proposed laws was obtained in only five states: Oklahoma, Florida, Tennessee, Mississippi, and Arkansas.

Tennessee's action led to high drama in 1925 when the American Civil Liberties Union sponsored a case to test the law's legality. John T. Scopes of Dayton, Tennessee, a young biology teacher, was prosecuted for violation of the law, and Bryan came to Tennessee to aid in the prosecution. The noted lawyer and free-thinker, Clarence Darrow, acted for the defense. The eyes of the world focused on Dayton, where the number of spectators necessitated moving the trial from the courthouse to a vacant lot. Though Scopes admitted violating the law, his defense was based on the law's unconstitutionality. Bryan, who also appeared as an expert witness on the Bible, was exposed by Darrow as naïve and uninformed. Though Scopes was convicted and fined $100, the Tennessee Supreme Court reversed the verdict on a technicality. In reality, Bryan's testimony ended the mass appeal of the Fundamentalists, who, though they obtained approval of anti-evolution measures in Mississippi and Arkansas after the Scopes trial, nevertheless were permanently damaged by it.

The nativist, anti-intellectual spirit of the 1920s divided America and produced tensions that left lasting scars. Catholics, Jews, blacks, Southern and Eastern Europeans, and intellectuals were not the only minority groups that were offended. The prosecuting groups themselves were motivated by frustrated desires, and many of their members were further alienated by their failures and public condemnation.

The Primacy of Business

While there were many divisive issues confronting the American people in the 1920s, most people were enamored with the achievements of American business. Industrial engineering arose, to a great extent, on the basis of the studies and philosophy of Frederick W. Taylor. The son of a prosperous Pennsylvania family, he left Harvard due to poor eyesight and became a patternmaker and machinist. Starting as a laborer at Midvale Steel, he became chief engineer of the company after

Clarence Darrow

earning a Master of Engineering degree at Stevens Institute. Taylor became enthralled at the possibilities afforded by higher productivity which resulted from increased specialization in the use of labor and machines. In the late nineteenth century, he promoted the use of time-motion studies, extra pay for increased productivity, and rigid discipline. Henry Ford applied many of Taylor's concepts and perfected use of the moving assembly line which wrought miracles in production. Largely because of a 40 percent increase in labor productivity, real wages generally increased over 25 percent during the decade 1919 to 1929. A short but sharp depression, due to international readjustments and decline in farm prices, hit the nation in 1921, but recovery came rapidly in 1922. Industrial profits rose over 60 percent between 1923 and 1929, and the automobile industry became the nation's largest with the electrical industry close behind.

Although the average worker's position was improving, there were signs of difficulty in the social fabric. An increasingly larger portion of wealth was concentrated in fewer hands. By 1929 almost 60 percent of the people received less than 24 percent of the nation's income. The masses lacked the purchasing power to sustain prosperity on a firm basis, much less enjoy the "good life" as Americans were coming to define it.

Labor unions were of little value to workers since their influence and membership declined constantly throughout the 1920s. Part of this decline came from the slackening support of the average laborer as his employer began the practice of "welfare capitalism." Group insurance, retirement benefits, in some instances profit sharing, and other programs by company experts in labor relations undermined union appeal. The National Association of Manufacturers and state manufacturers' associations led the fight which in many cases resulted in the

restoration of the open shop. By the end of the decade, union membership had fallen by almost 50 percent, and the decline in union influence in the coal mining and textile fields, two depressed areas, was particularly notable. Strikes in both fields led by small Communist-controlled unions were used to discredit labor organizations.

Throughout the 1920s business leaders found a receptive ear in Washington for many subsidies and supports. In 1920 they joined midwestern farm leaders burdened by falling prices in a crusade for a higher tariff. President Wilson, who correctly believed that duties would be of little value to farmers since the domestic surplus constituted the main problem, vetoed a measure placing high duties on many farm products in March, 1921. However, President Harding signed the reenacted measure, known as the Emergency Tariff, two months later. Over a year was required to enact the intricate Fordney-McCumber Tariff, which, like most tariffs, was greatly influenced by the mutual agreement of legislators to support each other's desired increases, a practice known as logrolling, and over two thousand amendments were added in the Senate. It returned the nation to a protectionist policy, increasing average rates above those of the Payne-Aldrich Tariff of 1909. Almost prohibitive duties were placed on many farm products as well as chemicals, silk and rayon goods, and other cheaply produced German and Japanese products. For most goods, however, the rates simply attempted to raise prices of foreign manufacturers to those of domestic production. This policy was similar to that underlying the earlier Underwood-Simmons Tariff of 1913 and was acceptable to most Americans.

Conservative business leaders were responsible for the appointment of Andrew W. Mellon, head of the aluminum monopoly, as secretary of the treasury. He urged wholesale reductions of taxes, especially on the well-to-do, and decreases in government expenditures. For four years, midwestern Republicans joined Democrats to frustrate his plans, but eventually in 1926, in the midst of national prosperity and treasury surpluses, Mellon prevailed. The maximum surtax on individual incomes and the estate tax were cut in half, the gift tax abolished, and in 1928 the corporation tax was reduced. There is little wonder that many agreed with Coolidge's description of Mellon as "the greatest Secretary of the Treasury since Alexander Hamilton." Few recognized that his policies actually lowered mass purchasing power and curtailed needed public services. The same results also came from a wartime decision of the Supreme Court in *Towne* v. *Eisner* which held that stock dividends were not taxable, thus enabling investors to buy more shares and escape taxation. Policies of this type contributed to an economic crisis which was to appear fully only in 1929.

Business influence also obtained generous federal subsidies for the merchant marine, especially under the Jones-White Act of 1928, and dominated the Federal Trade Commission (F.T.C.) and the Department of Commerce. As reconstituted under Republican control, the F.T.C. sought ways to avoid prosecution of monopolies and perpetrators of unfair practices. The commission obtained opinions from the attorney general to lessen its own power and invited businessmen accused of fraud or misrepresentation to appear before it and adjust matters. Secretary of Commerce Herbert Hoover sponsored meetings of trade associations whose activities in other periods would have been considered monopolistic. For many government leaders, business was the American people, and its interests were primary.

The Supreme Court assumed an equally conservative position, invoking the Fourteenth Amendment with the greatest frequency in history to invalidate welfare and regulatory laws. In *Bailey* v. *Drexel Furniture Co.* (1922), it prohibited the use of taxation to exclude children from mills. The following year, in *Adkins* v. *Children's Hospital,* it denied Congress the right to establish minimum wages for women in the District of Columbia, a reversal of an earlier, more progressive attitude.

The American Farmer

The most notable exception to the apparent prosperity of the 1920s was the farmer. Due to wartime overexpansion, inflation, and European recovery, farm prices plummeted in 1920 and generally remained below profitable levels throughout the decade. Farm income in 1921 declined to less than half of the 1919 level and did not rise above 70 percent of the 1919 level in the following years.

Under the severe pressure created by the situation, a Farm Bloc emerged in Congress led by midwestern Republicans and southern Democrats. Its greatest success came in obtaining intermediate credit for farmers. Previously, loans of five to forty years were obtainable from the cooperative farm loan associations underwritten by the Farm Land Banks established in 1916 and short-term loans from commercial banks, but a credit gap existed between the loans available. By the Agricultural Credits Act of 1923, twelve Intermediate Credit Banks were established to operate with the Federal Land Banks and extend loans for six months to three years. The Land Banks themselves were given additional capital, and the secretary of agriculture was empowered to regulate trading in grain futures as well as to preserve competition and reasonable rates in the stockyards.

Although these much-needed reforms were overdue, they did not alleviate depressed farm conditions. To do this, the Farm Bloc sponsored the McNary-Haugen Bill, which was originated by Senator George W. Norris in 1921 but was not accepted by the Farm Bloc until 1924. It proposed farm products be purchased by a government agency at "fair prices," which would be equivalent to the international prices plus the tariff levies. The surplus not consumed in the United States would be sold abroad at the prevailing price, but the difference in this return and the "fair" American return would be supplied by an equalization fee on farmers. The McNary-Haugen Bill, which was defeated in the House in 1924, passed Congress in 1927 and 1928, but on both occasions President Coolidge killed it by vetoes. Despite these rebuffs, the struggle contributed to farm unity and prepared the way for later government relief.

Prohibition

Paradoxically, the most idealistic motives led in the 1920s to mundane, materialistic results, especially in the case of prohibition, an appendage of Progressivism which in a number of states engulfed the entire movement. As early as 1869 the Prohibition party was organized, which was followed by the Women's Christian Temperance Union in 1874 and the powerful Anti-Saloon League in 1893. All indicted the morality of liquor drinking and traced many of urban America's intensified social problems to alcohol. In particular the intemperance of the "new immigrants" was indicted and in the South the spectre of alcohol's effect on blacks was portrayed. Also at the turn of the century, for the first time, alcohol's evil effect on the body was presented, and many intellectual leaders denounced its use.

By 1914 fourteen states had adopted statewide prohibition, and by 1918 the number had increased to thirty-two. The need to conserve grain for the war effort and to protect young draftees from liquor led Congress to forbid the sale of alcoholic beverages near military installations and prohibit the use of foodstuffs in liquor manufacturing. America had prohibition, but, to insure its permanency, Congress submitted the Eighteenth Amendment to the states on December 18, 1917, and it was ratified by the required number in January, 1919, to become operative January 16, 1920. Over President Wilson's veto, Congress passed the Volstead Act which excluded all beverages with more than one-half of one percent alcohol. Although this definition of what constituted an alcoholic beverage had long been used by the Revenue Service, it was a severe restriction which made light wines and beer unavailable and insured the failure of prohibition.

Once the wartime austerity was gone, millions of individualistic Americans chafed severely under prohibition. The federal government never employed more than 2,900 enforcement agents, and the law was unenforceable without converting the nation into a police state. In all states with large foreign-born populations and in larger cities opposition was overwhelming. Millions of Americans felt prohibition was an intrusion on their fundamental personal rights, and they openly violated the law by producing "bathtub gin" for themselves and patronizing the omnipresent bootleggers who purveyed poor quality and adulterated whiskey at exorbitant prices.

Ironically prohibition promoted the fashionableness of drinking, the increased consumption of hard liquors, and the use of alcohol by women. For many who aspired to sophistication, the search for establishments where an illegal drink could be bought (speakeasies) became an adventurous pastime. Often in these clubs the only available beverage was hard liquor because it returned more profit to the operators with no greater risk than the sale of less potent beverages. In the excitement and intimacy of these surroundings, newly liberated women first began to drink in public, and the cocktail hour became a regular feature of many women's days at home as well.

Not only did prohibition fail to end the consumption of alcohol, but it also spawned the growth and development of gangsterism to an astonishing degree. The profits made from the illegal sale of whiskey, wine, and beer enabled mobsters to extend their influence into local and state governments as well as many formerly legitimate businesses. No large city in America escaped some degree of gangster intrusion. In Chicago Al Capone became the richest of all the gang leaders and, due to his contemptuous defiance of the law, a hero to many Americans. The internal conflict among the various criminal elements led to gang wars which convinced many former advocates of prohibition that the law was destroying the society it was designed to save.

Eventually, even the proponents of prohibition had to admit its shortcomings, which were catalogued explicitly in 1931 by a special committee whose chairman was former Attorney General George W. Wickersham. Some, like President Hoover, continued to defend what he characterized a "noble experiment," but the Democratic platform in 1932 openly advocated repeal. The Twenty-first Amendment, which repealed the Eighteenth, was submitted to the states by Congress in February, 1933, and approved by December. Although prohibition may have reduced drinking in rural areas, nationally it promoted vicious aspects of American life and achieved unforeseen and unwanted results.

The Age of Disillusionment

Although the idealism which produced prohibition also found some expression in literature, a brazen materialism flourished during the 1920s as never before in American letters. Naturalism discarded what many proponents re-

Crowds buying liquor legally in a New York liquor store the day the Twenty-first Amendment was passed.

garded as the sentiment and pretense of an earlier generation and found avid readers who wished not only "to hear it as it was" but also to delve into the psychological reasons behind it. The effects of determinism in physical science, Freudian psychology, and loosened ethical and moral standards produced a "Lost Generation" of writers who renounced older values and glorified the new era of freedom.

In stylistically brilliant fashion, Ernest Hemingway debunked the false idealism of earlier times while celebrating the natural condition of man. Included in his works were *The Sun Also Rises, Men Without Women,* and, in 1929, *A Farewell to Arms,* which exposed the idealism of war in all its starkness.

No writer of the period was more popular with youth than F. Scott Fitzgerald, an alcoholic Princetonian still in his twenties. In *This Side of Paradise* the ultimate in cynicism was reached where, "All gods [were dead], all wars fought, all faiths shaken." Theodore Dreiser, a number of whose works had appeared earlier, reached the pinnacle of a mechanistic approach to life in *An American Tragedy,* which appeared in 1925. His portrayal of the murder of a

Ernest Hemingway

pregnant girl by her lover was stark realism. While some felt Dreiser's work lacked style and dexterous use of language, many believed *An American Tragedy* was the greatest novel of the decade.

Concern with small-town life characterized the works of Sherwood Anderson and Sinclair Lewis. In *Poor White, Many Marriages,* and *Winesburg, Ohio,* Anderson exposed, at times with sympathy, the foibles of much of middle America and attained greater influence with his fellow writers but less with the public than Sinclair Lewis. *Main Street,* which Lewis published in 1920, gave the nation its first literary shock of the new era. Subsequently, in *Babbitt, Arrowsmith,* and *Elmer Gantry,* he presented caricatures of the pretense and meanness behind much of the small-town, business-professional culture which enveloped the nation. John Dos Passos pictured an equally

meaningless existence for urbanites in *Manhattan Transfer,* while his *Three Soldiers* depicted the complete futility of wars. William Faulkner, the talented son of a once prosperous southern family, began his remarkable portrayal of degeneration and twisted passions in the 1920s. After writing some second-rate verse, he was persuaded by Sherwood Anderson to turn to fiction. His first two novels were somewhat shallow, but in 1929 one of his finest works, *The Sound and the Fury,* appeared which portrayed in unforgettable fashion the decomposition of the formerly distinguished Compson family. Perceptive critics immediately realized Faulkner's artistic ability.

Other popular American writers of the 1920s seemed to be absorbed with sex. Among the group was James Branch Cabell who in *Jurgen,* published in 1919, and later works, including *Something About Eve,* combined symbolism and a sophisticated style to win both wide approval and hearty condemnation by many readers. But not all writers abandoned the romantic, idealistic approach, and in 1929 the eccentric Thomas Wolfe began a short but brilliant career with the publication of *Look Homeward, Angel* which, while depicting the materialism and parochialism of his time, was a romance with life itself. Of those who continued to defend traditional values, perhaps the most successful was Willa Cather who in *Death Comes for the Archbishop* produced a work of enduring value which portrayed, in classic style, heroism and beauty in the midst of tragedy.

The poetry revival which began about 1914 increased in tempo, and St. Louis-born T. S. Eliot, who had moved to London during the war, became one of the most artistically influential poets of the times. Like many of the novelists, Eliot expressed the disillusionment and despair of the intellectuals, but in *The Waste Land,* a difficult work filled with brilliant imagery, he presented a striking plea for the necessity of faith. In this he was unlike his fellow expatriot, Ezra Pound, who used startling and difficult-to-decipher word pictures to convey meaning.

Robinson Jeffers, the poet who most nearly approached the naturalism of the novelists of the 1920s, found little to glorify and much to condemn in man. Most poets, however, did not share his pessimism. Robert Frost continued his romance with nature, and Edwin Arlington Robinson did not lose faith with man as he explored the depths of his ethical conflicts. Stephen Vincent Benet's *John Brown's Body* gave an emotional insight into the Civil War which earned it the status of the most popular of modern heroic poems. The search for new poetic forms was also evident in the works of e. e. cummings, Conrad Aiken, and others.

W.E.B. DuBois

The black poet Langston Hughes, who also experimented with almost every literary form, joined other writers such as Countee Cullen and performers such as Paul Robeson in initiating the "Harlem Renaissance" which portrayed every aspect of black life and exulted in black cultural achievements. It is difficult to determine whether such works as James Weldon Johnson's *The Weary Blues* (1926) and *Fine Clothes to the Jew* (1927) were more significant in arousing blacks' pride in themselves or in informing whites about black culture. The renaissance itself aided those black leaders who sought to enable their people to rise within the system. The most notable of these continued to be W. E. B. DuBois who in the NAACP publication, the *Crisis*, and in many

Robert Frost

magazine articles in particular continued to fight against discrimination and to preach independence to blacks.

The influence of DuBois and others proved far more effective and significant than that of Marcus W. Garvey who through his weekly newspaper, *Negro World,* preached a form of black chauvinism and urged American blacks to redeem Africa. After his steamship line, *The Black Star,* failed in 1923, Garvey was convicted of using the mails to defraud and sent to prison. Following his release in 1927, he was deported to his native Jamaica and his movement largely disappeared.

Black actors and actresses found the theater to be one area open to them, and they profited from the genuine native theater of distinction which emerged for the first time in the United States. Shortly before World War I, little theaters of quality came into being in Provincetown, Massachusetts, and New York City. These were followed in 1919 by the formation of the Theater Guild which brought the best of contemporary European and American drama to New York. Eugene O'Neill, a member of the Provincetown Players, became the nation's leading dramatist who in *Desire Under the Elms, Strange Interlude,* and other works demonstrated psychological insight and creativeness in the use of dramatic forms. However, his plays presented much of the seamier side of American life ·and were heavily Freudian in their orientation. The same was true of the dramatists who followed in O'Neill's tradition and sparked a national interest in drama which spread from Broadway to little theater and college productions throughout the country.

Scholarship flourished in many areas during the decade, much of it sustained by the colleges and universities whose enrollment doubled, for the first time exceeding one million students. Graduate schools abounded, the number of Ph.D.'s being awarded annually increasing over 400 percent. Interest in history and the social sciences grew and, under the influence of Charles A. Beard and others, these disciplines began to concern themselves with economic, social, and intellectual as well as political developments. Sociology obtained new status as a distinct discipline, relying heavily upon the use of data to form objective conclusions. In the physical sciences, American chemists led the world in developing synthetic products for practical use. In the more theoretical field of physics, leadership remained with Europeans, although American scholars fully integrated into their studies the new theories regarding the structure of the universe and the nature of matter and energy. Robert A. Millikan and Arthur H. Compton won Nobel prizes for their contributions in these areas.

Americans showed an increasing appreciation and support of the fine arts. Music training became much more widespread in the public schools, and American-born musicians were more frequently featured with the Metropolitan Opera and became members of leading symphony orchestras. In the field of lighter music, composers such as Cole Porter and George Gershwin produced lilting melodies that are still enjoyed today. Jazz, which originated among the blacks in New Orleans, arrived in Chicago by 1916, spread throughout the country, and became America's contribution to the world's music. Paul Whiteman and George Gershwin presented it in symphonic form, and Gershwin's *Rhapsody in Blue* and *An American in Paris* convinced many critics that jazz was worthy of the concert stage and should not be limited to the bandstand, the Victrola, and musical comedy.

In architecture, the functional designs of Frank Lloyd Wright had profound influence both in America and abroad. Insisting on construction being adapted both to the building site and to its use, he advocated bold experimentation with new building materials. The great majority of Americans, who found his ideas too unconventional for wide acceptance, were deeply impressed with the skyscraper, a style Wright generally deplored. The New York building code, which required receding facades for buildings as they increased in height, forced acceptance of a great deal of functionalism in the erection of many of these buildings. No architect more zealously promoted and defended the style for its utilitarianism and symbolic expression of efficiency than Harvey Wiley Corbett. The culmination of its development came with acceptance of plans for the 102-story Empire State Building, which was completed in 1931. Meanwhile a number of architects effectively created industrial structures of pleasing design while providing utilitarian working facilities. Of this group, perhaps most praise was bestowed on Albert Kahn for his designs of automobile plants.

America's painters and sculptors demonstrated much less originality than did its musicians and architects, although many were greatly influenced by the Armory Show which may have been the most significant event in the development of American art. Sponsored by the Association of American Painters and Sculptors, it opened at New York's Sixty-Ninth Regiment Armory on February 17, 1913, and introduced many Americans to modern European artists including Matisse, Van Gogh, Gauguin, and Cézanne. Although much of the press and public was scandalized by the break with traditional styles, the show inspired American artists to try their hand at Post-Impressionism, Cubism, and other innovations. It was over a decade before modernistic styles prevailed among American painters, but their emulation of European forms, such as Cubism and Surrealism in painting and Symbolism and Primitivism in sculpture, was notable. Artists of the Ash Can School such as Edward Hopper and Rockwell Kent did portray the unattractive but at times intently human side of American life, which was often overlooked.

Sculpture was less influenced by new forms although Charles Alston was representative of those who began an abstract approach to their work. Jo Davidson produced robust portrait busts of *Gertrude Stein* and *Dr. Albert Einstein,* and Hugo Robus created streamlined studies of figures including *Girl Reading* and *Girl Washing Her Hair.* The traditional style which emphasized monuments and memorials found greatest popular acceptance in the works of Gutzon Borglum who created gigantic monuments on Stone Mountain, Georgia, and Mount Rushmore, South Dakota.

As a whole, American intellectuals of the 1920s, as shown by the works of the nation's writers and artists, were in revolt against traditional assumptions and much of society as it was constituted. The joyous faith in man's innate goodness and the Progressive belief in his ability to rectify injustices was largely gone. H. L. Mencken, who began publication of *The American Mercury* in 1922, was an iconoclast and debunker whose biting criticism of Christianity, the average man, and democracy enjoyed vast popularity with the elite and seemed to epitomize the spirit of the times. His contempt for "the whole God-damn human race" reflected a serious malaise among America's most creative minority, which fortunately was overcome in the 1930s.

The Revamping of Popular Culture

Where the masses of people were concerned, equally significant developments were occurring in education, religion, and interpersonal relationships. Virtually free elementary education had become available to all children by 1920, but the decade saw a remarkable improvement in high school and college atten-

H. L. Mencken

dance. State departments of education became more effective in licensing teachers, and, even among conservatives, John Dewey's progressive theories began to have their impact. The number of high school students more than doubled, reaching almost 4.4 million by 1930. New curricula almost eliminated study of the classics, substituting more modern courses in art, music, the sciences, humanities, and social sciences. In addition, vocational courses, including home economics, manual training, secretarial science, and vocational agriculture, became quite popular. Obviously the schools were becoming training centers for a democratic society, not merely college preparatory centers. Higher education also grew rapidly and steadily broadened and diversified its offerings. Already some prophets were beginning to contend it should be available to all in a mobile, free society.

An increased demand for lighter reading material was one result of improved education.

Newspaper circulation rose markedly, although the number of city dailies declined by 20 percent and weeklies, unable to compete with larger journals in an era of rapid transportation, by more than 50 percent. Many consolidations occurred, and the Hearst and Scripps-Howard chains grew rapidly. In place of the vigorous personal journalism of an earlier era, syndicated features became commonplace, and many newspapers were similar in content. In 1920 the *New York Daily News,* a four-column tabloid dealing in sensationalism, made its appearance and was followed by other successful tabloids in New York and elsewhere. Although most of the new journals moderated their vulgar styles near the end of the decade, they did little to promote culture and intellectualism.

Comparable developments occurred in the magazine field. In 1922 the *Reader's Digest,* which purveyed condensed articles in simple language, was launched, and three years later, *Time,* the first of the weekly news magazines, appeared. *Collier's* and the *Saturday Evening Post* continued to prosper by presenting light fiction and moderately provocative nonfiction. However, the older quality reviews such as the *Outlook* and *World's Work,* which featured long works of major fiction and in-depth studies, declined and died by the 1930s.

Concurrently, religion played a vital role in most Americans' lives, and its leaders proved responsive to the intellectual changes of the times. The period from World War I until the outbreak of the depression in 1929 was one of extremely rapid growth in church membership. Although many rural churches were abandoned or consolidated, in the cities large congregations arose which had sizable property holdings and large incomes. Businessmen obtained status by serving as church leaders and stamped the business mold on many decisions and policies. Their leadership was of a different calibre from an earlier era, and they used proven methods to alleviate suffering and need. The social gospel made enormous inroads, leading the churches to undertake vast programs of social service and civic betterment. The Protestant percentage of total American churchmen continued to rise, and theological liberalism was widespread among clergymen and seminary students, especially outside the South.

A trend that many contended exerted an influence contrary to religion was the significant, sudden revision which came in the status of women, a change due in large measure to the assertion of independence by younger, middle-class women known as flappers. Realizing that dress and physical appearance could be used as symbols of a new position in society, they abandoned long hair and ankle-length dresses for short or bobbed hair, short often sleeveless dresses, high-heeled shoes, and entire ensembles complemented by long, double strings of beads, wrist bangles, and a hitherto inconceivable use of cosmetics. To emphasize the break with convention, the flappers frequently smoked and joined their male companions in drinking whiskey in public. By this means they

Henry Ford and his first car.

declared to all that they were human beings with the same rights as men.

Improved transportation affected women as much or more than any segment of society, providing many additional opportunities to get outside the home and to obtain employment and independence. No influence of the decade was more potent than the automobile, whose annual American production increased over 300 percent. Henry Ford, the leading manufacturer, completely revised production with the use of the assembly line and reduced the price of a car to less than $300, but General Motors became an effective challenger. By the use of mass advertising and installment plans, which other manufacturers copied, sales were rapidly promoted, and the auto industry became a principal source of the nation's economic development.

The automobile had profound economic and social consequences by expanding the production and market area for manufacturers and processors, ending much rural isolation, and increasing individuality by loosening the dependence on mass transportation. The mobility of the people was increased which decreased parental and neighborhood surveillance of personal conduct. Though the often expressed fear that the car was "a rolling house of prostitution" was incorrect, it did allow a degree of permissiveness previously unknown.

Motion pictures had a far more pervasive influence than the automobile on American life in the 1920s. As early as 1905 one-reel "nickelodeons" began to appear, and by 1914 technical improvements made possible the projection of pictures on large screens in sizable theaters. In 1915 David W. Griffith produced "The Birth of a Nation," a saga of the Civil War and Reconstruction which glorified the Ku Klux Klan and promoted racial hatred. In the 1920s the production center shifted from New York City and adjacent areas, Chicago, and Philadelphia to southern California whose climate afforded many advantages, and in 1927 "the talkies" were perfected. The works of such producers as Cecil B. De Mille, who specialized in spectaculars, and the use of the star system attracted over 100 million weekly movie admissions nationally by 1930. A potent force had emerged to influence conduct and attitudes.

The full impact of the radio, which came directly into the home, was reserved for the 1930s, but its early development came in the 1920s. The Westinghouse Corporation began the operation of the nation's first regular radio station, KDKA in Pittsburgh, in 1920. The number of stations grew to over 700 by 1927, by which time two major networks, NBC and CBS, had come into being. The former was controlled by the Radio Corporation of America, which in turn was largely owned by Westinghouse and General Electric. RCA also quickly came to dominate the manufacture of radios and radio equipment.

Although the major impact of the airplane did not come until after World War II, significant events in the 1920s prepared the way for later achievements. In October and December, 1903, Samuel P. Langley, third secretary of the Smithsonian Institution, tried unsuccessfully to fly a full-sized airplane carrying a man, a feat achieved by Wilbur and Orville Wright who made the first powered flight over the sand flats near Kitty Hawk, North Carolina, on December 17, 1903. In the following years the Wright brothers continued to perfect their craft and their skill as pilots. In 1905 they flew twenty-four miles in thirty-eight minutes and in 1909 formed the Wright Aviation Company from which the Glenn L. Martin Company obtained a license for plane production. Despite these advances, World War I found the United States lagging in aviation development, but the conflict was an enormous stimulus, and approximately 190,000 officers and men served in the Army Air Service. After the end of hostilities, a United States Navy plane became the first to cross the Atlantic in 1919, and in 1924 a United States Army plane became the first to circumnavigate the globe, although it took 175 days to do so. Also in 1925 domestic air mail service was begun in the United States.

Nevertheless a great lethargy settled on American aviation in the 1920s, a condition corrected by the accomplishment of Charles A. Lindbergh, a young pilot for the Air Mail Service, who in May, 1927, captured the imagination of the world by completing in thirty-three hours the first transatlantic solo flight. His achievement not only earned him an immediate promotion to colonel as well as the widespread interest and affection of the people but also enormously promoted the development of aviation. Companies were formed to develop domestic and international routes, investors attracted, and the basis of the modern aviation industry laid.

Charles A. Lindbergh and his plane, The Spirit of St. Louis.

The improved means of transportation and communication accelerated the educational and social revolution emerging across the land. Isolation was broken down as the same movies and radio programs began to be viewed everywhere. The peculiarities of regional and class speech and social concepts began to be removed, while easily accessible "store-bought" clothing destroyed the badge of distinctive dress. As never before the melting pot was functioning in the United States.

Hoover's Election

In 1928, in the midst of the rapid changes of the twenties, the Republican party nominated Herbert Hoover for president and Kansas Senator Charles Curtis for vice-president. Although a poor speaker, Hoover was one of the most respected Americans of his time. As secretary of commerce since 1921, he had been an effective champion of business interests and "rugged individualism." In the popular mind, however, his earlier feats as administrator of Belgian relief, wartime Food Administrator, and a successful international mining engineer who made a million dollars before he was thirty were paramount. Even his droll manner of speech contributed to his image as a no-nonsense expert who would apply scientific methods to solve every conceivable problem.

The Democrats, meeting in Houston, easily nominated Alfred E. Smith, the honest, somewhat conservative, unprecedented fourth-term governor of New York, who had emerged as the party's leading national figure. Due to his Tammany background, Roman Catholic faith, and opposition to prohibition, Smith was strongly opposed by many southerners. In an effort to conciliate the South, the platform pledged "an honest effort" to enforce the Eighteenth Amendment, but no reference was

Alfred E. Smith

made to the League of Nations nor was genuine tariff reduction promised.

In the campaign, Smith advocated federal operation of Muscle Shoals and a farm program similar to the McNary-Haugen plan, while Hoover opposed both. On other major issues, much to the disappointment of many liberals, few distinctions emerged between the candidates. Smith, working through John J. Raskob, chairman of the Democratic National Committee and a General Motors executive, worked for support of prominent capitalists as zealously as did the Republicans. In the South, where Protestant clergy were organized as Hoover partisans, Methodist Bishop James Cannon, Jr., and others were most concerned with the prohibition question, although anti-Catholicism was a factor. Due more to prosperity than any other factor since the people ascribed it to Republican policies, Hoover swept the nation. Outside six deep southern states, Smith won only in Massachusetts and Rhode Island, but he carried the larger cities, establishing the Democratic precedent as the party of urban liberals. Millions confidently expected Hoover to deliver on his promise to banish poverty from the land by going "forward with the policies of the last eight years."

The Depression

The new president and most of the nation confidently faced the future before a break in the stock market awakened them to a potential crisis in the economy. Serious weaknesses which threatened the nation's future had existed for some time in the economic structure. Most farmers had been in a depression since 1920 and able to maintain minimal purchases only by increasing debts. There was a concentration of wealth in a small percentage of the population, a condition promoted by the federal tax policy. The government had inadequate authority and machinery to control the amount of money in circulation and to regulate trade in stocks. The nation's failure to adjust to its creditor status and provide healthy, long-term means for Europeans to purchase American goods was especially significant.

The immediate crisis which initiated the depression was a collapse of prices in the stock market. In 1925 and 1926 a massive speculation in Florida lands revealed the nation's susceptibility to "get rich quick" schemes before it ended with economic ruination for many. This minor disaster was followed by a boom in the stock market in 1927; although a mild setback was sustained in June, 1928, it continued with minor declines until October, 1929. Between 1925 and 1929, the price of an average share of stock traded on the New York Stock Exchange increased by 300 percent as did the volume of shares traded. Much of the increase was due to speculation by short-term holders who obtained loans from brokers using the purchased stock as security. The immediate growth potential did not justify the fantastic increase in stock prices, and lack of confidence continued to grow. When the Bank of England raised its rediscount rate on September 26, 1929, forcing withdrawal of $200 million from the United States, stock prices declined sharply but recovered. On October 15, some of the larger investors began to sell their holdings, and on Thursday, October 24, a wholesale panic occurred when 13 million shares were sold. Despite the efforts of New York bankers to sustain prices and reassurances from the president that the economy was basically sound, panic occurred again on "Black Tuesday," October 29, 1929, when 16.5 million shares were sold in the most frenzied day in stock exchange history.

In the following months brief rallies occurred, but they were followed by greater declines, events which faithfully mirrored other economic developments. By 1932 the value of twenty-five leading industrial stocks was little more than one-fourth their October, 1929, price with even sharper declines in railroad and utility stocks. Unemployment rose from 3 million in 1929 to 14 million in March, 1933, when the very bottom was reached. New stock issues, to provide capital necessary for maintaining the nation's factories, fell to one-tenth their former level. Banks failed by the thousands, destroying the life savings of many at a time when the salaries of those fortunate enough to have jobs were declining by 40 percent.

In the crisis, state and local governments were called upon to provide unprecedented relief and, due to greatly decreased income, were unable to meet urgent needs. Across the nation, the dispossessed and poor took refuge in flimsy shacks on the edge of cities and towns, and beggars and breadlines became common. Women, many a family's sole support, were among the first fired. As families "doubled up," marital tensions increased, and the divorce rate rose, although the inability to pay lawyer's fees kept some couples legally married. Unfortunately, the schools and other public agencies were unable to fill the increased needs of children since nationally their income was cut approximately 20 percent between 1930 and 1934.

By mid-1931, the average American had ceased to believe the cheerful words of President Hoover and business leaders who held that the worst was over. As the withdrawal of American capital hit Europe, foreign conditions deepened the depression. At last, even the president of the U.S. Chamber of Commerce warned that business must develop a plan to alleviate unemployment and suffering or government would do so.

Surprisingly, in their despondency the masses of Americans resorted infrequently to radical action, although there were some notable exceptions. In 1932 the unemployed rioted in Dearborn, Michigan, and marches of the unemployed were staged in many cities. By force some midwestern farmers prevented mortgage foreclosures, but Minnesota's and North Dakota's prohibition of foreclosures or sales of foreclosed property kept major incidents to a minimum. The Communist party plied the discontented with its propaganda but with little result.

Nationally the most demonstrative event was the descent of over 1,200 veterans and unemployed persons on Washington, D.C., in the late spring of 1932. They demanded immediate cash payment of veteran's life insurance policies by the issuance of 2.4 billion paper dollars. When the Senate refused, about half of those who had settled in huts on Anacostia Flats accepted federal funds to return home. Following a riot on July 28, 1932, when police sought to remove the marchers from a building site, General Douglas MacArthur, army chief of staff, removed the remaining marchers and burned their shacks. The nearly seven hundred dispersed marchers found their way home or to other hobo jungles. Their existence was a sign of the people's suffering, but their small number was indicative of a lack of revolutionary spirit and of confidence the nation would right itself.

The Administration's Policies

Due to the natural tendency to find a scapegoat, the effective indictment of his political opponents, and the more advanced policies of the succeeding administration, Hoover has often been considered a do-nothing president in a time of gravest crisis. This evaluation is incorrect. An exponent of rugged individualism, he opposed government entry into fields such as electrical power which he believed could best be developed by private interests. Yet Hoover was far from an advocate of classical economics; as an engineer, he felt government must regulate enterprises which had a public nature. In the crisis of the depression, he responded with more extensive programs than any president had ever before attempted. Although there were many in Congress and the country who felt he did not go far enough, a case can be made that a "new deal" in the American government's attitude toward economic and social responsibility began under Hoover.

In the 1928 campaign Hoover had promised the farmers relief, a commitment he kept by obtaining enactment of the Agricultural Marketing Act of 1929 and the Hawley-Smoot

Herbert Hoover

rates of manufactured goods, giving the United States an all-time high tariff. Average duties on raw materials were increased from 38.10 to 48.92 percent and other commodities from 31.02 to 34.02. The average ad valorem duties, rates based on a percentage of customs value, rose to over 50 percent.

The raising of the American tariff, coming after the United States had become a creditor nation, had severe repercussions abroad, where barriers against American goods were erected in retaliation. Foreseeing this result, a thousand members of the American Economics Association urged Hoover to veto the measure. He refused because he believed the law would promote business confidence and aid in persuading business leaders to keep lay-offs to a minimum thus maintaining maximum operations. To encourage businessmen, he also obtained reductions in personal and corporate taxes in 1930, and, though some deficit financing was involved, federal appropriations for public works were substantially increased. Despite these efforts, production and employment began to deteriorate in the late spring of 1930.

Many criticized Hoover's state's rights policy under which relief was channeled through the states and his unwillingness to imbalance the budget to meet the crisis. Also liberal Democrats and Republicans urged that at least part of the veterans' bonus be paid and that the government promptly begin development of Muscle Shoals as a flood control project but especially as a source of cheap electrical power. In the November, 1930, elections, although the parties were almost evenly divided, the Democrats gained control of the Senate. The lame-duck Republican Congress, which ended in March, 1931, passed a bill authored by Senator Norris providing for government operation of Muscle Shoals, but it failed to override Hoover's veto of the measure. It did override the president in passing a bill authorizing veterans

Tariff the next year. The Agricultural Marketing Act not only endowed a board with $500 million, which could be lent to marketing cooperatives to increase efficiency and stabilize prices by making purchases when prices were falling, but also allowed the board through subsidiary corporations to purchase farm products directly. The board succeeded in maintaining prices above the international level until the European depression of 1931 had its repercussions in the United States. Its fatal weakness was lack of control over production, a deficiency the board urged Congress to remedy in late 1932.

Unlike the Agricultural Marketing Act, the Hawley-Smoot Tariff represented the past rather than the future. Although under it increased duties were provided for some seventy-five farm products, very little benefit came to farmers since there were international surpluses of these products, few of which were imported into the United States. Concurrently, the new law imposed over 900 increases in to collect in cash half the value of their insurance policies.

As the situation became more critical, in October, 1931, Hoover obtained a virtual moratorium on foreclosures from insurance companies and prompted the banks to form the National Credit Association with a credit pool of $500 million to aid salvageable companies and rediscount commercial and agricultural paper which the Federal Reserve Banks could not handle. After this scheme collapsed, the president, moving audaciously, proposed a greatly expanded public works program, extension of the lending capacity of the Federal Land Banks, the establishment of a system of home loan banks to aid in averting foreclosures, and creation of a large federal lending agency. He also recommended amendment of the Federal Reserve Act to make government bonds and an expanded variety of commercial paper the basis for paper money. In the crisis, gold had come to constitute about 70 percent of the nation's basis for paper money, and as the supply decreased something had to be done.

Congress complied, after some delay, with all these requests, but partisanship was intense at a time when action was needed. It was particularly unfortunate that months elapsed before the president's request for a lending agency, the Reconstruction Finance Corporation (RFC), was enacted in January, 1932. It was funded with $500 million and authorized to borrow $1.5 billion more to lend to companies and institutions throughout the country. Before the end of the year, the RFC had lent $1.5 billion to many railroads, banks, and other enterprises, an action which may have saved the American capitalistic system. The Glass-Steagall Act authorized the Federal Reserve banks to accept types of commercial paper formerly not acceptable for rediscount. It released approximately $1 billion in gold formerly required to back Federal Reserve notes by allowing U.S. government securities to serve as a portion of the 40 percent reserve required by law. Thus, by increasing the amount of gold, the act partially offset the contraction of credit due to the hoarding of gold and foreign withdrawals, but it did not stop the drain on gold. Congressional liberals also obtained enactment of the Norris-LaGuardia Act which enumerated union activities that could not normally be prohibited by federal injunctions and outlawed "yellow dog" contracts (those under which an employee agreed not to join a labor union). At last the labor provisions of the Clayton Antitrust Law became functional, although injunctions could still be issued when a court was shown that local police agencies were incapable of dealing with prevailing conditions and that without federal intervention an unlawful act would probably occur or that unalterable damage would be done to person or property.

As the election of 1932 approached, the administration could point to its unprecedented actions in combatting the depression, but liberals of both parties were displeased with its insistence that aid be channeled through the states and with the president's opposition to monetary inflation. Reluctantly, they voted for RFC loans of $300 million to states whose relief funds were gone and $1.5 billion for state and local government use in public works. Many began to believe that the administration had no qualms about aiding business directly but where the masses were concerned it subscribed to a "trickle down" philosophy.

The Election of Franklin D. Roosevelt

As the depression worsened, Democrats looked hopefully to the presidential election of 1932. Al Smith tried in vain to be renominated, but his successor as New York governor, Franklin D. Roosevelt, who had nominated Smith both in 1924 and 1928, attracted many of his former supporters and others who found Smith unacceptable. Roosevelt, who had been elected governor in 1928, tried unsuccessfully to develop large-scale public works to combat unemployment and was reelected in 1930 by the largest majority in New York's history despite the opposition of the Tammany organization. His nomination for president was shrewdly engineered by James A. Farley, a former Smith lieutenant, who gained a majority of delegates for Roosevelt, primarily from outside the East. At the convention, Farley withheld some votes on the first two ballots to give the impression his candidate was gaining strength. On the fourth ballot Roosevelt received the required two-thirds vote, but only after House Speaker John Nance Garner was promised the vice-presidency and Texas had swung into line.

The fifty-year-old Roosevelt had been born to wealth and position in upstate New York. He had never attended a public school, had cruised to Europe on his yacht as a young man, and had graduated undistinguishedly from Harvard and the Columbia University Law School. After admission to the bar, he accepted a comfortable position with a major New York City firm but bewildered many of his acquaintances by failing to settle down to a comfortable life. In 1910 he ran for the state senate from the upstate district which was his ancestral home, and, due to a Republican schism and vigorous campaigning, he won. At Albany he fought the Tammany organization and was a warm supporter of Wilson's candidacy in 1912. With the triumph of the Democrats nationally, Roosevelt became assistant secretary of the navy, a post he held for eight years and from which he learned much about government operations. In the meantime, he became a supporter of Tammany-backed Al Smith and as a

result was rewarded with the vice-presidential nomination in 1920. Though defeated, Roosevelt's warmth and charm attracted many followers who expected him to assume political leadership.

In August, 1921, Roosevelt was stricken with poliomyelitis and for years battled to regain partial use of his legs. His wife, Eleanor, a distant cousin whom he had married in 1905, and his faithful secretary, Louis M. Howe, helped him enhance his political following by writing to Democratic politicos throughout the nation. His suffering and struggle seemed to mellow his personality and burn out any traces of patrician haughtiness. In 1928 he acceded to Smith's personal request for him to run for the New York governorship and won, although Smith failed to carry the state.

In 1932 Roosevelt realized that he must convince the people of his physical ability to be president, and his political senses also told him the times called for a vigorous candidate. Therefore, breaking with precedent, he flew to the Chicago convention to accept his nomination in person. There he declared, "I pledge you, I pledge myself, to a new deal for the American people. . . . Give me your help, not to win votes alone, but to win in this crusade to restore America to its own people." From this time, Roosevelt retained the initiative in the campaign. He disregarded the Democratic platform, whose most radical feature was a promise to repeal the Eighteenth Amendment, and formulated appeals to various interest groups with the aid of his "Brain Trust," a group of intellectuals, several of whom were professors, who served as advisers to him. Although he made rash promises to balance the budget and cut expenditures, he also projected federal hydroelectric programs, national crop control, federal regulation of stock exchanges, and relief for the starving. In addition, he pledged to aid business leaders in developing programs to bring full employment.

President Hoover also campaigned widely, defending his policies and predicting doom should he be defeated. Although he pledged most vigorous action to alleviate suffering and extend credit, he proposed maintenance of the gold standard and an increase in duties on farm products as essential features of his program. The average voter was probably not greatly influenced by the arguments of either party. Roosevelt's political charisma, which was most effective over the radio, undoubtedly attracted votes, but in 1932 the desire for any change was paramount. Roosevelt swept the election, carrying all the states except six in the East.

The Republican ascendancy which had begun so hopefully in 1921 was at an end, partially a victim of its own success. During much of the 1920s its business-oriented leadership, overlooking the farmers' depression and international sore spots, had aroused hopes of increasing prosperity in an economy based on individualism and minimum controls. When the vision proved an illusion, the people reacted against their former idols.

Selected Bibliography

Interesting surveys include John D. Hicks, *Republican Ascendancy, 1921–1933** (1960); W. E. Leuchtenburg, *The Perils of Prosperity, 1914–1932** (1958); Arthur M. Schlesinger, Jr., *The Crisis of the Old Order, 1919–1933** (vol. I, *Age of Roosevelt,* 1957); and Harold U. Faulker, *From Versailles to the New Deal, A Chronicle of the Harding-Coolidge-Hoover Era* (1950).

Randolph C. Downes, *The Rise of Warren Gamaliel Harding, 1865–1920* (1970), is an exhaustive account of Harding's pre-presidential years. Andrew Sinclair, *The Available Man: The Life Behind the Masks of Warren Gamaliel Harding** (1969), enhances his reputation but Francis Russell, *The Shadow of Blooming Grove: Warren G. Harding in His Times* (1968), finds little to applaud. Robert K. Murray, *The Harding Era: Warren G. Harding and His Administration* (1969) assumes an intermediate position. The Harding scandals are covered in lively fashion in Samuel H. Adams, *Incredible Era: The Life and Times of Warren Gamaliel Harding* (1939), while Burl Noggle, *Teapot Dome: Oil and Politics in the 1920's** (1965), gives a full investigation of the most famous scandals. Coolidge's best biography is Donald R. McCoy, *Calvin Coolidge, The Quiet President* (1967), which largely supersedes William A. White, *A Puritan in Babylon: The Story of Calvin Coolidge** (1938).

Foreign policy of the 1920s is treated in L. Ethan Ellis, *Republican Foreign Policy, 1921–1933* (1968); Selig Adler, *The Isolationist Impulse: Its Twentieth-Century Reaction** (1957); Merlo J. Pusey, *Charles Evans Hughes* (2 vols., 1963); Betty Glad, *Charles Evans Hughes and the Illusions of Innocence: A Study in American Diplomacy* (1966); L. Ethan Ellis, *Frank B. Kellogg and American Foreign Relations, 1925–1929* (1961); and Robert H. Ferrell, *American Diplomacy in the Great Depression, Hoover-Stimson Foreign Policy, 1929–1933** (1970). The Washington Naval Conference is the subject of J. Chalmers Vinson, *The Parchment Peace: The United States Senate and the Washington Conference, 1921–1922* (1955), while Robert H. Ferrell deals with *Peace in Their Time: The Origins of the Kellogg-Briand Pact** (1969), and Alexander DeConde treats *Herbert Hoover's Latin American Policy* (1970).

Much social and cultural history may be gleaned from the contemporarily written books by Frederick L. Allen, *Only Yesterday, An Informal History of the 1920's** (1957) and *Since Yesterday** (1972), and P. W. Slosson, *The Great Crusade and After, 1914–1928** (1971). Nativism's effects may be studied in John Higham, *Strangers in the Land** (1963); Felix Frankfurter, *The Case of Sacco and Vanzetti** (1962); Julian F. Jaffe, *Crusade Against Radicalism; New York During the Red Scare, 1914–1924* (1972); Arnold S. Rice, *The Ku Klux*

---

*Available in paperback.

216

Klan in American Politics (repr. of 1962 ed., 1972); Charles C. Alexander, *The Ku Klux Klan in the Southwest** (1965); and Kenneth T. Jackson, *The Ku Klux Klan in the City, 1915–1930** (1967). N. F. Furniss deals with *The Fundamentalist Controversy, 1918–1931* (repr. of 1954 ed., 1963). No other work so effectively presents the plight of blacks as Gunnar Myrdal, *An American Dilemma: The Negro Problem and Modern Democracy** (2 vols., 20th an. ed., 1962). Reynold M. Wik, *Henry Ford and Grass-Roots America* (1972), shows how Ford came to epitomize the values of much of rural America.

On the role of business see Robert Sobel, *The Age of the Giant Corporations, . . . 1914–1970* (1972), and Alfred D. Chandler, *Strategy and Structure: Chapters in the History of the American Industrial Enterprise** (1969). Labor's status is presented in Philip Taft, *The A.F. of L., From the Death of Gompers to the Merger* (repr. of 1959 ed., 1969), and Irving Bernstein, *The Lean Years: A History of the American Worker, 1920–1933** (1972). The farmers' condition and actions are the subject of James H. Shideler, *Farm Crisis, 1919–1923* (1957); Theodore Saloutos and John D. Hicks, *Twentieth Century Populism: Agricultural Discontent in the Middle West, 1900–1939** (1951); and Gilbert C. Fite, *George N. Peek and the Fight for Farm Parity* (1954).

Andrew Sinclair, *Era of Excess: A Social History of the Prohibition Movement** (1964), is a balanced study of the "noble experiment." Literary trends may be sampled in John Hutchens, *The American Twenties: A Literary Panorama* (repr. of 1952 ed., 1972), and are analyzed in Maxwell Geismar, *Writers in Crisis: The American Novel, 1925–1940** (1971), and Frederick J. Hoffman, *The Twenties, American Writing in the Postwar Decade* (1955). Nathan I. Huggins deals with the *Harlem Renaissance** (1973), and Douglas C. Stenerson with *H. L. Mencken: Iconoclast from Baltimore* (1971). Developments in drama, painting, and architecture may be followed in A. H. Quinn, *A History of the American Drama: From the Civil War to the Present Day* (rev. ed., 1946); Edgar P. Richardson, *Short History of Painting in America** (1963); and John Burchard and Albert Bush-Brown, *The Architecture of America, A Social and Cultural History** (1961).

On educational changes see Richard Hofstadter and Walter P. Metzger, *The Development of Academic Freedom in the United States* (1955), Hofstadter's *The Progressive Historians* (1968), and H.G. Good, *A History of American Education* (1962). Paul A. Carter, *The Decline and Revival of the Social Gospel, Social and Political Liberalism in American Protestant Churches, 1920–1940* (rev. 2d ed., 1971), traces an important religious movement. Erik Barnouw, *A History of Broadcasting in the United States* (3 vols., 1966–1970), is the first large-scale history of the most important new means of communication.

Edmund A. Moore, *A Catholic Runs for President, the Campaign of 1928* (1956), is a good analysis. Oscar Handlin, *Al Smith and His America** (1958), is an intuitive study of Smith, his supporters and opponents. The events of Hoover's life may be gleaned from Eugene Lyons, *The Herbert Hoover Story* (1959). The depression's causes are analyzed in John K. Galbraith, *The Great Crash, 1929** (3rd ed., 1972), and Broadus Mitchell, *Depression Decade: From*

New Era to New Deal, 1929–1941 (1947). Hoover's presidential actions are treated in H. G. Warren, *Herbert Hoover and the Great Depression** (1967). Social developments are well covered in Dixon Wecter, *Age of the Great Depression, 1929–1941** (1971). An excellent account of Roosevelt's rise to the presidency is in Frank B. Freidel, *The Triumph** (vol. 3 of *Franklin D. Roosevelt,* 1956).

New Deal Attempts to Attain Prosperity and Reform

1933	Civilian Conservation Corps
	Federal Emergency Relief Act
	Agricultural Adjustment Act
	Tennessee Valley Authority
	The Federal Securities Act
	Wagner-Peysor Act
	Glass-Steagall Act of 1933
	National Industrial Recovery Act
	Civil Works Administration established
1934	Gold Reserve Act
	Securities Exchange Act
	Frazier-Lemke Farm Bankruptcy Act
	National Housing Act
1935	Works Progress Administration established
	Rural Electrification Administration created
	National Youth Administration established
	National Labor Relations Act
	Social Security Act
	Banking Act of 1935
	Rayburn-Wheeler Public Utilities Holding Company Act
	Frazier-Lemke Farm Mortgage Moratorium Act
1936	Soil Conservation and Domestic Allotment Act
1937	Bankhead-Jones Farm Tenancy Act
	Wagner-Steagall Act
1938	Second Agricultural Adjustment Act
	Fair Labor Standards Act

21

The Age
of
Roosevelt

Long-Range Developments

For Economics and Corporate Enterprise

National efforts to control agricultural production and guarantee parity prices produced astronomical surpluses until war conditions intervened in the 1940s.

For Democratic Government

The unprecedented actions taken by the New Deal permanently changed the average American's expectations of government and its role in national life.

The impressive growth of union labor under New Deal patronage led to popular disapproval of some labor practices and enactment of the Taft-Hartley Act and various state right-to-work laws.

For the Westward Movement,
Nationalism, and Expansion

The United States' improved relations with Latin America which developed under the Good Neighbor Policy were largely lost in the post-World War II period as America concentrated its attention on other regions.

The reciprocal trade program, though periodically attacked, has become a significant feature of United States policy.

The failure of American isolationist foreign policy in the 1930s prevented the reemergence of a significant isolationist movement until the coming of the Vietnam War.

For Civil Liberties, Freedom,
and Reform

President Roosevelt's realigned Supreme Court assumed a more progressive attitude toward social legislation and national power, setting precedents for more far-reaching decisions in the 1950s and 1960s.

The Dimensions of the Depression

The depths of depression were reached in the four-month interim between Roosevelt's election and inauguration.* Unemployment rose steadily, reaching an all-time high of over 14 million by March, 1933, and production declined at an unprecedented rate. In February national fear led to a run on the banks of intense proportions. To save sound institutions, the states declared bank holidays, and by inauguration day four-fifths of the surviving banks had been closed temporarily.

In the crisis, Hoover and Roosevelt's representatives failed to agree on an economic program for congressional consideration. Perhaps with justification, Roosevelt feared the outgo-

---

*In February, 1933, the Twentieth Amendment was approved which after October, 1933, ended the "Lame-Duck" session of Congress and moved subsequent inaugurations from March 4 to January 20.

An unemployed man is served in the Volunteers of America Soup Kitchen, Washington, D.C.

ing administration was seeking to commit him to policies which would hamper his efforts to combat the depression; this impasse contributed to national uncertainty and defeatism.

The Roosevelt Philosophy

Once in office, the new president electrified the nation by the manner in which he assumed leadership. In his inaugural address, he asserted a "firm belief that the only thing we have to fear is fear itself" and pledged, if necessary, to obtain from Congress "broad Executive power to wage a war against the emergency." Immediately the president declared a four-day national banking holiday and, using the Trading with the Enemy Act of 1917, prohibited the export of gold, silver, and currency. Within eight hours of the opening of a special congressional session, the president obtained passage of the Emergency Banking Act, which, in addition to confirming the action the president had taken, increased his power over currency transactions, allowed the Treasury to call in all gold and gold certificates to prevent hoarding, empowered it to license solvent banks to reopen, allowed the Reconstruction Finance Corporation to purchase preferred stock of national banks, and provided for government-appointed conservators of insolvent national banks. By these diverse steps, the currency panic was ended. Before the end of March an Economy Act designed to save the government 500 million dollars was passed, the Volstead Act was amended to permit sale of 3.2 percent beers and wines, and the Civilian Conservation Corps (CCC) was established to provide jobs for 250,000 young men, eighteen to twenty five, in reforestation, flood control, and other conservation projects. Soon afterwards, the CCC requirements were waived to give jobs to 25,000 needy World War veterans and 25,000 skilled woodsmen whose expertise was needed by the corps; in 1934, the CCC set up labor camps for women.

The special session of Congress which ended June 16, 1933, has often been called the "Hundred Days," since, after brief consideration, it enacted an unprecedented quantity of major legislation in a short time. The crisis was so intense that many business leaders who later came to oppose the New Deal gladly accepted Roosevelt's leadership. The president was fundamentally a conservative who had no intention of undermining capitalism. However, he was not well informed in economics, and, like the aristocrat that he was, he had a fundamental distrust of bankers and other money managers. As an intense admirer of Theodore Roosevelt and Woodrow Wilson, F.D.R. was in the Progressive tradition, yet he lacked the scholarly background to be firmly rooted to any ideology. Instead of studying, he preferred to obtain information from people, and he surrounded himself with a remarkably diverse group of advisers. The disparity of views was great between Secretary of State Cordell Hull, a low-tariff internationalist from Tennessee, and Secretary of Labor Frances Perkins, the first woman cabinet member and a former New York social worker. Equally divergent were the outlooks of Budget Bureau Director Lewis W. Douglas, a hard-money, "rugged individualist," and Harry Hopkins, a key adviser and exponent of organized planning. The result may have been an attempt to move in all directions at once, but at least the administration moved.

Many of the New Deal's programs arose from the "Brain Trust," a diverse group of advisers, a number of whom had assisted Roosevelt in the presidential campaign. Some of its members accepted secondary government positions while others did not. At first the group's leader was Raymond Moley, a Columbia professor whose fundamental conservatism led to a break with the New Deal. Another Columbia professor, Rexford G. Tugwell, served as an agricultural expert and advocate of national planning. Adolf A. Berle, Jr., was a major adviser on financial and tax matters. James M. Landis and Felix Frankfurter were two Harvard Law School professors who were important members of the group after 1934.

Roosevelt's efforts to deal with unemployment illustrated his receptivity to new ideas and his pragmatism. In May, 1933, the Federal Emergency Relief Act (FERA) allotted $500 million to the states, half on a matching basis, for aid to the destitute. The FERA found most of the states so devoid of funds, however, that in all except three cases it was forced to provide more than half of the relief funds. In June, 1933, Congress passed the Wagner-Peysor Act which established the U.S. Employment Service in the Department of Labor. The act required federal matching of state appropriations and cooperative action in seeking to aid the unemployed in finding jobs. Harry Hopkins, the Relief Administrator, advocated programs to provide work, not a dole, and in November, 1933, the Civil Works Administration (CWA) was established and given $950 million to create jobs during the next fifteen months. Many of its projects, such as community clean-ups and leaf-raking, were hastily contrived and evoked criticism, but almost 4 million unemployed were put to work before the CWA was abandoned, partly due to skyrocketing costs, in late March, 1934.

Roosevelt had hoped many of Hopkins' objectives would be met by the Public Works Administration (PWA), established to undertake major public improvements and endowed with $3 billion in June, 1933. However, the PWA administrator, Secretary of the Interior Harold L. Ickes, an old Bull-Moose Progressive from Illinois, was so careful in seeing that the government obtained proper return on its investment that the program did not bring needed job relief. Therefore, Roosevelt capitulated to the Hopkins forces in May, 1935, creating the Works Progress Administration (WPA). As an adjunct of it, the National Youth Administration (NYA) was established in June, 1935, to aid high school and college youths by providing part-time jobs. Some 600,000 young men and women were subsidized by the NYA in 1936, and approximately 750,000 in 1939–1940, its peak year.

Though often attacked for inefficiency and even involvement in politics, within a year the WPA was employing 3.4 million persons on major construction projects and such diverse undertakings as theater productions, translating, cataloguing and writing historical works, record inventories, and musical productions. In eight years the WPA gave jobs to 8.5 million persons and expended approximately $11 billion. Its cumulative effect convinced the masses the government was concerned and would attempt to provide work, not a handout, for employables in times of depression.

The administration's attitude toward inflation also indicated a divided mind. Early attempts to reduce expenditures, to protect the gold standard, and to cooperate in international currency stabilization were followed by contrived inflation. Secretary Hull had his orders countermanded while en route to the London Economic Conference in June, 1933. Instead of supporting the gold-bloc nations' efforts to stabilize currencies, he was ordered to negotiate only for bilateral tariff reductions. Earlier actions had taken the United States off the gold standard, and by the Gold Reserve Act of 1934 the president was permitted to reduce the gold content of the dollar to 50 to 60 percent of its former content. He promptly set the percentage at 59.06. This action did not produce notable price increases, but it had a salutary effect on the economy and was another example of Roosevelt's willingness to experiment.

One Roosevelt innovation which received almost universal approval was the establishment of the Federal Deposit Insurance Corporation (FDIC) which was one feature of the Glass-Steagall Act of 1933. The FDIC insured deposits in member banks up to $2,500 and in 1935 up to $5,000. All national banks were required to join the system, and many state institutions chose to do so, thus guaranteeing the savings of small depositors and increasing confidence in banking. In addition, the Glass-Steagall Act divorced commercial from investment banking and empowered the Federal Reserve to curtail bank lending for speculative purposes.

The First and Second New Deal

Historians have often referred to the "First New Deal" and the "Second New Deal" to differentiate between the cumulative effect of the administration's policies. The First New Deal came during Roosevelt's initial two years and was closely related to policies begun under Hoover. It sought to raise prices and consumption through controlled production and utilized much centralized planning, making it in some ways more radical than the Second New Deal. More closely related to Teddy Roosevelt's New Nationalism than Wilson's New Freedom, the First New Deal was ideologically opposed by such important administrative advisers as Supreme Court Justice Louis D. Brandeis and Harvard Law Professor Felix Frankfurter, whom Roosevelt elevated to the high court in 1939.

The cornerstone of the First New Deal was bold experimental attempts to establish a planned economy in agriculture and industry. One of its foundations was laid in May, 1933, when the Agricultural Adjustment Act (AAA)

*President Roosevelt greets workers
on a stock water dam in
North Dakota.*

was passed which sought to obtain parity prices for corn, cotton, wheat, rice, pork, dairy products, and tobacco. Parity prices were those which would give the farmer the same purchasing power he had enjoyed in an earlier prosperous period; for all commodities except tobacco this was in the years 1909–1914. To attain this goal, producers were authorized by their own votes to limit acreage or crops, and when they did so the government agreed to maintain prices by extending loans or purchasing crops which it would store. It also agreed to pay for lands withheld from cultivation. The cost of the entire program was defrayed by a processing tax on the affected commodities.

Initially, Secretary of Agriculture Henry A. Wallace, whose Republican father had held the same office in the 1920s, had crops plowed under and pigs destroyed, a sordid event when millions of Americans were hungry and threadbare, but after a few months, this phase of the program ended. Aided by droughts which reduced production, it produced an approximate 50 percent increase in prices, which were approaching parity by 1936.

The major industrial planning program of the First New Deal had a less successful experience. The National Industrial Recovery Act (NIRA), passed in June, 1933, was extremely complex. Drawing on the precedent of the fair trade codes of the 1920s, it sought to attain industrial self-regulation through codes formulated by representatives of industry, labor, and government and approved by the president. Exemption from the antitrust laws was granted, and in section 7a the right of workers to organize and bargain collectively was guaranteed. General Hugh S. Johnson, the gruff draft administrator of World War I, became head of the National Recovery Administration (NRA) and promptly set up a blanket code for all industry until the separate codes could be established.

Over 550 basic and 200 supplementary codes were drafted between 1933 and 1935. Each set minimum wages and maximum hours, forbade child labor, and acknowledged the right of collective bargaining, but serious difficulties arose. The codes were formulated primarily by representatives of big business, whom the smaller concerns often unjustly indicted because they disliked the codes' prolabor features. Moreover, by attempting to limit production without giving the NRA power to establish or enforce quotas, the law assigned an impossible task. It may also have actually impeded recovery by discouraging investments and production. Conscious of difficulties, Roosevelt fired Johnson and asked Congress for authority to revise the codes. Before it could act, the Supreme Court invalidated the act in May, 1935. Many in the administration, including the president, were probably relieved.

Confronted by a need to revamp the policy, the administration in 1935 embarked on the Second New Deal which sought to restore competition, protect the small businessman, and provide more directly for the needs of the ordinary American. Some aspects of this policy had begun earlier including substantial relief for homeowners through government-backed refinancing of home loans. The Federal Securities Act had required full disclosure on all new securities issues and their registration with a government agency; and the Securities Exchange Act had provided for federal control of stock sales including limits on credit (margin) use. Now the administration obtained passage of the Banking Act of 1935 which greatly enhanced the federal government's control over banking and the volume of credit. Under it the Federal Reserve Board, reorganized as the Board of Governors of the Federal Reserve System, obtained final authority over the regional Federal Reserve Banks' rediscount rates, reserve requirements and operations in the open market. After a bitter struggle, the Rayburn-Wheeler Public Utilities Holding Company Act was passed which gave the Federal Power Commission the authority to regulate the interstate transmission of electricity and the Federal Trade Commission the same regulatory power over gas. In addition, the Securities and Exchange Commission was given authority over public utility holding companies who were restricted to a single, concentrated operation in one area. Under a "death sentence" clause, at the end of five years companies which could not show the local and efficient nature of their operations were to be dissolved.

In taxation, the administration committed itself to increases primarily on rich persons and on larger corporations. A graduated income tax was imposed on corporations, the estate tax was raised to a maximum of 70 percent, and a surtax placed on larger personal incomes. Concurrently, the WPA was established, and new legislation providing security for the average worker was enacted. Clearly a new approach favored by workers, farmers, social workers, and the unemployed had begun. Although it involved less centralized planning, it appealed to the Populist tradition which wished government intervention in behalf of the masses.

Labor's Development

Under the NIRA, limited advantages came to labor, and membership in the A.F. of L. increased by almost 50 percent to 3,045,000. In many industries, however, employers, refusing to abide by section 7a, prevented unionization and challenged the NIRA in court. Almost as many employees were organized in company unions as were affiliated with the A.F. of L., and many intense strikes, frequently unsuccessful, occurred in 1933–34. A National Labor Board, chaired by New York's Senator Robert F. Wagner, mediated a number of disputes and, transformed into the National Labor Relations Board (NLRB) in 1934, it conducted many polls of workers to determine their desire for unionization. But due to lack of authority to impose its decisions, the board accomplished little.

Confronted by labor's chaotic state, Senator Wagner introduced additional legislation to protect unions in 1934 which received the administration's support after the invalidation of the NIRA in 1935. In July the National Labor Relations Act (also known as the Wagner Act) became law, reenacting the basic provisions of section 7a but specifically defining a number of unfair labor practices which interfered with unionization or penalized workers for union activities. The NLRB was authorized to conduct elections to determine by majority vote who would be the sole representative of workers in a plant, company, or other bargaining unit. Employers who violated the law were subject to the board's "cease and desist" orders which were to be enforced through the federal courts.

Supported by the new legislation, which reflected a vigorous antibusiness attitude among the people, organized labor began a spectacular growth. Much of this success came through the organization of strong industrial unions which organized workers on an industry rather than a craft basis. Except for a few unions, the largest of which was the United Mine Workers, the A.F. of L. was craft organized, which presented difficulties in unionizing an industry such as steel. The Mine Workers' head, John L. Lewis, and such aggressive leaders of the Amalgamated Clothing Workers as Lithuanian-born Sidney Hillman and David Dubinsky formed the Committee for Industrial Organization in 1935, confident that only through such organization could a number of major industries be unionized. Their action was taken after the 1935 A.F. of L. convention disapproved their plans, and, when the C.I.O. refused to obey orders to dissolve, the A.F. of L.'s Executive Committee expelled the unions associated with the movement.

Under Lewis' presidency, rapid growth was experienced by the C.I.O. (whose name was changed to the Congress of Industrial Organization in 1938). Failure was experienced in the southern textile field, but by herculean efforts the rubber, automobile, steel, electrical, and some other basic industries were organized. Despite the Wagner Act, employer opposition was vigorous, and, especially in 1936 and 1937, the sit-down strike became a major union weapon. By taking over a facility, the workers not only made the introduction of strikebreakers difficult but also threatened costly machinery. Violence occurred in a six-week sit-down at General Motors plants in Flint, Michigan, and, although a federal court

John L. Lewis

order was obtained requiring evacuation, the prolabor stand of the federal and state government resulted in mediation and union recognition.

One of the most violent labor episodes occurred in the steel industry in May, 1937. Rather than risk a strike, United States Steel recognized the union, the Steel Workers' Organizing Committee (SWOC), the predecessor of the United Steel Workers organized by Philip Murray, a close associate of John L. Lewis; however, many of the smaller steel companies, known as "Little Steel," did not. Strikes were called against the nonunionized companies, and in a Memorial Day conflict with police at

Republic Steel's South Chicago plant ten strikers were killed and scores injured. This episode contributed to the unpopularity of the sit-down strike, and even President Roosevelt denounced the C.I.O. for its use. "Little Steel" was able to break the 1937 steel strike, postponing unionization until 1941, but before that time, in 1939, the Supreme Court declared sit-downs illegal. Despite some reverses, the number of union members grew to 9 million by 1939, and to 10.5 million by 1941.

Part of organized labor's success in attracting members was due to the invocation of the president's name. Certainly Roosevelt supported unionization in general and felt it was one means to increase purchasing power and alleviate sweatshop wages and working conditions. However, his concern included all workers, and following the invalidation of the NIRA he sought to reestablish not only the right to unionize but some of its other benefits as well. In 1936 Congress met part of the need in the Walsh-Healey Act by stipulating that holders of government contracts of more than $10,000 must pay local prevailing wages, not employ children, and observe an eight-hour day. Though this provided an excellent beginning, it was entirely inadequate.

In 1937 the president sponsored a general wage-hour law which was killed in the House, but the next year it was enacted as the Fair Labor Standards Act and, with the exception of sizeable groups such as agricultural workers, covered employees involved in interstate commerce or producing goods for it. It set a minimum wage of 25 cents an hour which was to be raised to 40 cents by 1945, and maximum hours were set at 44, to be lowered to 40 by 1940. Any overtime pay was to be compensated at time-and-a-half rates. Labor of children under sixteen was forbidden and under eighteen in industries found to be hazardous by the Children's Bureau. The law immediately raised the wages of 300,000 workers and

shortened the hours of 1.3 million. Its enactment and New Deal guarantees of the right to bargain collectively gave the worker a new status in America and produced a powerful political bloc on which the Democratic party could rely.

Personal and Regional Security

In haphazard fashion and in response to a variety of pressures, the New Deal extended protection to the average American which he had not known before. Much of this gain came in the Social Security Act of 1935, a most important measure which provided subsistence for unemployed, disabled, and retired individuals. Although benefits were initially low, the act was the first under which the federal government assumed responsibility for the public welfare in a number of critical areas. The states were coerced into establishing unemployment insurance by levying a 1 percent payroll tax on employers, but the law allowed most contributions to state plans to be charged against the federal tax.* Extensive federal funds were made available to the states on a matching basis to aid mothers, children, the crippled and blind as well as those over sixty-five for whom the newly established system of old age and survivors insurance was coming too late. This annuity program was the act's most essential feature and was financed by levying a payroll tax of 1 percent in 1937, gradually increasing to 3 percent in 1949, to be jointly shared by employers and employees. From its beginning in January, 1942, pensions, varying from $10 to $85 a month, were to be paid retirees sixty-five years of age or older. The taxes, benefits, and

---

*Employers still paid 10 percent of the levy to the federal government, but most of this was remitted to the states to pay for the administration of their programs. Under the law the unemployment tax was raised to 3 percent in 1937.

A migrant workers' "shacktown."

covered groups have been increased over the years, and protection given to millions. No New Deal measure has been more popular.

No segment of the people caused the administration more concern than the farmers who were among the most depressed groups in the nation. The plight of migrant workers, brilliantly presented in John Steinbeck's *Grapes of Wrath,* was a national disgrace, and Roosevelt was thinking primarily of the rural people when he described the South as "the nation's No. 1 economic problem." In addition to laws dealing with production and prices, the New Deal sought to aid farmers in many other ways. A number of actions were taken in efforts to prevent loss of farm lands through foreclosures. In March, 1933, President Roosevelt consolidated all government agencies related to farmers' credit into a Farm Credit Administration which received additional funds to refinance long-term loans at low interest. In 1934 the controversial Frazier-Lemke Farm Bankruptcy Act provided funds for farmers to repurchase their properties, after reappraisal of their value, at an interest rate of only 1 percent. If a creditor objected, farmers were assured possession of their lands for five years by making "fair and reasonable" payments. After the law was declared unconstitutional in 1935, it was replaced by the Frazier-Lemke Farm Mortgage Moratorium on farm foreclosures for farmers who obtained court permission and paid a reasonable rental.

The Resettlement Administration was created in May, 1935, to relocate a million farmers who lived on submarginal lands. It did build three model "Greenbelt towns" near Cincinnati, Milwaukee, and Washington, D.C., demonstrating the feasibility of this needed construction for lower-income city workers, but only 4,441 farmers were resettled, largely due to fear of collectivization and racial integration. In 1937 these objections were partially overcome when, with strong southern support, the Bankhead-Jones Farm Tenancy Act was passed. Its accompanying report revealed that over half of the South's farmers did not own the lands they cultivated, nor did a third of those in the North or a fourth in the West. The act created the Farm Security Administration which assumed the functions of the Resettlement Administration and provided low-interest, forty-year loans to enable farmers to purchase lands; it also furnished loans for operational and educational expenses and established camps for migrant workers. By 1945 it had lent over a billion dollars, three-fourths in short-term rehabilitation loans, over 90 percent of which were repaid.

The Rural Electrification Administration, established in 1935 and expanded in 1937, provided loans and, through the WPA, labor to extend power lines into rural areas. Though private utilities often opposed the federally endowed cooperatives which led in expanding facilities, much of rural America was electrified. In 1935 only 10 percent of farm homes had electricity, but by 1950, 90 percent did.

Less spectacular but highly significant gains were also made in federally developed urban housing. By 1937 the PWA had constructed projects in thirty-six cities with units for over 21,000 families, but Roosevelt decided the action was too slow and aided in the passage of the Wagner-Steagall Act. A United States Housing Authority (USHA) was established with $1 million initial capital and wide-scale borrowing powers for extension of loans to public housing authorities in all major cities for the clearing of slums and building of low-cost housing. By 1941 over $750 million were loaned by the USHA in a program which at last began to grapple with this major problem of the cities' poor.

Many felt that the more comprehensive effort at regional planning and rehabilitation undertaken by the Tennessee Valley Authority (TVA) would provide a blueprint for the future. Although the private power interests, led by Commonwealth and Southern Corporation's Wendell L. Willkie, strenuously objected, TVA was established as an independent agency in May, 1933. It was authorized not only to construct dams and power sites throughout the seven-state Tennessee Valley but also to sell electricity, produce fertilizers, and develop the region economically and socially. In addition, it was to provide a "yard-

stick" by which the government could judge the cost of producing electricity.

Although the TVA's extent of regional planning was not as great as some desired, it achieved remarkable results. By the construction of twenty new dams and the improvement of five older ones, flood control was obtained on one of the nation's most turbulent rivers, which also aided control of portions of the Ohio and Mississippi. A 650-mile waterway system was created which yearly carried increased traffic. The people of the valley were greatly influenced by farm demonstration work, CCC reforestation, cheap fertilizers, and electricity, and industry was drawn in as the region became more attractive. TVA's expansion of electrical generating capacity was hindered by private utility lawsuits until 1939 when the Supreme Court ruled against the Tennessee Electric Power Company in a suit which sought to restrict TVA competition. After this decision, the Commonwealth and Southern Corporation sold the Tennessee Company to TVA, and its generating capacity

Fontana Dam, the highest (480 ft.) of the TVA dams. It is located on the Little Tennessee River in North Carolina and bordered by the Great Smoky Mountains National Park.

was increased in time to play a crucial role in industry's World War II efforts.

TVA's potential success led Roosevelt to ask Congress for establishment of six other similar regional projects in 1937. Apparently he was thinking of long-range developments which would propably have been initiated had rearmament not diverted the nation's interests. As it was, nuclei for such developments were laid by the erection of Hoover Dam on the Colorado River, Grand Coulee Dam on the Columbia, and Ft. Peck Dam on the Missouri.

The Election of 1936

Long before the 1936 elections, the persuasive national support Roosevelt received upon taking office had disappeared. As the economic crisis lightened, conservatives, many of whom disliked much of the NRA, turned against the administration. In 1934 the DuPonts and others formed the Liberty League, which attacked the New Deal for its inroads on free enterprise and state's rights. Among its adherents were two former Democratic presidential candidates, John W. Davis and Al Smith.

More distressing to the president was the substantial support gained by some outspoken critics on the left. Dr. Francis E. Townsend, a Californian, claimed five million members had joined his clubs which urged the federal government to give $200 a month to every unemployed person over sixty. In Detroit, Father Charles E. Coughlin, the "Radio Priest" whose weekly programs had been popular since 1926, turned against the New Deal in 1935. He indicted the administration for not turning to wholesale inflation, mercilessly attacking it as well as the business community. Though his claim of nine million followers was exaggerated, he did have much support.

The most severe challenge to Roosevelt's leadership was that of Senator Huey P. Long,

who by 1933 had come to control Louisiana. Though crude and poorly educated, Long provided unprecedented state welfare and educational services in Louisiana while eliminating many racial barriers. By 1935 his "Share-Our-Wealth" movement had attracted over 4.5 million members nationally. He proposed to give every family a homestead, a car, a $2,000–$3,-000 guaranteed annual income, and many social services by confiscating estates of over $5 million and annual incomes of over $1 million. In September, 1935, Long was assassinated, and by 1936 his removal and the launching of the Second New Deal had quieted much criticism from the left. Roosevelt and Garner were renominated by acclamation, and the southern Democrats were so mesmerized by the political climate that they agreed to abandon the two-thirds rule for nominating candidates.

The Republicans had only one strong contender, Kansas Governor Alfred M. Landon,

Huey P. Long as he delivered the radio address in which he attacked the Roosevelt administration and also outlined the plan for his "Share Our Wealth" program.

"FDR splitting the Democratic party
with his New Deal."

one of very few members of their party to be reelected governor in 1934. An old "Bull Mooser" who supported government regulation of business, Landon's first ballot nomination represented a resurgence of liberalism within the Republican party. *Chicago Daily News* publisher Frank Knox was chosen as the vice-presidential candidate, and the party platform, like Landon, confined its criticism of the New Deal mainly to its tax laws and tariff reductions. To many voters the Republicans seemed only to promise to do better what Roosevelt was already doing. Although Landon campaigned hard, he lacked warmth and color, critical weaknesses in a campaign with Roosevelt.

The president, though certain of reelection, also campaigned vigorously, defending his administration and promising to expand economic and social opportunities. For the first time, a majority of blacks, many of whom had profited by New Deal programs for the poor, voted Democratic. Organized labor also supported the Democrats to an unprecedented degree. Its Non-Partisan League raised over $1 million and aided in getting out the vote.

On the far left, the radical North Dakota farm leader, Representative William Lemke, received the support of many followers of Dr. Townsend, Father Coughlin, and Reverend Gerald L. K. Smith, a protofascist and Long's successor. He polled 900,000 votes but did not break into the electoral column.

Roosevelt's broad popular support earned him one of the most impressive presidential triumphs in which he won every state except Maine and Vermont and carried many Democratic congressmen with him to victory. In the new Congress, there were only eighty-nine Republican representatives and sixteen senators. With confidence, Roosevelt promised in his Second Inaugural to alleviate the conditions of the one-third of the nation which remained "ill-housed, ill-clad, ill-nourished. . . ." Never had an American president appeared to be in a stronger position to obtain congressional approval of his programs.

Court Reorganization

In February, 1937, shortly after his second inauguration, President Roosevelt presented a Judiciary Reorganization bill to Congress which had major political repercussions. It authorized the appointment of fifty new federal judges including a new Supreme Court justice for each incumbent who upon reaching the age of seventy did not retire within six months, until the Court reached a total of fifteen members. Provision was made for appeal of lower court decisions directly to the Supreme Court in cases involving constitutional issues and for a more efficient organization of the lower courts.

Roosevelt's action, taken without consulting his own party leadership, evoked a storm of criticism. His bold recommendation was provoked by a constitutional impasse which threatened to destroy the major New Deal reforms. Associate Justices Pierce Butler, James McReynolds, George Sutherland, and Willis

Van Devanter were militant reactionaries. Chief Justice Charles Evans Hughes, who wrote some notable civil rights decisions, and Justice Owen J. Roberts occupied a middle ground but, in 1935 and 1936, joined the Court's right-wingers in important conservative decisions. Although some decisions were by five-to-four splits, most of the major ones were not, indicating substantial agreement of at least six of the justices in the major cases. Under the circumstances, liberal Justices Louis D. Brandeis, Benjamin N. Cardozo, and Harlan F. Stone constituted a helpless minority.

In its decisions, the Court defined commerce as only the movement of goods, just as an earlier high tribunal had done in the notorious *E. C. Knight* case in 1895. Partially on this basis, it invalidated the Railroad Retirement Act of 1934, the NIRA (in *Schechter Poultry Corp.* v. *United States,* 1935), and the AAA (in *United States* v. *Butler,* 1936). On "Black Monday," May 27, 1935, in addition to destroying the legal basis for the NIRA, it invalidated the Frazier-Lemke Farm Bankruptcy Act, on the grounds that it took creditors' property without due process of law, and in *Humphrey's Executor* v. *United States* (1935) condemned the president's action in removing an obstructionist reactionary, William E. Humphrey, from the Federal Trade Commission, holding that the regulatory agencies were a part of the congressional branch of government whose members could be removed only on terms Congress dictated. In August, 1936, the Guffey-Snyder Bituminous Coal Stabilization Act, which attempted to salvage portions of the NRA codes as they applied to the soft coal industry, were invalidated, a clear indication that the Court would continue to defy the will of the other two branches of government. Not satisfied with restrictions on the federal government alone, the Court, using the Fourteenth Amendment, also denied New York the right to use its police powers to set minimum wages for women and children.

The Court in a few notable cases did sustain New Deal reforms. In three of four *Gold Cases* in 1935, it sustained the government's right to nullify the clause in private contracts calling for repayment in gold, and in the fourth case, *Perry* v. *United States,* refused the plaintiff the privilege of suing the government to force honoring of gold contracts in U.S. bonds on the grounds the plaintiffs had suffered only nominal damages. In 1936, in *Ashwander* v. *TVA,* the TVA was sustained as an operation necessary for control of navigable streams and a provision for national defense. Despite these exceptions, to many New Dealers it seemed only a matter of time until the Social Security and National Labor Relations Acts would be declared illegal. With much justification, Roosevelt acted to prevent perversion of the popular will by "nine old men living in the horse and buggy days."

The heavy Democratic majorities in the new Congress did not give the president the votes he anticipated on court reorganization. Surprisingly, a number of strong New Deal supporters, led by Montana's Senator Burton K. Wheeler, joined the opposition. Many congressmen sympathized with Roosevelt's objectives but believed only a constitutional amendment could do what he was attempting. Accusing him of trying to make a coequal branch of government subservient, they effectively used a letter from the chief justice which refuted the charge that the Court was behind in its work. For the first time, Roosevelt found he could not command a majority in Congress when the New Deal coalition divided, a development that was to occur frequently on major issues in the years ahead. In the midst of the dispute, Senator Joseph T. Robinson, the majority leader, died, and Roosevelt, regaining his political finesse, accepted a compromise on which Democrats could agree. As a result, the Judicial Procedure Reform Act was passed in August, 1937. Although it made no provision for appointing additional judges, it expedited movement of cases where constitutional questions were involved from district courts to the Supreme Court and allowed the attorney general to participate in such cases from the beginning.

Congressional reaction to the president's attempted "court packing" resulted in a two-year delay in enactment of his proposed Executive Reorganization bill, a piece of legislation the administration labeled as a "must" but did not obtain until 1939. It gave the president wide authority to consolidate and reorganize government agencies and furnished six administrative assistants to expedite the work of the executive branch.

Though public reaction to Roosevelt's proposed Court changes contributed to the loss of his invincible image, it was instrumental in breaking the Supreme Court's hamstring of progressive legislation. Chief Justice Hughes began to take a more liberal stance, and Justice Roberts, influenced by the threat to the Court's independence and by Hughes' pressure, reversed his previous stand on a number of critical votes in the spring of 1937. A Washington state minimum wage law was upheld (*West Coast Hotel Co.* v. *Parrish*) in a decision which seemed to open the way for large-scale wage and hour legislation. In the next two months, both the National Labor Relations Act and the Social Security Act were also sustained. On June 1, 1937, Justice Van Devanter retired, and Roosevelt nominated Alabama's Senator Hugo Black, a neo-Populist, as his successor. Black had earned a national reputation through Senate Investigations of government favors granted business, and, before the enactment of the NIRA, had embarrassed the administration by pressing for a law establishing a thirty-hour work week. After his confirmation, it was revealed that he had been a member of the Ku Klux Klan, but the president's confidence in him was soon sustained by the liberal positions he assumed. Thus, in the midst of the Court

reorganization dispute, Roosevelt obtained the prevailing attitude essential for his political success.

The Renewed Depression

It was fortunate that the president made peace with his party since the economy took a sudden, severe slump in September and October, 1937. This development came after a spectacular economic improvement beginning in the spring of 1936, in which, over a fifteen-month period, production, employment, and income rose above 1929 levels. Frightened by fear of inflation, the Federal Reserve system severely tightened the money supply, and the WPA cut its jobs in half, which contributed to the drastic economic reversal.

Roosevelt, realizing the new crisis required action, called Congress into special session in October, 1937, to deal with a number of problems concerning the worsening state of agriculture. Following invalidation of the First AAA, a Soil Conservation and Domestic Allotment Act had been passed in 1936 under which two-thirds of the nation's farmers were paid for conservation practices, especially the planting of soil-enriching crops. The act contained a major inadequacy, however, since it lacked effective production controls. Now, under presidential leadership, the Second Agricultural Adjustment Act was passed in February, 1938. It continued payment of $500 million annually for conservation practices but reestablished quotas and guarantees of prices somewhat below parity for corn, cotton, rice, tobacco, and wheat through government loans and storage of surpluses. The new law proved of great value to farmers until wartime demands removed many farm problems by creating an international scarcity of agricultural goods.

Reduction in wages and employment spurred the administration to obtain passage of the Fair Labor Standards Act and a greatly expanded job creation program under which the WPA, the Farm Security Administration, and other agencies received millions of dollars of additional funds. Concurrently, the Federal Reserve loosened funds, and large sums were made available to the states for matching purposes in building programs. These efforts contributed to improved conditions in the late summer of 1938, but the economy did not again reach the 1937 level until rearmament began in 1940.

In the midst of the renewed economic emergency, Roosevelt remained committed to the spirit of the Second New Deal, and in 1938 he inaugurated the most rigorous antitrust campaign since the Progressive Era. Thurman Arnold of the Yale Law School was appointed head of the Justice Department's Antitrust Division and given a large staff to ferret out unlawful combinations. Hundreds of investigations were made and scores of companies prosecuted. In a message to Congress, the president indicted the increasing concentration of economic power and obtained establishment of the Temporary National Economic Committee. After extensive hearings in 1941, it recommended only mild reforms, such as an amendment to the Clayton Antitrust Act lessening concentration of corporate resources. By that time the rearming effort made antitrust action inexpedient.

Elections of 1938

As the 1938 elections approached, Roosevelt was painfully aware of the need for the selection of additional congressmen committed to his policies. In foreign affairs many midwestern and western Democrats, who were as isolationist as Republicans from their region, warmly supported the Ludlow Amendment, which would have required a national referen-

dum to declare war unless U.S. territory was invaded. Only by strenuous efforts did Roosevelt obtain its defeat in the House by a 209 to 188 vote. On the other hand, numerous conservative, international-minded, southern, Democratic congressmen increasingly voted with Republicans on domestic questions. Many were ardent opponents of the Fair Labor Standards Act, the Farm Security Administration, and an antilynching bill which was defeated by a Senate filibuster.

Under the circumstances, Roosevelt intervened in a number of Democratic party primaries, supporting candidates to his liking. The result was disastrous, the only notable victory being the defeat of a New York City congressman. In the South, Senators Walter F. George of Georgia, Millard F. Tydings of Maryland, and "Cotton Ed" Smith of South Carolina were elected over the president's opposition after effectively using the "underdog" position in which they were placed. Roosevelt's efforts actually hurt the liberal cause, forcing progressives to take a defensive position.

The president learned his lesson well and henceforth stayed out of party primaries, but his failure had far-reaching consequences. In November, 1938, Republican gains of seven Senate and eighty House seats and the election of a number of conservative Democrats forced an end to bold administrative leadership in domestic affairs. In 1939 Roosevelt asked for additional funds to meet the economic reversal through established programs, but no new ones were projected.

The Results of the New Deal

Domestic political reaction alone did not end the reform era of F.D.R. since by 1939 his intentions had been accomplished. The essentially conservative Roosevelt, who wished to make the capitalist system work, had obtained basic reforms which gave labor, farmers, and small businessmen a new status in the American economy. Government had at last recognized that it could never be neutral in the fundamental struggles between classes and economic groups. Instead, without overturning the economic structure or destroying a class of Americans, it had embarked on taxation, regulation, welfare, and job-creation programs that guaranteed minimum returns to every producer and a measure of security to all.

In a sense the New Deal was an old-fashioned movement, many of whose leaders were more attuned to the concepts of 1910 Progressivism than modern radicalism. Yet it was caught in titanic changes and forced to experiment for viable resolutions of tremendous problems. Its answers were never ultimate and frequently subject to alteration. In seeking solutions to fundamental problems, it commanded the allegiance of a great majority of American intellectuals, many of whom abandoned the lethargy so characteristic of their class in the 1920s.

Although the changes induced by Social Security, the Fair Labor Standards Act, the AAA, TVA, and other historic measures were great, probably the most fundamental significance of the New Deal lies in its effect on the outlook of Americans. Regardless of party, except for a small minority, the scope and role allotted government in America was enormously enlarged by the New Deal experience. The leadership role of the president was magnified and the political status of hitherto neglected social, economic, and racial groups elevated. Few would deny that Roosevelt achieved much of his desire to promote social and economic democracy throughout the land.

Literature and Social Concern

The social trauma which affected America in the 1930s had a tremendous impact on the nation's intellectuals and, in particular, served as stimulus for outstanding writing. Among those most sensitive to the nation's problems was John Dos Passos who presented a panorama of American society during the first third of the century in his trilogy *U. S. A.* (1930–1936). Although he was to become a reactionary in the 1950s, in *U. S. A.* he was a caustic critic of capitalism, whose weaknesses he vividly portrayed, using a stream-of-consciousness, impressionistic depiction of what the economic system had done to many Americans.

At the time of Dos Passos' greatest achievement, James T. Farrell produced his trilogy, *Studs Lonigan* (1932–1935), which presented a naturalistic portrayal of Irish life in the Chicago slums. His work lacked the craftsmanship of Dos Passos but breathed the disdain and contempt of the oppressed. The same was true of the novels of John Steinbeck, whose *Grapes of Wrath* (1939) was probably the most popular and poignant presentation of the effects of the depression. In this work, as well as *Tortilla Flat* and *Of Mice and Men* which described the travail of the California poor, Steinbeck revealed an element of hope and understanding even of the oppressors which was lacking in Dos Passos and Farrell.

The thirties also was a period in which the historical novel became a major literary form. Most of those which appeared were syrupy accounts of the past, but there were notable exceptions. An Atlanta housewife, Margaret Mitchell, produced *Gone With the Wind,* a masterful Civil War saga of the death of the old South and the struggle of its people to survive. Though she never wrote another novel, her romanticized version of a bygone era and the realistic response to its decay etched themselves into American thought.

Two other southerners proved to be among the best of modern writers. Before his premature death in 1938, North Carolina's Thomas Wolfe wrote four major novels—*Look Homeward Angel, Of Time and the River, The Web and the Rock,* and *You Can't Go Home Again,* the last two published after his death. Like their author, Wolfe's works were oversized, inundating the reader with vivid descriptions of individual personalities and their confused, frustrated, but at times beautiful world. William Faulkner, who was also strongly influenced by his region, depicted the adversities of the Snopes, Compsons, McCaslins, and others in Yoknapatawpha, an imaginary northern Mississippi county. Though he described recognizable southern types so vividly that he stamped his own imprimatur on them, Faulkner, like all great artists, was primarily a portrayer of the human mind and spirit, a master psychologist who probed the depths of the soul. At times obscure and overly subtle, his novels, extending in time from *Soldier's Pay* in 1926 to *The Reivers* in 1962, displayed a uniformly high quality which won him Nobel and Pulitzer prizes.

Ernest Hemingway was the only American writer who challenged Faulkner for preeminence as a modern literary figure. His terse, manly style, which was at its best in describing violence and action, attracted imitators around the world. Much of his life was spent abroad —in Spain during its civil war and in France during World War II. From his Spanish experience came *For Whom the Bell Tolls* in 1940, the last of his truly successful full-length novels. In 1952, however, he published the moving saga of an elderly fisherman who, in the role Hemingway best portrayed, assumed a heroic individual struggle to survive and to conquer, in this case a great fish. *The Old Man and the Sea* earned Hemingway the Pulitzer prize in 1953.

The Good Neighbor Policy

While American authors were producing significant works and major domestic reforms were being attained in the 1930s, the United States government instituted some policies of comparable importance in foreign affairs. When Roosevelt assumed the presidency, the patchwork relationship which had maintained the postwar international settlements was coming apart. Fortunately, the new administration continued and amplified the policies of President Hoover which drew the nations of the Western Hemisphere closer together. Had it not done so, the crises of the 1930s and 1940s would have been an even greater menace to the United States. All the while, it was obvious that Latin American weakness and U.S. strength, especially in economics, would make the United States dominant in hemispheric affairs.

Early in his first term, Roosevelt was confronted with a variety of treacherous Latin American situations. Paraguay and Bolivia were at war; tension was great between Colombia and Peru; Cuba was ready to revolt against its dictator; and everywhere depression and bankruptcy increased discontent and contributed to anti-Americanism. In the midst of this turmoil, Roosevelt not only pledged himself to a "Good Neighbor" policy but also acted upon it.

One of the most critical areas concerned Cuban policy, where the president's forbearance paid handsome dividends in Latin American goodwill. With the close cooperation of Secretary of State Cordell Hull, he stayed out of two Cuban revolutions, the second of which ensconced Fulgencio Batista as ruler, and, in 1934, he formally abandoned the Platt Amendment, giving up all special concessions in Cuba except the renewed privilege granted by Cuba of maintaining a naval base at Guantanamo. Also, to aid the island's economic recovery, duties on sugar were reduced over 60 percent.

Meanwhile, the policy of disentanglement was pursued elsewhere in Latin America. Marines were withdrawn from Haiti in 1934, and the protectorate mutually agreed to in 1916 was permitted to expire in 1936. The same year, the United States negotiated a treaty with Panama which abandoned the unlimited right to intervention granted in 1903. As eventually ratified by the Senate in 1939, the United States could intervene to protect the canal against aggression but agreed to consult with Panama before doing so. In 1940 a new agreement with the Dominican Republic ended U.S. collection of Dominican customs in 1941, four years earlier than treaty agreements stipulated. By these actions, the United States removed itself from intervention in the internal affairs of Latin America, at the risk of substantial property losses of its own citizens.

The new U.S. policy transformed hemispheric relations and forestalled the plans of the Argentine foreign minister who had intended to vigorously assail the United States at the 1933 Inter-American Conference in Montevideo, Uruguay. Instead, after Secretary Hull agreed to sign a nonintervention pact, friendship for the United States increased. Roosevelt attended a special 1936 Inter-American Conference in Buenos Aires called at his instigation because of the worsening world situation. He was cordially received and obtained, in modified form, approval of plans for unified action should war threaten the hemisphere. The na-

tions agreed to refrain from military action against each other for six months should war erupt and to conduct mutual consultations. Roosevelt and Hull wanted establishment of a permanent committee to deal with aggression and war but refrained from pressing their wishes. As a result hemispheric relations continued to improve.

Disengagement was not confined to the Western Hemisphere but was also extended to the Philippines. Pressure for independence came from U.S. producers of sugar, cotton, and other commodities who wished to lessen Philippine competition, and in January, 1932, a Democratic Congress passed over President Hoover's veto the Hawes-Cutting Act which provided for independence ten years later. The measure was rejected by the Philippine legislature, but in 1934 it unanimously accepted the Tydings-McDuffie Act which decreed the Philippines would become independent in ten years but, unlike the earlier measure, provided for removal of U.S. military installations, negotiations over naval bases, and a ten-year period for gradual imposition of the U.S. tariff.

Reciprocal Trade

Secretary Hull was as firmly committed to the lowering of international economic barriers as he was to the Good Neighbor policy. During 1933 Roosevelt, who was unconvinced such a program would work, prevented its pursuit and even withheld American support of international currency stabilization. By 1934, however, the president, pleased by the decline of the dollar in international exchange, came to accept Hull's faith in tariff reduction as a means of promoting trade and friendship abroad. Therefore the Trade Agreements Act was pushed through Congress in June, 1934, authorizing the president to raise and lower rates by 50 percent in return for concessions

Cordell Hull

from other countries; to benefit, other states had to grant their lowest rates to the United States. The act was renewed in 1938, in 1940, and periodically since that time. Under Hull's zealous leadership, by 1940 agreements had been reached with powers with whom two-thirds of American foreign trade took place. By 1951 the number had grown to fifty-three countries who accounted for more than 80 percent of U.S. foreign trade. The reciprocal tariff program cut the average ad valorem tariff rate by more than two-thirds, reducing it to approximately 15 percent by 1951. Though it proved no panacea, the program increased U.S. commerce, removing one barrier in international relations.

Since Roosevelt's policies precluded U.S. political involvement to protect investments, the administration was most pointedly challenged when, after 1933, Mexican President Lázaro Cárdenas began to nationalize American land holdings and, in 1938, the property of American oil companies. Due to the astute intervention of American Ambassador Josephus Daniels and Secretary Hull, Mexico offered and Americans accepted compensation for their losses, the oil companies receiving $40 million. Relations with Mexico improved, and all Latin America gained new confidence in the United States.

The Neutrality Acts, 1935–37

While Western Hemisphere relations improved, the world situation worsened, but U.S. concern with the depression largely precluded its interest in world affairs. When the strengthening of China's position in Manchuria led Japan to occupy the area in 1931, Secretary of State Stimson in 1932 recommended the application of economic sanctions, but President Hoover, reflecting the nation's pacifist attitude, prevented action. The most Stimson could achieve was the promulgation of a doctrine named for him which asserted that the United States would recognize no treaty or agreement in the Far East obtained through force which impaired U.S. treaty rights, the integrity of China, or the Open Door policy. Soon afterwards, the League of Nations adopted the Stimson Doctrine in essence but did not back it with force.

No appreciable change in America's role was initiated by the Roosevelt administration when it assumed office, although recognition was extended the Soviet Union after Russian leaders pledged to end propaganda activities in the United States and to bolster it against possible Japanese aggression. Pacifist, isolationist attitudes grew markedly as congressional investigations, sparked by old-line Progressives, purported to show that the U.S. munitions industry was a significant cause of American entry into World War I. North Dakota's Senator Gerald P. Nye began three years of sensational hearings in 1934, culminating in a report which held incorrectly that U.S. bankers seeking to protect their Allied loans were greatly responsible for American participation. Among intellectuals the "war to end wars" was downgraded by such historians as Charles A. Beard and Charles C. Tansill, who refurbished Germany's image as a victim of propaganda and economic ruses.

Responding to popular pressure, the Congress, in hopes of avoiding war, passed a series of acts which abandoned the high-toned concept of neutrality so forcefully asserted by Woodrow Wilson in the years before World War I. In May, 1935, when the Italian dictator Mussolini instigated border clashes with the ancient African state of Ethiopia, those fearful of American involvement pressed for strict neutrality legislation. Roosevelt felt such action was futile and might even drag the country into war. Seeing the inevitability of a law, however, he indicated a preference for a measure that would allow the president to tailor his actions to favor victims and punish aggressors, but he offered no overt opposition to the bill fathered by Senate isolationists. The Neutrality Act of 1935, a short-term measure, stated that when war occurred the president must prohibit the export of arms and munitions from the United States and must not allow its ships to carry them to a belligerent power. American citizens were to be warned that travel on belligerent vessels was at their own risk.

The administration succeeded in limiting the Neutrality Act of 1935 to six months' duration, but the Neutrality Act of 1936 stiffened the law and extended it fifteen months. However, the president was given authority to determine when war existed. After he proclaimed such a condition, the extension of loans and credits to the belligerents was prohibited. Secretary Hull tried in vain to get some presidential discretion in applying the laws so that aggressors might be penalized.

As America retreated from responsibility, foreign dictators increased their conquests and plans for expansion. In October, 1935, Mussolini led Italy in a full-fledged invasion of Ethiopia, a country whose pride was exceeded only by its military impotence. Though the president immediately applied an arms embargo and would have joined in sterner sanctions, France and Britain refused, and Italy defied the League of Nations. Fear of Hitler, who had come to power in 1933 and had renounced the Versailles Treaty's limitation on Germany's military development in 1935, was paramount in determining free Europe's attitude.

In 1936 civil war erupted in Spain, and, in an effort to stay out of the conflict, the administration led Congress in January, 1937, to pass a joint resolution extending the neutrality laws to cover civil wars. It soon became apparent that Hitler and Mussolini, who had formed the Rome-Berlin Axis, were giving decisive support to General Francisco Franco, the Spanish dictator. Roosevelt made no effort to revise his policy, in part because of strong Catholic sympathy for Franco.

The ultimate in America's effort to isolate itself came in the Neutrality Act of 1937. Though the president was given more discretion in determining when war existed, he received no greater leeway in embargoing arms and credit. Significantly, for the first time, sale of nonmilitary goods to belligerents was placed on a strictly "cash and carry" basis for a two-year period.

Soon after the Neutrality Act of 1937 was passed, the world moved closer to a major war. In July, 1937, Chinese resistance to Japanese movements near Peking initiated full-scale war in China, although a formal declaration of war was not issued, and Japan began wholesale construction of warships. Since President Roosevelt refused to classify the conflict as a war, the neutrality legislation was not invoked against China who still received loans and goods, but this policy also allowed Japan to buy arms in America. In March, 1938, Hitler moved into Austria, annexing it to Germany, and in September, 1938, Britain and France surrendered the Czechoslovakian Sudetenland at Munich. During all these developments, America had done nothing to strengthen the democracies' resistance to aggression but had contributed to the appeasement which made war inevitable.

The Quarantine Speech

Roosevelt, who had never agreed with the neutrality legislation, was able to do little to reverse the course of aggression. Concern with domestic economic problems and the prevailing isolationist spirit limited American action in 1937 to a plea for international reaffirmation of moral action and the dispatch of 1,200 additional troops to Shanghai, where they joined some 2,000 other American troops in China.

In October, 1937, conscious of the increasingly serious situation, the president, prompted by Hull, delivered a plea for international cooperation in a speech in Chicago, the heart of isolationist country. By an impetuous gesture, typical of Roosevelt when aroused, the president castigated "the present reign of terror and international lawlessness" and urged an international quarantine of aggressors. He warned that if aggression was not contained the American people would not escape and advocated the severance of all relations with its perpetrators.

The president's rational appeal shocked a nation which had not come to grips with current realities. In part he was responsible for not devoting more of his unique ability in mass communication to foreign affairs. Uninformed and frightened, thousands of Americans deluged the White House with protests. Reluctantly, Roosevelt, who was again confronted with a revived depression, abandoned efforts to obtain a more vigorous foreign policy. A nine-power Brussels conference, in which the U.S. participated, confined itself to sanctimonious pleas. Following this evidence of weakness, the Japanese sank three Standard Oil tankers and the U.S. gunboat *Panay* in Chinese waters, after which the U.S. government contented itself with demands for apologies and reparations. The Japanese willingly apologized for the *Panay's* destruction, paid a $2 million indemnity, and contended the incident had been the result of mistaken identity.

In early 1938, Roosevelt did propose to the British government the calling of an international conference which would attempt to revive international law, reduce armaments, and promote economic security. At first Prime Minister Neville Chamberlain, who was attempting to appease Hitler, refused, but Foreign Secretary Anthony Eden forced acceptance. Eden's resignation in February, 1938, and Hitler's Austrian invasion in March, 1938, led to a scuttling of these efforts. As the international outlook deteriorated, Congress, in May, 1938, over vigorous pacifist protests, approved a naval construction program which envisioned a billion dollars' expenditure within a decade. Later, in response to the president's prompting, additional appropriations were made to allow construction of a true "two-ocean" navy.

The European Situation Worsens

Large additional military expenditures were obtained by the administration in late 1938 and 1939 as Hitler's actions began to arouse the people. Many Americans became alarmed when he began vicious persecution of Jews in November, 1938, increased subversive activities in Latin America, and, in March, 1939, seized most of the remainder of Czechoslovakia. Over Argentine opposition at a Lima conference in December, 1938, Secretary Hull obtained Pan-American rededication to prevent "all foreign intervention or activities that may threaten" the Western Hemisphere.* The administration's main goal became modification of the neutrality laws so that the United States could aid Hitler's opponents.

From spring until the early fall of 1939 Roosevelt tried earnestly to obtain amendment of the Neutrality Act of 1937 to permit the sale of arms and other war materials on a cash and carry basis. Despite a state visit of King George VI and Queen Elizabeth of Great Britain, a majority of the Congress refused to budge. When World War II began in Europe in early September, 1939, following Hitler's invasion of Poland, the president invoked the Neutrality Act but stated that he did not ask Americans to be neutral in thought. Soon thereafter he called Congress into special session to consider his previous proposals for changes in the neutrality laws and exclusion of American ships from the war zones. Within a month Congress complied, an indication that American public opinion was at last beginning to change. The American people were indignant at Hitler's conquest of Poland and horrified at Russia's participation in the process and its invasion of Finland in November, 1939, a prelude to

---

*In September, 1939, at Panama the American states agreed to a common policy if transfer of European possessions in America threatened the hemisphere.

months of gallant resistance before surrender in March, 1940. In February, 1940, Roosevelt dispatched Undersecretary of State Sumner Welles to the major European capitals, but, due to Hitler's unwillingness to compromise, no overtures for peace could be developed. After months of quiet in the West, Hitler's blitzkrieg moved with shocking rapidity in April, 1940, when Denmark and Norway were taken. The low countries fell in May, and, following the occupation of Paris on June 13, France surrendered.

In this gravest crisis, Roosevelt moved as rapidly as he could to lead public opinion. To aid in obtaining Republican support for a bipartisan foreign policy, he named two Republicans to strategic cabinet positions—Henry L. Stimson, who had held the same position in Taft's cabinet, as secretary of war and Frank Knox as secretary of the navy. In April, 1940, to avert Nazi capture of Greenland, he announced its American protection under the Monroe Doctrine. As France fell, he proclaimed the end of American isolation by stating the United States would furnish supplies to the opponents of aggression, and he pressured Congress for a billion dollars in additional defense funds. Large quantities of military supplies were furnished private firms who in turn sold them to Britain. This aid was critical, since much British equipment had been lost when the evacuation was made from Dunkirk as the Germans overran France. From August to October, 1940, the German *Luftwaffe* directed thousand-plane attacks against British cities in an effort to destroy the will to resist. Instead, led by Winston Churchill, who had become prime minister in May, 1940, the Royal Air Force and the British people resisted superbly. After losing almost twice as many planes as the British, the Germans converted to night raids and "the Battle for Britain" continued through the winter of 1940–41.

Churchill quickly indicated to Roosevelt

A Sheffield street after night bombing during the Battle for Britain, December 14, 1940.

The Election of 1940

Inevitably the international crisis projected itself into the 1940 presidential election. Until near the convention, it seemed certain the Republican nominee would be an old-line isolationist like Senator Robert A. Taft of Ohio, who had only begun to change his views. However, stirred by the fall of France only days before, the delegates chose Indiana's Wendell L. Willkie, a former Democrat and advocate of aid to Britain. Though as president of Commonwealth and Southern he was one of the nation's most successful business tycoons and an ardent opponent of TVA, he was a moderate on domestic issues who accepted much of the New Deal.

Roosevelt engineered his own nomination for an unprecedented third term by keeping

that Britain must have sizable quantities of supplies and forty to fifty destroyers to survive. Against the advice of some military planners, who urged concentration on self-defense, the president decided to back the British. Throughout the summer and fall of 1940, a great public debate ensued. Pro-Nazi forces, including Father Coughlin, Gerald L. K. Smith, and Anne Morrow Lindbergh, joined militant liberals, such as Senators Gerald P. Nye and Burton K. Wheeler, in opposing the abandonment of isolationism. Their most effective organization, the America First Committee, headed by Sears, Roebuck and Company Chairman Robert E. Wood, staged massive rallies and distributed much propaganda urging America to concentrate on defending itself. Its work was effectively countered by the Committee to Defend America by Aiding the Allies, which even obtained inclusion of a plank in the Republican party platform approving aid to those people "fighting for liberty." Daily, pro-Allied sentiment grew in the United States though an isolationist minority remained until December 7, 1941.

Wendell L. Willkie

The Age of Roosevelt 243

quiet and not repressing his supporters. When the Democratic convention opened, he sent a message stating his desire to retire but implying he would accept a draft. Though many of the party pros would have preferred someone else, Roosevelt was quickly renominated. He insisted on the selection of Secretary of Agriculture Henry A. Wallace as the vice-presidential candidate in the belief that a more liberal running mate was essential both to win and to advance the reform program. Opposition of many professional politicians and conservatives, especially southerners, was overcome only by vigorous political pressure.

For several months, Roosevelt neglected the campaign to concentrate on the nation's rearmament and diplomatic efforts. In July, 1940, he obtained from the Pan-American foreign ministers' meeting in Havana a declaration that an attack on one American republic would be considered an attack on all. In September an agreement was reached whereby Great Britain received fifty reconditioned World War I destroyers in return for a ninety-nine year lease of eight bases extending from Newfoundland to British Guiana. This obvious abandonment of neutrality was quickly followed by the enactment of the first peacetime draft in American history which provided for the training of 1,200,000 troops and 800,000 reserves in a one-year period.

While Roosevelt wrestled with foreign affairs and rearmament, Willkie, whose good nature and Hoosier background made him a good campaigner, took his views to the people. He questioned New Deal efficiency and Roosevelt's threats to constitutional government through personal rule while advocating an internationalist foreign policy. Yet by October, when it was obvious Willkie's campaign was proving ineffective against Roosevelt, he began to attack the administration for policies which he predicted would lead to war within five months if the president were reelected. Spurred by fear of defeat, Roosevelt made five major speeches in which he defended the New Deal reforms and his foreign policy. In a Boston address he made an unwarranted pledge which would return to haunt him: "I have said this before, but I shall say it again and again and again. Your boys are not going to be sent into any foreign war."

Encouraged by his assurance, the electorate proved unwilling to abandon Roosevelt's experience in time of crisis, especially when many feared Republican control would jeopardize New Deal reforms. As a result, the president was easily reelected, carrying all the states except ten, most of which were in the midwest and plains area. He had almost a 5 million vote majority and received 449 electoral votes to Willkie's 82. Both at home and abroad, his reelection was interpreted as an endorsement for aid to Britain and continued opposition to Nazi tyranny.

To many, perhaps even the president, 1933 seemed far away. Under Roosevelt's leadership, substantial changes had been effected in domestic life; the depths of isolationism had been reached; and, although some suspected it was too late, the nation had begun to play an important role in world affairs. Whether it could avert military disaster and continue domestic reform remained major questions.

Selected Bibliography

The period is effectively surveyed in W. E. Leuchtenburg, *Franklin D. Roosevelt and the New Deal: 1932–1940** (1963). The most complete study of the New Deal is being written by Arthur Schlesinger, Jr.; two of its volumes, *The Coming of the New Deal** (1959) and *The Politics of Upheaval** (1960), carry the story to 1936. Brief but informative studies include Dexter Perkins, *The New Age of Franklin Roosevelt, 1932–1945** (1957), and John A. Woods, *Roosevelt and Modern America* (1967).

The most adequate biographies of Roosevelt are multivolume works which do not reach the presidential years. They are Frank Freidel, *Franklin D. Roosevelt* (3 vols. to date, 1952–1956), and Kenneth S. Davis, *F.D.R.: The Beckoning of Destiny, 1892–1928, A History* (1972). Useful one-volume biographies of Roosevelt include James M. Burns, *Roosevelt: The Lion and the Fox** (1956), and Rexford G. Tugwell, *The Democratic Roosevelt; A Biography of Franklin D. Roosevelt** (1969). M. S. Venkataramani, *The Sunny Side of F.D.R.* (1973), provides much insight by a study of his humor. The opinions of two important cabinet members are given in Frances Perkins, *The Roosevelt I Knew** (1946), and John M. Blum, *From the Morgenthau Diaries: Years of Crisis, 1928–1938* (repr. of the 1959 ed., 1965) and *Years of Urgency, 1938–1941* (1965).

The plight of the people is well presented in Dixon Wecter, *The Age of the Great Depression, 1929–1941** (1971); Walter J. Stein, *California and the Dust Bowl Migration* (1973), and Sophonisba P. Breckinridge, *Women in the Twentieth Century: A Study of Their Political, Social and Economic Activities* (repr. of 1933 ed., 1972). The administration's effort to promote recovery by inflation is covered in Broadus Mitchell, *Depression Decade, From New Era through New Deal, 1929–1941** (1969). Raymond Moley and Elliot A. Rosen treat *The First New Deal* (1966). Hopkin's important role in changing administrative policies is analyzed in Searle F. Charles, *Minister of Relief: Harry Hopkins and the Depression* (1963).

Labor's new role is assessed in Philip Taft, *The A.F. of L. from the Death of Gompers to the Merger* (repr. of 1959 ed., 1970), and Walter Galenson, *The C.I.O. Challenge to the A.F.L., A History of the American Labor Movement, 1935–1941* (1960). Sidney Fine, *Sit Down: The General Motors Strike of 1936–1937* (1969), presents in detail one method used effectively by the C.I.O. Horace R. Cayton and George S. Mitchell describe the relationship between *Black Workers and the New Unions* (repr. of 1939 ed., 1969). Gunnar Myrdal, *An American Dilemma: The Negro Problem and Modern Democracy** (2 vols. 20th an. ed., 1962), deals with black problems generally.

Paul K. Conkin, *F.D.R. and the Origins of the Welfare State* (1967), chronicles the reform of the Second New Deal. Edwin E. Witte presents

---

*Available in paperback.

*The Development of the Social Security Act** (1962). David E. Lilienthal, *TVA, Democracy on the March* (1953) and *The Journals of David E. Lilienthal* (5 vols., 1964–1971) are accounts of TVA from one of its major architects.

Donald R. McCoy, *Angry Voices: Left-of-Center Politics in the New Deal Era* (repr. of 1958 ed., 1971), recounts the role of left-wing movements while T. Harry Williams, *Huey Long* (1969), is a biography of the most important of their leaders. Donald R. McCoy, *Landon of Kansas* (1966), is a fine study of Roosevelt's 1936 opponent. J. Joseph Huthmacher, *Senator Robert F. Wagner and the Rise of Urban Liberalism** (1971), gives much insight into the growth of liberal strength, while George Wolfskill presents *The Revolt of the Conservatives: A History of the American Liberty League, 1934–1940* (1962). Norman D. Markowitz, *The Rise and Fall of the People's Century: Henry A. Wallace and American Liberalism, 1941–1948* (1973), analyzes Wallace's career and the forces which supported it.

The court controversy is reviewed in Robert H. Jackson, *The Struggle for Judicial Supremacy, A Study of a Crisis in American Power Politics* (1941), and Edward S. Corwin, *Constitutional Revolution* (1941).

For a survey of developments in fiction see Willard Thorp, *American Writing in the Twentieth Century* (1960), and Robert E. Spiller et al., *Literary History of the United States* (3rd ed., 3 vols. in 2, 1966), for essays on major writers. Incisive appraisal of the nation's two most eminent modern writers is in Dean Schmitter, *William Faulkner** (1973), and Carlos Baker, *Hemingway: The Writer As Artist** (4th ed., 1973).

Roosevelt's foreign policy to 1940 is surveyed in Robert A. Divine, *The Reluctant Belligerent: American Entry into World War II** (1965); Dexter Perkins, *The New Age of Franklin Roosevelt, 1932–1945;* and John E. Wiltz, *From Isolation to War, 1931–1941** (1968). Secretary Hull's important career is carefully detailed in Julius W. Pratt, *Cordell Hull, 1933–1944* (2 vols., 1964) and *The Memoirs of Cordell Hull* (2 vols., 1948). *Roosevelt's Good Neighbor Policy* (1950) is the subject of Edward O. Guerrant and of Bryce Wood, *The Making of the Good Neighbor Policy** (1967). D. M. Dozier, *Are We Good Neighbors?* (repr. of 1959 ed., 1972), questions its altruism.

Isolationism and Roosevelt's troubled reactions toward it and aggression are presented in Robert A. Divine, *The Illusion of Neutrality** (1968); Donald F. Drummond, *The Passing of American Neutrality, 1937–1941* (repr. of 1955 ed., 1968); and Manfred Jonas, *Isolationism in America, 1935–1941** (1969). Selig Adler deals with *The Isolationist Impulse: Its Twentieth Century Reaction* (1957). The fullest account is by the moderately pro-Roosevelt William L. Langer and S. Everett Gleason, *The Challenge to Isolation, 1937–1940* (1952), which emphasizes the complexity of foreign relations. Basil Rauch, *Roosevelt From Munich to Pearl Harbor; A Study in the Creation of a Foreign Policy* (1967), is full of praise for the president; the opposite view is taken in Charles A. Beard, *American Foreign Policy in the Making, 1932–1940: A Study in Responsibilities* (repr. of 1946 ed., 1968).

Events
Leading To
War

1940   **Rome-Berlin-Tokyo Axis formed**

1941   **Lend-Lease Act**

               United States embargo on sale of oil and other materials to Japan

               Meeting of Roosevelt and Churchill

               American navy ordered to attack German ships and aircraft in United States "defensive waters"

               Final negotiations begin with Japan

               Attack on Pearl Harbor

Major United States
Military Encounters

1942   **Battles of Macassar Strait, the Java Sea, the Coral Sea, and Midway**

1942–43   **Guadalcanal and North African campaigns**

1943–45   **Sicilian and Italian campaigns**

1944   **D-Day**

               Battle of Leyte Gulf

               Invasion of southern France

1944–45   **Battle of the Bulge**

1945   **Iwo Jima campaign**

               Germany invaded

               A-bomb attacks

22

World War II and Its Aftermath

Long-Range Developments

For Economics and Corporate Enterprise

The enormous industrial and military development of the United States during World War II resulted in its emergence as one of the world's two major powers.

The use of government wartime controls prompted the return to price and wage controls when an economic crisis emerged in the early 1970s.

For Democratic Government

Diplomatic and military experience gained during the war permitted the United States effectively to lead the anti-Communist coalition after 1946.

The close wartime relationship between Great Britain and the United States became the basis for a significant postwar collaboration which greatly influenced international affairs.

American leadership in the rehabilitation of non-Communist countries and support of NATO and other military opponents of Communism made possible the relative stability of the 1970s and détente with Russia and China.

For the Westward Movement, Nationalism, and Expansion

American wartime military achievements resulted in immense national self-confidence and contributed to postwar disillusionment, in the 1950s especially, when many national and international problems proved extremely difficult.

For Civil Liberties, Freedom, and Reform

The improved standard of living attained by many Americans during the war served as the basis for further advances after 1945.

The U.S. Abandons
Its Neutrality

Roosevelt's third inauguration in January, 1941, came at a time of American concern with the European war, and a small segment of Americans would have welcomed war with Germany because of their sympathy with the Allies and fear that Hitler's ultimate goal was conquest of the United States. However, Roosevelt reflected the view of the great majority, who wished to stay out of the war while, at the same time, contributing to Hitler's defeat. The incongruity of these desires produced tension and debate before the constant erosion of U.S. neutrality led to war.

In December, 1940, Prime Minister Winston Churchill in a forceful letter correctly presented the British plight to Roosevelt. Over two-thirds of British funds in America had been expended; Hitler could be defeated only if the United States would provide the supplies which the British had been obtaining on a cash and carry basis. Moreover, Churchill pointed out, the submarine menace was growing, and America must aid in keeping the vital North Atlantic route open.

By mid-December, 1940, Roosevelt had developed a program to aid Britain whose essential features were presented to the people. Unabashedly he proposed to make the United States "the great arsenal of democracy" whose goods would be loaned or leased to the Allies and payment decided upon after the coming of peace. Using a masterful comparison, he likened the Allied condition to that of a man whose house was afire. In such a crisis, his neighbor would quickly been him a garden hose, and only after the fire had beed put out would any consideration be given to compensation.

To implement this philosophy, Roosevelt proposed the Lend-Lease bill, which contained an initial allocation of $7 billion, and, though popularly approved, encountered stern opposition in Congress for two months. It was enacted in March, 1941, passing the House by a vote of 317 to 71 and the Senate by 60 to 31. Two weeks later, the Germans intensified their submarine campaign, sending large numbers of additional craft into the North Atlantic and extending the war zone beyond Iceland almost to Greenland.

German action threatened to neutralize the Lend-Lease Act by impeding the flow of goods to Britain. Over 500,000 tons of merchant shipping were lost in March and May, 1941, and over 650,000 tons in April, results which would have been worse had the president not begun steps to counteract the German policy. In late March and early April, he opened American navy yards to repair British vessels, gave the British ten Coast Guard cutters for antisubmarine use, signed an agreement with Denmark to defend Greenland, and extended American patrol of the Atlantic almost to Iceland. While American vessels were not authorized to attack German submarines, they served as spies for the British, informing them of German submarine locations. Following the German torpedoing of the *Robin Moor,* an American freighter, in May, 1941, the president disclosed his actions and pledged steps would be taken to keep goods flowing to Britain.

The attention of the world was diverted on June 22, 1941, when Hitler launched a surprise attack against Russia. In July Roosevelt sent Harry Hopkins to Moscow, and his report that Russia would assume the offensive in the summer of 1942 led to the extension of Lend-Lease aid. Meanwhile, the international crisis required an extension of draftees' terms of service for eighteen months and permission to send them outside the Western Hemisphere. After a month's consideration, the measure passed in early August, 1941, with a close vote in the House of 203 to 202.

Concurrently, the necessity of keeping the North Atlantic open led to increasingly provocative American actions. In July, Iceland agreed to occupation by U.S. Marines, and the U.S. Navy began to convoy American and Icelandic vessels between the United States and Iceland. If molested, the navy was ordered to attack.

In August, 1941, as a result of Hopkins' July stopover in London en route to Moscow, Roosevelt and Churchill met aboard the U.S.S. *Augusta* off Argentina, Newfoundland. To obtain the meeting, Churchill agreed not to discuss U.S. entry into the war or territorial or

President Roosevelt and Prime Minister Churchill on board the Augusta *during the Atlantic Charter meeting in August 1941. Standing at left are Harry Hopkins and Averell Harriman.*

economic changes. Despite this, the talks were highly significant since mutual goals were articulated and rapport enhanced.

Earlier in the year, the president in his State of the Union message had enunciated "Four Freedoms" to which all mankind was entitled: freedom of speech and expression, freedom of worship, freedom from want, and freedom from fear. These concepts were reaffirmed when the president proclaimed a state of unlimited national emergency in May, 1941, and he and Churchill issued the Atlantic Charter which reiterated the Four Freedoms and outlined policies to attain them. The Charter renounced territorial aggrandizement, proposed the peoples involved should approve territorial changes and the form of government under which they lived, and advocated easing trade restrictions and equal access to raw materials. It supported cooperative action to improve the economy and security of people while urging establishment of freedom of the seas and disarmament of aggressor nations until a permanent peace structure was established.

The president's policy in effect launched the nation in an undeclared naval war, the actual aggressive step being taken in September, 1941, when, following a U-boat attack on the destroyer *Greer,* which had been spying for the British, Roosevelt ordered the U.S. Navy to attack German and Italian aircraft, submarines, and surface raiders in U.S. "defensive waters" which included the route to Iceland. October 9, 1941, Roosevelt belatedly asked Congress to revise the Neutrality Act of 1939 to permit the arming of merchant vessels and the carrying of goods to belligerents. While a fierce debate ensued in Congress on the question, a German submarine torpedoed the destroyer *Kearney,* killing 11 sailors, and sank another destroyer, the *Reuben James,* with the loss of 115 men. In early November, 1941, the president's recommendations regarding neutrality were ap-

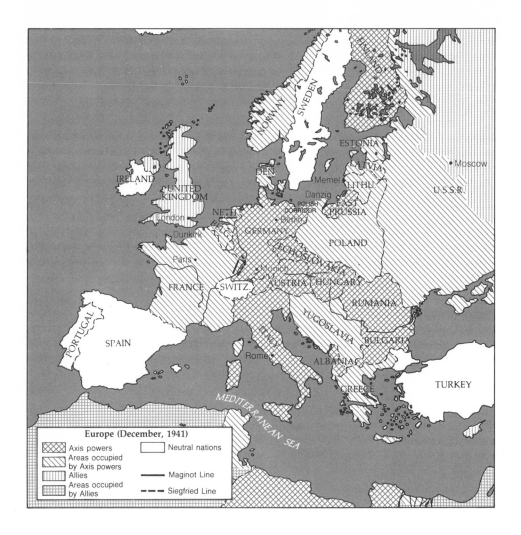

Europe (December, 1941)

⊠ Axis powers	☐ Neutral nations
⊘ Areas occupied by Axis powers	
⊟ Allies	── Maginot Line
⊞ Areas occupied by Allies	- - - Siegfried Line

proved by votes of 50 to 37 in the Senate and 212 to 94 in the House. To all well-informed persons, it was apparent that a declared war with Germany might come at any time.

The Embargo on Japanese Trade

The rupture of relations with Japan came after much more extensive contacts and negotiations than the United States had with Ger-many. It was also characterized by a vacillation of attitude during which the two countries almost reached a compromise.

Shortly before its resignation due to popular opposition to its appeasement policies, the Chamberlain government in Britain recognized Japanese control of the Far Eastern areas it occupied. Stunned, Roosevelt abrogated a 1911 Japanese-American commercial treaty, serving warning that within six months the U.S. would possibly end sale of such vital war materials as oil, iron, and steel. Public opinion in the United

States, partially due to racism, was strongly anti-Japanese and would have welcomed such action, but when the Tokyo government proved willing to talk, Secretary Cordell Hull and others obtained delays, hoping to gain Japanese concessions in China. Apparently these conciliatory moves would have been forthcoming had war not erupted in Europe in the fall of 1939, leaving the United States and Russia alone to face Japan in Asia. In July, 1940, a more militant government headed by Prince Fumimaro Konoye came to power, and General Hideki Tojo became war minister. Among its first triumphs was an alliance with Hitler and Mussolini in September, 1940, the Rome-Berlin-Tokyo Axis, which projected Japanese conquests of British, Dutch, and French holdings in Asia.

As the American government perceived changes in Japanese policies after the Konoye government took command, its position hardened, and it levied an embargo on prime scrap metal, aviation gasoline, and other petroleum products to Japan. To insure its success, on September 26, 1940, a complete embargo aimed at Japan was placed on scrap iron and steel excluding their shipment outside the Western Hemisphere except to Great Britain. When the Japanese concluded an agreement with Hitler's puppet Vichy government in France to establish bases in northern Indochina, the U.S. extended a $25 million loan to China. This was followed by a $100 million loan to Chiang Kai-shek's government in late November, 1940, after Japan recognized a rival Chinese regime.

Alarmed by these developments and joint American, British, and Dutch military planning for the Western Pacific which began in January, 1941, the Konoye government in March and April, 1941, obtained a pledge of Russian neutrality and assurance from Germany's Foreign Minister Joachim von Ribbentrop that Germany would go to war with Russia if it attacked Japan after Japan had gone to war with the western democracies. Concurrently, Japan attempted to come to terms with the United States. In January, 1941, Konoye, using a Roman Catholic bishop and priest as message carriers, indicated he was willing to abandon his German alliance, withdraw the military from China, and improve economic relations in return for U.S. considerations. As always in Japanese matters, Hull was skeptical, but when a new ambassador, Admiral Kichisaburo Nomura, arrived, he began discussions with him in March, 1941. Hull demanded withdrawal from China and renouncement of aggression, an unimaginatively stiff position which the incompetent Nomura garbled in relaying to Tokyo. In May, 1941, under the influence of the militant foreign minister, Yosuke Matsuoka, Japan proposed a complete U.S. retreat as the basis for an understanding, including resumption of trade, an end to U.S. immigration restrictions against Japanese, the end of U.S. aid to Britain, and use of its influence to force Chiang Kai-shek to come to terms.

The Roosevelt administration continued negotiations because it knew that strong forces in Japan wished to reach an understanding. These more moderate elements almost gained the ascendancy in June, 1941, before Hitler's invasion of Russia lessened fears of war. After that event, Japan made plans to move into southern Indochina while Matsuoka urged an attack on Russia and an end to U.S. negotiations. Although his radicalism led to his removal in July, 1941, the government committed itself to advance to the south even at the risk of war with the United States and Britain. Concurrently, it attempted to end hostilities in China and, at least temporarily, avoid war with Russia.

The Roosevelt administration's decisive reaction to the Japanese agreement with Vichy France for occupation of southern Indochina led to potentially fruitful negotiations with Japan. The president, in an interview with the Japanese ambassador, threatened war if the Dutch East Indies were molested. At the same time, he promised to obtain raw materials for Japan and a neutralization of Indochina if Japan would withdraw. On the other hand, he impounded Japanese funds in the United States, closed the Panama Canal to Japanese shipping, and, on August 1, 1941, placed an embargo on the sale of oil to Japan, which might be converted to aviation gasoline and other strategic materials.

Under great pressure from naval leaders to avoid a U.S. war, the Konoye government tried desperately to avert it and retain Indochina. Konoye twice urged a direct meeting with Roosevelt, but the president replied that the United States would take steps to protect itself and that it would resume negotiations only if Japan wished to reach an agreement along earlier proposed lines. Konoye replied that Japan would withdraw from Indochina when the dispute in China proper was settled, pledged not to move southward or against Russia, and even acknowledged that the American principles formed the basis for peace. In September, 1941, the Japanese government agreed not to be obligated by its German alliance to go to war with the United States should the U.S. wage a "defensive war" with Germany.

Secretary Hull's intervention at this point insured war. Roosevelt was prepared to agree immediately to a conference with Konoye, but Hull insisted on a proper China settlement as a preliminary. Roosevelt followed Hull's policy in the mistaken belief that Japan would not attack, but Japan, confronted by apparent American unwillingness to come to reasonable terms and the necessity of obtaining embargoed materials, turned to army leaders who advocated movement to the south. Konoye sent a special representative to Washington who, on October 13, 1941, proposed an evacuation of China to Undersecretary of State Sum-

ner Welles. In Japan, however, General Tojo, the war minister, vetoed such a proposal, and Konoye resigned October 16. His fall, to which American intransigence contributed, hastened the coming of war.

The Attack on Pearl Harbor

After Konoye's fall, the debate between the Japanese army and navy intensified. Shigenori Togo, the new foreign minister, urged relinquishment of China to avert conflict, but the army preferred the risks of war to economic strangulation. November 5, 1941, the army leaders consented to one final effort for compromise, but the Emperor endorsed the issuance of orders for an attack in early December should the negotiations fail. Discussions continued uninterruptedly in Washington from November 7 until December 7, and after November 17, Saburo Kurusu, a special envoy, joined Ambassador Nomura in presenting the Japanese position. The key question hinged on U.S. demands for evacuation of southern Indochina, while Japan insisted on a package deal but included in it some major concessions. It proposed a joint guarantee of access to raw materials in the Dutch East Indies, restoration of Japanese-American trade, no U.S. intervention in Japanese efforts to make peace with China, Japanese agreement to evacuate all of Indochina upon conclusion of a Sino-Japanese peace, and a mutual promise not to invade any area in Southeastern Asia or the South Seas except Indochina.

Nomura was certain the Japanese proposals would avert war, but the United States was unwilling to accept them, feeling it would make the nation a party to Japan's conquest of East Asia. Acting on the president's orders, the State Department countered by preparing proposals which modified those of Japan primarily by providing for immediate, unconditional evacuation of southern Indochina. Unfortunately the counterproposals were not submitted due to British and Chinese opposition and news of Japanese troop movements off Formosa. On November 22, 1941, an intercepted Japanese message, translatable because the Japanese code had been broken, revealed that Japan would refuse a true compromise and that after November 29 "things are automatically going to happen." On November 26, Secretary Hull demanded Japan evacuate not only southern Indochina but China also and that it support Chiang Kai-shek's Nationalist government. Even then war was not unalterably decided upon until December 1, after Roosevelt had rejected Nomura and Kurusu's personal overtures.

By November 25, 1941, a carrier fleet had left the Kurile Islands with planes which on order would attack Pearl Harbor, while troops were amassed in southern Indochina to strike at Malaya. Washington knew of the latter movements and that an attack was imminent. On December 6 the president appealed to Emperor Hirohito to avert war, but he and the U.S. military were completely surprised by the attack on Hawaii. The final sections of the reply to Hull's November 26 note were not decoded and delivered until after the attack.

American military and naval leaders in the Pacific had been warned of the likelihood of surprise attacks as early as November 24, 1941, but no action was taken to protect the vulnerable U.S. fleet at Honolulu. Admiral Husband E. Kimmel had concentrated most of his Pacific fleet at Pearl Harbor, an unwise policy which his predecessor had opposed so zealously that he had been removed, and General Walter C. Short dispersed his planes and antiaircraft guns to avoid potential sabotage in such a manner that they were largely ineffective. But the military and political leaders in Washington were also responsible for the tragedy since they failed to assess the intelligence they received and to communicate it to Pacific leaders.

Two waves of almost 200 planes each which struck at 7:55 and 8:50 A.M. on December 7, 1941, were unopposed except by a few army planes and antiaircraft guns. Two battleships, the *Arizona* and *Oklahoma,* were sunk, six others in the harbor damaged, virtually every plane on the island destroyed or damaged, over

Burning and damaged ships after the Pearl Harbor attack. Left to right:
U.S.S. West Virginia, *U.S.S.* Tennessee, *U.S.S.* Arizona.

2,300 servicemen killed and half as many wounded. Never had U.S. forces suffered such a shattering blow. At the same time, Japanese attacks were launched against the Phillippines, Wake and Midway Islands, Malaya, Hong Kong, and other areas. War was declared against both the United States and Great Britain. A daring, surprise attack had given the Japanese a great advantage in a conflict many of their leaders did not believe they could win. Yet fortunately for the United States, the carriers and cruisers operating out of Pearl Harbor were not at the base at the time of the attack, and the Japanese did not try to destroy the torpedo shop, submarine base, or valuable ammunition supplies. Neither did they attempt a landing in Hawaii which would probably have succeeded and driven the U.S. defense line

President Roosevelt signing the declaration of war against Japan.

back to the Pacific coast, although some high-ranking Japanese naval officers had advocated such a plan before the attack.

Immediately after the tragedy at Pearl Harbor, on December 8, 1941, President Roosevelt, before a joint session of Congress, described December 7 as "a day that shall live in infamy" and castigated Japan for its "unprovoked and dastardly attack." His request for a declaration of war quickly passed the Senate unanimously and the House with only one dissenting vote. On December 11, Germany and Italy, complying with Japanese wishes, declared war against the United States; the Axis alliance was working exactly as it was designed to work. On the president's recommendation, Congress declared war against them later the same day.

The nature of the sneak, surprise attack united the American people in a way nothing else could. Shock was soon replaced by anger and almost universal desire to participate in the war effort.

Organization for Victory

America entered World War II better prepared than in previous wars, due to the mobilization which had begun months earlier. On September 16, 1940, the Burke-Wadsworth Act had established the nation's first peacetime draft, and when war came approximately 1.6 million men were in the U.S. Army and 400,000 in the U.S. Navy and Marine Corps. Congress quickly approved the registration of all men between twenty and forty-four for potential drafting, and by November, 1942, the age for draftees was lowered to eighteen and an upper limit placed at thirty-eight. Over 15 million were drafted or had volunteered by 1945. They received training of a diversity hitherto unknown due to the requirements of more sophisticated equipment and the prospects of fighting under varying conditions.

The U.S. war machine was based upon an enormous industrial expansion which took place without seriously disrupting the civilian economy. Manufacturing output almost doubled during the war, and farm production increased 22 percent. Difficulties arose, however, particularly in the first eighteen months of war, in the allocation of scarce materials and coordination of industrial efforts. Roosevelt, who was superb in galvanizing popular support, experimented with centralized direction. In May, 1940, nineteen months before American involvement, the National Defense Advisory Commission (NDAC), a World War I agency, had been reestablished to direct industrial mobilization. As the crucial need for materials both for rearmament and for the allies increased, the NDAC's power proved inadequate, and it was superseded by the Office of Production Management in January, 1941. Its

Civilian women producing plane parts in a Michigan plant.

limited authority, which many ascribed to the president's fear of concentrated production control, was insufficient to deal with full-scale war.

Therefore in January, 1942, Roosevelt obtained establishment of the War Production Board, headed by Donald Nelson, a Sears, Roebuck and Company executive, to direct economic activities and make specific allocations of strategic materials. It achieved a great deal despite Nelson's failure to take assignment of priorities out of military hands and to see that smaller companies received a just share of war contracts. In May, 1943, the president transferred much of the board's authority to the Office of War Mobilization whose head, James F. Byrnes, resigned from the Supreme Court to become the nation's economic czar.

Byrnes also dealt effectively with inflation, an achievement that had eluded the government over a period of almost two years. As early as August, 1941, the president had established the Office of Price Administration (OPA), but it lacked power to hold the line even after an April, 1942, general price and rent freeze. Wages and farm prices were not effectively controlled, the latter being allowed by law to rise to 110 percent of parity. In January, 1942, the War Labor Board had been established to settle disputes, and in July it allowed workers for the "Little Steel" companies to receive a 15 percent cost of living wage increase. This formula, which tied wage increases to that of the cost of living, was applied to other industries but was rejected by John L. Lewis, who called a national strike of mine workers in May, 1943. The strike was broken when Roosevelt seized the mines and threatened to draft the miners, but Lewis obtained a raise larger than the prescribed formula by obtaining compensation for shorter lunch periods and travel time.

The drift toward inflation was broken in the spring of 1943 under Byrnes' leadership when Roosevelt vetoed a law allowing exclusion of government payments in determining parity levels, and the OPA began a campaign which reduced retail prices of meat, coffee, and butter by 10 percent. The Anti-Inflation Act of October, 1942, which authorized the president to stabilize wages and salaries, was vigorously enforced, and in the next two years the cost of living increased less than 2 percent. Rationing of canned fruits and vegetables, meats, gasoline, and some other items was imposed, but adequate goods were available to maintain the nation's health and vital services. Most Americans lived far better than they had during the depression.

The control of inflation made the war years profitable for labor. Not only was unemployment ended, but also a worker shortage led many women and youths to take jobs. Worker income almost doubled, and agricultural prices more than doubled. Union membership, which was carefully protected by the War Labor Board, increased to almost fifteen million.

At the beginning of the war the A.F. of L. and C.I.O. adopted no-strike pledges for the duration, commitments honored by most of labor, although some notable work stoppages occurred. Following the 1943 coal strike, Congress passed the Smith-Connally War Labor Disputes Act over Roosevelt's veto. It required a workers' vote and a thirty-day waiting period before a strike began and empowered the president to seize struck war plants. Though negligible in its effects, the act indicated a rising wave of popular anti-union sentiment which resulted in the passage of many states laws prohibiting the closed shop and such union practices as secondary boycotts and mass picketing.

While the federal government's policies may have contributed to anti-union sentiment, they also promoted the workers' and the nation's economic well-being. During the war the national debt increased almost 540 percent to $260 billion, but approximately 41 percent of war costs were paid from current revenue. Income and corporation taxes were raised to record highs with a straight 90 percent excess profits tax (increased to 95 percent in 1944). Many excise or "luxury" taxes were levied, and a maximum salary limit of $25,000 per year was imposed. For the first time, millions of Americans were subject to the income tax, whose payment was insured by payroll deduction. A gigantic national effort also resulted in public purchase of almost $100 million in war bonds which, by removing money from circulation, aided in controlling inflation.

The prosperity and common purpose of the people did much to avert domestic crises during the war. Unlike World War I, there was no large-scale abuse of the civil rights of national groups except for the Japanese. In February, 1942, in response to a frenzy on the West Coast and among military leaders, the president ordered removal of Japanese-Americans from large sections of the Pacific Coast states and Arizona. Some 110,000 persons were placed in

A group of Japanese-Americans being relocated.

concentration camps and later in ten relocation centers. Ultimately, all but 18,000 of the most suspect were freed to live in the interior or the East. Unquestionably, the civil rights of Japanese-Americans were violated, but as late as December, 1944, the Supreme Court refused to condemn the actions taken against them.

Blacks comprised another important segment for whom the war brought many trials, but, in their case, many opportunities as well. Almost a million blacks, in response to job availability, migrated to northern cities where, though employment was found, they encountered heightened racial tensions. A number of riots occurred, the most serious in Detroit in June, 1943, in which twenty-five blacks and nine whites died.

Although at times discouraged by the prevailing conditions, almost a million blacks served in the armed forces where segregation continued in full force. However, officer rank was increasingly open to blacks, and during the war the army utilized the services of its first black general, Brigadier General Benjamin O. Davis, Jr., who, following his elevation in 1940, became commanding general of the 4th Cavalry Brigade.

Everywhere blacks were encouraged to take a more militant stand for their rights. Even before war erupted, A. Philip Randolph, president of the Brotherhood of Sleeping Car Porters, called for a 50,000-person march on Washington to protest defense industries' discrimination. To avert the march, the president issued Executive Order 8802 in June, 1941, which established a Fair Employment Practices Committee. It helped blacks by prohibiting exclusion from job training programs or discrimination by employers holding defense contracts. As the economic status of blacks improved, they obtained increased opportunities and were better able to defend their own rights.

The European Plan

Developments at home furnished the basis for eventual victory, but the early months of the war were bleak for the United States. Large areas of the Pacific fell into Japanese hands; Hitler's forces penetrated deeply into Russia, and in North Africa they almost reached Alexandria. Throughout 1942, German submarines took a frightful toll in Allied shipping with over 600,000 tons sunk in each of ten months during the year.

Soon after Pearl Harbor, Prime Minister Churchill came to Washington, accompanied by a number of British leaders, for the first of many wartime conferences. The easy rapport and confidence shared with President Roosevelt were powerful factors in the eventual victory. Quickly a Combined Chiefs of Staff was established in Washington as well as a joint command, including the Dutch in the Pacific, and a common Munitions Assignment Board.

It was agreed that primary consideration would be given to defeating Germany since it posed an immediate threat to Europe and America, while Japan did not. If Russia collapsed or the German General Erwin Rommel severed the Suez Canal, Great Britain could fall, leaving America alone to face Hitler. Russia pressed strongly for the immediate establishment of a second front in Western Europe to divert German strength. In a May, 1942, Washington meeting with Russian Foreign Minister Molotov, Roosevelt promised to seek a continental invasion before the end of the year. In June, however, Churchill and British military leaders vetoed the plan. In July, General George C. Marshall, army chief of staff, and General Dwight D. Eisenhower, commander of the European Theater of Operations, compromised with Britain and developed plans for a fall invasion of North Africa, where the British Eighth Army, commanded by General Bernard Montgomery, had in June,

The combined British-American convoy unloading at Oran, Algeria.

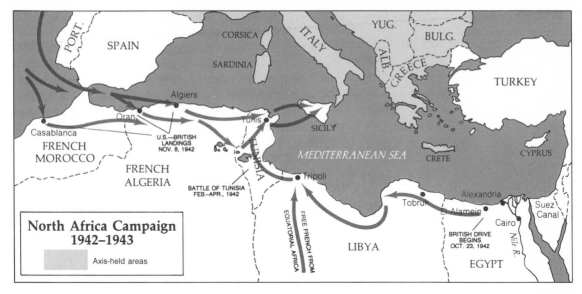

North Africa Campaign 1942-1943

Axis-held areas

1941, stopped the German forces, ably led by General Rommel, at El Alamein, only seventy miles from Alexandria. On October 23, 1942, Montgomery launched a drive to the west which forced Rommel's forces to flee from Egypt by November 12 and led to the capture of Tobruk in Libya, November 13.

Meanwhile on November 8, 1942, an Allied army, led by Eisenhower, moved into French North Africa which was ruled by the Vichy government with landings being made at Casablanca, Oran, and Algiers. Eisenhower was accompanied by General Henri Giraud, an escapee from a German prison who contended he could lead the French in North Africa to support the allies. In Algeria there was little opposition, and heavy fighting in Morocco came only near Casablanca. When Giraud proved ineffective, Eisenhower recognized the Vichy Admiral Jean Darlan as the *de facto* head of Algeria and signed an armistice with him. General Charles DeGaulle, leader of the Free French government-in-exile, was horrified by this action, and the British were skeptical. Although Darlan was assassinated in December, 1942, and the Free French came to control the

region, DeGaulle's anti-Americanism was accentuated. In mid-November, 1942, the Germans and Allies began a six-month struggle for North Africa in Tunisia. Tripoli in Tunisia was taken by the British Eighth Army in January, 1943, opening the way for its invasion of the country. Soon afterwards, on February 6, 1943, General Eisenhower was made commander of all allied forces in North Africa, and the Tunisian conflict became intense. In mid-February Rommel's forces launched a drive forcing the

General Rommel (the "Desert Fox") in North Africa.

Americans from Kasserine Pass, but the position was retaken and by February 23 Rommel's offensive was stopped. In March the audacious Major General George S. Patton, Jr., assumed command of the U.S. II Corps, and it took the offensive in late March, at approximately the same time that Montgomery's forces did so in the East. They completed encirclement of the Axis forces on April 7, although Tunis did not fall to the British and Bizerte to the Americans until May 7. As a result of the North African campaign, fifteen German divisions had been removed from the war, the Mediterranean secured, and American experience vastly increased.

Meeting with Churchill in Casablanca in January, 1943, the president tried unsuccessfully to obtain the prime minister's approval of an invasion of France. Instead agreement was reached to move through Sicily and Italy, plans were formulated for a Sicilian campaign, and a declaration was issued stating that the Allies would insist on unconditional surrender. Roosevelt explained such surrender did not mean the destruction of peoples but of the philosophies which sought to conquer and subjugate other nations. Although some held the declaration discouraged Hitler's German opponents and may have prevented Japanese efforts to seek a negotiated settlement, little evidence exists to support these views.

The turning point of the European War, it was later recognized, came in the spring of 1943 when the menace to the vital North Atlantic life line was largely removed, Russia assumed the offensive on the Eastern front, much of Italy was conquered, and the Allies formulated strategy for an invasion of the continent. By the use of sonar, unprecedented air patrols, and destroyer escorts, the loss of shipping was cut by 75 percent in the North Atlantic (and virtually eliminated a year later). The Russians, who had held at Stalingrad, began to push the enemy westward, and plans were completed

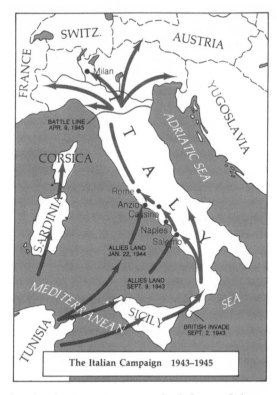

The Italian Campaign 1943–1945

for the Sicilian invasion which began July 10, 1943. On July 25 Italy's King Victor Emmanuel II aided in deposing Mussolini, and Marshal Badoglio, leader of the new Italian government, agreed on September 3 to surrender in return for protection against the Germans. Before the Allies could move in, however, the Germans entrenched themselves. Though Naples fell to U.S. forces October 7, 1943, and the British cleared the South and East, the Allied advance was stopped below Monte Cassino, halfway from Naples to Rome, early in 1944. A bold attempt to establish a front behind the German lines at Anzio, near Rome, established only a bloody beachhead where Allied soldiers fought furiously for weeks. Rome did not fall until June, 1944, and months were required to take Northern Italy. Although the Italian campaign did not succeed as Allied leaders wished, it was significant. By occupying many of Hit-

The Normandy Beach assault.

ler's finest divisions, it relieved other theaters and gained strategic air bases for attacking Central Europe and the Balkans.

Two days after the fall of Rome, June 6, 1944, the long-awaited opening of the Western front was accompanied by an Allied invasion of Normandy on the French coast. At conferences in Washington and Quebec in May and August, 1943, Roosevelt and Churchill had agreed on the approximate date. Russia, already distressed by delays in establishing a second front in the West, was conciliated at a lengthy October, 1943, meeting in Moscow in which Secretary Hull obtained Stalin's approval of tentative postwar plans for Germany and a pledge to enter the war against Japan when Germany was defeated.

In November, 1943, Roosevelt met with Churchill and Generalissimo Chiang Kai-shek of China in Cairo. Although Roosevelt would have preferred a major invasion of Burma as a prelude to movement into China, Churchill dissuaded him and plans were formulated only for a Burma campaign to open a supply route to China. In the Declaration of Cairo, the powers declared the war would be waged until Japan surrendered unconditionally and promised to deprive Japan of all Pacific islands acquired after 1914, to return territories to China taken by Japan, and to free Korea. Following the Cairo Conference, Roosevelt and Churchill proceeded to Teheran where for the first time they held a conference with Joseph Stalin, who had not been present at Cairo since Russia was

Stalin, Roosevelt, and Churchill at Teheran.

not in the Far Eastern war. Teheran was chosen as the meeting site because Stalin insisted he could not get further away since he was the ultimate military leader of Russia. In the conferences, he convinced Roosevelt that he could be relied upon and pressed Churchill and Roosevelt to set a definite date for a French invasion to be coordinated with a drive in southern France and a Russian offensive in the East. They agreed to open the second front in May or June, 1944, and all three leaders concurred in plans to support the forces of Marshal Tito in Yugoslavia, to partition Germany among the three major powers with each having an occupation zone, and to allow Russia to retain the areas of Poland taken in 1939. Under Roosevelt's tutelage, a general plan for an international peace-keeping organization, which later became the United Nations, was also formulated.

The Second Front

In January, 1944, plans were pressed for the French invasion. Reluctantly, Roosevelt decided he could not spare General Marshall in Washington and sent General Eisenhower to London to become the Allied Expeditionary Forces' Supreme Commander. After the arrival in February, 1944, of large numbers of auxiliary fighters in Britain, daylight raids on Germany were resumed. As "D-Day" approached, devastating assaults were made on the German transportation system and major industries as well as the invasion area.

On June 6, 1944, 200,000 American invaders landed in France, encountering little opposition except at Omaha Beach. The Germans, who had believed the incursion would come at the narrowest channel crossing near Calais, felt the Normandy movements were a diversion.

A strategic planning session with the officers of the American European Forces during the spring of 1944. General Dwight D. Eisenhower, supreme commander of the AEF, is seated in the center, General Sir Bernard L. Montgomery, commander-in-chief of British forces, is on his right, and Lt. General Omar N. Bradley, senior commander of U.S. Ground Forces, is on the left, standing.

By June 18 the U.S forces had reached the west coast of the peninsula where they had landed. Cherbourg was taken June 27 and Caen by the British on July 2. By July 25 General George Patton, whose audacity earned him the title "Old Blood and Guts," led a breakthrough which forced German withdrawal to their border by mid-September. Meanwhile, on August 15, 1944, an invasion of southern France by Allied forces including the U.S. Seventh Army under General Alexander M. Patch was made at St. Tropez and St. Raphaël. The important port of Marseilles was taken and a drive launched up the Rhone Valley which diverted much German strength. Meanwhile Paris fell August 25, and Brussels, Antwerp, and Luxembourg soon afterwards. Concurrently, the Russians began a general offensive freeing Finland, reaching the Baltic, and moving into Rumania in August, 1944.

As Germany suffered inevitable defeat, an abortive plan to assassinate Hitler by planting a bomb in his headquarters was carried out on July 20, 1944. As a result, almost 5,000 leaders, some high in military circles, were executed. In the fall of 1944, a quick Allied victory could probably have been won by following General Montgomery's plan for a concentrated thrust through the north German plain. However, Eisenhower vetoed the proposal, but in later independent action failed to turn the northern German flank. On December 16 Hitler launched a last great counteroffensive through the relatively weak Allied center in the Ardennes Forest. In the hotly contested Battle of the Bulge, the Germans almost split the Allied forces, but the ground abandoned was regained by the end of January, 1945; the Germans never recovered from the losses sustained. Capturing the Ludendorff Bridge across the Rhine at Remagen before it could be destroyed, the Allies in March established a base for penetration into Germany.

Roosevelt's Fourth Election

In the midst of the war, America demonstrated its political strength by holding a presidential election, a luxury which most of the Western democracies did not emulate. The Republicans had gained forty-seven House and nine Senate seats in 1942 due to a prosperous economy and emphasis on a bipartisan war effort. Although the Democrats had nominal majorities in both chambers, control rested with a conservative coalition composed of Republicans and many southern Democrats. Influenced by the political as well as military conditions, the president chose largely to inter reform for the war's duration. Congress curtailed such New Deal agencies as the Farm Security Administration, ended the $25,000 salary limitation, and passed the Smith-Connally Act over the president's veto, but it was cooperative in supporting the war effort.

The bridge at Remagen.

The conservative resurgence was also present at the state level. In 1943 twenty-six of the forty-eight states, a group which cast a majority of electoral votes, had Republican governors, and a number of Democratic governors in the South were quite conservative as well. Wendell Willkie, the titular Republican head, was eliminated as a presidential candidate by the spring of 1944. As a former Democrat without the professional politician's finesse, he lacked appeal for party regulars, many of whom were offended by his close relationship with the Roosevelt administration. The president sent him on a round-the-world trip which in 1943 resulted in the publication of *One World,* an effective plea for internationalism. His book aided many Republicans in sloughing off isolationism but did not endear him to the party element he most needed to cultivate. After defeat in the Wisconsin primary, Willkie withdrew from the race.

Following Willkie's withdrawal, the only Republican candidate except favorite sons was

Thomas E. Dewey, a forty-two-year-old leader who had gained respect as a crusading district attorney and in 1942 had been elected as New York's first Republican governor since 1920. Dewey was nominated for president on the first ballot and a platform adopted reflecting his progressive views, including advocacy of Social Security expansion, agricultural price supports, and protection of labor. As a concession to his opponents, Dewey chose the conservative, isolationist Governor John W. Bricker of Ohio as his running mate.

Roosevelt waited until a week before the Democratic convention before indicating that "as a good soldier" he would accept a fourth nomination. A highly divisive contest emerged for the vice-presidency when he did not insist on Henry A. Wallace's renomination. Strong elements, including southerners and party leaders in the larger cities, opposed his selection. Roosevelt stated that if he were a delegate he would vote for Wallace, but he apparently

Thomas E. Dewey

planned for the choice to be James F. Byrnes, on whom he had come to rely heavily. Byrnes' labor record, attitude toward blacks, and departure from the Roman Catholic faith posed difficulties. His selection was vetoed by Sidney Hillman, a C.I.O. vice-president and the organizer in 1943 of its Political Action Committee, whose support Roosevelt felt to be essential. The president then stated he would be happy to run with either Supreme Court Justice William O. Douglas or Missouri Senator Harry S Truman. Labor initially supported Wallace but, as prearranged, shifted to Truman, who was nominated on the third ballot. As chairman of a special Senate committee investigating military spending, second-term Senator Truman had achieved wide respect for saving the government millions of dollars.

In the campaign Dewey had difficulty finding issues, since he agreed with much of the Roosevelt program. Like Willkie four years earlier, he criticized the administration's inefficiency, and, at least by inference, he raised doubts regarding Roosevelt's health. Following the president's poor showing in a Bremerton, Washington, speech, questions began to mushroom regarding his ability to continue. These were largely killed by a Teamsters' Union address given on September 23, 1944, and by lengthy tours made in the last weeks of the campaign.

The Allied victories of 1944 assured Roosevelt's reelection, permitting the Democrats to use effectively the slogans "Don't change a winning team," and "Don't change horses in midstream." The Political Action Committee,

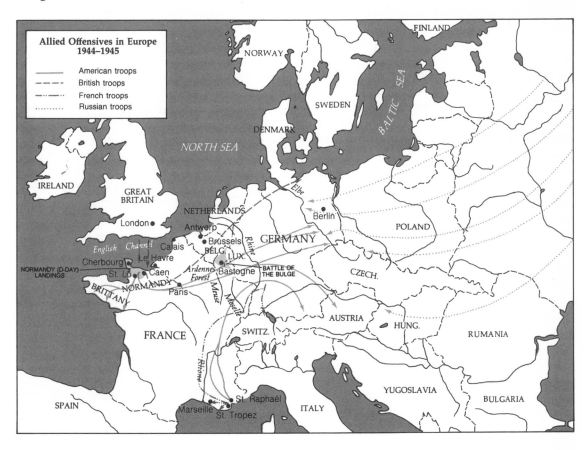

spurred by the president's pledge to expand liberal policies after the war, also contributed handsomely to Democratic victory. Roosevelt was reelected by a 3.5 million vote popular majority and carried thirty-six of the forty-eight states. He could clearly feel that his program to win the war and write the peace had been approved by the people.

The Yalta Conference

In February, 1945, shortly after his fourth inauguration, Roosevelt met Stalin and Churchill for a week of conferences at Yalta in the Crimea. The meeting was an urgent one since the end of the war was coming without a common approach to fundamental questions. In the fall of 1944, the president temporarily accepted the Morgenthau Plan, which would have given large sections of Germany to other powers and have converted the small remaining state into an agricultural community. But this decision was soon abandoned, and the fate of Germany remained a major issue. So did the status of Eastern Europe, especially Poland, which was being occupied by the Russian Army, and the structure of the United Nations. From August 21 to October 7, 1944, representatives of the United States, Great Britain, Russia, and China (with the last two meeting separately with the other major powers) conferred at Dumbarton Oaks, near Washington, where they drafted tentative proposals for a permanent charter of the United Nations. Russia, over U.S. objections, insisted that each of the great powers, as permanent members of the Security Council, have a veto over the *consideration* of disputes to which it was a party. The failure to settle this point posed a threat to establishment of the entire organization.

At Yalta, each of these critical issues was resolved to the satisfaction of the major powers. It was agreed that additional study would be given to German dismemberment, and France would have a zone of occupation along with Britain, Russia, and the United States. Berlin, though deep in the Russian zone, was to be under joint control of the major powers. At this time, sanction was given to Russian and Polish annexation of much of East Prussia. Russia was given permission to take sections of former Eastern Poland, and, as compensation, Poland was to receive territory in East Germany. Although Russian demands for $20 billion in reparations for the Allies, half of which would go to Russia itself, were refused, the reparation principle was accepted and provisions made for a Reparations Commission to meet in Moscow.

The questions relating to Eastern Europe proved to be the most difficult since Russia demanded a Polish state friendly to her and proposed acceptance of the Soviet-sponsored government in Lublin. Churchill and Roosevelt refused to accept this regime even with the incorporation of leaders from the Polish government-in-exile in London. Stalin then agreed to a reorganization which would include opposition leaders at home, and, more importantly, he promised to conduct genuinely free elections in Poland and throughout Eastern Europe.

The other major questions considered at Yalta were settled with little dispute. Russia accepted the American position on the United Nations, removing the Security Council veto on questions involving consideration of disputes. No one proposed to restrict the veto's use when actions on actual disputes were being considered. In additon, Russia reduced its demands from seventeen to three seats in the General Assembly and allowed the United States the same privilege, which it never exercised.

In regard to the Far East, Stalin, in secret agreement with Roosevelt, pledged to declare war on Japan within two to three months after victory in Europe, to recognize Chinese control of Manchuria, and to sign a treaty of friendship with the Nationalist Chinese government. To obtain these concessions, which Roosevelt considered vital to an early end of the Japanese war, the president recognized Russian control of Outer Mongolia and consented to Russia recovering its losses in the Russo-Japanese War plus the Kurile Islands.

The Yalta negotiations were harmonious, and, though tired, the president was a skilled diplomat in his discussions, obtaining marked concessions from the Russians on UN organization and agreement to democratic procedures in Eastern Europe. Confronted by Soviet occupation in Eastern Europe, there was little else he could have demanded without risking war with Russia. In addition, he was accustomed to strict Russian compliance with wartime agreements and discounted reports of Russian wartime murders of Polish officers and opposition leaders. The tragedy of the Yalta agreements was not their terms but the Russian failure to comply with them. Had they been carried out, the postwar period would have been entirely different.

Germany Surrenders

The inadequacies of the Yalta agreements were accentuated by the position General Eisenhower took in the last days of the European war. Though a staunch patriot and master organizer of victory, his innocence of politics led him to make decisions which plagued the postwar world. For purely military reasons, as his forces advanced into Germany, he refused General Montgomery's pleas to take Berlin, preferring instead to split the German forces by driving to the Elbe and cutting off the city. Opposing this decision, Churchill made personal appeals to the general and to Roosevelt, but to no avail. Churchill also pressed the

Western powers to take Prague, which would have given the West a decided advantage in Czechoslovakia, but, when Stalin protested, General Patton was recalled, allowing the Russians to take the city. In late April, American and Russian forces met at the Elbe, and, on April 30, 1945, Hitler and his newly married former mistress, Eva Braun, committed suicide in a Berlin bunker. German forces began to surrender May 2, and all fighting had ceased by May 8 (victory in Europe or V-E Day), when a German representative signed the unconditional surrender papers at the Allied headquarters in Reims.

War Strategy in the Pacific

While the war was being won in Europe, equally decisive events were occurring in the Pacific. By March, 1942, the Japanese had captured the East Indies, New Britain, and northern New Guinea and had forced the Philippine defenders to take a last stand on the Bataan Peninsula. General Douglas MacArthur, the American commander in the Philippines, was ordered to Australia on March 17, 1942, to become commander of the army in the South Pacific, leaving General Jonathan Wainwright to surrender the Philippines forces in May. Meanwhile, in the naval battle of Macassar Strait, on January 24, 1942, severe damage was inflicted on a Japanese invasion convoy, but in the battle of the Java Sea, February 27 to March 1, the participating Allied naval forces were wiped out except for four destroyers. The immediate question became whether Australia and India could be defended.

In this taut situation the Allied position in the Pacific was saved by two major naval encounters, both of which were fought by carrier planes, the vessels never sighting each other. At the Battle of the Coral Sea, May 7 and 8,

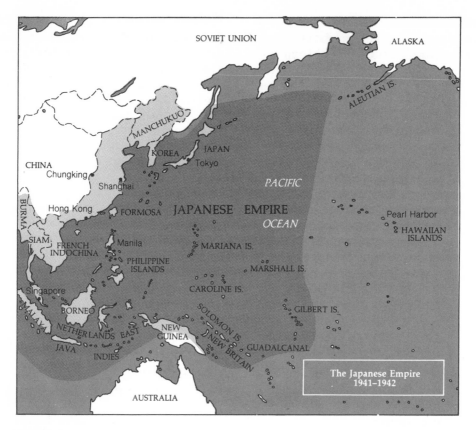

The Japanese Empire
1941–1942

1942, a Japanese expedition aimed at Port Moresby, southern New Guinea, was forced to turn back, and the critical route from Hawaii to Australia was kept open, although the carrier *Lexington* and two other U.S. vessels were lost. This encounter was followed by a superb American victory at the Battle of Midway, June 3–6, 1942. The prelude for this battle began on April 18 when Colonel James Doolittle, flying from the carrier *Hornet,* raided Tokyo, and the Japanese government, incorrectly assuming the raid had been launched from a Central Pacific island, resolved to avoid repetitions by cutting American supply lines and establishing bases there. Capture of their initial goal, Midway Island, would have jeopardized Hawaii, and therefore U.S. leaders met the Japanese threat head on. American victory

came in the Battle of Midway when Admiral Chester Nimitz, forewarned after the U.S. broke the Japanese code, skillfully deployed his craft and obtained remarkable results. American dive bombers and torpedo-planes sank four Japanese carriers and their 275 planes, a heavy cruiser, three destroyers, and other craft.

The decisive Midway victory enabled the Allies to begin a grueling, three-year island-hopping offensive. The first major advance was against Guadalcanal, to the east of New Guinea in the Solomon Islands, where six months of hand-to-hand combat were required before the Japanese pulled out in February, 1943.

In the following year, 1944, the South and Central Pacific fell into American hands. A dual approach was followed when MacArthur and Nimitz could not agree on a single strategy. The army strongly urged a central approach, including movement through the Marianas and Formosa. Painfully, the MacArthur forces moved up the New Guinea coast and, backed by strong naval support, cut off New Britain by taking the central and northern Solomons and the Admiralty Islands. Meanwhile, to the east, Nimitz's forces, including army and marine units, took strategic locations in the Gilbert Islands and began to attack Saipan in the Marianas, part of Japan's inner defense line which was only 1,300 miles from the homeland.

In June, 1944, Japan sent nine carriers, five battleships, and other craft to challenge the Saipan invasion. Although the U.S. Navy used 500 aircraft, it suffered only minimal damages while destroying four-fifths of the attacking planes. Pursuing American submarines and airplanes destroyed much of the Japanese strength in the Battle of the Philippine Sea, including three carriers and two destroyers.

In the summer of 1944, the controversy over Japanese invasion routes intensified. Naval leaders urged an immediate attack on Formosa, but MacArthur insisted on first honoring his promise to liberate the Philippines. Eventually MacArthur prevailed, and Leyte Island in the Philippines was invaded October 20, 1944. Realizing conquest of the Philippines would cut Japanese communications with the East Indies, Malaya, and Indochina, the Japanese navy waged the all-important Battle of Leyte Gulf, October 24 and 25. The encounter, the greatest in naval history, virtually eliminated the Japanese navy. Manila fell in February, 1945, and, although resistance in the mountains continued until July, the islands were for all practical purposes in American hands after April, 1945.

American troops moving up on Japanese positions in the Philippines.

Direct aerial attack of Japan began in June, 1944, following the sending of B-29's to China.* It was greatly accelerated when Saipan fell in July, 1944, and Iwo Jima, only 750 miles from Tokyo, was taken following a month's battle in March, 1945. After four months of concentrated raids on aircraft factories, in March a firebomb attack on Tokyo inaugurated intense bombing of civilian areas. In a short time, a third of a million people were killed, and a majority of the nation's industry destroyed.

On April 1, 1945, Okinawa, a large island only 350 miles from Japan, was invaded. Realizing that its loss spelled complete defeat, its defenders fought ferociously and over 110,000 men were killed before surrender on June 21. Among those who died were a number of *kamikaze* pilots, who willingly committed suicide by crashing their bomb-laden planes into American vessels in an attempt to destroy them.

While Japan was under relentless raids from land and carrier-based planes, important elements in the government worked for a negotiated peace. The army remained adamant, however, although the Emperor instructed the cabinet to seek Russian intercession with the United States.

Truman Assumes Office

After returning from the Yalta Conference, the weary President Roosevelt went to his retreat at Warm Springs, Georgia, where he died

*Unfortunately, the Nationalist government of China made only relatively small contributions to victory. General Joseph ("Vinegar Joe") Stillwell led in building a road across northern Burma to China but was removed as American commander in China at Chiang Kai-shek's request when the Joint Chiefs of Staff proposed Stillwell assume command of the Chinese army. The Nationalists would not relinquish absolute control of the army and were notably diverted in their war efforts by its use to destroy the growing Chinese Communist movement.

A kamikaze *dive bomber attacking the U.S.S.* Missouri.

unexpectedly of a cerebral hemorrhage on April 12, 1945, and the leadership of the United States in the last days of the war passed to Vice-President Harry Truman. Roosevelt's sudden death left the American people, many of whom had never known another president, grieved and apprehensive regarding the nation's future.

President Truman assumed office grossly uninformed regarding the national situation since Roosevelt had not made him privy to many important developments including work on the atomic bomb. In his new role, however, Truman's sincerity and humility quickly earned widespread respect, even though subsequent actions cost him much goodwill. He lent his full support to the organizational session of the United Nations (UN), which, meeting from April to June, 1945, in San Francisco, drafted a charter that was signed on June 26 and ap-

proved by the United States Senate on July 28, 1945; it was proclaimed in effect on October 24, 1945. Bearing a striking resemblence to the Covenant of the League of Nations, it provided for a General Assembly representing all member nations and authorized it to discuss and recommend actions. The more important Security Council was composed of five permanent members—China, France, Great Britain, Russia, and the United States—and six others elected annually by the General Assembly. It was empowered to investigate disputes and to take measures, including the use of armed force, to end them when they threatened peace. The Council's action was limited by the veto of each of its permanent members but, through direct intercession with Stalin by Secretary of State Edward R. Stettinius, who had succeeded Hull in November, 1944, Russian compliance with the Yalta agreement on the use of the veto was obtained and procedural matters were exempt from it. Nevertheless Russia used the veto over one hundred times by 1972, and the United States only used it once.

Due in part to the veto's imposition, many felt some of the UN's most effective work was done in a number of its affiliated agencies such as the United Nations Relief and Rehabilitation Administration (UNRRA). Following its creation in 1943, UNRRA distributed vast quantities of goods to the destitute throughout the world. The International Monetary Fund and the World Bank (International Bank for Reconstruction and Development) sought to bring economic stability and to supply capital to underdeveloped countries. The United Nations Educational, Scientific, and Cultural Organization (UNESCO) promoted cultural exchange between nations and provided much aid to backward countries. Many of these and other UN-affiliated agencies received much of their support from the United States since the Communist nations frequently failed to participate in them, and a number of prominent Americans assumed leading roles in their work.

The Assembly Hall of the United Nations.

Japan Capitulates

In military matters Truman relied on the judgement of his commanders, and the war was quickly terminated when the United States used the atomic bomb. A sequence of events leading to its development began in 1939 when President Roosevelt, acting on the advice of Albert Einstein, began sponsoring research on splitting the atom. Progress was sufficient to lead to the establishment of the Manhattan Project in May, 1943, which over the next twenty-six months spent approximately $2 billion before achieving its goal. On July 16, 1945, a bomb with the destructive force of 20,000 tons of TNT was exploded over the New Mexican desert.

President Harry Truman's decision to drop A-bombs on major Japanese cities seemed the only means to avoid an invasion of Japan with as many as a million American casualties. The Japanese had shown no indication of abating their suicidal resistance; moreover, only two bombs were available, and no one could be certain each would detonate properly. Therefore, after the Japanese prime minister flatly rejected a surrender demand, the bomb was dropped August 6, 1945, on Hiroshima, a city of 344,000. Over 75,000 people were killed, a larger number injured, and the city destroyed. Three days later the second bomb was dropped on Nagasaki with devastating but less pervasive destruction. On August 8, 1945, Russia declared war on Japan, and on August 10, 1945, Japan sued for peace. Hostilities ended when the Japanese accepted the Allies' terms on August 14. The formal surrender took place aboard the battleship *Missouri* in Tokyo Bay on September 2, 1945 (V-J Day).

Victory over the Axis had cost the United States dearly—almost 300,000 combat-related deaths, 671,000 wounded, and billions of dollars in expenditures. Yet the nation emerged from the war almost unscathed compared to

The ruins of Hiroshima following the explosion of the first atomic bomb.

General of the Army Douglas MacArthur signs as the supreme allied commander during formal surrender ceremonies on the U.S.S. Missouri.

most combatants, and with its economic, military, and diplomatic strengths at all-time highs. Only Russia, which had sustained enormous internal losses, ended the war in a position approaching the U.S. as a major power. The world's future would depend, in great degree, on the use made of American strength.

Attempts at Collective Action

Immediately after the war, United States foreign policy was characterized simultaneously by charity and vindictiveness. Through the United Nations Relief and Rehabilitation Administration and the army, vast quantities of supplies were furnished the Japanese, Germans, and the peoples of Eastern and Central Europe. Though President Truman summarily ended Lend-Lease shipments, a mistake which he later admitted came from signing an order without reading it, short-term loans kept U.S. goods flowing abroad. Never before had such concern been demonstrated for newly defeated peoples.

At the same time, the United States was authoritarian and naïve in attempting to remake Germany and Japan in its own image. During the war, the Allies had agreed that reparations could be obtained from the Axis in a number of ways including the taking of capital goods. Therefore nothing could be done to prevent the Russians dismantling a sizable segment of German industry and removing it to Russia and Poland. This policy weakened a major deterrent to Communist aggression and necessitated additional support for many people that could have come from German industry. Reformation was even more the order of the day in Japan where the United States succeeded in keeping other powers out of the reconstruction process. General Douglas MacArthur enforced demilitarization, land redistribution, and removal of social distinctions, winning much support in Japan and enabling a startling change to take place.

The most questionable practice in both Germany and Japan was punishment of so-called militarists and alleged war criminals. In Germany, over half a million former Nazis received some form of punishment, as did thousands of comparable Japanese. The most serious development was the trial of twenty-two Nazi officials at Nuremberg in 1945 and 1946 and twenty-eight Japanese officials between 1946 and 1948. Of these, twelve Nazis were sentenced to death as were seven Japanese. Though many of these men had been guilty of bestial decisions, and some precedents existed in international law for conducting such procedures, their trials by military courts under *ex post facto* laws was questioned by many in a nation which prided itself as being governed by laws rather than men.

Punishment of war criminals was one issue that did not disrupt relations between the United States and Russia, but others did. Before Roosevelt's death, Soviet conduct in Eastern Europe had become a matter of grave concern. President Truman and Secretary of State James F. Byrnes, who came to office in June, 1945, were troubled by the imposition of a Red government in Rumania, failure to move toward free elections in Poland, and Stalin's allegation that the U.S. had attempted to negotiate a separate peace with Germany. In desperation, Harry Hopkins was dispatched to Moscow in May, 1945, where he joined Ambassador W. Averell Harriman, who was

highly skeptical of Soviet intentions. They obtained Stalin's promise that non-Reds would be admitted to the Polish government and his assent to hold a "Big Three" meeting in July, 1945, at Potsdam, a Berlin suburb. Little of a fundamental nature was achieved at the conference, but, in return for more freedom for Western observers, Russia was, in effect, confirmed in its occupation of Poland and German lands east of the West Neisse-Oder line although Russia had taken the area west of the East Neisse River without approval of the other Allied powers. The Soviets were permitted to take reparations from the German zone they controlled, and the other three occupying powers agreed to give 10 percent of capital equipment in their zones to Russia and to transfer 15 percent in return for food and raw materials. A Council of Foreign Ministers, composed of representatives of the major powers, was also established and entrusted with the settlement of outstanding territorial questions as well as the framing of peace treaties with Austria, Hungary, Bulgaria, Rumania, and Finland.

For a year and a half, Truman and Byrnes labored diligently to cooperate with the Russians, though the president never shared his secretary's belief that Russia and America must come to terms if peace were to prevail. Although the Soviets would not agree to an Austrian treaty which would have removed their excuse for keeping troops in Hungary and Rumania, under Byrnes' pressure they joined the Western powers in negotiating treaties with Bulgaria, Hungary, Rumania, and Italy in February, 1947. (The Russians finally agreed to a treaty establishing a neutralized Austria in 1955.) In effect, America recognized Russian domination of the Balkans in return for the West's control in Italy and North Africa.

The Russians repeatedly refused to join the Western powers in a twenty-five-year guarantee against German militarism and would not accept the U.S. plan for international control of atomic energy. The American proposal, presented to the UN Atomic Energy Commission by Bernard M. Baruch, provided an international authority would own and control all atomic production facilities. The United States agreed to turn over its atomic secrets provided there was international control and inspection which was not subject to a veto of the UN Security Council. The Russians, fearful the authority would be controlled by the West, would never agree to international inspection and sought merely to outlaw the atomic bomb.

While relations with Russia were worsening, the United States suffered a major defeat in China where the Russians also had misjudged conditions and, as late as 1945, had signed a treaty with Nationalist China. From their base in northwestern China to which they had retreated in the mid-1930s, the Chinese Communists expanded, and by the end of the war had control of much of the northern countryside. By 1945 the U.S. Foreign Service in China was convinced that Chiang Kai-shek's Nationalists were too corrupt to be relied upon. Despite this, General Patrick J. Hurley, U.S. ambassa-

Chiang Kai-shek (center)

dor to China, recommended support be given Chiang to stabilize conditions.

In 1945 the U.S. sent large quantities of Japanese goods to the Nationalists and flew their forces to regions falling into Communist hands; at the same time, American marines occupied a number of northern cities until Nationalists arrived. Meanwhile Russia, which had become aware of its Chinese mistake, began investing Mao Tse-tung's Communist forces with vast stores of materials. Civil war on an unprecedented scale was imminent, and General Albert C. Wedemeyer, American commander in China, warned in November, 1945, that Chiang's forces could not resist the popular opposition without American aid.

No major segment of American opinion favored wholesale American intervention in China, and many believed the Chinese Reds were more agrarian reformers than genuine Communists, a conclusion given credence by Russian failure to champion their cause. Therefore the decision was made to send General George C. Marshall to China with instructions to seek peace through the establishment of a coalition government, and Truman warned Chiang Kai-shek that China must bring the influence of militarists and reactionaries under control or America would have to alter its policy. For over a year, before his departure from China in January, 1947, Marshall attempted unsuccessfully to obtain compliance with his instructions. However, the civil war became intense early in 1947 and by mid-year turned in the Communists' favor. Believing that the Nationalists' defeat was not due to lack of supplies, the Truman administration made only small additional quantities of military goods available to them and removed American forces.

In July, 1947, the president sent Wedemeyer to China again, and, in a September report, for the first time he clearly pictured the Reds as genuine Communists and tools of Russia whose victory would be a menace to the United States. He proposed massive aid to the Nationalists, which would have brought major U.S. involvement. Truman not only rejected what he believed was an undesirable action but also kept Wedemeyer's report secret until after the mainland had fallen in 1949. For years the "China Lobby," which included leading American conservatives, severely indicted Truman for China's loss without assessing the multiple causes for it. The United States had suffered a stupendous blow which Washington had not foreseen but which probably could not have been prevented.

Truman Fights Communism

The administration's hands-off attitude in China was not indicative of its approach to foreign affairs generally. In 1946 it supported the opponents of Argentine strong-man Juan Péron and publicly denounced his thrust for power immediately before the Argentine national elections. This action aided Péron to come to power and seriously damaged inter-American relations.

Better results were obtained by American policy in other Latin American states. In 1947 the representatives of the American republics, meeting in Rio de Janiero, put some force in the 1945 Act of Chapultepec by which they had agreed to act as a unit if any one power were attacked. By the Inter-American Treaty of Reciprocal Assistance, they declared that, upon the vote of two-thirds of the American states, diplomatic and economic relations would be severed with an aggressor. Significantly, no state was required to use military force, but a variety of alternatives were provided for crisis use including military power to resist aggression collectively. In 1948 at Bogotá the Inter-American Conference established the

Organization of American States (OAS) providing for frequent conferences and consultations. An Advisory Committee was established, and a Council, with one representative from each country and headquarters in Washington, came into being.

Though apparent progress was made, the United States' role in Latin America had greatly deteriorated. Internal struggles motivated by the desire of the masses to improve their lot in highly stratified societies were partially to blame as were depressed economic conditions in a period of peace when the U.S. purchased fewer raw materials. The fiasco in Argentina was a contributing factor, but even more important was United States' neglect when it concentrated on the foreign affairs of other areas.

The Truman administration's success in European affairs was in contrast to its performance in China and Latin America. By 1947 it was painfully apparent that Russia had rejected cooperation with America and was seeking to expand its control in a variety of ways. The term "Cold War" began to be applied to the conflict between the Russian-led and the Western world, a real, menacing encounter which, though intense, stopped short of an all-out, hot war. In a Fulton, Missouri, speech delivered in March, 1946, in the presence of President Truman, Winston Churchill declared, "From Stettin in the Baltic to Trieste in the Adriatic an iron curtain has descended across the continent [Europe]." He warned that strength was the quality most admired by Russia and military weakness earned only its disrespect. In early 1946, George F. Kennan, counselor at the American Embassy in Moscow, cautioned that Russia's main goal was American destruction. In the July, 1947, issue of *Foreign Affairs,* he elaborated his argument, pleading for "containment" of Communism and contending only a strong, vigilant United States could, through patience and agility, inhibit Russian expansion. After Secretary of Commerce Henry A. Wallace was fired for criticism of the hard line being pursued against Russia, Truman placed Kennan in a position to promote his policy by making him head of the planning staff in the State Department.

The U.S. revision of its Russian policy required it to play a creative role in the Middle and Near East. In 1946 the Truman administration, aided by concern in the UN Security Council, successfully pressured the Soviets into withdrawing their support of a puppet government in the Iranian state of Azerbaijan. The following year, it supported in the UN General Assembly proposals leading to the partition of Palestine into Jewish and Arab states with the city of Jerusalem being internationalized. On the day the new state of Israel came into being, May 15, 1948, the United States extended recognition. Difficulties with Israel's Arab neighbors proved endemic, however, and the UN mediator, Count Folke Bernadotte of Sweden, was assassinated in

Dr. Ralph J. Bunche, center, acting UN mediator for Palestine, in conference with General A. Lundström, chief military observer, in Haifa.

Jerusalem on September 17, 1948. Following this event, Ralph J. Bunche, an American black man, continued the delicate mediation assignment and successfully arranged an armistice between Israel and the Arab states.

Meanwhile, a Russian threat to the Eastern Mediterranean developed in 1947 when efforts were made to gain Turkish territory, including naval bases on the Bosporus, and to capture Greece by supporting a Communist government. In February, 1947, Britain informed the United States that, due to economic conditions, it would have to remove its forces completely from Greece. Truman and his new secretary of state, General George C. Marshall, responded with vigor. The president enunciated what has been known as the Truman Doctrine which stated U.S. policy was "to support free peoples who are resisting attempted subjugation by armed minorities or by outside pressures. . . ." The Senate affirmed the Truman Doctrine in April, 1947, when, by a vote of 67 to 23, it approved aid to Greece and Turkey, and the House followed in May by a vote of 287 to 107. Angered, Russia responded by reestablishing the Cominform, an international agency to promote revolution.

Under the Truman Doctrine, over $650 million of aid was given the Turks and Greeks which enabled both countries to resist the Reds. The stable, efficient Turks achieved notable economic and military reforms also, while in Greece a reactionary regime overcame Communist guerrillas, who were crushed after Yugoslavia's Tito broke with Moscow in 1948 and withdrew his support. Discontent continued in Greece, however, and the United States was in the unfortunate position of supporting a dictatorship.

In 1947 a real danger also existed that France and Italy would fall to Communism from within, outflanking any stability achieved to the east. As American economic relief came to an end, some plan had to be developed which would sustain the economies of Western Europe, an action Undersecretary of State Dean Acheson called for in May, 1947. Speaking before the Delta Council in Cleveland, Mississippi, he demonstrated the necessity of aiding those governments which were attempting "to preserve their independence and democratic institutions and human freedoms against totalitarian pressures." At Harvard in June, Secretary Marshall proposed that all European countries develop a recovery plan which the United States would support. He avowed the Marshall Plan was directed "against hunger, poverty, desperation, and chaos," and not against "any country or doctrine." Its purpose was "the revival of a working economy in the world so as to permit the emergence of political and social conditions in which free institutions can exist." Since Russia had been consolidating the economies of Eastern Europe as a means of economic warfare, there seemed little chance it would cooperate.

The British, French, and Russian foreign ministers met in Paris three weeks after Marshall's address and formulated plans to implement the Marshall Plan. When Molotov, the Russian representative, found he could not wreck the proceedings, he withdrew, but non-Communist European plans continued apace with the British and French inviting twenty-two countries to participate in a general meeting. The eight nations most vulnerable to Soviet seizure declined, but at a July meeting sixteen nations including Turkey helped develop a master plan envisioning U.S. extension of $22.4 billion in aid and loans to themselves. They approved creation of the Committee for Economic Cooperation, on which each was represented, whose duty was to supply the U.S. estimates of goods the European countries had available and of their needs. On September 22, 1947, the participants signed a report outlining a four-year European Recovery Program and suggesting the sixteen nations form a permanent organization. At another Paris conference in March, 1948, a constitution was authorized for the Organization for European Economic Cooperation (OEEC) which was signed on April 16, 1948. Membership included the sixteen original conference participants and military representatives from the American, British, and French zones of Germany. Later the German Federal Republic and Spain were included, bringing OEEC membership to eighteen. In addition, the United States, Canada, and Yugoslavia participated in some phases of its work.

While these events were occurring, groundwork was being laid in the United States for acceptance of the Marshall Plan. Extensive studies were made on the country's ability to furnish aid and the influence of such aid on the U.S. standard of living. As the result of reports given by the House Select Committee on Foreign Affairs, chaired by Representative Christian Herter, and committees headed by Secretary of Interior Julius A. Krug, Secretary of Commerce W. Averell Harriman, and presidential economic advisor Edwin G. Nourse, Truman requested $17 billion in aid to be furnished the European countries over a four-year period. Although the request met some opposition, Communist seizure of Czechoslovakia in February, 1947, aided the pro-Marshall Plan coalition, including business, labor, and internationalist Republicans led by Senator Arthur Vandenberg, to attain victory. The initial appropriations were cut to $5.3 billion for one year, but the program was approved in April, 1948. Paul G. Hoffman, president of the Studebaker Company and chairman of the board of the Committee for Economic Development, was chosen as administrator of the Economic Cooperation Administration, a position he held during the crucial period until September, 1950. The success achieved was spectacular, permitting reduction of expenditures under the program (which was supplanted by the Mutual

Security Agency in December, 1951) to approximately $12.5 billion. The danger of Communist victories in the West was eliminated, industrial production increased over 60 percent, and a base for European self-defense laid. Concurrently, large expenditures for direct military aid went to many countries.

In 1949 Truman, in his inaugural address, also proposed a $45 million program of technical assistance and public and private investment in the underdeveloped countries. The proposal was named the Point Four program since, according to the president, it was the fourth point on which American foreign policy was based; the other three were commitments to resist Russian expansion, to support the United Nations, and to provide military and economic aid to those nations who were targets of Russian aggression. By developing healthy economies and improved living standards in backward areas, Truman believed the growth of Communism internally could be averted. Although Congress supported the first three of the president's points, it initially appropriated only $10 million for Point Four. By 1953 its yearly allocation had increased to $140 million, which was still only a small portion of the monies expended abroad. Despite the relatively small sums involved, technical aid was given to over thirty underdeveloped countries, and substantial results were obtained in human betterment and goodwill for the United States.

America needed all the support it could obtain from other nations in the early postwar years as a confrontation emerged with Russia over conditions in Germany. Twice at 1947 foreign ministers' meetings, the Soviets rejected Western efforts to reunite Germany while demanding a commanding voice in control of the Ruhr Valley and, with it, much of Europe's industrial development. With difficulty, due to French fears, the Western powers united their German zones and in October,

1948, brought a West German government into being. In retaliation, the Russians had Communist-dominated unions call strikes in France and Italy and, beginning in April, 1948, restricted movement to the four-power controlled city of Berlin, which was 110 miles within the Russian zone. After withdrawing from the four-power Berlin council, the Russians ended all traffic to the city on June 23, 1948.

President Truman, rejecting the alternatives of withdrawing from Berlin or using armed convoys, cooperated with the British in instituting an airlift which captured the imagination of the non-Communist world. For almost eleven months it supplied the 2,100,000 West Berliners with essential goods. On May 12, 1949, the Russians withdrew the blockade in return for a face-saving foreign ministers' conference on Germany which accomplished little.

Russian audacity in establishing the Berlin blockade did much to promote Western unity and rearmament. In March, 1947, Great Britain and France had signed the Treaty of Dunkirk establishing a fifty-year military alliance which British Foreign Secretary Ernest Bevin declared was not aimed at Russia but was designed to establish a "perfect pattern for universal peace." A year later, in March, 1948, this alliance was expanded by the Brussels Pact under which Britain, France, the Netherlands, Belgium, and Luxembourg committed themselves to fifty years of military alliance and economic cooperation. Assessing the critical nature of the times, Bevin persuasively contended America also must be committed. In response, Senator Arthur Vandenberg sponsored a resolution which provided a basis for U.S. affiliation with the Atlantic alliance. The Vandenberg Resolution, which passed the Senate by a sixty-four to six vote on June 11, 1948, advocated United States participation "with such regional and other collective arrangements as are based on continuous and effective self-help and mutual aid, and as affect its national security."

While the Brussels Pact was being expanded to include Scandinavia, Italy, Ireland, and the new German Republic, negotiations began in the summer of 1948 to establish the North Atlantic Alliance. The draft was completed in December, 1948, signed in April, 1949, and approved by the U.S. Senate in July, 1949, by a vote of eighty-two to thirteen. The treaty provided an attack on any of the twelve signatory members (Belgium, Britain, Canada, Denmark, France, Iceland, Italy, Luxembourg, the Netherlands, Norway, Portugal, and the United States) would be considered an attack on all and projected the creation of a common military force. For the first time since 1800 the United States had entered a permanent, military alliance, in no small measure because of Truman's success in obtaining bipartisan support. Like the Organization of American States, NATO had a Consultative Council with, of course, the right to decide on a course of action in case of aggression, but, unlike the OAS, NATO was to have a military force under its command. In the event of war, U.S. troops attached to NATO would be attacked as part of the total force, and the United States would be involved in the war. In the fall of 1949, Congress expanded U.S. commitment to NATO by appropriating a billion dollars under the Mutual Defense Assistance Act for arming the member countries. This action was taken none too soon, since by September, 1949, the Russians had exploded an atomic bomb of their own. As international tensions increased, rearmament took place, and in 1951 the North Atlantic Treaty Organization's unified forces came into being with General Eisenhower recalled to duty as their commander. With four U.S. divisions as its backbone, the NATO forces came to be a strong deterrent. The emergence of NATO permitted the rearming of West Germany, and in 1954, when West Germany was admitted to NATO, its strength was increased even more. The challenge to Red aggression had been effectively met in the West.

The Korean Conflict

The nemesis of the Truman administration came not in Europe but in the Korean War. Secretary of State Dean Acheson, who had mistakenly believed that nationalism not Communism was the dominant force in Asia, was under a barrage of criticism because of the failures of the administration's Chinese policy. In January, 1950, he prepared the way for increased difficulties by listing an Asian perimeter which the United States would defend. Running from the Aleutians to Japan and the Philippines, it excluded Korea, a region which had been jointly occupied by a Communist regime north of the 38th parallel and a republic under UN supervision in the south. The declaration was unwise since Korea was a territory traditionally coveted by both Russia and Japan.

Freed of fear of American reprisal, on June 25, 1950, the Communist North Koreans invaded the south. Due to the absence of the Russian delegate, who was boycotting the session because of failure to seat Red China, the United Nations Security Council condemned the aggression and called on UN members to aid the Korean Republic, which throughout the ensuing conflict furnished the vast majority of the troops opposing Red aggression. Soon nineteen nations contributed military forces, but 90 percent of the foreign troops came from the United States. Initially Truman ordered the Seventh Fleet to prevent attacks on or from Formosa and General MacArthur to provide arms and air support to the South Koreans. When this proved insufficient, and after Russia denied any responsibility for the attack,

U.S. ground troops were ordered in on June 30, 1950.

By early September, when it seemed the Reds would overrun the peninsula, General MacArthur demonstrated the brilliant generalship worthy of an officer who graduated first in his West Point class. Landing troops at Inchon on the western Korean coast near the 38th parallel, his forces overran the south and were ready to invade the north by October 1, 1950.

President Truman characterized the Korean conflict a "police action" and sponsored a tax increase designed to produce $4.5 billion in additional revenue to meet its cost. He also obtained standby authority under a Defense Production Act to impose price and credit controls, allocate scarce materials, and underwrite industrial construction. These powers were held in abeyance in a belief the conflict would soon be over; the great fear was that Russia would invade Western Europe or the Middle East.

A step toward more serious difficulties in Korea was taken on September 11, 1950, when President Truman endorsed a National Security Council recommendation that American forces continue their operation beyond the 38th parallel provided there was no "threat of entry of Soviet or Chinese Communist elements in force. . . ." In early October the UN General Assembly authorized MacArthur's troops, who had paused at the 38th parallel, to bring all of Korea under UN control. The Communist Chinese Foreign Minister Chou En-lai warned this action would lead China to send troops to aid North Korea, but MacArthur, meeting with President Truman on Wake Island on October 15, discounted the threat. In less than a month, American forces moved within fifty miles of the Chinese border at the Yalu River where advanced U.S. units encountered large concentrations of Chinese troops. On November 24, 1950, MacArthur launched an offensive to drive the enemy beyond the Yalu. Only South Korean troops were used, but Red China strenuously protested, amassed some 850,000 men in Manchuria, and sent volunteers to aid in the North Korean defense. On November 26 massive Chinese forces moved into Korea, splitting the UN line. A major American disaster was averted only by a large-scale amphibious evacuation from the east coast port of Hungnam.

In the crisis, President Truman proved a wise leader. The standby controls he possessed were imposed, largely under the direction of Charles Edward Wilson, former president of General Electric, and the Office of Defense Mobilization which he headed. By a determined stand vigorous efforts to retreat from NATO responsibilities, led by former President Hoover, Senator Taft, and others, were resisted, and, most significantly, General MacArthur was prevented from pursuing actions which could have led to a full-scale war with China.

MacArthur, who felt he should make policy in the Far East, had publicly called for incorporation of Formosa within the American defense area. To avert difficulties, the president, in the October, 1950, Wake Island meeting, ordered him to make no more policy statements and assured him that the United States was resolved to avoid a major Chinese war.

After China entered the Korean conflict with massive forces, MacArthur demanded the right to bomb its bases beyond the Yalu, as well as blockade the Chinese coast and use the Formosa troops of Chiang Kai-shek. The Joint Chiefs of Staff, rejecting this advice, felt its policy was vindicated when General Matthew Ridgway's Eighth Army halted the invasion of southern Korea in January, 1951. MacArthur would not accept a limited victory, however. Though informed in March, 1951, that the Korean conflict was to be settled by diplomacy, he defiantly replied in two public statements, and the second, a letter to House Minority Leader Joseph W. Martin, Jr., demanded the U.S. attain victory. Reluctantly, Truman relieved MacArthur of command on April 10, 1951.

General MacArthur had not returned to the United States since the war, and the circumstances under which he now arrived led to a tumultuous reception in city after city. On April 19, 1951, addressing a joint session of Congress, he eloquently called for complete triumph. His support continued to grow until the Senate Armed Services Committee, judiciously chaired by Senator Richard Russell, exhaustively examined the entire dispute in May and June. Its work led most Americans to see Truman had acted properly.

The unpopular involvement in Korea continued, ultimately costing the United States over 33,000 dead and 103,000 wounded. The Chinese casualties were many times this number, many of which were sustained in unsuccessful offensives in April and May, 1951. Secretary Acheson obtained a UN embargo against the shipment of war-related materials to mainland China, and, spurred by the war, completed plans to improve anti-Communist strength in the Far East. In September, 1951, a conference of fifty-two nations, meeting in San Francisco, with only Russia, Poland, and Czechoslovakia dissenting, adopted a generous peace treaty with Japan which left the state virtually intact except for its overseas possessions. The same day the treaty was signed, the United States negotiated a security treaty with

American troops work their way over the mountains about ten miles north of Seoul, Korea, attempting to locate the Communist lines.

Japan which granted the U.S. the right to maintain troops indefinitely in Japan. (In February, 1952, a joint pact gave the United States the right to maintain bases in Japan. The peace treaty and security pacts were approved by the Senate in March, 1952.) In anticipation of fears which would be aroused by the Japanese peace treaty's failure to place restrictions on the military forces and by the U.S. alliance with Japan, the United States signed mutual defense pacts with the Philippines, Australia, and New Zealand. The Philippines' pact of August 30, 1952, implemented earlier agreements continuing free trade until 1954, providing rehabilitation aid, and furnishing military assistance. The ANZUS pact of September 1 with Australia and New Zealand provided for military assistance and periodic consultations on defense matters.

Undoubtedly due to U.S. military and diplomatic achievements, in June, 1951, Russia proposed an ending of the Korean conflict by reestablishment of the 38th parallel as a dividing line between North and South Korea. In July, 1951, the U.S. opened negotiations with representatives of China and North Korea and urged acceptance of the battle line rather than the 38th parallel as an armistice line, a condi-

tion the Communists accepted in November. Just when peace seemed near, the Reds demanded the repatriation of upwards of 50,000 North Koreans and Chinese who had indicated they would not return to the North. The negotiations remained stalemated until the Reds terminated them in October, 1952. Meanwhile, the UN forces maintained their position, preventing, through wholesale air strikes, development of Communist strength sufficient to launch a major invasion.

An armistice at last came in July, 1953, along the lines the United States had consistently demanded. The new Eisenhower administration through Indian Prime Minister Nehru warned that peace would be obtained at whatever the cost. Apparently the Communists assumed this threat implied the use of atomic weapons and capitulated. President Syngman Rhee of South Korea threatened to continue the war because all of Korea was not liberated, but American pressure as well as extension of a million dollars in economic aid and a promise to establish a twenty-division South Korean army obtained his acquiescence. A U.S.-South Korean mutual security treaty was initialed in Seoul on August 8, 1953, and became operative when ratifications were exchanged in Novem-

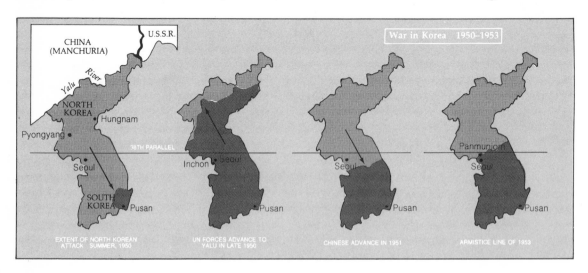

ber, 1954. Under it the United States pledged "armed aid" to the Republic of Korea should it be subjected to "external armed attack."

The long, bloody Korean conflict had intensified the contest with the Communist bloc and brought serious division in the United States where many found a negotiated peace hard to accept. The idealism which inspired U.S. participation in World War II, formation of the United Nations, and mobilization to resist Red aggression seemed strangely betrayed in accepting less than the establishment of a united, democratic Korea. Americans were learning the price of world leadership the hard way, but in their frustration scapegoats were sought at home for the less than ideal achievements abroad.

Selected Bibliography

The events of 1940 and 1941 leading to war are presented in Donald F. Drummond, *The Passing of American Neutrality, 1937–1941* (repr. of 1955 ed., 1968); William L. Langer and S. Everett Gleason, *Undeclared War, 1940–1941* (1953); Robert A. Divine, *The Reluctant Belligerent: American Entry Into the Second World War** (1965); and Herbert Feis, *The Road to Pearl Harbor: The Coming of the War between the United States and Japan**(1950). Critical of the U.S. role are Charles A. Beard, *President Roosevelt and the Coming of the War, 1941: A Study in Appearances and Realities* (repr. of 1948 ed., 1968), and Charles C. Tansill, *Back Door to War; The Roosevelt Foreign Policy, 1933–1941* (1952). The attack on Pearl Harbor is analyzed in Roberta Wohlstetter, *Pearl Harbor: Warning and Decision**(1962), and Walter Millis, *This is Pearl: The United States and Japan, 1941* (repr. of 1947 ed., 1971). Formidable domestic opposition to intervention is revealed in Wayne S. Cole, *America First; The Battle Against Intervention, 1940–1941* (1953).

The nation's organization for victory may be studied in Eliot Janeway, *The Struggle for Survival* (1968); Donald M. Nelson, *Arsenal of Democracy: The Story of American War Production* (1946) by the head of the War Production Board; James P. Baxter, *Scientists Against Time**(3rd ed., 1968), which deals with the influence of research and experimentation; and William L. White, *Bernard Baruch, Portrait of a Citizen* (1950).

Joel Seidman, *American Labor from Defense to Reconversion* (1953), deals with labor's wartime gains and struggles. Robert C. Weaver, *Negro Labor: A National Problem* (repr. of 1946 ed., 1969), shows the effects of mass migrations to industrial centers and should be supplemented for black problems generally by Gunnar Myrdal's *An American Dilemma: The Negro Problem and Modern Democracy**(2 vols., 20th an. ed., 1962). The mistreatment of Japanese Americans is recounted in Roger Daniels, *Concentration Camps, U.S.A.: Japanese Americans and World War II**(1972), while Edward S. Corwin, *Total War and the Constitution* (fasc. ed., 1947), is concerned with civil rights generally.

Military aspects of the war are comprehensively covered in A. Russell Buchanan, *The United States and World War II** (2 vols., 1964); Kenneth S. Davis, *Experience of War: The United States in World War II* (1965); and Charles B. MacDonald, *The Mighty Endeavor, American Armed Forces in the European Theater in World War II* (1969). Samuel E. Morison, *The Two-Ocean War: A Short History of the United States Navy in the Second World War* (1963), summarizes his fifteen-volume study. Military strategy is studied with varying conclusions in Morison, *Strategy and Compromise** (1958); Kent R. Greenfield, *American Strategy in World War Two: A Reconsideration** (1963); and Hanson W. Baldwin, *Great Mistakes of the War* (1950).

---

*Available in paperback.

Herbert Feis, *Churchill, Roosevelt, Stalin: The War They Waged and the Peace They Sought** (2d ed., 1967), deals brilliantly with wartime diplomacy. Other useful works include Gaddis Smith, *American Diplomacy During the Second World War, 1941–1945**(1965), and John L. Snell, *Illusion and Necessity: The Diplomacy of Global War, 1939–1945**(1963). Robert E. Sherwood, *Roosevelt and Hopkins: An Intimate History* (rev. ed., 1950), depicts the president as an earnest, able diplomat, a contrary picture from that presented in Gabriel Kolko, *The Politics of War: The World and United States Foreign Policy, 1943–45**(1970). John L. Snell, ed., *The Meaning of Yalta: Big Three Diplomacy and the New Balance of Power* (1956), and Herbert Feis, *Between War and Peace: The Potsdam Conference**(1960), judiciously review the two major diplomatic encounters with Russia. Feis analyzes Truman's method of ending the war in *The Atomic Bomb and the End of World War Two* (rev. ed., 1966).

Martin F. Herz, *Beginnings of the Cold War** (1966), and Norman A. Graebner, *Cold War Diplomacy, American Foreign Policy, 1945–1960** (1962), sympathetically present U.S. entrance into and pursuit of the cold war. A contrary view characterizes Denna F. Fleming's *The Cold War and Its Origins, 1917–1960* (2 vols., 1968), and Gar Alperovitz, *Atomic Diplomacy: Hiroshima and Potsdam; The Use of the Atomic Bomb and the American Confrontation with Soviet Power**(1966). Specific studies include Harry B. Price, *The Marshall Plan and Its Meaning* (1955); Robert E. Osgood, *NATO, The Entangling Alliance* (1962); and Walter P. Davison, *The Berlin Blockade; A Study in Cold War Politics* (1958). The memoirs of leading participants are quite useful, especially Harry S Truman's *Memoirs* (2 vols., 1958); James F. Byrnes, *Speaking Frankly* (1947); George F. Kennan, *Memoirs, 1925–1950* (1967); and Dean Acheson, *Present at the Creation: My Years in the State Department** (1970).

The debacle in China is scrupulously analyzed in Herbert Feis, *The China Tangle: The American Effort in China from Pearl Harbor to the Marshall Mission** (1953), and Tang Tsou, *America's Failure in China, 1941–50* (1963). The Korean War is treated generally in Carl Berger, *The Korean Knot: A Military-Political History* (1957), and David Rees, *Korea: The Limited War* *(1970). John W. Spanier, *The Truman-MacArthur Controversy and the Korean War** (1965), is an unbiased view of that conflict. Norman A. Graebner, *The New Isolationism: A Study in Politics and Foreign Policy Since 1950* (1956), deals with the internal divisiveness caused by the war and disputes over Asian foreign policy.

Postwar Reforms and Counter-Reforms

1946	Employment Act
1947	Taft-Hartley Act
	Presidential Succession Act
1949	Housing Act of 1949
1950	Displaced Persons Act
	McCarran Internal Security Act
1951	Passage of Twenty-second Amendment
1952	McCarran-Walter Act
1953	Creation of Department of Health, Education and Welfare
1954	St. Lawrence Seaway approved
	Agricultural Adjustment Act
	Brown v. *Board of Education of Topeka* decision
	Dixon-Yates contract dispute
1957	Civil Rights Act of 1957
1958	National Defense Education Act
1960	Civil Rights Act of 1960
1961	Peace Corps and Alliance for Progress announced
	Twenty-third Amendment approved
	"Freedom Riders" crusade
	Aid for Distressed Areas Act
1962	Trade Expansion Act
	End decreed to discrimination in federally financed housing
1963	Civil rights march on Washington
	Expansion of National Defense Education Act
1964	Twenty-fourth Amendment

23

The Postwar Search for Prosperity and Equality

Long-Range Developments

For Economics and Corporate Enterprise

The relative control of inflation in the 1950s resulted in much popular discontent with the substantial inflation of later years.

For Democratic Government

The G.I. Bill of Rights has been extended to Vietnam War veterans.

The pro-business image of the Eisenhower administration, which was promoted by some of its leaders, had an adverse effect on the Republican party, particularly in the 1960 and 1964 national elections.

For Civil Liberties, Freedom, and Reform

Reaction against "McCarthyism" has continued to the present, and no comparable movement questioning the loyalty of the nation's civil servants has developed.

The Department of Health, Education and Welfare has grown to become the largest single department in the federal government.

The Twenty-fifth Amendment, ratified in 1964, provided the basis for Representative Gerald Ford's selection as vice-president of the United States in 1973.

Widespread compliance with the *Brown* v. *Board of Education of Topeka* decision has come only in recent years, as has the realization of many civil rights goals set by President Truman.

Truman's
Domestic Policies

The Second World War left the average American citizen with a new affluence which stimulated enormous economic, social, and political changes. Economic indexes indicated over a third of the nation's families still had poverty-level incomes, but, having enjoyed some of the luxuries of an industrial society, many of their members were determined to improve their positions. No group was more frustrated than the million blacks whose armed service experiences motivated them to seek improved jobs, housing, and social conditions. Everywhere the urge to leave the war behind and to create a new and better world was accompanied by fear of the nation's economic inadequacy and possible depression.

Fate decreed that an unusual man would fill the presidency in the trying postwar years. Harry Truman had risen to the rank of major in World War I, had failed in the haberdashery business in the 1920s, and had served as county judge in Independence, Missouri, for years before the Pendergast machine tapped him for the U.S. Senate in 1934. At the same time, he had proven himself a man of courage, remaining personally honest and losing an election rather than coming to terms with the Ku Klux Klan. As president, his loyalty to unworthy friends, brash tongue, and taste for personal controversy caused him difficulties, yet he became a courageous, liberal leader whose administration revived the reform movement of Franklin D. Roosevelt's prewar years.

The nation plunged into peace, demobilizing its armed forces and abandoning controls faster than Truman wished. Though generous provision was made for veterans, including the establishment of the G. I. Bill of Rights which provided free college tuition, funds were drastically cut for the military establishment. The president's plan for universal military training was rejected, but at last a single Department of Defense was created in which the air force received coequal rank with the army and navy. After a violent struggle, the civilian-controlled Atomic Energy Commission received exclusive control of the nation's atomic power, although means were provided for the military to contribute to its policy-making decisions.

In a refreshing change of emphasis to non-military affairs, in September, 1945, the president presented to Congress a program which challenged it to interject the government into the private economy on behalf of the masses. Included were recommendations for slum clearance, increase in the minimum wage, extension of Social Security, national health insurance, reorganization of the executive branch, extension of wartime controls, and full employment legislation. The southern Democratic-Republican coalition which controlled Congress was unfriendly to this program. In February, 1946, an Employment Act was passed, but it was quite different from Truman's bill which would have had the president submit an annual production and employment budget and establish a congressional Joint Committee on the National Budget to see laws were enacted to insure full employment and production. Instead the Employment Act established a three-man Council of Economic Advisers and a joint congressional committee to advise the president and Congress on needed economic action. The measure was weaker than the president wished but unabashedly assumed federal responsibility for managing the economy.

The president was less successful in obtaining controls extension even though prices skyrocketed in the summer of 1946, after Congress refused to continue a strong Office of Price Administration. Farmers withheld their meat from market, and the public generally blamed the administration. Conservatives, frightened by Truman's program, deserted him in the 1946 congressional elections, as did many liberals and union leaders who were offended by his policies. To counterbalance the loss of overtime pay and a drop in real income after the coming of peace, many unions demanded wage increases of approximately 30 percent. When management refused to concede, a number of crippling national strikes, including walkouts in the automobile, electrical, and meat packing industries, occurred in the winter of 1945–46. Under pressure, the administration allowed price increases to permit the wage increases necessary to maintain labor's purchasing power. However, this concession failed to end major difficulties, and national impatience with what many considered unwarranted labor demands led to the call for legislation to regulate union practices and actions. The president opposed most of these requests, feeling they were punitive and injurious, but he did not fail to act in crisis situations.

In April, 1946, Truman seized the coal mines, following John L. Lewis' failure to come to terms with management, and the railroads in May, 1946. After the Engineers and Trainmen, two of the twenty railway brotherhoods, walked out despite federal seizure, Truman asked Congress to draft strikers in vital industries under federal control. However, the action did not need to be taken since the unions finally complied, but many union men were alienated by the president's stance. Other liberals were offended when Harold L. Ickes resigned as secretary of the interior, correctly charging the president with nominating a corruptionist, Edwin W. Pauley, a California oil man, as undersecretary of the navy,* and when Secretary of Commerce Henry Wallace was dismissed for opposition to the administration's Russian policy. Therefore it was not surprising that the Republicans gained control of

*Pauley was not confirmed but became a reparations agent.

both houses of Congress in 1946 for the first time since 1928. The Eightieth Congress had 246 Republicans to 188 Democrats in the House, and 51 Republicans to 45 Democrats in the Senate.

In the ensuing two years, the president and Congress were in perpetual disagreement, a condition promoted by the difficulties which beset the country. Inflation rocked the nation, stimulated by two tax reductions opposed by Truman and by failure to give the president effective controls. In a period when housing was in short supply, Congress defeated administrative efforts to enact the Taft-Ellender-Wagner bill which would have provided extensive public housing. Though in June, 1948, farm price supports were continued at 90 percent of parity through 1949, adequate funds were not provided for storage facilities. In July, 1947, the Presidential Succession Act was passed revising succession procedure prescribed in 1886. It made the speaker of the House and the Senate president pro-tempore next in line of succession to the presidency following the president and vice-president; placed next in order were the secretary of state and other cabinet members in the sequence of their offices' creation. Since in the Eightieth Congress both the speaker and president pro-tem were Republicans, the political motivation behind the law was obvious.

Although Truman suffered many reverses, his most spectacular defeat came in the enactment of the Taft-Hartley Bill over his veto in June, 1947. This amendment to the Wagner Act, which reflected public loss of confidence in unions, still permitted industry-wide bargaining, but it offended labor by providing additional use of federal injunctions, imposing new requirements, and outlawing a number of union practices. In cases involving the national health or safety, the government was authorized to obtain an eighty-day injunction preventing strikes. Both unions and employers were required to give sixty days' notice of contract termination or modifications. Union officers were forced to sign loyalty oaths; unions became liable for breach of contracts, were required to publish financial statements, and were prohibited from making financial contributions to political campaigns. Secondary boycotts and the closed shop were among the practices forbidden. Union leaders feared the law would be used to break their organizations, and, though these fears proved largely unfounded, Truman's veto sealed labor's devotion to him.

The Fair Deal

After experiencing a number of defeats and reversals, Truman appeared to be headed for defeat in the 1948 presidential election, and therefore a vigorous contest arose for the Republican nomination. Although Harold Stassen won the Wisconsin and Nebraska primaries, neither he nor Senator Robert A. Taft, who had emerged as the party's most effective leader, could stop the renomination of Governor Thomas E. Dewey on the third ballot. Dewey's splendid organization, his progressive, internationalist record, and a conviction that he had the best chance to win were factors in his selection. The attractive, moderately liberal California governor, Earl Warren, was chosen as his running mate. The party platform committed it to support the United Nations and the European Recovery Program but pledged tax reductions and an effort to destroy internal Communism. Significantly, it advocated slum clearance, low cost housing, and expansion of Social Security.

Disenchantment with Truman led Democrats of various philosophies to attempt the drafting of General Eisenhower as a presidential candidate. When he refused, a number of liberals unsuccessfully turned to Supreme Court Justice William O. Douglas, but, because no alternative became available, Truman was renominated. The popular Democratic leader of the Senate, Alben W. Barkley, was chosen as his running mate.

The convention's most exciting event came in the adoption of a minority platform committee report on civil rights. Led by Mayor Hubert Humphrey of Minneapolis and a number of liberals belonging to Americans for Democratic Action, the convention narrowly endorsed creation of a permanent Fair Employment Practices Commission, federal antilynching and antipoll tax laws, and strong federal machinery to protect civil rights. In making his acceptance speech, Truman electrified the convention and assumed an initiative retained during the campaign. He announced he was calling a special session of Congress to enact the liberal features of the Republican platform, laws he had been trying to obtain for two years. After Congress met perfunctorily and did nothing, Truman, in a 30,000-mile "whistle stop" campaign, denounced "the do-nothing, Republican Eightieth Congress" as the worst in American history.

Governor Dewey, confident of victory, conducted a low-key campaign. Two schisms from the Democrats seemed to confirm his views. One was led by Henry Wallace and Senator Glen Taylor of Idaho, who were nominated by a new Progressive Party which urged nationalization of major industries, an end to racial injustice, and cooperation with Russia. The party came increasingly under Communist control, however, which enabled Truman to divert criticism of left-wing influence in the Democratic Party by denouncing Wallace's Communist support. Departing from a prepared text in a nationwide address, he asserted "We are going to win, and we are going to win without the help of Henry Wallace and his Communists," a declaration that largely dissipated the issue.

The adoption of a strong Democratic civil rights plank led to the organization of a States' Rights party which nominated South Carolina Governor J. Strom Thurmond and Mississippi Governor Fielding L. Wright as its candidates. Though the party carried Alabama, Mississippi, Louisiana, and South Carolina, it polled only 1.1 million votes, approximately the same number as the Progressives. On the other hand, its existence stimulated many blacks and northern liberals to support the president, an opposite result from that it wished to attain.

Backed by labor, blacks, and normally Republican farmers in the Midwest who were offended by the inadequacy of government provision of agricultural storage bins, Truman scored the upset victory of the century. He received over 3 million more popular votes than Dewey and 303 electoral votes to Dewey's 189. West of the Mississippi, only Oregon, the Dakotas, Kansas, and Nebraska went Republican. Both houses passed into Democratic hands, where majorities of 12 and 23 were obtained in the Senate and House.

Truman interpreted his victory as an endorsement of liberal policies and, as a result, in January, 1949, launched his "Fair Deal" program. The opposition of the southern Democrat-Republican coalition, which had for years functioned well on numerous issues, and the eruption of war in 1950 contributed to the death of many of his plans, although substantial results were obtained from them. The minimum wage was increased from 40 to 75 cents, and, for the first time in the postwar era, a significant federal commitment was made to low-cost housing. The Housing Act of 1949 provided funds for some 810,000 low-cost units to be built over a five-year period. Social Security was extended to ten million additional persons in 1950 and seven million in 1952 while benefits were also increased. The modern conservation movement was initiated by gaining substantial funds for the Reclamation Bu-

President Truman signing the Fair Labor Standards Act, which raised the minimum wage to 75 cents an hour.

reau's water control programs in the West. Significant aid for smaller farmers was obtained through the Farm Security Administration and increased allocations for TVA and REA.

The administration and liberal forces, however, suffered some reverses which were indicative of the generally conservative attitude of the people. In March, 1947, the Eightieth Congress submitted the Twenty-second Amendment to the states, and it was adopted in February, 1951. The amendment, which many regarded as aimed at the deceased President Roosevelt, made two terms the limit for the presidency and placed a limit of one term in cases where a person had held the office for more than two years of a term to which someone else had been elected. The amendment became operative with President Truman's successor.

Truman, who was most sensitive to the plight of displaced persons and those subject to Communist persecution, was also disappointed in some actions taken regarding immigration. In December, 1945, he directed the speedup of admissions of persons under the quota system, and, in 1948, when he advocated a liberalized immigration policy, Congress passed a law admitting 205,000 European displaced persons including 3,000 nonquota orphans. The president was displeased, however, feeling the law unjustly discriminated against Catholics and Jews. He strongly supported the Displaced Persons Act of 1950 which removed these discriminations and increased the number of visas to be issued over the following three years.

A major reversal came with the enactment over the president's veto of the McCarran-Walter Act in 1952. Although the act removed the ban on the immigration of Asian peoples, it retained the basic provisions of the 1924 immigration law, including the quota system, incorporated screening procedures to keep out subversives, and authorized the attorney general to deport immigrants for Communist and "Communist-front" affiliations.

The president sustained even greater defeats on farm, labor, health insurance, and civil rights legislation. After failing in Congress to obtain civil rights laws, he used executive powers broadly to implement the report of his Committee on Civil Rights, which urged the end of discrimination. The strengthened Civil Rights section of the Justice Department began to assist individuals in private cases. At the same time, segregation began to be phased out in 1948 in the government and military services, while blacks in number were welcomed for the first time at the White House.

Since his first year in office, Truman had advocated a program of compulsory national health insurance, but the powerful American Medical Association, waging a relentless campaign against it as a form of "socialized medicine," defeated the administration's bill. Approval was obtained, however, of the Hill-Burton Act which provided federal matching funds for constructing nonprofit hospitals and clinics.

In labor policy, outright repeal of the Taft-Hartley Act became the president's goal. Stubbornly he refused to accept less than this and defeated what could have been prolabor amendments to the law. However, the act was amended in 1951 to permit the negotiation of union-shop contracts without first taking votes of employees.

More ingenuity was demonstrated in farm policy after prices began a continuing decline in 1948. The administration program, proposed by Secretary of Agriculture Charles Brannan, included conventional support for nonperishable commodities but, while allowing perishable goods to sell at market prices, provided payment of the difference between this return and a just price from the treasury. The plan probably would have lessened storage problems and reduced food prices but was defeated by a combination of large farmers and foes of what many conservatives felt to be the gradual imposition of socialism (creeping socialism).

One of the major deterrents to the administration's success was a growing fear of Communist influence in government. Part of the anxiety sprung from an effort to find a scapegoat to explain America's precarious position in world affairs and part was a natural reaction to revelations of the penetrations Communists had made in labor movements in the United States.

Moreover, the Truman administration was attacked for allowing Communists to remain in government. In the summer of 1947 the president, after realizing that some Reds had become employees during and immediately after the war, began a loyalty review of all government employees. By 1951, of 3 million employees, 2,000 were allowed to resign because they were regarded as security risks and 212 were dismissed. Although no evidence of espionage was uncovered, fear of Communist subversion continued to grow in the United States. In August, 1948, a *Time* magazine editor and confessed former Communist, Whittaker Chambers, testified before the House Un-American Activities Committee that Alger Hiss, a long-time State Department employee who had been present at the Yalta Conference, was also a Communist. After extensive congressional hearings and two trials, in 1950 Hiss was convicted of perjury and sentenced to five years in prison. Truman, perhaps unwisely, labeled the charges against Hiss a "red herring," and Secretary of State Acheson, even after his conviction, declared that he did "not intend to turn my back on Alger Hiss." These statments contributed to the fear that the government was soft on Communists.

Fears were also increased in 1950 when the public learned that Klaus Fuchs, a German-born physicist who had been arrested by the British government for espionage, admitted that he had been part of a spying operation while working on the atomic bomb in 1944 at Los Alamos, New Mexico. As a result of his information, the FBI arrested a couple, Julius and Ethel Rosenberg, and Morton Sobell. In March, 1951, Sobell was sentenced to thirty years in prison and the Rosenbergs sentenced to death, a sentence which, after many appeals, was carried out on June 19, 1953.

Congress reflected the fearful, popular mood when in September, 1950, it overrode the president's veto of the McCarran Internal Security Act which Truman felt would punish men for their opinions rather than their actions. The McCarran Act was broad and ill-defined in nature. It required individual Communists and Communist organizations to register and submit their records to the attorney general, barred members of Communist organizations from defense plants, prohibited entry into the United States of anyone who had belonged to a totalitarian organization, made punishable by law acts which contributed to the erection of a dictatorship in the United States, and established a Subversive Activities Control Board to watch internal Communist developments. Yet the McCarran Act did not quiet the fears of those who felt the country was being destroyed from within. Many wondered if the failure of government investigations to unearth any appreciable number of Reds on the payroll was due to a deliberate covering up of their presence. In February, 1950, Wisconsin's Senator Joseph McCarthy initially charged that there were a number of Reds in the State Department who were known to the secretary of state.

A shocked Senate appointed an investigating subcommittee headed by Maryland's Senator Millard Tydings, a conservative Democrat whom Roosevelt had unsuccessfully tried to purge in the 1938 primaries. In the summer of 1950, the committee reported McCarthy's charges were a "fraud," and constituted "perhaps the most nefarious campaign of half-truth and untruth in the history of the republic." The angered McCarthy obtained revenge by contributing to Tydings' defeat in the fall elections through the use of smear tactics such as a fake photograph showing Tydings with Earl Browder, a leading Communist. No person in public life was secure from McCarthy's smears; even General George C. Marshall and General Dwight D. Eisenhower were attacked in 1951 as tools of the international Communist conspiracy. McCarthy's influence was so potent that those who challenged him frequently were defeated at the polls or felt compelled to retire from public life. In addition to Senator Tydings, Senators William Benton, Ernest MacFarland, and Scott Lucas were among his victims, but the main brunt of his attack was the Truman administration.

Eisenhower's Nomination

As the 1952 elections approached, discontent with the administration darkened chances of

Democratic victory. In addition to fears of Communist influence, disgust with the Korean involvement, a limited conflict in which intense fighting still continued, was primary. Contributing to the disillusionment was an inflationary spiral, which caused an increase of 12 percent in the wholesale price index within eighteen months, and concern with corruption in government. In 1951 a congressional investigation revealed Reconstruction Finance Corporation loans had been purchased through the payment of 5 percent kickbacks to government officials. Soon afterwards, similar graft was shown to exist in the Internal Revenue Service and the Tax Division of the Department of Justice. The public was also inflamed by televised hearings of Senator Estes Kefauver's Senate Crime Investigating Committee, and it often failed to distinguish between the activities of exposed city machines and that of the national administration.

Though Truman began to clean up federal corruption, even removing Attorney General J. Howard McGrath, he moved too slowly and with insufficient moral zeal to dispel doubts regarding his administration. The Republican nomination again assumed great value since many believed the party's nominee would be elected.

Ohio's Senator Taft became the leading Republican contender after his reelection over vigorous labor opposition in 1950. By the 1952 convention he had garnered almost 500 first-ballot votes, only one hundred less than the number needed for victory. His support came primarily from the Midwest and from the coterie of officials dominating the party in the South.

In spite of his impressive strength, Taft's nomination was blocked by the eastern Republican establishment, controlled by the Dewey organization, which, distrusting his commitment to progressivism and internationalism, doubted he could be elected. Appealing to General Eisenhower's fear of isolationism, its leaders persuaded him to become a candidate. Massachusetts' Senator Henry Cabot Lodge, Jr., effectively obtained Eisenhower primary victories in New Hampshire, Pennsylvania, and New Jersey, and after Taft won in Wisconsin and Nebraska, the general resigned his NATO command to campaign. By the time of the convention, he, like Taft, had obtained almost 500 first ballot votes. Minnesota and California were committed to favorite sons, and it was generally concluded that the nomination would go to the candidate who obtained the 68 contested votes of Texas, Georgia, and Louisiana.

The well-versed Eisenhower managers knew from a study of the 1912 Republican convention that if normal procedures were followed Taft would probably win. These procedures allowed temporarily seated but contested delegations to vote on all credential disputes except their own. Therefore the Eisenhower managers obtained issuance of a "fair play" demand by twenty-three of the twenty-five Republican governors, asking that all disputed delegates stand aside when the vote was taken on contested seats. Under intense popular pressure, the convention adopted this procedure by a 110-vote majority which led to the seating of the Eisenhower delegates from Georgia and Texas and the general's nomination. As a concession to conservatives, the vice-presidential nomination went to the young California Senator Richard Nixon, who in 1950 had taken a prominent role in the exposure of Alger Hiss.

Eisenhower's Appeal

After refusing early overtures, including those of President Truman, Illinois Governor Adlai Stevenson bowed to a genuine draft and accepted the Democratic nomination. To conciliate the South, Alabama's liberal Senator John Sparkman was chosen as his running mate. Stevenson, a grandson of Grover Cleveland's vice-president, had run ahead of the national ticket in Illinois in 1948, and as a candidate raised the tone of American politics by witty, intellectual speeches which dealt with basic issues. The university community especially responded to him with a devotion seldom bestowed on any political candidate. The support of labor leaders was retained by a commitment to repeal the Taft-Hartley Act and that of blacks by firm advocacy of civil rights legislation.

Stevenson's appeal, however, was no match for that of Eisenhower who based his campaign on a promise to "clean up the mess in Washington" and, developing a theme of the Republican platform, to end mismanagement

Adlai Stevenson

of foreign affairs. If elected, Eisenhower promised to end the "containment" of Communism and pursue policies that would enable the captive peoples to free themselves. He never spelled out the means by which this could be done, but to many Americans the election of Eisenhower, the master of armies and liberator of Europe, offered a chance to assume the initiative in foreign affairs.

Two fall events sealed Eisenhower's victory. On September 12, 1952, he assured himself of right-wing Republican support by signing a policy statement drafted by Senator Taft which held that the main campaign goal was to defeat creeping socialism. If elected president, Eisenhower agreed to defend the basic features of the Taft-Hartley Act and to see that Taft's partisans received a just portion of the patronage. A second significant event occurred on October 24, 1952, when Eisenhower, speaking in Detroit, promised to go to Korea in an effort to bring the war to a quick and "honorable end."

When the returns were in, Eisenhower carried all except nine southern and border states, attaining a popular vote majority of 5.5 million and 442 electoral votes to Stevenson's 89. The new president assumed office at sixty-two with little political experience and an intense desire to avoid rough and tumble politics. His army experience had conditioned him to rely on information and decisions made by subordinates, a practice he continued in the presidency. A major heart attack in 1955, a serious ileitis operation in the spring of 1956, and a mild stroke in November, 1957, necessitated even greater dependence on those around him. Former Governor Sherman Adams of New Hampshire, who kept the presidential calendar and determined who saw the president, served as virtual "assistant president" until Eisenhower was forced to remove him in September, 1958, for receiving gifts from a New England industrialist.

Eisenhower's executive style was conditioned by a sincere belief in state's rights and a conviction that the government should be kept as close to the people as possible. Little was achieved in accomplishing these goals, however. The President's Commission on Intergovernmental Relations made a number of suggestions, but, harrassed by problems, the nation's governors were reluctant to reassume additional responsibilities, even when the president asked their aid.

In dealing with Congress, Eisenhower, reacting against the style of his immediate predecessors, assumed a distant attitude which left wide leeway for congressional action. He proposed policies and laws but made few efforts to coerce congressmen into supporting them. This approach, he believed, would re-

Dwight D. Eisenhower

store the balance of power envisioned by the founding fathers, but the result was a failure of many bills desired by the administration and a disturbing floundering of national leadership.

Despite inadequacies, Eisenhower retained the respect and even the affection of a large portion of the people. Many, tired of three decades of reform and war, welcomed the respite his administration offered. Moveover, he was a man of immense personal charm and goodwill who evoked a warm response from most Americans. Throughout his years in office, his earlier military successes inspired confidence in his foreign and defense policies. Regardless of statistical or rational objections, the masses believed that the president would pursue the best policies for the nation.

Such faith enabled the "nonpolitical" Eisenhower to win renomination easily in 1956 and command overwhelming popular support, even though he had experienced two major illnesses and the Democratic party was increasing its lead as the nation's major political organization, as demonstrated by its gaining majority control in the House of Representatives in 1954. Stevenson was again the Democrat's nominee, although ex-President Truman had given his support to former New York Governor Averell Harriman. In the campaign, the Democrats attacked the administration's reduction of defense expenditures and failure to provide greater concessions to the poor, the elderly, and smaller businessmen; also the question of Eisenhower's health was raised. The Democrats were not able to find an issue, however, and the Republican appeal based on peace, prosperity, and confidence in Eisenhower was overwhelming. When international difficulties arose in Hungary and the Near East just before the election, the desire to continue the experienced Eisenhower in office was intensified, although his policies may have contributed to the coming of the crises.

Eisenhower was reelected by a 9 million vote majority and received 457 electoral votes. Stevenson won only 73 electoral votes of seven southern and border states, but the Democrats accomplished the unprecedented feat of winning both houses of Congress while losing the presidency.

Eisenhower's Domestic Problems and Achievements

When Eisenhower first assumed office in January, 1953, he was committed to a program that would enhance the power of the states and preserve and expand the free enterprise system while maintaining the basic reforms of the New Deal and Fair Deal. As Eisenhower expressed it, his program was "conservative when it comes to money and liberal when it comes to human beings." The president felt he was pursuing a middle-of-the-road policy which accounted for attacks from both the right and the left.

Early in the administration, many were disappointed when it failed to deal effectively with Senator Joseph McCarthy. Without proving his allegations, McCarthy continued to attack various segments of the government, especially the State Department, charging that Communist officeholders had influenced policies leading to national surrender. Many hoped Eisenhower, who personally despised McCarthy, would end his reign of terror. The sly Senator Taft, who also disliked him but did nothing to impede his forays against Democrats, attempted to end McCarthy's power by making him chairman of the Committee on Government Operations, while the Internal Security Committee was placed in moderate hands. The ruse backfired since McCarthy proceeded to hunt Communists throughout all areas of government by using the permanent Subcommitteee on Investigations of the Gov-

ernment Operations' Committee in an unprecedented manner. The Voice of America program, which attempted to promote pro-American opinion by beaming broadcasts around the world for the United States Information Agency, was thoroughly indicted. Most humiliating of all was an international "witch-hunting" expedition conducted by two young committee employees, Roy Cohn and G. David Schine, which resulted in purging of State Department libraries and demoralization of the International Information Administration. Under the engendered hysteria, the government began to remove a number of employees, not because of any proven disloyalty but because they were considered poor security risks. On these grounds, the Atomic Energy Commission in 1953 even barred J. Robert Oppenheimer, one of the key scientists in the development of the atomic bomb, from access to classified material.

Eisenhower, who was aware of McCarthy's influence, avoided a direct confrontation with him for over a year after coming to office. At last, in the spring of 1954, he denounced the Wisconsin demagogue in unmistakable terms after McCarthy began to lose status as a result of nationally televised congressional hearings. These hearings occurred following McCarthy's indictment of the army for promoting a reserve corps dentist who refused to sign a loyalty oath and his attack on Secretary of the Army Robert Stevens. In the resulting dispute, Roy Cohn's efforts to obtain preferential treatment for G. David Schine, who had recently been drafted, were presented, and McCarthy's bullying, unfair techniques were scrutinized by millions during thirty-five days of hearings. At their conclusion, McCarthy's power was broken, and a resolution to censure him was introduced in the Senate in July, 1954, and passed December 2.

Fortunately the administration's position on other issues was more effective than on

McCarthyism. A coterie of successful business leaders and attorneys accepted cabinet positions, including the steel magnate George Humphrey as secretary of the treasury and General Motors' Charles Erwin Wilson as secretary of defense. In one year the federal budget was cut almost 10 percent, sizable tax reductions introduced, credit tightened, and the Federal Reserve rediscount rates raised to counteract inflation. Yet the administration proved to be very pragmatic in dealing with economic situations, and, when recessions occurred in 1953–54, 1957–58, and 1960–61, credit was eased and deficit spending used. "Modern Republicanism," as the president described his philosophy, was fully committed to government intervention in the economy to promote the general welfare. Debate centered on the degree and type of action, with Democrats charging that the administration welcomed some unemployment as necessary to maintain a stable dollar. Denying the charge, Republicans pointed with pride to the relative control of inflation. Though prices rose approximately 8 percent between 1955 and 1958, they were practically stable during the remainder of the Eisenhower years.

Among Eisenhower's most conservative policies was opposition to federal expansion in the electrical power field as illustrated by his defeat of Democratic attempts to build a high dam on the Snake River at Hell's Canyon in Idaho, after which the Idaho Power Company received authorization for three small dams in the area. When TVA discovered it lacked facilities to supply adequate electricity to the plant of the Atomic Energy Commission (AEC) at Paducah, Kentucky, the president endorsed the Dixon-Yates contract under which a newly created private utility group would construct a plant to fill the need. Critics, who felt the president was sabotaging TVA, defeated the plan after it was shown the government expert rec-

ommending the contract was an officer of the firm that would sell the Dixon-Yates securities. Later the government of Memphis, Tennessee, built a plant to generate the needed power, and both sides in the controversy were reasonably well pleased. The advocates of private power were satisfied since TVA was prevented from expanding its facilities, and the proponents of public power were pleased that the extra power for the AEC came from a municipal project.

The president proved equally conservative in reversing an executive order of President Truman which set aside "the submerged lands of the Continental Shelf as a naval petroleum reserve." With Eisenhower's approval, a law was enacted in 1953 returning to state possession the tidelands oil deposits within the "historic boundary" of each state but retaining federal ownership of the oil resources in the outer continental shelf. Court decisions defined the historic boundaries, with the result that California obtained approximately half of the gas and oil off its coast, but the other states received much less.

In other fields, however, Eisenhower maintained and expanded progressive programs, frequently over the opposition of the right-wing of his party. In April, 1953, a number of agencies concerned with social welfare and education were consolidated into a cabinet level Department of Health, Education and Welfare, and Oveta Culp Hobby, wartime head of the Women's Army Corps, became its first secretary. The minimum wage was increased to a dollar an hour in 1955; Social Security benefits were broadened and extended to millions not previously covered in 1954 and 1956. Extensive flood control and power production were undertaken in the Missouri, Rio Grande, Colorado, and Columbia River valleys and elsewhere. The St. Lawrence Seaway, whose development had been blocked by the railroads since the 1920s, was approved in 1954 and opened in 1959. In 1956 a 42,000-mile system of interstate highways, 90 percent of whose cost was to be federally paid, was authorized. In 1959 statehood was granted to both Alaska and Hawaii, in part due to their recent impressive growth in population.

The administration also acknowledged federal responsibility in the critical field of housing and education, obtaining the underwriting of approximately 35,000 low-income housing units each year, fewer than many liberals would have liked but enough to be of aid. Concurrently, FHA requirements for home purchases were made more lenient. Facing the education crisis produced by the bountiful postwar crop of babies, in 1956 the president sponsored an education bill to provide the states with funds based on per capita income and the percentage of state expenditures on schools. However, this and a similar bill in 1957 were defeated after desegregation amendments were added to them.

The administration's major educational achievement came in 1958, while the nation was still in shock from Russia's launching of its first *Sputnik* satellite the previous year. To aid the United States in catching up, especially in science and language study, the National Defense Education Act provided long-term, low-interest loans to teacher education students, half of whose loans would be remitted if they taught five years in elementary or secondary schools following graduation. Fifty-five hundred graduate fellowships were also established and matching grants made available to the states to provide public school facilities and books in mathematics, the sciences, and foreign languages. These funds were quickly absorbed but, because they did not provide new buildings or pay salaries, met only a portion of the need. Meanwhile, a national debate of major proportions raged as to why the educational

systems of other countries seemed to be achieving more than that of the United States.*

The Economic Condition of the People

The improvement in the standard of living which began for most Americans with rearmament for World War II continued in the 1950s, 1960s and 1970s, although moderate recessions slowed economic developments every four or five years. Progress was not uniform, of course, but the application of advanced technology, to the point where automated equipment in many instances was truly self-regulating, resulted in many benefits. Production in most fields advanced rapidly, providing a sound base for wage increases, at least in the 1950s. Although the automobile industry remained the nation's largest, such new industries as electronics and aviation rose to important positions.

Despite inflation and increased taxes, the average industrial worker gained over 25 percent in real income between 1940 and 1960. After 1960, increases in productivity did not keep pace with wage increases, which contributed to the substantial inflation of the 1960s and early 1970s, a trend by no means confined to the United States. Between 1958 and 1960 the annual increases in prices averaged 2.2 percent, but they were to skyrocket in later years.

---

*The demand for a return to basic studies with less emphasis on tailoring the curriculum to each student, a movement discernible since the end of World War II, was omnipresent. Long before the new educational crisis, most colleges had modified the elective system to require courses giving students some familiarity with the basic arts and sciences. The emphasis was soon changed, however; with the curtailment of the government's rocketry program in the late 1960s a serious temporary surplus of engineers and other scientists developed. This fact in conjunction with more assertive student bodies which demanded a voice in shaping curricula resulted in a loosening of general requirements and greater flexibility in course choices.

Despite adversities, the average citizen had greater real income and more material goods than ever. This was not true of the farmer, whose increase in productivity was the basis of his problems. In the 1950s alone, individual production per man-hour on farms increased by 84 percent—three times as fast as that in industry. The size of farms constantly grew and their number declined, as did farm population. The total number of persons employed on farms decreased from 10,012,000 in 1946 to 8,773,000 in 1959. Net farm income suffered terrific losses, being 40 percent lower in 1960 than it had been in 1945.

The agricultural problem defied the most strenuous efforts made to resolve it. The government guaranteed many prices at a substantial percentage of parity, but the rapidly rising costs of farm operation ate up potential profits. Secretary of Agriculture Ezra Taft Benson led the Eisenhower administration in the Agricultural Adjustment Act of 1954 to adopt a system of flexible supports that dropped as low as 70 percent of parity. Although the parity ratio, a comprehensive measure of farmers' purchasing power, declined to 80 in 1960 (and hit 75 in 1970, the lowest figure since 1933), government price supports were largely responsible for an astronomical 600 percent increase in federal expenditures for agriculture in a six-year period ending in 1958.

Since 1954, good use has been made of agricultural surpluses as food has been given to destitute nations and exchanged for foreign currencies; also at home much has been used in school lunch programs and distributed to the poor. Payment for conservation practices and withdrawal of lands into "soil banks" became a prominent government policy under the Agricultural Act of 1956. In an effort to reduce surpluses, farmers were compensated for withdrawing lands from cultivation and the government practice, in use since the 1930s, of paying for conversion of lands to soil-conserv-

ing crops was abandoned. Though the new policy offered some advantages, it often failed to reduce surpluses since farmers intensified cultivation of the lands being farmed and productivity rose. Disgusted with their lot, hundreds of thousands of rural people moved to the cities where they contributed greatly to the increasing urbanization of the nation.

The Civil Rights Movement

Among the largest migrant groups in the nation during and after the Second World War were southern blacks who sought greater opportunities in northern and border cities. Although a bloody race riot occurred in Detroit in 1943, and interracial tension became intense in other cities, no other major riots occurred until the 1960s. In many areas public facilities were gradually opened, and some jobs formerly reserved for whites were made available to blacks. In the South, also, a new tolerance was evident, especially in the cities whose growth reflected most of the region's progress. Nevertheless, limited opportunities and wartime experiences made the omnipresent repression and, in many cases, segregation intolerable to many blacks.

The modern civil rights movement received its greatest advancement not from the actions of discontented blacks but from decisions of the U.S. Supreme Court. Since the 1930s the Court has been chipping away at the dual system of privileges afforded the American people. In the case of *Missouri ex rel. Gaines* v. *Canada,* the Court held in 1938 that blacks in Missouri had a right to equality of educational opportunity, and, since no provision was made for black legal training, the University of Missouri's law school must be opened to them. In 1941, in *United States* v. *Classic,* the right of the federal government to regulate a primary election when it was an integral part of the process of choosing a federal official was first recognized. As a result, three years later the decision in *Smith* v. *Allwright* ended exclusion of blacks from Democratic party membership in Texas since the party's primary was a vital part of the election process. In *Shelley* v. *Kraemer* in 1948 government sanctions of restrictive covenants prohibiting minority groups from buying houses in certain neighborhoods were invalidated as a violation of the Fourteenth Amendment protection clause. From 1946 to 1953, under Chief Justice Fred M. Vinson, the Court chose to abide by the 1896 *Plessy* v. *Ferguson* decision, which sanctioned "separate but equal" conditions, but it was careful to discern the presence of inequality. Blacks were admitted to the University of Oklahoma as a result of *Sipuel* v. *University of Oklahoma* (1948) and the University of Texas law school following the decision in *Sweatt* v. *Painter* (1950), when it was demonstrated that facilities available to them were not equal. As a result graduate and professional schools began to be opened to blacks.

The "separate but equal" approach began to be seriously questioned by the Vinson Court, and, in 1950, in *Henderson* v. *United States,* which like the *Plessy* case dealt with a common carrier, the Court used the commerce clause to strike down racial discrimination in interstate transportation and came close to ruling that segregated facilities were unequal.

To avoid integration, most southern and border states greatly increased their appropriations for black schools, hoping to avoid desegregation by providing equal but dual facilities. This effort failed when the Supreme Court under Chief Justice Earl Warren revised its attitude toward segregation in education. In 1954 it handed down an epochal decision in a suit brought by the National Association for the Advancement of Colored People, which had concentrated its efforts on court battles. In one of a series of grade school cases, *Brown* v. *Board of Education of Topeka,* the Court accepted much of the psychological and sociological arguments of the NAACP counsel, Thurgood Marshall, who was later elevated to the Court himself. Considering the impact on the child, it held in public schools separate education was "inherently unequal." Within a year it ordered the federal district courts to see that school systems had made a "reasonable start" toward integration and were moving with "all deliberate speed" to comply. In the next two years, the Court ended segregation in publicly owned facilities and interstate transportation. In 1956 and 1957, in several decisions which horrified many conservatives, it placed additional safeguards on the right of dissent.

Grudgingly but effectively the border states and most of the upper South began to comply with the desegregation decisions. In the deep South, however, White Citizens Councils began to be formed in 1954 which proclaimed the *Brown* decision unconstitutional and aided in the passage of legislative subterfuges. The federal district courts and especially the Fifth Circuit Court of Appeals in New Orleans invalidated these laws as they were passed. In 1957 at least a few blacks were integrated in white schools in North Carolina, Tennessee, Texas, and Arkansas. In the latter state, however, the governor's opposition forced President Eisenhower to modify his race relations strategy.

The president, who believed that racial attitudes could not be legislated nor determined by court decrees, feared that outside pressure would impede progress, and he tried to keep the federal government out of intense controversy. His strategy seemed to be working when southern senators allowed passage of the Civil Rights Act of 1957, the first since Reconstruction. It established a Civil Rights Commission, whose life was periodically reextended, with wide powers to investigate interference with voting rights and equal protection of the laws. An assistant attorney general was also empowered to bring suit in district courts to protect voting rights, while the courts were authorized to issue injunctions and take other measures to enforce their orders.

Although some progress was made under Eisenhower's approach, the president was forced into a major confrontation with a state over civil rights in September, 1957, when Arkansas' Governor Orval E. Faubus stationed national guardsmen in state service outside Little Rock's Central High School to prevent entry under federal court orders of nine blacks. The president had no alternative but to federalize the Arkansas National Guard, which, backed by federal troops, obtained entrance of the black students. Feelings ran so high that a district court judge in September, 1958, gave the Little Rock school board a two-and-a-half year respite before requiring compliance. When the Supreme Court reversed this decision, Arkansas closed Little Rock's four high schools until 1960, when they were reopened on an integrated basis.

Opposition to federal court orders emerged elsewhere, including Virginia where, in compliance with a "massive resistance" policy chosen by state leaders, administrators closed some public schools in 1958 rather than integrate them. In early 1959 the Virginia Supreme Court held school closings, private tuition grants, and cut-off of funds from integrated schools violated the state constitution, and a federal district court ruled that closing schools to prevent compliance with federal court decisions violated the Fourteenth Amendment. Token integration then began in several regions of the state. By 1961 all states had made some effort to comply with the *Brown* decision except Alabama, Mississippi, and South Carolina.

Blacks and other concerned Americans had reason for discontent over the speed with which the *Brown* decision was implemented since in 1960 only 6 percent of black students in the South were in integrated classes. It would have taken a farsighted man indeed to see that many barriers were to end within a decade and the center of the controversy shift to other regions.

One reason for hope came in the passage of a second federal civil rights bill within three years. President Eisenhower lent his support to bipartisan efforts for its enactment, but equal credit was due the southern Democratic majority leader of the Senate, Texas' Lyndon B. Johnson, who was instrumental in obtaining its passage after weeks of continuous Senate sessions. The Civil Rights Act of 1960 levied heavy fines for interference with voting rights and authorized federal courts to appoint referees with power, upon demand, to investigate state voting laws. When a charge of discrimination was brought, the aggrieved persons were authorized to "vote provisionally" until the courts decided the merits of their case. By vigorous court action, the ballot was extended to many people, and with it a means of self-protection.

A series of constitutional amendments in the 1960s and 1970s also broadened the civil rights of many Americans and made important changes regarding the vice-presidency. The ratification of the Twenty-third Amendment in 1961 gave predominantly black Washington, D.C., a voice in presidential elections through the choice of electors for president and vice-president. In 1964 the Twenty-fourth Amendment outlawed the poll tax as a requirement for voting in federal elections in those few states where it was retained. The Twenty-fifth Amendment, ratified in 1967, provided that, when a vacancy occurred in the office of vice-president, the president would nominate a candidate for the office, who would be elected by a majority vote of both Houses of Congress.* The Twenty-sixth Amendment, ratified in less than four months after its submission to the states in 1971, forbade the state and federal governments to deny or abridge voting rights on account of age to any U.S. citizen who was eighteen years old or older.

Peaceful Protest

In the mid-1950s much of the momentum for black elevation to first-class citizenship passed directly into black hands. Passive resistance was perfected and utilized most effectively by followers of Martin Luther King, Jr., an Atlanta-born Baptist minister who received a Ph.D. from Boston University in 1955, a year after he had become pastor of a Baptist church in Montgomery, Alabama. In December, 1955, following the arrest of a black woman for failure to move to the rear of a bus, he organized the Montgomery Improvement Association, which led a successful boycott of the local bus system. Following a 1956 court decision outlawing segregated seating, the bus company capitulated.

King, who was deeply influenced by the philosophy of Gandhi and Thoreau, combined genuine organizational ability with a genius for communication. Thousands who heard him speak, read his articles or his three books were captivated by his concept of nonviolent resis-

Martin Luther King, Jr.

tance. He aided in the formation of the Student Nonviolent Coordinating Committee which, with the Congress of Racial Equality, took a leading role in conducting sit-ins at lunch counters throughout the South in 1960 and 1961. As a result, though some counters were closed, many stores began to serve blacks on a nonsegregated basis.

To more effectively advance black rights, in 1960 King aided in founding the Southern Christian Leadership Conference and became its president. It cooperated with other groups in challenging segregation in a variety of ways and in pressuring the federal government for action. In the spring of 1961 "freedom riders,"

---

*It also stipulated that the vice-president should become acting president when the president transmitted a declaration to Congress that he was unable to serve or when the vice-president and a majority of the principal executive department officers "or such a body as Congress may by law provide" declared him to be unable. The president would reassume office when he declared he was able unless the vice-president and a majority of the executive heads or the congressionally designated group objected. In that case, Congress would decide the question.

who chartered private buses and traveled throughout the South, demonstrated the hold segregation still retained. As outside troublemakers, they were enormously resented when they entered facilities reserved for whites, including terminals, rest rooms, and restaurants. A number were mobbed, and only the intervention of federal marshals and proclamation of martial law in Montgomery, Alabama, prevented carnage. As a result, late in 1961 the Interstate Commerce Commission demanded bus companies end segregation in all aspects of interstate travel.

The cost of demonstrations led to their more infrequent use after 1961 and an even heavier reliance on court decrees and legislation, although much of the impulse for equality continued to come from King-directed programs. From Atlanta, where he returned in 1959 to be co-pastor with his father of the Ebenezer Baptist Church, he conducted highly publicized protests which aroused the nation. By 1963 King had come to place top priority on ending discrimination in employment and chose this as well as an end to segregation in eating establishments and stores as a goal for a crusade in Birmingham, Alabama. The day before sit-ins and picketing began, the city's ardent segregationist police commissioner, Eugene "Bull" Connor, had been defeated in a race for mayor by a racial moderate, by deep South standards. In his closing days of office, Connor, defying the protesters, used police dogs and high-pressure water from fire hoses to contain the demonstrations, which increasingly were composed of school children. Although, after a month, a truce was arranged with business leaders granting many of King's demands, conditions remained tense for weeks. The bombing of a demonstrator's home and a black-owned motel in May, 1963, and in September of a black church where four girls were killed contributed to the confusion. Fortunately, the new Birmingham government and many local business leaders worked hard to improve racial relations.

Kennedy's Election

John F. Kennedy, the Democratic presidential candidate in 1960, had great regard for the civil rights movement, and this attitude played a major part in his election. In his humanistic approach toward civil rights and in other ways, Kennedy injected much life into the 1960 campaign. The forty-two-year-old Massachusetts senator became one of the nation's youngest presidential candidates following a well-organized and strenuously fought series of primary contests. His victory in Wisconsin was discounted, due to the vote received from his Roman Catholic coreligionists, but when he won resoundingly in West Virginia, his major opponent, Senator Hubert Humphrey, withdrew. Other victories followed, and Kennedy entered the convention with over 600 of the 761 votes needed for the nomination. The psychology of victory and excellently applied pressure earned him a first ballot nomination, defeating Missouri's Senator Stuart Symington and Texas' Senator Lyndon B. Johnson. Much to the public's surprise, Kennedy drafted Johnson for the vice-presidency, an action which probably enabled him to carry several southern states and win the election.

There was no open challenge of Vice-President Richard Nixon for the Republican nomination after New York's liberal Governor Nelson A. Rockefeller withdrew in January, 1959. However, Rockefeller threatened to disrupt the convention with a floor fight and even encouraged a group to draft him as a presidential candidate if the platform failed to reflect his views. Intimidated by this threat, Nixon accepted planks which by implication were critical of some phases of the Eisenhower program. They called for a greatly expanded defense program, increased government stimulation of the economy, and strong federal intervention in behalf of civil rights. As a vice-presidential candidate, Nixon chose Henry Cabot Lodge, Jr., the U.S. ambassador to the United Nations and a former U.S. senator from Massachusetts whose seat Kennedy had taken in 1952.

The Democratic and Republican platforms were quite similar, and in the campaign the candidates seemed to share the same basic views. To a great extent the contest became one of personalities, relying on a difference in style and outlook to attract votes. Kennedy, projecting an image of youth and vigor, contended the United States was in a declining position abroad and at home. Citing a loss of the military superiority previously enjoyed by the United States and a decrease by one-half in the annual rise in gross national product, he pledged to "get America moving again." Nixon contended that Kennedy was incorrectly depicting America's condition but also avowed he would take all necessary action to keep the nation strong and prosperous.

Kennedy scored two triumphs which did much to aid his election. Appearing before the Ministers Association of Houston, he largely removed his Catholic faith as a campaign issue by clearly enunciating his commitment to separation of church and state. Second, in four nationally televised debates with Nixon, he appeared the keener, more attractive personality. By mid-October Kennedy, according to the opinion polls, was in the lead. Although herculean television usage and a series of speeches by President Eisenhower reversed the trend immediately before the election, when the results were tabulated Kennedy was the winner in the closest race in American history. His popular majority was 120,000 in a total vote of 68,335,000; the electoral vote was 303 to 219. Kennedy took southern New England, New York, Pennsylvania, Michigan, and Illinois,

while losing most of the West. The votes of blacks and other minorities were essential to his victory as were the large Democratic majorities produced, at least partially, by the party machines in several major cities. Republican criticism was concentrated on Major Richard Daley of Chicago, where alleged election irregularities were held to have given the Illinois vote to Kennedy. Wisely, for the country's sake, Nixon did not push for a disruptive investigation.

Both the 1960 candidates had committed themselves to maintain and advance the reforms of the last thirty years, but Kennedy was conceded to be the more advanced in his philosophy and the more eager for change. His election, even by the most minute margin, was felt by many to be a vote for renewed and intensified government action at home and abroad. As a candidate, Kennedy had referred to the 1960s as a "New Frontier" whose challenges offered opportunities as well as threats. With anticipation, millions of Americans awaited his leadership to guide the nation in fulfilling its destiny.

The Arts and Letters

It was symptomatic of Kennedy and the America with which he was in rapport that the poet Robert Frost participated in his inaugural ceremony. A new era of presidential patronage of the arts began, extending from efforts to restore authentic period furniture in the White House to federal subsidies for writers and artists.

Since the 1930s the nation's increasing literacy and educational level provided an expanded market for literature and the arts. The results were not always acclaimed by the critics, but no one could deny the broadening of the popular base. Many of the older, prestigious magazines died, but new ones which concentrated on news and contemporary developments such as *Time* and *Newsweek* and picture-stories such as *Life* and *Look** enjoyed vast circulation. The number of newspapers was drastically reduced, and most cities ceased to have competing publishers, but the remaining newspapers frequently had sales that would have seemed incredible to an earlier generation. The paperback book, which had its advent shortly before World War II, had a fantastic sale expansion in the 1950s and afterwards. Every conceivable type of work became available in paperback, and, to the surprise of many, sales of the cheaper editions seemed to stimulate demand for hardbacks.

More people than ever before tried their hand at writing, and authors' groups enjoyed a vigorous growth. The increasing cost of printing, however, made many publishers more cautious than ever in accepting works. One leader in the industry estimated only one in ten thousand unsolicited manuscripts was published. Novelists particularly faced a rough time, but the rewards of the successful were often great due to royalties from book clubs and movie and television rights.

Novelists of recent years have had less concern with moral problems or the dilemma of society generally. Many, such as John Updike who wrote *The Centaur,* were quite introspective. Two exceptions were favorites with the young—J. D. Salinger, whose most important work was the best-seller, *The Catcher in the Rye,* and James Gould Cozzens, author of *By Love Possessed.* Both authors portrayed human failure but called on man to transcend his limitations. James Baldwin presented the plight of blacks in such a manner that readers were moved beyond race to consider the problems of men everywhere. In *Catch-22,* Joseph Heller

---

Look ceased publication in 1971 and *Life* at the end of 1972.

revealed the utter absurdity of war, quite a different approach from some of the immediate post-1945 novels which glorified conflict.

Most critics contend that the quality of American poetry and drama has moved in divergent ways in the last few decades. Poetry came of age in the post-World War II era, relying less on foreign styles and, at least in the works of such writers as Phyllis McGinley and Richard Wilbur, losing some of the obscurity which came from the imitation of Ezra Pound and T. S. Eliot. Meanwhile, drama declined from the quality attained in the 1930s when Sherwood Anderson and Eugene O'Neill were at their peaks, although some notable figures emerged. William Inge in such plays as *Come Back, Little Sheba* and *Bus Stop* presented a sympathetic, realistic portrayal of the trials and tribulations of average Americans. Tennessee Williams emerged in the postwar era as a superb craftsman whose concern with sex, perversion, and violence held audiences' interest in such plays as *The Glass Menagerie* and *A Streetcar Named Desire,* productions which made theater history. Arthur Miller proved to be one of the most potent critics of modern, middle-class society. Some were offended by his portrayal of the less than whole mid-century man, which in itself was a tribute to Miller's works such as *Death of a Salesman* and *A View from the Bridge.*

Although little theater groups flourished throughout the country and a number of off-Broadway theaters continued to do exciting experimental works, by the 1970s the commercial theater appeared to be declining. High costs which resulted in high-priced theater tickets led to smaller audiences, and, in turn, resulted in fewer new productions each year. The most successful long-runs were the lavish musicals such as *Hello Dolly, The Sound of Music,* and *Fiddler on the Roof,* but for each that succeeded there were several failures with increasingly drastic losses.

The movies and television supplanted the theater in providing much of the nation's entertainment, as technical competence increased notably in the years following World War II. By the 1970s there was a marked loosening of the earlier restraints imposed by the major networks in the television medium. As it saturated the nation with its coverage after the late 1940s, television had an enormous impact. No one could deny its value as a news medium, yet some questioned the inevitable bias that emerged when film was edited and decisions made as to what was newsworthy. The increased practice of prerecording programs on videotape enabled more elaborate programs to be staged. It also permitted the development of the Public Broadcasting System (PBS), which at times presented complete coverage of congressional hearings and in-depth analyses economically impossible for the commercial networks.

In recent years the fine arts of painting, architecture, and music have received greater public concern and patronage than ever before. As early as the 1930s such regional painters as Thomas Hart Benton and Grant Wood with their presentation of the simple values of rural America won wide acclaim. The primitive scenes of Grandma Moses were highly regarded after the war, but it was the work of American abstract expressionists, led by Jackson Pollock until his death in 1956, that came to be studied around the world. Retreating from the concrete, they often distorted objects or even eliminated them in favor of color or designs. Many of their canvases were large, bold, and emotion provoking—truly art for art's sake. Though repulsive to some who expected a specific message, their paintings reflected faith in individuality and a commitment to their own perception of truth.

In architecture, the availability of new, lighter, and stronger building materials provided opportunities for experimentation and creativeness. Ranch and split-level homes superseded more conventional styles, while Frank Lloyd Wright and his disciples effectively used concrete and dome-shaped styling to build utilitarian structures which often looked as if they were nestling near the ground. Other architects, such as Gordon Bunshaft, whose Lever Building was completed in 1952 in New York, utilized glass and steel to create extremely simple, attractive structures. As time passed, the starkness of their design was broken by various additions, but its basic features remained.

Music also experienced comparable signs of maturity as popular purchase of a wide variety of recordings and tapes reached unanticipated proportions. An increase occurred each decade in musical training from grade schools through the university, and the appreciation of jazz and folk music spread to every age category. Rock music became a symbol with youth of the 1960s, a means of communication which transcended barriers and united those from diverse backgrounds. At the same time, country and western music enjoyed a new sophistication which made it popular with many who had only disdain for hillbilly music. Some critics felt that the most creative popular writing was being done in this field in the early 1970s. Meanwhile, more serious American composers began to enjoy international recognition. Among the most original was Charles Edward Ives who discovered uses of dissonance and polytonality before his European counterparts, the completely romantic Paul Creston, and Samuel Barber whose opera *Vanessa* was widely acclaimed. It was usually conceded, however, that the work of native Americans was generally inferior to that of Igor Stravinsky, Arnold Schönberg, Bela Bartók, and Paul Hindemith, foreigners who spent much of their career in the United States and greatly influenced U.S. composers. Leonard Bernstein, conductor of the New York Philharmonic

Symphony Orchestra, was considered by some to be the nation's leading composer, although his reputation arose primarily as a conductor. It was most appropriate that when a single memorial was chosen for President Kennedy, it should be a splendid Washington center for the performing arts and that Bernstein should compose and conduct a mass for its dedication.

The New Frontier

When John F. Kennedy was inaugurated in January, 1961, he continued a theme used in his nomination acceptance speech. Kennedy challenged all peoples everywhere to join in an attack on "the common enemies of man: tyranny, poverty, disease, and war itself." He advised his fellow countrymen, "ask not what your country can do for you—ask what you can do for your country."

Kennedy, grandson of two first-generation Irish-Americans who became Boston Democratic leaders, had received every advantage which his wealthy father, Joseph P. Kennedy, could afford. Graduating with distinction from Harvard in 1940, he served as a naval officer during World War II. When his PT boat was sunk off the Solomon Islands in 1943, he rescued several members of the crew, earning the Navy and Marine Corps Medal for bravery. In the episode, he sustained spinal injuries which required extensive surgery even after the war and left him in constant pain. In spite of this handicap, in 1946 he was elected to the House of Representatives and to the Senate in 1952, where his image for politically acceptable progressivism made him increasingly attractive as a national political figure. While recovering from back surgery, he wrote the impressive book, *Profiles in Courage,* which describes the actions of American leaders who put their country ahead of their own self-interest. Ken-

John F. Kennedy

nedy received a Pulitzer Prize for biography in 1957 for this work.

As president, Kennedy pressed for enactment of laws to fulfill his campaign promises. Little difficulty was encountered in obtaining substantial increases in military funds including allocations for the space program to put a man on the moon before 1970. Equal enthusiasm led to approval of programs to help foreign countries help themselves: a Development Loan Fund pledging $7.2 billion over five years to underdeveloped countries and the beginning of the Alliance for Progress committing over $10 billion for use in Latin America within a ten-year period. The Peace Corps was established, which provided volunteers to furnish skilled services in needy countries, a mission which as much as any other captured the imagination of young America. The administration also succeeded in 1962 in enacting the significant Trade Expansion Act which permitted the reduction and, in some cases, elimination of tariffs with European Common Market countries on items largely supplied by them and the U.S. in world trade. Only in the direct extension of foreign aid, a program whose value the people had begun to question, were rebuffs met, and cuts of over 15 percent were imposed on the president's requests in 1961, and 20 percent in 1962.

Domestically the New Frontier encountered much rougher treatment at the hands of the southern Democratic-Republican coalition which controlled Congress. The president, cognizant of the situation, moved slowly, especially in areas dealing with fiscal policy and racial discrimination. Though the country was in a recession and a balance of payments deficit when he assumed office, he chose to counteract their effects through loosening federal funds for various projects rather than asking for additional appropriations. Conditions improved in the spring of 1961 and, aided by House adoption of an administration measure expanding the Rules Committee from twelve to fifteen members, important laws were passed which the president hoped would help obtain an annual growth in gross national product of more than 5 percent and remove many individuals from poverty. The minimum wage was increased over a two-year period from $1.00 to $1.25 an hour, and 3.6 million additional workers were covered. For the first time, the federal government moved on a large scale to aid distressed cities by appropriating $5 billion over a four-year period for urban renewal. Concern with blighted economic areas was reflected in a $400 million program for "distressed" regions with high unemployment.

For a president with less drive than Kennedy the administration's achievements would have seemed admirable, but he was thwarted by a number of congressional failures. Catholic insistence on aid for parochial schools killed a federal aid to education bill which would have provided $2.3 billion to higher education. A Medicare program providing national health insurance for senior citizens was rejected, a plan for which the president had strongly contended in the 1960 campaign. A proposal to create a cabinet Department of Urban Affairs met a similar fate, in part because of fears that Kennedy would name a black man as its secretary. While Congress passed a law allowing additional tax credits for capital developments in business, a measure Kennedy favored to aid economic growth, it rejected other revenue reforms, including withholding of income taxes on dividends and interest as well as closing loopholes in expense account deductions. He was refused standby authorization to begin a public works program in case of recession and to place an effective limitation on wheat and cereal crop production.

Disgusted, the president decided to campaign boldly in 1962 for pro-administration candidates in a fashion which had backfired for both Presidents Franklin D. Roosevelt and Dwight D. Eisenhower. When the Cuban missile crisis emerged in October, 1962, however, he abruptly ended his excursion. Partially due to the crisis, the Democrats, as the party in power, suffered the least attrition in congressional seats since the early New Deal.

In the new Congress which opened in January, 1963, the president obtained approval of a number of laws. In building community health centers, $150 million was appropriated for state use; the National Defense Education Act was extended; and funds were appropriated for medical and dental education including loans to students. However, on the major questions of foreign aid, the race in space, and economic growth, the administration again suffered reversals. The foreign aid program was cut by one-third and appropriations to the National Aeronautics and Space Administration by 10 percent. Despite the president's pleas for substantial tax reductions, action was prevented by congressional reluctance to lower expenditures and fear of offending business and labor, each of which wanted reductions more favorable to itself.

Civil rights was another area in which the president accomplished much but was frustrated by congressional opposition. Realizing that a zealous campaign would encounter defeat and jeopardize other parts of his program in Congress, Kennedy moved with caution while taking broad executive action to aid blacks. Much of the inspiration and leadership

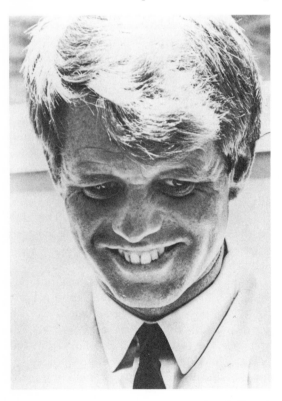

Robert F. Kennedy

came from the president's brother, Robert F. Kennedy, the attorney general whose appointment at the age of thirty-five had drawn a great deal of criticism, especially from conservatives who disliked his vigorous drive. An important advance on the employment front was made by the appointment of Vice-President Johnson as chairman of a newly created Committee on Equal Employment Opportunity which effectively pressured defense contractors to accept equal opportunity clause contracts. Ultimately, the president issued an antidiscrimination order requiring that all firms holding contracts valued at more than $10,000 file reports showing they were in compliance with the committee. He also ordered an end to all discrimination in federally financed housing and appointed a number of blacks to important administrative positions, including Robert C. Weaver as Federal Housing Administrator.

When James H. Meredith was denied admission under court order to the University of Mississippi in September, 1962, the president moved with resolution tempered by charity. Federal marshals were ordered to enforce the law, the Mississippi National Guard was federalized, and federal troops placed on a standby basis. In an eloquent national address, the president appealed to the chivalrous tradition of Mississippians in asking compliance with the law. Instead, serious rioting occurred, and the federal marshals were saved only by the arrival of troops, after which Meredith was registered and began attending classes.

The civil rights struggle intensified following the Birmingham crisis in 1963, and over 700 demonstrations occurred in other cities throughout the nation. These led to the gigantic "March on Washington" when over 200,000 demonstrators moved on the nation's capital in an orderly expression of determination to end black proscription. This action prepared the way for eventual approval of a civil rights law Kennedy first urged Congress to enact in February, 1963, which included protection of individual rights and aid in school desegregation. The president declared the nation faced a moral crisis and proposed extensive legislation which became the important Civil Rights Bill of 1964. Although a long congressional fight lay ahead before approval, victory seemed likely, but the president chafed when he reflected on the discontent delay engendered.

To enhance his political leverage, on November 22, 1963, Kennedy began his drive for reelection by a trip to Texas, whose vote he felt to be critical. The state's Democratic party was severely divided, a liberal faction being led by Senator Ralph W. Yarborough and a conservative segment by Governor John B. Connally. The president was warmly received as his motorcade moved from Love Field to downtown Dallas, but, as it turned toward the freeway for the trip to Ft. Worth, shots were fired from an upper story of the Texas Book Depository Building, hitting Kennedy and Governor Connally, who was riding in the front seat of the same automobile. Apparently the president died instantly; thirty minutes after being shot

The March on Washington.

he was pronounced dead at Parkland Memorial Hospital. Governor Connally, though critically wounded, recovered and became a leading representative of the Nixon administration in the early 1970s and, after his conversion to the Republican party, a potential Republican presidential candidate.

The nation and world were profoundly shocked by Kennedy's senseless assassination. Millions watched every step of the distressing drama by television from the events in Dallas immediately following the shooting until the interment took place three days later in Arlington National Cemetery. Almost immediately a twenty-four-year-old psychotic, Lee Harvey Oswald, was arrested for the murder. Before the former president's burial, however, he too was assassinated by a Dallas nightclub operator while millions watched on television. Speculation arose that Oswald was killed to cover a major plot; however, no evidence for this belief was unearthed in the exhaustive investigation conducted by Chief Justice Earl Warren and a special commission.

Like Lincoln, in death the image of Kennedy was enhanced. His style, words, and philosophy became more potent than in his lifetime, and under the leadership of the congressionally astute President Johnson, many of his reforms, some of which had first been advocated by President Truman twenty years before, were enacted.

Selected Bibliography

Eric F. Goldman, *The Crucial Decade and After: America 1945–1960** (1961), and John N. Brooks, *The Great Leap: The Past Twenty-five Years in America* *(1966), present excellent views of recent trends in American life and their interrelationship. *Harry S. Truman** (1974) by his daughter, Margaret Truman, is the best biography available but should be supplemented by Jonathan Daniels, *The Man of Independence* (repr. of 1950 ed., 1971); Frank McNaughton and Walter Hehmeyer, *Harry Truman, President* (1948); and Alfred Steinberg, *The Man from Missouri; The Life and Times of Harry S. Truman* (1962). Cabell Phillips, *The Truman Presidency** (1969), follows political developments closely, while Truman's own views are in his *Memoirs* (2 vols., 1958).

Lester V. Chandler, *Inflation in the United States, 1940–1948* (1951), is the story of a major postwar problem. The stormy account of labor relations is recounted in R. Alton Lee, *Truman and Taft-Hartley, A Question of Mandate* (1966); Foster R. Dulles, *Labor in America: A History* (3rd ed., 1966), and the agricultural crisis in Allen J. Matusow, *Farm Policies and Politics in the Truman Years* *(1970). Arnold M. Rose depicts *The Negro in Postwar America* (1950), and Richard Davies treats *Housing Reform During the Truman Administration* (1966). Irwin Ross, *The Loneliest Campaign: The Truman Victory of 1948* (1968), presents Truman's strengths and Dewey's mistakes.

Eisenhower's nomination is well analyzed in Wilfred Binkley, *American Political Parties* (4th rev. ed., 1958). Samuel Lubell, *Revolt of the Moderates* (1956), explains much of his broad public appeal. Robert J. Donovan, *Eisenhower: The Inside Story* (1956), is a contemporary account of his first four years, and Emmet J. Hughes, *The Ordeal of Power, A Political Memoir of the Eisenhower Years* (1963), records the observations of a perceptive speech writer. Dean Albertson, ed., *Eisenhower As President* *(1963), contains interesting evaluations. The president's and vice-president's views on major developments are presented in Eisenhower's Memoirs, *The White House Years: Mandate for Change, 1953–1956* (1963) and *Waging Peace, A Political Memoir of the Eisenhower Years, 1956–1961* (1965) and in Richard M. Nixon's *Six Crises* (1962).

Richard Hofstadter, *Anti-Intellectualism in American Life* *(1963) and *The Paranoid Style in American Politics and Other Essays* (1965), provides insight into the public acceptance of McCarthyism. Truman receives much of the blame in Athan Theoharis, *Seeds of Repression: Harry S. Truman and the Origins of McCarthyism* (1971). The story of the Wisconsin senator's rise and fall are in Richard H. Rovere, *Senator Joe McCarthy* (1959), while Seymour M. Lipset and Earl Raab find McCarthyism to be part of *The Politics of Unreason, Vol. V, Right-Wing Extremism in America, 1790–1970* (1970).

---

*Available in paperback.

The U.S. Economy in the 1950's, An Economic History (1963) is skillfully portrayed in a work by Harold G. Vatter. John K. Galbraith challenges the administration's policies in The Affluent Society *(rev. ed., 1970). Aaron Wildavsky, Dixon-Yates: A Study in Power Politics (1962), reveals its attitude toward public power and its capacity for political bungling. The recurring agricultural crisis is analyzed in W. H. Peterson, The Great Farm Problem (1959), and Edward C. Higbee, Farms and Farmers in an Urban Age (1963).

No better introduction to the civil rights controversies can be found than Martin Luther King, Jr., Stride Toward Freedom: The Montgomery Story* (1958) and Why We Can't Wait* (1964); Malcolm X, The Autobiography of Malcolm X* (1973); and James Baldwin, The Fire Next Time* (1970). Inside America: A Black African Diplomat Speaks Out (1972) reveals an African observer's shock at American racism. Charles E. Silberman spells out the Crisis in Black and White *(1964). Southern racism and resistance to change is clearly pictured in John B. Martin, The Deep South Says "Never" (1957), and James W. Silver, Mississippi: The Closed Society *(enl. ed., 1966). Neil R. McMillen examines The Citizens Council: Organized Resistance to the Second Reconstruction, 1954–1964 (1971), while J. W. Peltason shows the influence of Fifty-Eight Lonely Men: Southern Federal Judges and School Desegregation* (1971). Hopeful views are contained in Howard Zinn, The Southern Mystique (1964), and Larry L. King, Confessions of a White Racist *(1971). Reed Sarratt traces The Ordeal of Desegregation, The First Decade (1966). The continuing ferment and change in black life is depicted in Louis E. Lomax, The Negro Revolt *(1971), and Stokely S. Carmichael and Charles Hamilton, Black Power: The Politics of Liberation in America *(1968). Black nationalism is analyzed in E.U. Essien-Udom, Black Nationalism* (1972), and John H. Bracey, Jr. et al., Black Nationalism in America *(1969).

The vital role of the Supreme Court in other areas as well as civil rights is portrayed in Alpheus Mason, The Supreme Court from Taft to Warren *(rev. ed., 1968), and Archibald Cox, The Warren Court: Constitutional Decision As an Instrument of Reform* (1968).

In addition to works on literature cited in chapter 21, see Stephen Stepanchev, American Poetry Since 1945 *(1965), which reveals the renaissance that has occurred. Barbara Rose, American Art Since 1900 *(1967), is informative while Oliver W. Larkin, Art and Life in America (rev. ed., 1960), correlates developments in the nonliterary arts with other aspects of life. Marshall McLuhan, Understanding Media: The Extensions of Man *(1971), and with Quentin Fiore, The Medium Is the Massage* (1970), deals with television's impact.

Theodore H. White's volumes, The Making of the President, 1960,* 1964* (1961, 1965), provide excellent analyses of presidential politics. The most useful studies of President Kennedy include Arthur M. Schlesinger, Jr., A Thousand Days: John F. Kennedy in the White House* (1971), and Theodore C. Sorensen, Kennedy (1965). The Kennedy assassination is covered in William Manchester, Death of a President* (1968). There is A Concise Compendium of the Warren Commission Report on the Assassination of President Kennedy (1964) which is challenged by Edward J. Epstein in Inquest: The Warren Commission and the Establishment of Truth* (1966).

Contemporary Events

1964	Civil Rights Act of 1964
	Economic Opportunity Act
1965	Medicare instituted
	Voting Rights Act
	Watts riots
1967	Detroit riots
	Passage of Twenty-fifth Amendment
1968	Report of National Advisory Commission on Civil Disorders
	Civil Rights Act of 1968
	Assassinations of Dr. Martin Luther King, Jr., and Senator Robert Kennedy
	Court orders end of *de facto* segregation
	Omnibus Crime Act
1969	Moon landing of Apollo 11
	Massive antiwar demonstrations
1970	Education Bill of 1970
	Omnibus Crime Control Act
	National Environmental Policy Act
	Comprehensive Drug Abuse and Control Act
1971	Passage of Twenty-sixth Amendment
	Price-wage freeze instituted
1972	Revenue sharing legislation enacted
	Watergate burglaries
1973	Confrontation at Wounded Knee
	Senate Watergate hearings
	Resignation of Vice-President Agnew
1974	Resignation of President Nixon and inauguration of President Ford

24

The Continuing Struggle for the American Way of Life

Long-Range Developments

For Economics and Corporate Enterprise

Spiraling inflation continued to pose major problems for most Americans, but no adequate solution has been found.

For Democratic Government

The New Federalism policy increased state demands for national funds whose limited availability necessitated lower allocations than frequently expected.

For Civil Liberties, Freedom, and Reform

The Voting Rights Act of 1965 provided leverage for blacks in the South which promoted black advances in many fields in addition to politics.

Governor George C. Wallace's neo-Populist opposition continued to attract support, and following his attempted assassination he attained increased national approval.

Extension of the right to vote to eighteen-year-olds may have diverted the activities of a number of potential protesters into regular political channels.

Although the U.S. Supreme Court recently rendered some conservative decisions, there have been no reversals of earlier liberal decisions whose impact continues to transform American life.

Heroic efforts continue to be made to improve minority rights, control pollution, and obtain true equality for women, with slow but notable progress being made in each area.

Johnson Assumes Office

For many Americans the death of President Kennedy assumed the proportions of a personal tragedy and symbolized for them the interment of many of the dreams and ideals they shared with the martyred leader. A sense of frustration and apprehension pervaded the outlook of many who sensed the extreme difficulties besetting the nation and the magnitude of the tasks before its government.

President Lyndon Baines Johnson, who took the oath of office in Dallas aboard *Air Force I,* the presidential plane, shortly after Kennedy's death, was a product of the Texas frontier and the New Deal. After working his way through Southwest Texas State Teachers College, he went to Washington as secretary of a Texas representative and proved so capable that at the age of twenty-seven he was appointed National Youth Administrator for Texas. Five years later, he was elected to the national House of Representatives, where, under the tutelage of his mentor, Speaker Sam Rayburn, he became one of the most staunch and able supporters of President Roosevelt. In 1949, following a contested election which he won by eighty-seven votes, he moved to the Senate where four years later, while still a freshman senator, he was elected minority leader. Despite a serious heart attack, he served as one of the most effective majority leaders in congressional history, following Democratic recapture of the House in 1955. An intense partisan and at times cruel opponent, he also had profound respect for the opposition. He was, to a great extent, responsible for Congress' approval of many Eisenhower measures, including the Civil Rights Acts of 1957 and 1960.

Johnson, who was fifty-five when he became president, was an old-fashioned liberal whose commitment to national honor and the rights of the oppressed was deep and sincere. As chief executive, his previous experience in Congress aided him in obtaining enactment of laws, at least during his first years in office. Although singularly devoid of political philosophy other than a pragmatic concern for results, his open use of power, as time elapsed, tended to discredit him with many. He worked and moved at a frantic pace, without the urbane wit, charm, and comic relief of a Franklin Roosevelt or a John Kennedy which delighted the more modern minded. In another time, he would undoubtedly have left office as one of the nation's most highly regarded presidents—his quaint eccentricities being regarded as period pieces not without their own captivating qualities. As it was, a new issue arose, the war in Vietnam, whose political import Johnson may have misjudged. Or it may well have been that the president pursued the policies he did in full knowledge of their domestic import. Ironically, time may yet reveal Johnson as the least compromising of modern presidents on what he believed a paramount moral issue.

The Civil Rights Acts of 1964 and 1965

Johnson was equally committed morally to obtaining first-class citizenship for the nation's blacks, and, drawing on the popular support engendered by the 1963 demonstrations, he obtained enactment of the Civil Rights Act of 1964 after the Senate limited debate (cloture) for the first time on such a measure. Under the new law, the Justice Department received the most extensive powers to prosecute civil rights violators; blacks were guaranteed equal access to public accomodations; the government was authorized to file suits to end school segregation and to curtail programs and end payments where discrimination was practiced. Moreover, discrimination in employment was forbidden because of sex, religion or nationality, and the maintenance of an Equal Employment Oppor-

Lyndon B. Johnson is sworn into office aboard Air Force I, *flanked by Mrs. Johnson and Jacqueline Kennedy.*

tunity Commission was made mandatory. The popular crisis which had arisen made possible a law that would have been unthinkable a short time before.

After passage of the Civil Rights Act of 1964, few foresaw that demonstrations led by Martin Luther King, Jr., would result in enactment of another far-reaching civil rights law within a year. Events leading to its approval began in January, 1965, when King began a drive for voter registration at Selma, in the heart of the Alabama "Black Belt." When only fifty blacks were enrolled in two months, King

decided to stage a fifty-mile march from Selma to the capital in Montgomery. Local and state police, who held the movement would impede traffic, used electric cattle prods and clubs in an attempt to prevent the march. This action, which the nation saw on television, led many sympathizers, especially clergymen, to come to Alabama to participate. After a federal judge ordered Governor George C. Wallace to permit the march, the Alabama National Guard was federalized, and the march took place. Meanwhile, President Johnson, angered by developments, asked Congress for a law insuring black voting rights. The Voting Rights Act of 1965, passed in the late summer, voided tests that interfered with registering. It authorized federal supervision in states and counties which had tests before November 1, 1964, and where less than half of the adults had registered or voted in the 1964 presidential election. If state officials failed to register applicants, federal examiners were authorized to do so.

With the passage of the 1965 act, passive resistance and presidential leadership had scored their greatest triumphs. In 1966 King conducted his first major northern demonstrations, where fewer results were obtained than anticipated. As discontent rose in the ghetto, major eruptions came in the next few years, and the truly national nature of the racial crisis became clear, a fact President Johnson had recognized and frequently described in his numerous addresses and interviews dealing with civil rights.

Johnson's Domestic Policy

In other aspects of his domestic program, President Johnson attained congressional victories comparable to those in civil rights. Shortly after coming to office in 1964, he pushed most of the Kennedy program through Congress: acts providing for tax reduction, the planning and development of urban transit systems, incorporation of federal wilderness areas into a preservation system, and a foreign aid bill with fewer reductions than ever before. In response to Johnson's declared "war on poverty," the Economic Opportunity Act was passed, appropriating almost a billion dollars for use over three years in a variety of programs, including a Domestic Peace Corps, the Job Corps to train youths, and many joint federal-state activities to improve the health and job readiness of the poor. In appreciation of his leadership, Johnson was nominated for president without difficulty

by the Democrats in 1964, and he chose Minnesota's Senator Hubert H. Humphrey, an Americans for Democratic Action liberal, as his running mate.

The Republican party took a turn to the right in 1964 in nominating Senator Barry M. Goldwater of Arizona and New York Representative William M. Miller for the nation's highest offices. Following Nixon's defeat in 1960, Goldwater had worked constantly for his party, gaining support with many of its professionals. He repeatedly charged defeat was due to a failure to offer a conservative alternative to Democratic policies and suggested participation in Social Security might be placed on a voluntary basis and that NATO commanders should have the right to decide when nuclear weapons would be used. Following his victory in the 1964 California primary, Goldwater's nomination was assured.

In other primaries, evidence came to light which led many to conclude that there was a strong conservative movement sweeping the nation. Alabama Governor George C. Wallace captured 42 percent of the Democratic primary vote in Maryland, 33 percent in Indiana, and almost 30 percent in Wisconsin, following attacks on liberal court decisions, "coddling of criminals," and government "giveaway programs." Despite this appearance and the eruption of race riots which contributed to a spirit of anxiety, Goldwater steadily lost ground in the contest with Johnson. In part this was due to his advocacy of a firmer policy with Russia which led many to fear that as president he would plunge the nation into war. In mid-October when Khrushchev was ousted as Russian premier and Red China exploded its first nuclear weapon, the heightened international tension increased Johnson's appeal. When Goldwater's opponents labeled him an extremist, he made the mistake of defending "extremism in the defense of liberty" and "in the pursuit of justice" which was interpreted by

Barry M. Goldwater

some as evidence of a dangerous reactionism. Later, many of his supporters blamed the news media for conveying a wrong impression of their candidate; however, Goldwater's own lack of finesse in gauging popular opinion and his own expressions were primarily at fault. Johnson won the election by a landslide, losing to Goldwater only in Arizona and five deep South states. The electoral vote was 486 to 52, and Johnson's popular majority was 16 million. Militant conservatism had taken a defeat from which it might never recover.

In 1965, when he became president in his own right, Johnson pushed plans for "the Great Society," in which poverty would be eliminated and America would come to grips with the problems of the cities and blighted regions. During the next two years, a remarkable number of laws were enacted. In 1965 the Appalachian Regional Development Act made $1.1 billion available for improvements and people-development in an area extending from Pennsylvania to Alabama. The Medicare program, a proposal first made by President Truman, was initiated for persons over sixty-five. It provided hospital and nursing home care and, with a premium payment (initially of $3 per person per month), 80 percent of most doctors' bills. The Housing and Urban Development Act of 1965 appropriated funds for 240,000 units over a four-year period and almost $3 billion for urban renewal. Robert C. Weaver became the first black cabinet officer when he assumed the headship of the newly created Department of Housing and Urban Development. After decades of controversy, the Elementary and Secondary Education Act of 1965 allocated $1.3 billion to aid schools with low-income children. The Higher Education Act provided $500 scholarships to 140,000 low-income college students and authorized establishment of a Teachers Corps for schools in poorer areas. A fitting climax to this battery of impressive legislation, most of which was designed to improve the status of the downtrodden, was enactment through the president's vigorous support of the Voting Rights Act of 1965, which virtually guaranteed the right to vote.

Despite the administration's remarkable legislative achievements, in 1966 it began to lose the confidence of many Americans. Intensified war efforts in Vietnam,* increased urban crime, and black rioting, which was openly defended in the name of "Black Power" by a number of new militant leaders, all took their

*See chapter 25 for a treatment of the Vietnam war and American foreign policy related to it.

toll. Some important laws were enacted that year, however. A new Department of Transportation was established and additional funds made available for health and educational programs.

Although Johnson attained some successes, in the 1966 elections the Republicans gained three Senate seats and forty-seven House seats. However, in the face of adversity, Johnson remained determined, and, remarkably, achieved many of his domestic goals in 1968. After rioting, particularly in Detroit, startled the nation in 1967, the president appointed a National Advisory Commission on Civil Disorders, headed by Governor Otto Kerner of Illinois. Its report, in March, 1968, warned that the United States was "moving toward two societies, one black, one white—separate and unequal" unless the Commission's extensive recommendations to alleviate poverty and urban deterioration were enacted. Although most of its proposals were ignored or defeated,* the Civil Rights Act of 1968 incorporated its open-housing provisions for which the president had contended for two years. Many felt that, with the possible exception of inequities in employment and education, discrimination in housing was the most basic deterrent to black advancement. Although limited by smaller allocation of enforcement funds than was desired, the act was a breakthrough since it prohibited discrimination in the sale or rental of housing where federal financing was involved in any way. After a year's agitation, approval was also obtained for a 10 percent tax surcharge to aid in financing the war, but, of necessity, its enactment had to be linked with spending cuts in other areas. However, $1.9 billion was allocated to the antipoverty program, the largest grant in its history, and Congress appropriated $5.3 billion

*Among its recommendations which were implemented were an increase of blacks in National Guard units and an improved Guard riot control program.

for use in a three-year period for housing and urban development, even more than the president requested. Concurrently, the Omnibus Crime Act authorized many new programs in an area of increasing concern but contained provisions for wiretapping which the president strongly opposed.

Even though the administration's accomplishments were great, the continued unpopularity of the Vietnam war led approval of Johnson to decline below 40 percent in public opinion polls early in 1968. March 31, shortly before the Wisconsin Democratic primary where many predicted he would be defeated by Senator Eugene McCarthy, a dove, the president announced his withdrawal from the presidential race. In doing so, he declared he wished to remove the war issue from politics and be able to devote all his energies to the quest for peace. In his withdrawal address, the president announced an end to bombing of North Vietnam except in the areas of military buildup just above the demilitarized zone, which threatened allied positions and lives. For months strenuous efforts were pursued to end the conflict, Johnson going so far as to end all naval, air, and artillery bombardment on November 1, 1968. His dream for achieving peace was not realized, however, and, because of his Vietnam policy, he was rejected by many of his own party. In 1972, his name was scarcely mentioned at the Democratic national convention, and candidates where chosen whose major issue was opposition to his Southeast Asian intervention.

Nixon's Election

Following President Johnson's retirement, Senator McCarthy won the primary in Wisconsin and was victorious over Senator Robert Kennedy in Oregon, the only contest he won against an active opponent. However, by early

June Kennedy was emerging as the leading Democratic contender. The president's younger brother had gained valuable experience as counsel to important Senate committees in the 1950s and was the Democratic campaign manager in 1960. He became the attorney general in John F. Kennedy's cabinet in 1961, where he demonstrated a special interest in minority rights, and was elected senator from New York in 1964. Tragically his career was ended shortly after he won the California Democratic primary in June, 1968, when he was assassinated in Los Angeles' Ambassador Hotel by Sirhan B. Sirhan, a Jordanian nationalist.

Vice-President Hubert Humphrey announced his candidacy a month after Johnson's withdrawal, and, although he entered no primaries, he amassed many delegates before the convention. Because of his association with the administration and his refusal to renounce its Vietnam position, he found himself regarded by many as an establishment candidate, a new role for an old liberal.

When the Democratic convention met in Chicago, it was turned into a shambles by various leftist groups who strongly opposed Johnson's Vietnam policy. These were organizations, such as the Coalition for an Open Convention, which for two months had formulated plans to challenge the credentials of many delegates and force adoption of a platform repudiating the Johnson administration. Thousands of youths descended on the convention, where they were given no concessions by its managers. Frustrated, they taunted some members of Mayor Richard Daley's 13,000-man police force into vicious attacks. The worst encounter came immediately in front of the Conrad Hilton hotel and received excellent television coverage, demoralizing both the Democratic party and much of the public. In the midst of the confusion, Humphrey was nominated with Maine's liberal Senator Ed-

mund Muskie as his running mate. The convention outlawed the unit rule which gave a majority the right to cast all of a delegation's vote, and, after a bitter two-hour debate, sustained the platform committee's moderately hard-line Vietnam plank by only a 60 percent vote.

By comparison the Republican convention was sheer tranquility. Although he had renounced politics for a lucrative New York law practice following his defeat as a candidate for governor of California in 1962, Richard M. Nixon reappeared as a campaigner for party

Hubert H. Humphrey

Spiro T. Agnew

recent Czechoslovakian invasion. Until mid-October, Humphrey's addresses were largely howled down by antiwar protesters, and he trailed Nixon badly in the polls. Then, aided by Lawrence O'Brien, a former Kennedy leader, his organization began to hum. After pledging to stop all bombing of North Vietnam if elected, he won many converts including Senator Eugene McCarthy. Five days before the election, President Johnson adopted this policy as his own, an action comparable to Eisenhower's "I shall go to Korea" statement in 1952. Partially as a result, Humphrey gained much strength in the closing days of the campaign, and Nixon received only .7 percent more popular votes than he.

The most interesting development of the campaign was the success of former Alabama Governor George C. Wallace, who ran for president as a candidate of the newly formed American Independent party. He received substantial support in widely diverse sections of the North, although his rallies were frequently disrupted by hecklers. Some, sensing that his appeal was broader than racial prejudice, began to call him a modern populist due to his attacks on corporate interests and identification with the less affluent groups. His strength crested in late September, apparently because many were frightened by his choice as a vice-presidential candidate of former Air Force Chief of Staff Curtis E. LeMay who publicly advocated use of any weapons necessary, including nuclear ones, to win the war in Vietnam.

When the votes were in, Nixon carried thirty-two states with 301 electoral votes, and Humphrey thirteen and the District of Columbia with 191. There was only a 500,000 vote difference between the two men although a total of 63 million votes were cast for them. Wallace made the greatest impact of any third-party candidate since Theodore Roosevelt in 1912, winning 9.9 million popular votes but only the 46 electoral votes of five southern

candidates in every section of the country in 1964 and the years thereafter. A new Nixon emerged, a much smoother, more knowledgeable man than before, who not infrequently made allusions to the basic values and eternal verities, but without the emotionalism and bitter partisanship of earlier years. He was quickly nominated in 1968 when favorite son candidates failed to stick together. One of these, Maryland's first-term Governor Spiro T. Agnew, was chosen as the vice-presidential candidate.

Nixon assumed an early lead in the campaign, attacking Humphrey as naïve on the question of law and crime and defending delay on the nuclear nonproliferation treaty as necessary for a reassessment of Russia after its states. Though the Republicans reduced the Democratic majorities in both houses of Congress, Nixon became the second president elected in 120 years not to have his party in control of at least one chamber. He emerged from the campaign, however, with increased stature as a result of moderation in meeting Democratic challenges, especially the president's last minute bombing halt. To many, his rise from a crushing defeat in California to the presidency seemed almost a political resurrection. This feat was only the first of a number of unlikely Nixon surprises in the next few years.

Major Internal Challenges

Fifty-six-year-old Richard Nixon assumed the presidency in January, 1969, in one of the most trying times in American life. The war in Vietnam increasingly divided the nation, although the president began the deescalation of the conflict in June, 1969, by the first of many announcements of troop withdrawals. Massive nationwide demonstrations including rallies, candlelight marches, and teach-ins were staged on October 15 and November 15, 1969. On the latter occasion, a quarter million people

The inauguration of Richard M. Nixon.

marched down Pennsylvania Avenue and staged a rally at the Washington monument. Over 45,000 participated in a forty-hour march from Arlington National Cemetery to the Capitol, each bearing the name of a U.S. soldier killed in Vietnam or a Vietnamese village supposedly destroyed by U.S. forces.

For several years demonstrations, often led by nonstudents, had been growing on the nation's college and university campuses. The first major one, which began at the University of California at Berkeley in September, 1964, and continued for the remainder of the academic year, focused on removal of restrictions on campus political activity and university treatment of students in and out of class. Although few changes came as a result, the demonstrators felt they made some gains by forcing the resignation of a number of university officials, including President Clark Kerr. The campus protesters quickly came to devote much attention to the Vietnam war, and teach-ins in opposition were staged at some one hundred colleges and universities in the spring of 1965.

As the 1960s progressed, some observers found a correlation between economic uncertainty and unrest. A drop occurred in study in the sciences as job opportunities declined in engineering, physics, and other formerly lucrative areas while increasing numbers of students majored in the social sciences and became activists who wished to see needed changes implemented at once. They succeeded in obtaining a larger voice in university affairs, winning membership on many faculty committees and even some boards of trustees, but often the change did not come soon enough or in adequte measure to please the disaffected.

In 1968 student unrest was intensified with the most notable eruption coming at Columbia University in late April when demonstrators seized five buildings to protest the school's contribution to military research and planned construction of a gymnasium in a park area largely used by blacks. They were ejected only after city police were summoned and a great deal of destruction occurred; 150 persons were injured, 700 arrested, and the educational process was interrupted for the remainder of the term. San Francisco State, Howard, Harvard, Yale, and a number of other schools suffered similar but less destructive disruptions. As a result, many schools, including some in the Ivy League, met one of the rioters' major demands by establishing Afro-American courses of study.

Campus crises were precipitated in late April, 1970, when President Nixon ordered American forces into Cambodia to clear sanctuaries used by the Viet Cong and the North Vietnamese. Calls for a nationwide students' strike met with success at a number of schools; in Ohio, where the National Guard was called to contain a demonstration at Kent State University, four students were tragically killed by guardsmen firing M-1 rifles into an unruly crowd. This event gave impetus to a Washington protest demonstration on May 9, 1970, when more than 100,000 protesters converged on the capital. By May 10, almost 450 colleges or universities were closed or on strike, but these events marked the high watermark of student protest.

Student demonstrations declined after 1970 as the president continued to deescalate the war and as many of the malcontents found an effective means of expressing their views within regular political channels.* Without realizing it, many political leaders modified their views to accept much of the peace movement's philosophy. In 1972 the Democratic party's presidential nominee, South Dakota's Senator George McGovern, a long-time opponent of

---

*Two weeks of Washington antiwar demonstrations in April and May, 1971, were an exception. Though the number participating was less than expected, 7,000 were arrested for attempting to block bridges and streets.

the war, met wide student acceptance, although almost half of the nation's voting students voted for Nixon. McGovern made the conflict one of the major compaign issues, promising in his convention acceptance speech to end the fighting within ninety days of his inauguration if he were elected.

A major concession to youth came in 1970 when Congress passed a law giving eighteen-year-olds the right to vote in national elections, an action quickly emulated by most states for their elections and one that made eighteen to twenty-one-year-olds a potent political force. These changes were followed in 1971 by the passage of the Twenty-sixth Amendment which guaranteed the same voting rights to those eighteen or over as enjoyed by other U.S. citizens.

Although the youth protests declined, financial problems and inflation continued to plague almost every aspect of American life. As costs rose, the federal government became the primary source, in many cases, of new revenue, but each increase in federal appropriations contributed to the inflation. For that reason, President Nixon vetoed a $4.4 billion aid to education bill in 1970, which passed over his veto. In 1971, due to inflation, he postponed consideration of his revenue-sharing program, designed to rejuvenate the states, but it was enacted in October, 1972, as part of his New Federalism. Unlike earlier legislation providing funds to state and local governments, the new law placed few restrictions on use of the appropriations. A complex formula provided some 38,000 governmental units approximately $5.3 billion during the program's first year and grants of $30 billion were projected during the first five years. Meanwhile, the president consistently refused pleas for the federal government to provide approximately one-third of the educational dollar. After vetoing major educational appropriations bills in 1971 and 1972, however, he accepted others

which increased federal appropriations to more than $5 billion annually. The administration sought to effect savings by curtailing a number of educational programs in fiscal 1973–74, but Congress overrode many of its recommendations, providing $6.44 billion for the Education Division of the Department of Health, Education and Welfare, $1.17 billion more than the president's budget requested.

The cost spiral continued to affect everyone, however, with prices rising even in recessions. During 1970 the number of unemployed almost doubled, reaching five million people or 6 percent of the labor force in December, a level at which it remained in late 1971. At the same time, prices increased on the average of 6 percent in 1970 and 4.6 percent in 1971. The 1971 rate would have been higher if the president had not declared a wage-price freeze on August 15, 1971, an action which came as a surprise due to Nixon's commitment to as free a market as possible. The president ordered a ninety-day freeze on wages, prices, and rents; ended the convertibility of the dollar into gold; placed a 10 percent surcharge on the importation of dutiable goods; proposed a $4.7 billion reduction in federal expenditures, an end to automobile excise taxes, and new tax incentives for industry. After Phase I of the freeze ended in November 1971, the Cost of Living Council, a group responsible to the president and endowed with authority to pass on proposed price and wage increases, continued to attempt to hold prices and wages within noninflationary ranges, passing through various degrees of regulation known as Phases II, III, and IV. Direct controls were removed on price increases except on food by early 1973, but they were reimposed as a virulent inflation developed in mid-1973. However, the controls proved a major factor in reduction of production, particularly of food, and most were removed by the fall of 1973. Prices continued to rise, however, attaining an annual increase of

8 percent in 1973 and 12 percent in 1974. The 100 cents dollar of 1960 would purchase only 76 cents in comparable goods and services in 1970. Though national income increased per capita from $2,115 in 1958 to $3,910 in 1970, much of the increase was absorbed by the higher cost of living.

The nation's farmers, whose number of employees declined from 8,773,000 in 1959 to 5,251,000 in 1971, remained among the most unstable economic groups. In 1970 the parity ratio hit 75, the lowest figure since 1933, and major new legislation granted cotton and grain growers more freedom after meeting basic allotment requirements. In 1973, however, when international shortages placed a severe strain on American production, a number of restrictions were removed and many farm producers found the most brisk, high-priced market for their goods in history. Yet the high costs which they were forced to pay for many goods and services led many to operate in the red.

One of the major factors contributing to the farmers' economic difficulties was the increased cost of fuel. Following the Arab-Israeli War in the fall of 1973, the Arab nations curtailed their oil exports to the United States and much of the rest of the world, reducing America's available supplies by 15–20 percent and creating an energy crisis of major proportions. Nixon requested Congress to delegate extensive authority to the president to deal with the situation since the difficulties the crisis engendered proved among the most troublous in recent American history. In 1974 the Arab nations enlarged the quantity of oil for sale to the U.S. but also greatly increased their prices, compounding the inflation which was already of major proportions.

In an effort to deal with another economic crisis, the nation's balance of payment deficit with foreign countries, in December, 1971, the president obtained agreement from leading non-Communist countries to a devaluation of the dollar by approximately 12 percent. It was hoped that within three years this action, which would lessen the cost of U.S. goods sold abroad, would wipe out the unfavorable balance of trade which in 1971 amounted to $9 billion, a goal that, following a second devaluation in 1973, was apparently being achieved. To obtain this concession, Nixon agreed to remove the 10 percent surcharge on imports. In 1972 the employment situation improved, but by early 1974 the unemployed again exceeded 5 percent of the labor force.

In addition to inflation and unemployment, the continued increase in crime and drug abuse posed major problems for the administration and the American people which appeared far from solution. Between 1960 and 1970 there was a 73 percent increase in the number of men and a 200 percent increase in the number of women arrested for serious crimes. Many of these occurred in urban areas where 74 percent of America's 212 million people lived in 1974 and increasing numbers were in the suburban areas where, since 1940, over 75 percent of urban growth took place. By 1971 skyjacking had become a serious problem, particularly for the giant 747's, whose rear door provided an escape exit for ransom extortionists. As a result, in 1971 air marshals were assigned to some craft, and in January, 1973, the federal government imposed costly, elaborate inspection procedures for boarding areas at all commercial airports, measures which proved quite effective in combating the menace. The government also increased its activities in the crime control and drug abuse fields. The Omnibus Crime Control Act of 1970 greatly expanded federal authority in the area, establishing the death penalty for anyone convicted of a fatal bombing and allowing FBI agents to investigate and the U.S. to prosecute those accused of arson and of bombing college campuses and institutions receiving U.S. aid.

By the early 1970s, the extent of the drug problem was becoming well known. In 1969 the nation had an estimated 250,000 heroin users, a million LSD addicts, 4 million who took amphetamines orally, 10 to 20 million who smoked marijuana, 2 million dependent on barbiturates, and an untold number of others who injected amphetamines, sniffed inhalants, and used barbiturates mixed with other drugs. At the height of the American military operation in Vietnam, 5 percent of the American forces there were also believed to be dependent on drugs. Addiction had ceased to be a problem primarily affecting derelicts and was moving into every segment of society.

In response, Congress in 1970 adopted a Comprehensive Drug Abuse Prevention and Control Act, which provided for greatly expanded treatment, research, and education programs. In 1971 the president created the Special Office for Drug Abuse Prevention to direct all federal programs in the field. Although the hard-core drug areas in some cities seemed to be declining, it was still too early to tell if the spread of drug abuse had been contained.

Due to its concern with the rights of the accused, some critics of the liberal-oriented U.S. Supreme Court under Chief Justice Earl Warren blamed it for a portion of the increase in crime. In 1963, in *Gideon* v. *Wainwright* the court held that Florida must supply defense counsel to indigent defendants in noncapital as well as capital cases. The following year, in *Escobedo* v. *Illinois,* it decreed a conviction was invalid when a defendant was denied an attorney during questioning or was not specifically told of his right to remain silent. These decisions were broadened and amplified in 1966 and, in the opinion of some, interfered with police operations and conviction of obviously guilty criminals. In *Miranda* v. *Arizona* (1966), for example, comprehensive rules on the use of confessions were established as were guide-

Earl Warren

lines for local police and standards for lower courts based on those used in the federal system.

Meanwhile, earlier judicial decisions continued to have repercussions. In 1962 in *Baker* v. *Carr* the Supreme Court took jurisdiction in a Tennessee case involving inequitable representation in the legislature, an action it had declined to take since 1946 on the grounds that the issue was a purely political one. In a six-to-two decision, the Court held that it must consider suits concerning apportionment of state legislatures when allegations were made that the equal protection clause of the Fourteenth

Amendment had been violated. In 1964 the Court, ruling in fourteen apportionment suits, held the states concerned had not met the requirements of the equal protection clause. In *Reynolds* v. *Sims* it laid down the "one man, one vote" principle declaring that both houses of the state legislature had to be chosen from districts having approximately equal representation. Few denied that the "one man, one vote" decision was a great strike for democracy which would eventually destroy the stranglehold of rural areas over many legislatures, but many questioned whether the Court had assumed legislative power in denying to the state upper houses the same type electorate enjoyed by the U.S. Senate. Equally controversial was the outlawing in public schools of required Bible reading and prayers as violations of the First Amendment in the 1962 and 1963 decisions in *Engel* v. *Vitale* and *School District of Abington Township* v. *Schempp*. These decisions were, however, only two of many which broadened the interpretation of the First Amendment.

Soon after taking office in 1969 President Nixon began an attempt to change the Supreme Court's approach by appointing strict constructionists. He successfully named Warren E. Burger, a judge of the U.S. Court of Appeals for the District of Columbia, to succeed Warren as chief justice in 1969. Controversy arose when he tried to choose a successor to Justice Abe Fortas, who resigned after it became known he had received $20,000 from a family foundation of Louis E. Wolfson, a man charged by the Securities and Exchange Commission with selling unregistered securities, although the money was returned. Nixon's first nominee, Circuit Court of Appeals Judge Clement F. Haynsworth, Jr., of South Carolina, was opposed by labor and civil rights leaders and was rejected. The president's next choice, Florida's Judge G. Harrold Carswell, was also rejected after he was indicted for mediocrity

and racism. The angered Nixon, charging sectional bias was the real reason for his defeats, turned to Minnesota for a new nominee, and U.S. Court of Appeals Judge Harry A. Blackmun was confirmed without difficulty. In 1971, when John M. Harlan and Hugo Black retired, the president appointed two other associate justices, Lewis Franklin Powell, Jr., a corporation lawyer from Richmond, and Assistant U.S. Attorney General William Rehnquist. Powell was confirmed without difficulty, but Rehnquist's approval by a Senate vote of 68–26 came after liberal groups questioned his commitment to civil rights.

In the 1971–1972 Court year a number of decisions of a conservative nature were reached by five-to-four votes, with the four Nixon appointees voting together on 54 of 67 decisions; often they were joined by Justice Byron White. The total impact of the new decisions was to broaden police rights to search suspects; to allow states to continue to issue licenses to private clubs excluding blacks; to validate court convictions with less than a majority vote if state constitutions and laws permit this; to restrict use of the First Amendment by reporters in protecting their sources; to limit civilians in their prohibition of military surveillance only if they could show harm from it; and to allow the Amish to remove their children from school in the eighth grade as a right guaranteed by the First Amendment. Apparently the court's approach was changing, but the extent of the change would not be known for some time, although the main thrusts begun in 1971–1972 were present in decisions delivered in the following years.

The Persistence of Major Problems

In the midst of concern and heroic efforts, some major problems such as race relations seemed to defy solution. In 1969 President Nixon sanctioned use of the "Philadelphia Plan," which required that a specific portion of blacks be hired by contractors doing federally assisted construction work in the Philadelphia area. Since then similar plans have been instituted elsewhere, but, though some success has been obtained, blacks have continued to occupy the lowest positions in the economy. Often ruses have been found to subvert the most carefully laid plans; for example, blacks have been transferred to nonfederally financed projects to avoid federal rules. Significant concessions by segments of industry and education to admit blacks with lower standards than whites have emerged in recognition of the handicaps under which blacks have lived. Despite these and similar efforts, some blacks have come to feel that they can never receive justice in American society and have resorted to violence. The Black Panthers, a military disciplined group, adopted the philosophy of Mao Tse-tung and Che Guevara, the Marxist who became Castro's principal lieutenant and instigator of revolutions throughout Latin America. After challenging police in several cities in the late 1960s and early 1970s, a number of Panthers were arrested and indicted. Although some people expressed fear that they could not receive a fair trial, a surprising number were acquitted, as was Angela Davis, the most celebrated black brought to trial in recent years. She was indicted for supposedly smuggling murder weapons into a California courtroom in 1970, which led to the abduction and death of a San Rafael judge.

Much of the concern about black rights stemmed from a recent subtle but significant change in national attitudes. In 1966 Martin Luther King, Jr., conducted his first northern drive in Chicago, where he achieved less than he had hoped. A number of younger blacks did not feel that his approach was radical enough, and some, particularly among the poorer, less educated, joined the Black Muslim movement which wished to make war on whites and maintain a separate black society. Many northerners who had sympathized with passive resistance when aimed at southern conditions were less appreciative of it nearer home. The severe 1965 race riot in Watts, a lower-middle class Los Angeles suburb, which killed thirty-four and inflicted $40 million in damages, was followed by riots in Atlanta, Chicago, Cleveland, Los Angeles, and San Francisco in 1966. Watts-type destruction resulted from 1967 riots in Newark and Detroit. In April, 1968, King was assassinated in Memphis, Tennessee, where he was leading a protest movement in behalf of striking sanitation workers, after which violence erupted throughout the nation's cities with predominantly black Washington, D.C., evidencing the greatest turmoil.

The wave of fear engendered by these ghetto eruptions moderated white sympathy with blacks. Before King's death, plans had been completed for a Poor People's March on Washington to demand better living conditions, education, and employment opportunities. Without King's leadership, only about 2,600 persons were attracted to "Resurrection City," the Poor People's encampment near the Lincoln Memorial; yet at the movement's end some 50,000 demonstrators did converge on the capital. While plans were being developed for the movement, an act was passed in April, 1968, outlawing discrimination in housing other than owner-sold single dwellings or apartments of less than four units. Soon afterwards, in June, 1968, the Supreme Court upheld an 1866 law giving all citizens the right to sell, lease, or hold property equally.

In 1968 also black demands for educational equality received substantial support when South Holland, Illinois, was ordered by the Supreme Court to end *de facto* school segregation created by neighborhood schools. In the following years the federal government cut federal funds to school districts that did not abide by its guidelines to end segregation, an imposition of standards which proved in many instances to be an effective means of speeding up the desegregation process. The federal courts also increasingly required more than token integration as a reasonable expectation, and by 1971 they had instituted extensive busing to correct racial imbalance, a policy which drew emotional criticism from both black and white parents. The problem was more intense outside the South than within it. By the fall of 1970, 38 percent of black children were attending primarily white schools in the South, but only 28 percent of blacks were in such schools outside the South.

In 1972 after Alabama Governor George Wallace, who pledged to end busing, won a majority in the Democratic presidential primary in Florida and a plurality of the votes in Michigan and Maryland, President Nixon advocated a moratorium on additional busing. This action was opposed by his Civil Rights Commission and many liberals, who felt it would lessen black opportunities. Many of the president's supporters contended the issue was not racial but involved safety and the quality of instruction provided whites who were forced to attend classes with less well-prepared students.

Blacks continued to gain additional rights and opportunities but confrontation, having served its purpose, gave way to jockeying for economic advantage and other less explosive gains. Barriers to voting and public school attendance had been broken in the South, although in some rural Black Belt counties the whites had virtually left the public schools. Business America had accepted blacks, at least in token numbers, in administrative and supervisory positions, yet blacks continued to furnish less than 4 percent of the nation's managers and supervisors. In a period of recovery from recession, black unemployment was

George C. Wallace

50 percent higher than white, and various economic indexes indicated that, while blacks were continuing to make progress, the disparity was increasing between black and white living standards. No end was seen to white escape from the core of the nation's cities nor was a decrease evident in the cities' black population. In the 1960s the white population of central city areas declined 2.5 million, while their black members increased by 3 million, and, as industry moved to the suburbs, blacks found that transportation to jobs, even when available, was a major difficulty. The crisis of urban America remained intensely racial in nature. The most frightening aspect of the racial problem was stated by the Reverend Theodore Hesburgh, president of Notre Dame and chairman of the U.S. Civil Rights Commission, who found, though the problems were tremendous,

there was "a lack of moral commitment both in and out of government" to deal with them.

By the 1970s American Indians, Puerto Ricans, and Chicanos (Mexican-Americans) were emulating blacks in a search for identity and security, although there was frequent conflict between the various groups. In November, 1969, Indians dramatized their aspirations by seizing Alcatraz Island and demanding it as an area of their own. Demonstrations staged in Washington and elsewhere pricked the conscience of the nation, which recognized justice demanded payments be made for many unjust seizures of tribal lands. In February, 1973, after weeks of clashes, 200–300 members of the militant American Indian Movement seized the trading post and church at Wounded Knee on the Oglala Sioux reservation in South Dakota, site of the last major conflict between Indians and the U.S. Army in 1890. Almost three months of intermittent sieges, cease-fires, and negotiations occurred before the Indians surrendered their weapons and the government removed its armed personnel.

President Nixon in July, 1970, proposed the formulation of a national policy which would turn over to the Indians control of many of the government aid programs that fostered dependency. Concessions were made to Indian-Americans when $12.3 million was awarded to the Seminoles for Florida land seized in the 1830s and when the Taos received title to 48,-000 acres in New Mexico's Carson National Forest. There was no solution to the Indian problem, however. Cultural alienation remained a major difficulty with dualistic forces pulling at many of the young who had contacts with the white world but were also bound to their people.

Chicanos formed another significant racial group affected by discrimination and exploitation. Much of the attention given them came from the unionization efforts among agricultural workers undertaken by Cesar Chavez,

which resulted in national boycotts of a number of products. In 1972 the Democratic National Convention gave much publicity to a boycott of lettuce when various delegates, even in roll-call votes, managed to express their support of Chavez's program.

Chicanos constituted a large portion of the 7 percent of U.S. residents who were of Latin birth. Concentrated in the Southwest, they often felt discriminated against not only in employment, housing, and education but also in police treatment as well. Credence was given their dissatisfaction in 1970 when the U.S. Civil Rights Commission asserted the Justice Department had been remiss in investigating Chicano complaints of civil rights violations and urged Congress to pass laws to end police misconduct in the Southwest.

The daily migration of Mexicans to perform agricultural work in border regions, a long-standing problem, was a contributing factor to Chicano unrest. In 1970 the U.S. Civil Rights Commission estimated 100,000 made the illegal trek daily and were forced to work for low wages in fear of exposure. Their presence contributed to the poverty of other Mexican-Americans who were either denied jobs or forced to work for starvation pay.

The effects of discrimination were by no means confined to race. America's women assumed a new militancy for equality in the late 1960s, and after twenty-two years in committee, in August, 1970, the House of Representatives submitted a constitutional Equal Rights Amendment (ERA) to the states which would end discrimination on the basis of sex. Though thirty-three states ratified it by 1974, it still needed the approval of six legislatures. Much lobbying against it came from various women's groups who felt the measure would destroy advantages enjoyed by women, an allegation hotly contested by various pro-ERA organizations. Nevertheless, the reaction of Congress and many state legislatures was indicative of a new urgency in the women's rights movement. The federal government itself responded to it in 1970 by bringing the first suit against a major company for job discrimination based on sex, an act made illegal by the Civil Rights Act of 1964.

Though women had made notable gains by obtaining entry into most colleges and universities, the right to vote, and opportunities to advance in many companies, the average woman still was at a disadvantage in most economic activities. In 1970 average salaries paid women were 42 percent lower than those of men, and women were concentrated in inferior positions with promotions usually going first to men. Some jobs which women could perform were barred to them entirely, and some public places were closed to their entry.

In the 1970s, however, under the attack of committed women and a not inappreciable number of men, many barriers were falling. Although the Supreme Court sanctioned a bar for men only, New York City prohibited sex barriers in public places in 1971 and followed this action by forbidding sexual discrimination in employment. After New York State's Human Rights Commission began an even broader investigation, many barriers fell while both state and federal court decisions opened additional opportunities. In *Phillips* v. *Martin Marietta* the U.S. Supreme Court ruled employers could not deny jobs to women solely because they had small children unless men were denied on the same basis, and in New Jersey and California state courts declared women had the right to work as bartenders. As these and other decisions were rendered, a number of employers voluntarily relaxed their discriminatory rules, but the crusade for true equality had far to go.

Though concerned with many questions, the cutting edge of the women's rights movement, often called women's liberation, came by 1972 to concentrate on easing restrictions on abortion. Its goal was abortion on demand for any woman, which was achieved in New York in 1970. A number of other states had liberalized their laws, but President Nixon indicated his opposition, and Senator George McGovern, the 1972 Democratic presidential candidate, carefully avoided the issue. In an important 1971 decision, *United States* v. *Vuitch,* the U.S. Supreme Court upheld a District of Columbia law which permitted abortions only when necessary to preserve the mother's life or health. The majority five-to-two opinion was one of the last written by Justice Hugo Black, whose concern with civil rights had characterized his long tenure on the court. However, in January, 1973, the Supreme Court in *Jane Roe* v. *Henry Wade* held that any state interference with the termination of pregnancy during its first three months was an invasion of an individual's right to privacy. During the second three months laws could only require certain prescribed procedures to be followed in performing abortions. However, the state was allowed to deny abortions during the last three months when the fetus had a chance of independent survival. The momentous decision invalidated laws in over forty states and led to an increased number of abortions.

Liberalized abortion was only one aspect of the more permissive sexual standards in America. Despite the widespread availability of effective oral contraceptives and antibiotics for the treatment of venereal diseases, many unwanted pregnancies occurred, and a growing epidemic of syphilis and gonorrhea developed. In 1974 penicillin-resistant venereal diseases were second only to the cold as the nation's most common illnesses. One caustic critic declared that contemporary Americans might well be characterized as "the careless generation." While the extent of promiscuity was debatable, none could deny that a flood of books, magazines, and films dealing explicitly with sex proliferated.

Pollution also posed major problems which were as emotionally laden as abortion and pornography for many Americans in the 1970s. Its deadly significance came not only from population increase, which had been slowed markedly, but also from the tremendous rise in waste and pollutants produced by a society which had traditionally disregarded conservation. Millions were taken unaware when streams literally began to die and scientists revealed that air pollution had reached the danger level, at times in entire regions. In 1970 President Nixon committed the nation to a repayment of its debt to the past "by reclaiming the purity of its air, its waters, and our living environment." With urgency he added, "It is literally now or never."

As a result, the National Environmental Policy Act was passed, establishing the Council on Environmental Quality in the executive branch of government. By executive order, in July, 1970, the president established the Environmental Protection Agency, consolidating many of the government's operations dealing with the environment, which in fiscal 1971 had a budget totaling $1.4 billion.

The Council on Environmental Quality made important recommendations which have been incorporated in many federal programs. Moreover, the government canceled projects and refrained from undertaking others whose conservation damage or polluting effects were considered too great. For example, the president ended construction in 1971 of the Cross-Florida Barge Canal, to which $50 million in federal funds had been committed, and Congress, over strong administration protests, stopped additional appropriations for a supersonic transport plane. As the energy crisis became severe in late 1973, however, a number of standards were relaxed or their attainment postponed. It was only then that approval was finally granted, over environmentalist reservations, for the building of a trans-Alaskan pipe-line whose completion four years hence would increase the availability of petroleum. Meanwhile, the states, aided by federal regulations and requirements, undertook their own programs and interested private groups began many legal cases in an attempt to preserve the natural balance of various areas.

The Second Nixon Administration

The nation's ability to grapple with domestic problems began to be seriously impeded in 1973 when the Nixon administration lost the confidence of many Americans and became so concerned with its own internal problems that it was unable to concentrate on other issues. This unexpected development was all the more amazing since the president and Vice-President Agnew had been renominated by acclamation at the 1972 Republican National Convention and proceeded to effectively meet the challenge of the Democratic contenders.

Fragmentation in the Democratic party began in the preconvention struggles between its various candidates. Maine's Senator Edmund S. Muskie, the party's 1968 candidate for vice-president, stopped active campaigning in April, 1972, after making a poor showing in several primaries, and Governor George C. Wallace was forced to withdraw after he was seriously wounded in May at a Laurel, Maryland, shopping center by Arthur Bremer, a twenty-one-year-old psychopath from Milwaukee, Wisconsin. Senator Hubert Humphrey, the 1968 nominee who announced his candidacy in January and received strong labor support, was unable to gain sufficient strength to stop the front-runner, the even more advanced liberal, Senator George McGovern of South Dakota.

McGovern amassed a large plurality of delegates both from primaries and state conventions due, in many cases, to the party's adoption of rules formulated by a commission he had headed following the disastrous 1968 convention. Although designed to insure adequate representation of women, blacks, and young people, the new rules alienated many professional party workers and were greatly modified in 1973. After the entire convention decided California and Illinois credential disputes in favor of McGovern, he was easily nominated on the first ballot. Following the refusal of the vice-presidential nomination by Senator Edward Kennedy and several others, McGovern chose the impressive, young junior senator from Missouri, Thomas F. Eagleton, as his running mate. Within two weeks it became known that Eagleton had been hospitalized three times during the previous twelve years with psychiatric problems and had received electric shock therapy. After initially declaring he was "1,000 percent" behind Eagleton, McGovern changed his mind and pressured him to resign from the ticket. He was replaced by Sargent Shriver, Senator Kennedy's brother-in-law who had served as the first head of the Peace Corps, as director of the Office of Economic Opportunity, and ambassador to France.

The Eagleton episode injured the Democratic campaign, but alienation of large groups of normally democratic voters insured defeat. At the convention, the Illinois delegation, led by Chicago's Mayor Daley, had been replaced by a new one whose composition met the guidelines laid down by the McGovern Commission. This rejection greatly offended Daley, and comparable actions alienated party leaders in other states. Jewish voters, some of whom felt McGovern was a belated supporter of Israel, inherently distrusted a quota system required by the McGovern Commission's rules, and many representatives of labor, ethnic groups, and the South felt the rules were rigged against them. Moreover, McGovern's advocacy of ending the Vietnam war by any possible means and of greatly expanded welfare programs was unacceptable even to many liberals.

In the campaign, Nixon and Agnew effectively aroused the fear that the Democratic candidates would surrender national honor, reduce U.S. military power until it was at the mercy of the Communist states, and indulge the indolent to the point that they would destroy the productive elements of society. As a result, the Republican candidates carried every state except Massachusetts, and the District of Columbia, although their popular vote was slightly less than Johnson's and Humphrey's in 1964.

The second Nixon-Agnew administration was initiated with great self-confidence in January, 1973, although extensive dismissals and reshuffling of leadership at the cabinet and subcabinet level and a renewed effort to hold down federal spending through cutbacks and cancellations of a number of programs created a great deal of uncertainty. However, by the early spring of 1973, the nation was on the verge of the greatest constitutional crisis since Reconstruction, and many Americans could scarcely believe the continuing incriminating revelations which became public in the following months.

By bits and pieces it became known that at least with the knowledge of men close to the president, on May 28, 1972, the Democratic headquarters in the Watergate building complex in Washington, D.C., were burglarized, and the phones "bugged" and documents photographed. When the quality of the stolen material proved inferior, a second burglary occurred on June 17, 1972, but five men were apprehended and arrested in the process, including James McCord, a former CIA agent and security officer of the Committee to Reelect the President who was fired from his position only after his arrest. Although the Democratic National Committee sued for $1 million damages,

McGovern was unable to exploit the issue with much effect during the presidential campaign.

Due in large measure to the exposés of the press, on April 30, 1973, the president acknowledged that "top men" in his organization were responsible for the Watergate affair, but he denied knowledge of its seriousness or of the efforts to cover it up before March, 1973. He summarily fired presidential counsel John W. Dean, III, and accepted, regretfully, the resignations of White House Chief of Staff H. R. Haldeman and Domestic Affairs Assistant John D. Ehrlichman. Attorney General Richard G. Kleindienst resigned stating that individuals with whom he had close "personal and professional associations" could be involved in law violations. He was replaced by Secretary of Defense Elliot Richardson who, in response to mounting public and congressional pressure, was authorized to appoint a special Watergate prosecutor. On May, 18, 1973, he chose Archibald Cox, a Harvard Law School professor, to fill this office.

Meanwhile, startling revelations had occurred in the case of Daniel Ellsberg and Anthony J. Russo, Jr., who were being tried for espionage, theft, and conspiracy in connection with the release of the "Pentagon Papers," secret government documents dealing with its Vietnam policy which were leaked to the press. It was revealed that two of the principals in the Watergate affair had, on government orders, broken into the office of Ellsberg's psychiatrist to steal his medical records and that the trial judge had been approached with the possibility of becoming F.B.I. director. Quite properly, Judge William M. Byrne refused to discuss the potential position while the case was before him, and on May 11, 1973, he dismissed it on the grounds that the government's conduct had "placed the case in such a posture that it precludes the fair, dispassionate resolution of these issues by a jury."

On May, 22, 1973, President Nixon acknowledged that he had exerted efforts to restrict investigations into some aspects of the Watergate matter because of their impingement on national security, but he did not clarify the nature of this impingement. He also acknowledged that following the Pentagon Papers leak, in 1971, he had authorized the establishment of a small intelligence unit under the supervision of John D. Ehrlichman known as "the plumbers" and that he ordered one of them to find out all he could about Ellsberg; he contended, however, that he never sanctioned illegal action.

Meanwhile on May 17, 1973, the Senate Select Committee on Presidential Campaign Activities, known popularly as the Watergate Committee, began public hearings, the first series of which continued until August and shocked the people with the daily revelations carried in their entirety by nationwide television. Under the chairmanship of seventy-seven-year-old Senator Sam J. Ervin of North Carolina and vice-chairmanship of Senator Howard H. Baker of Tennessee, the Committee heard James McCord, by this time a convicted Watergate conspirator, testify that he had been offered executive clemency, financial aid, and a

President Nixon holding a press conference.

job by a former aide of Ehrlichman and Dean. Jeb Stuart Magruder implicated former Attorney General John Mitchell, Dean, and Haldeman in the effort to cover up the Watergate affair. Dean contended that the president had also been involved in the cover-up for as long as eight months, a charge the White House denied when it alleged Dean was the "mastermind" behind the cover-up. Nixon's former personal attorney, Herbert W. Kolmbach, acknowledgd he had raised $220,000 for use of the seven Watergate defendants and that his orders came from Dean with assurances from Ehrlichman.

An opportunity to resolve the charges and countercharges seemed to present itself after former presidential Deputy Assistant Alexander P. Butterfield testified on July 16, 1973, that President Nixon had recorded his White House and Executive Office Building conversations since March, 1971. The Watergate Committee and Special Prosecutor Cox immediately asked for the tapes of those conversations, but the president refused, vigorously asserting compliance would represent an intrusion on the executive branch of government.

A turning point in the Watergate affair came in October, 1973, when the president seemed to be violating an order of U.S. District Court Judge John J. Sirica requiring him to furnish the tapes to Special Watergate Prosecutor Cox. When Cox refused a proposed White House compromise under which the president would submit a personally edited summary of matters related to Watergate from the tapes, Nixon ordered Attorney General Richardson to fire him. Rather than do this, Richardson resigned, and his deputy, William D. Ruckelshaus, was fired by the president; Cox was replaced as special Watergate prosecutor by Leon Jaworski of Texas. When public reaction became intense, the president agreed on October 23 to obey the court order, but subsequently the White House stated two of the most critical tapes (a conver-

sation with Dean on April 15, 1972, and Mitchell on June 20, 1972) no longer existed, and an eighteen and one-half minute erasure was found to exist in a crucial conversation with Dean.

Under this barrage of incrimination, the president stoutly defended his innocence and attempted to shift emphasis to non-Watergate matters. The issue refused to die, however, and public opinion polls showed a majority of the people felt he should resign while impeachment proceedings began in Congress. The president's image was not helped by former Attorney General Richard G. Kleindienst's statement to the Watergate Committee that Nixon had ordered him personally not to press an antitrust suit against the International Telephone and Telegraph Company which led the way to an out-of-court settlement. In addition, many were infuriated to learn that Nixon's tax lawyers had apparently predated forms which enabled the president to claim over $400,000 in a tax deduction for vice-presidential papers given the National Archives, a deduction that enabled him to pay less than $900 one year in federal income taxes. Moreover, the resignation of Vice-President Agnew in October, 1973, though not directly related to the president, damaged the entire administration. After allegations were made that Agnew received bribe money from Maryland contractors both while he was a state official and vice-president, he pleaded guilty to a charge of tax evasion, was sentenced to a three-year probation and fined $10,000; following these events Agnew resigned his office, the second vice-president in American history to do so, and was barred from the practice of law in Maryland. President Nixon, acting under the Twenty-fifth Amendment adopted in 1967, selected Representative Gerald R. Ford, the respected minority leader from Michigan, to succeed Agnew, and he was confirmed without difficulty.

Ford Succeeds Nixon

Every effort of the Nixon administration to inter the Watergate scandal or to divert attention from it failed, and in the summer of 1974 the national debate surrounding it came to a climax. After months of exhaustive investigation, the House Judiciary Committee, headed by Representative Peter Rodino, a New Jersey Democrat, came to a vote on the articles of impeachment of President Nixon. The final days of its deliberations were nationally televised, and the intensity of the members' concern and the care with which they proceeded made a marked impression on public opinion. When leading southern Democrats and some Republicans on the committee indicated their condemnation of the president's action, there was no doubt as to the outcome.

On July 27, 1974, by a vote of twenty-seven to eleven (twenty-one Democrats and six Republicans voting yes), the committee approved the first of three articles of impeachment. It held that the president "has prevented, obstructed and impeded the administration of justice" by using his powers of office "in a course of conduct or plan designed to delay, impede and obstruct the investigation" of the Watergate burglaries and "to cover up, conceal and protect those responsible; and to conceal the existence and scope of other unlawful covert activities."

Subsequently, the committee passed by a twenty-eight to ten vote (twenty-one Democrats and seven Republicans voting yes) the second article of impeachment. It accused the president "of abusing the powers of his office and failing to take care that the laws be faithfully executed." It held he "has abused the powers invested in him as President . . . either directly or through his subordinates or agents. . . ." The third article was passed by a smaller vote, twenty-one to seventeen (nineteen Democrats and two Republicans

voting yes). It charged the president with deliberately disobeying lawful subpoenaes for White House tape recordings from the House Judiciary Committee. Other proposed articles based on purported secret orders to bomb Cambodia and an attempt "to willfully evade" federal income taxes were defeated.

The House Judiciary Committee's action obviously commanded sufficient support in the full House of Representatives to lead to the president's impeachment and trial before the Senate. This certainty and a ruling of the U.S. Supreme Court on July 24, 1974, proved decisive in the Watergate struggle. The president had sought Court sanction to withhold certain of the White House tapes on the grounds of executive privilege. By a unanimous eight-to-zero decision, the Supreme Court in effect declared that even the president is under, not above, the law and that his right of executive privilege is limited. It asserted "neither the doctrine of separation of powers, nor the need for confidentiality of high level communications . . . can sustain an absolute, unqualified presidential privilege of immunity from judicial process under all circumstances." It clearly stated, "When the ground for asserting privilege as to subpoenaed materials is based only on the generalized interest in confidentiality, it cannot prevail over the fundamental demands of due process of law in the fair administration of criminal justice."

As early as May 6–7, 1974, President Nixon, after listening to some of the Watergate tapes, had abandoned a proposed compromise under which twelve of them would have been turned over to Special Prosecutor Jaworski, apparently due to the fact that they would reveal he was not innocent of aiding in the Watergate cover-up. On July 26, 1974, District Judge Sirica asked President Nixon's attorney, James St. Clair, if he had personally listened to the tapes in question and was amazed to find he had not. On July 31, 1974, St. Clair received and read transcripts of three July 23, 1972, conversations between the president and H. R. Haldeman. These appeared to indicate that six days after the second Watergate burglary Nixon was aware that former Attorney General Mitchell and two former White House consultants, E. Howard Hunt and G. Gordon Liddy, had been involved and that Nixon proposed their actions be covered up.

It was obvious to St. Clair that under the recent Supreme Court decision the incriminating tapes would become public, at least at the trials of six former presidential aides who had been indicted for conspiracy in the cover-up. When this information was made known to White House Chief of Staff, General Alexander Haig, Secretary of State Henry Kissinger, and other leaders of the administration, they shared it with leading congressional Republicans, including Representative Charles Wiggins of California who had led the Nixon defense in the House Judiciary Committee. Support for the president collapsed, and prudence demanded he resign.

On August 8, 1974, President Nixon announced in a nationwide television address that he would resign the next day, a historic first in American history. Although he conceded that he had made mistakes, he in no way admitted his guilt and based his resignation on a desire to place the country's well-being ahead of his own.

In a poignant scene, President Nixon bade his associates good-bye in a televised session held in the East Room of the White House on the morning of August 9, 1974, and boarded *Air Force I* for his San Clemente, California, home. A few hours later, when the resignation became effective at noon, Gerald Ford was sworn in as president.

The new president began the difficult transition of power by pledging to continue his predecessor's foreign policy, a fact symbolized by Secretary of State Kissinger's retention in

Gerald R. Ford

office, and by acknowledging that inflation was the nation's major domestic problem. Although he proposed no immediate solution, he called a national economic summit conference on inflation and promised continued, sustained efforts to meet the challenge.

The relations of the new administration with Congress began auspiciously due to the president's close connections on Capitol Hill. In his first address to a joint session, President Ford asserted that he did not want "a honeymoon but a marriage" with the Congress and pledged he would work to that end.

The first disruption of cordial relations with Congress and many other Americans came only thirty days after Ford's inauguration. Without notice and in contradiction of indications he had given to congressional committees when his nomination as vice-president was being considered, he granted former President Nixon "a full, free and absolute pardon" for all offenses he might have committed against the United States between January 20, 1969, and August 9, 1974. The president contended his decision was based primarily on a desire to save the nation at least another year of agony which would have occurred had Nixon been placed on trial for his conduct in the Watergate affair. Many feared, however, that the president was creating a dual system of justice and questioned his action.

As the new Ford administration attempted to come to grips with the problems before it, the dreams of a peaceful, prosperous America which former President Nixon had projected only eighteen months before seemed far away. Only time would tell the results of the newest challenges to the country's development and its very existence.

Selected Bibliography

The works on contemporary politics and problems are voluminous. In addition to a number of works cited in the previous chapter, excellent accounts of the most recent presidential elections are given in Theodore H. White, *The Making of the President, 1968,* * *1972* * (1970, 1973). Useful studies of Presidents Johnson and Nixon include Eric F. Goldman, *The Tragedy of Lyndon Johnson: A Historian's Personal Interpretation* * (1969); Rowland Evans and Robert Novak, *Lyndon B. Johnson, The Exercise of Power, A Political Biography* * (1966) and *Nixon in the White House: The Frustration of Power* * (1972); Tom Wicker, *JFK and LBJ: The Influence of Personality upon Politics* * (1969); and Earl Mazo and Stephan Hess, *Nixon, A Political Portrait* (1968). The newspaper reporters who were most influential in breaking the Watergate story chronicle their experiences in Carl Bernstein and Bob Woodward, *All the President's Men* (1974).

Interesting studies of present-day conditions are found in Alphonso Pinkney, *The American Way of Violence* * (1972), which charges the economy begets people at war with each other, and David Boesel and Peter Rossi, eds., *Cities Under Siege: An Anatomy of the Ghetto Riots, 1964–1968* (1971), which provides an informative introduction to the urban riots. For works dealing with blacks see the previous chapter.

Perceptive studies of other minority groups include Matt S. Meirer and Feliciano Rivera, *The Chicanos: A History of Mexican Americans* * (1972); Alvin M. Josephy, Jr., *Red Power, The American Indians' Fight for Freedom* (1972); and Kal Wagenheim, *Puerto Rico: A Profile* (1971). Christopher Jencks and David Riesman portray *The Academic Revolution* * (1968). A sympathetic view of rebellious youth is in Kenneth Keniston, *Young Radicals: Notes on Committed Youth* * (1968) and their new life styles kindly treated by Theodore Roszak, *The Making of a Counter Culture* (1969), and Kenneth Keniston, *Youth and Dissent: The Rise of a New Opposition* (1972). Donald B. Louria, *The Drug Scene* * (1968), outlines the dimension of that problem. Poverty's extent and significance is treated by Chaim I. Waxman, ed., *Poverty: Power and Politics* * (1968). Council on Population and Environment, Noel Hinrichs, ed., *Population, Environment and People* * (1971), presents the urgent problems created by numbers and pollution. An interesting background to conservation problems is found in Roderick Nash, *Wilderness and the American Mind* * (rev. ed., 1973). Judith Hole and Ellen Levine, *Rebirth of Feminism* (1973), and Betty Friedan, *The Feminine Mystique* * (1970), deal with the inequities promoting the women's rights movement and its psychology. William H. Chafe, *The American Woman, Her Changing Social, Economic and Political Role, 1920–1970* (1972), traces the movement during the last fifty years, challenging many stereotypes of it. Examples of organized religion's response to change are found in Urban G. Steinmetz, *The Sexual Christian* * (1972), and Joseph J. Reidy, *The Sensitivity Phenomenon* * (1973).

---

*Available in paperback.

Foreign Policy
Achievements and Failures

1950	Beginning of American aid to French Indochina
1954	Doctrine of massive retaliation
	Division of Vietnam
	Formation of Southeast Asia Treaty Organization
1955	Protection extended to Taiwan, the Pescadores, and closely related localities
	Geneva Summit Meeting
1958	Vice-President Nixon attacked in Latin America
	American troops sent to Lebanon
1959	Castro's assumption of power in Cuba
	Bilateral United States agreements with Iran, Turkey, and Pakistan
1960	U-2 incident
1962	Cuban Missile Crisis
1964	Gulf of Tonkin Crisis
1965	United States troops sent to the Dominican Republic
	First army units sent to Vietnam
1967	NATO renunciation of massive retaliation
	Six-Day War
1968	Temporary end of United States bombing in Vietnam
	Vietnam peace talks began
1969	Nixon visit to Europe and Southeast Asia
	Signature of Nuclear Non-Proliferation Treaty
1971	People's Republic of China admitted to UN and Republic of China expelled
	United States support of Pakistan and East Pakistan revolt
1972	Presidential visits to China and Russia
1973	Peace settlement in Vietnam
	Yom Kippur War
1974	Disengagement of forces in Middle East

25

Foreign Affairs
1953-1974

Long-Range Developments

For Democratic Government

American experiences in earlier wars contributed to pursuit of policies in Vietnam which produced staggering numbers of casualties without victory until popular pressure in the United States led to disengagement, an action that left Southeast Asia's future in doubt.

For the Westward Movement, Nationalism, and Expansion

Some of Secretary of State Dulles' pronouncements on foreign policy aroused hopes of Communist reversals whose failure to occur damaged American credibility.

The exigencies of modern foreign relations have forced modification of the "massive retaliation" policy.

The lack of reality in American isolation from Communist China resulted in abandonment of the policy in 1972 and a continued search for understanding between the two powers.

Acceptance of President Eisenhower's "falling domino" theory promoted increasing United States involvement in Vietnam until experience exposed some of the theory's fallacies.

American support of West Germany has proved one of the most stabilizing factors in the Cold War and a major deterrent to Communist expansion.

The Dulles Foreign Policy

Domestic problems by no means had a monopoly on the difficulties and challenges confronting the American people in contemporary times. The nation's strength and its unabated struggle with international Communism led to a continued succession of crises—a position many Americans, unaccustomed to their country's leadership in world affairs, found hard to accept. Compounding the difficulties were rapid changes in the United States power base as industrial and military advances occurred in Russia and China, as West Germany and Japan recovered, and as neutralist states came into being.

From 1953 until his resignation in April, 1959, one month before his death, John Foster Dulles, Eisenhower's secretary of state, dominated American foreign policy. No man assumed the office with finer credentials. As the grandson of Benjamin Harrison's secretary of state, John W. Foster, and the nephew of Robert Lansing, Wilson's secretary of state, he had grown up in an atmosphere attuned to diplomacy. From 1907, when he served as secretary to the Chinese delegation at the Hague Conference, until 1951, when he was primarily responsible for terms of the Japanese peace treaty, Dulles was often a representative and adviser of the State Department. He formulated the Republican party's 1952 foreign policy plank which promised a "dynamic" foreign policy designed to "liberate" countries that had fallen under Communist control. By implication at least, the Yalta Conference was castigated when the promise was made to renounce "secret understandings," and Dulles promoted the belief that Chiang Kai-shek would be unleashed to attack the Chinese mainland.

After assuming office, Dulles punctuated his extensive travels with moralistic statements which aroused unattainable hopes and, on occasion, alienated staunch U.S. allies. At the same time, in part due to the president's fear of war, a restrained but firm policy was maintained which was similar to the Truman-Acheson containment program. As the costs of military weapons increased and the business-minded Eisenhower administration wrestled with budget deficits, Dulles in 1954 promulgated the doctrine of "massive retaliation." It proposed to deter aggression by threatening a major attack using the powerful hydrogen bomb developed in 1952; this approach, which would carry the nation to the very "brink of war," permitted large savings in conventional weapons. However Dulles, when accused of advocating a policy that would give the United States only the alternatives of either a nuclear war or tolerance of an aggressor, denied the allegation. He believed the United States would still have to be prepared to wage "brush fire" wars and that the nature of its response in a crisis would depend on the challenge. Yet he held that less reliance need be placed on conventional weapons to avert a major conflict provided the United States was audacious enough to convince the potential major aggressors that it would use strategic air power to deliver nuclear weapons. Due to the acceptance of this policy, by 1960 the size of the army had been cut to half what it had been in 1953, but increases in air force appropriations and the missile program, as well as inflation, did not permit a decrease in defense spending.

Severe critics of the massive retaliation policy also appeared, among the most effective being Harvard Professor Henry A. Kissinger. He contended massive retaliation limited America's options in crisis situations and encouraged Communists to chip away at the free world, taking bits and pieces over which the United States would not risk nuclear war. The Russian development of a hydrogen bomb in 1953, nine months after the United States, supported his argument.

The Dulles "liberation" rhetoric may have contributed to revolts in East Germany in 1953 and Hungary in 1956, which were brutally crushed by Russia, but the United States did not project itself into the struggle. Chiang Kai-shek was not "unleashed" either, and Chiang agreed, in notes exchanged in December, 1954, not to attack the mainland without prior consultation with the United States. In a halting fashion, the United States clarified its position regarding the Nationalist Chinese following Red China's pledge to conquer Taiwan. In September, 1954, the mainland Chinese first bombarded the Nationalist-held islands of Quemoy and Matsu, which were near the Chinese mainland. Dulles prepared the way for later difficulties by not guaranteeing them protection in a December, 1954, mutual security treaty signed with Chiang. Under it, each power recognized an armed attack in the Western Pacific directed against the territories of the other would be dangerous to its own safety and stated it would act to meet the danger in accordance with its constitutional processes. Territories included in the protected area were the U.S. islands in the Western Pacific, Formosa, Taiwan, and the Pescadores, and provision was made to extend the secured area to other territories that were mutually agreed upon. In January, 1955, the administration rectified its error by leading Congress to pass a resolution authorizing defense not only of Taiwan and the Pescadores but also other "closely related localities." After this, bombardment of Quemoy and Matsu continued for three months but was temporarily ended in April, 1955. In August, 1958, when bombardment was resumed, Dulles contended the islands were probably covered by the congressional resolution and cautioned their invasion would likely lead to a larger conflict. Sizable U.S. naval and air force units were assembled in the Formosa Strait, and Nationalist Chinese ships were convoyed to Quemoy. After Russia promised support for Red China in any American conflict, public opinion became alarmed in Western Europe and the United States. Both sides backed away from the crisis, however. Dulles advocated a cease-fire as a prelude to reducing Nationalist forces on the islands; the mainland Chinese stopped the bombardment for three weeks in October, 1958, and then, after several months of periodic shelling, totally ceased the attack.

Eisenhower Struggles to Contain Communism

The Dulles foreign policy was more successful in use of the collective security framework to contain Communism than in liberating countries or advancing Chiang Kai-shek's cause. Grave problems arose among America's European allies to which only partial solutions were found, but the alliance system did not disintegrate and NATO remained a major deterrent. The Eisenhower-Dulles program called for a well-integrated European Defense Community with strong military forces and centralized leadership. Many factors made this unattainable, including fear of a rearmed Germany, the lessening of fear of Russia following a mild thaw in anti-Westernism which came after Stalin's death in 1953, and concern with material well-being as prosperity returned. Secretary Dulles did not help the resolution of the problem when he threatened an "agonizing reappraisal" of American policy, which many interpreted as U.S. abandonment of Europe. Fortunately, a compromise was developed in the fall of 1954 under which plans were projected for a sovereign West Germany with armed forces under NATO control. The United States and Britain pledged maintenance of large numbers of troops in Europe, and the continental powers accepted greater NATO control over their armed forces.

In protest over German rearmament, Russia formed a military alliance of Eastern European nations known as the Warsaw Pact. It effectively intimidated many Western Europeans with threats of destruction in case of war at a time when regard for America was seriously weakened by disputes over colonialism as the colonies of Britain, the Netherlands, and France either revolted or became independent. The United States urged rapid acceptance of independence, winning the contempt of many Europeans. Together the combination of Russian threats and internal disunity almost destroyed the Western alliance in the fall of 1956.

Groundwork for increasing factionalization was laid in late 1954 when Dulles courted Arab favor by pressuring Britain to abandon the Suez Canal to Egypt's new nationalist leader, Colonel Gamal Abdel Nasser. To obtain this concession, Egypt promised to allow British reentry if any alien power attacked Turkey or the Arab states. Dulles' plans for collective security in the area, which envisioned a strong Middle East Defense Organization relying heavily on Egypt, aborted, however, when Nasser refused to cooperate and set the Arab world aflame with nationalism. The much weaker defensive Baghdad Pact, creating the Middle East Treaty Organization, was concluded between Turkey, Iraq, Iran, Pakistan, and Great Britain. Only one of the northern tier Arab states was a member and the United States remained officially outside. The Baghdad Pact frightened Russia who feared encirclement, and it moved to establish an alliance of its own behind that engineered by the United States. Nasser, who was also infuriated by the Baghdad Pact, signed an agreement in September, 1955, with Russia providing for the exchange of cotton and rice for large quantities of military equipment. The United States attempted to regain Nasser's favor by refusing military aid to Israel and, in conjunction with the British, offering $200 million in financing to build the Aswan Dam, a tremendous power project on the upper Nile designed as a key factor in improving Egyptian life. After Nasser stepped up his raids against Israel and incited a revolution in Jordan and after it became known that Russia could not provide funds for the Aswan Dam, Dulles withdrew the Anglo-American offer for its financing. Insulted and humiliated, Nasser on July 26, 1956, nationalized the Suez Canal Company, whose charter ran until 1968.

Egypt's action led to a break in communications between the United States and Britain and France. When Nasser would not agree to international control of the canal, plans were made for an Anglo-French-Israeli attack on Egypt. The invasion was begun on October 26, 1956, by Israel, whose ships Egypt had consistently excluded from the canal. Israeli forces quickly occupied most of the Sinai Peninsula, but British and French troops moved into the Suez area so slowly that the Egyptians were able to block the canal before withdrawing.

British and French action in the Middle East was taken without American consultation or approval; the United States joined Russia in condemning the invasion but rejected overtures for a joint military movement to pacify the area. Humiliated by a UN General Assembly demand for a cease-fire, British and French forces withdrew. The Suez Canal remained under Egyptian control but was closed for months until it could be cleared. In the aftermath of the dispute, the president obtained congressional approval in March, 1957, of the Eisenhower Doctrine in a Joint Resolution to Promote Peace and Stability in the Middle East. In a vague fashion, it proclaimed the United States' vital interest in preserving the independence of Middle Eastern countries, pledged military assistance to any country facing Communist aggression, and authorized use of up to $200 million for military and economic assistance to Middle Eastern nations. The doctrine did not specify the countries covered nor did it deal with the serious problems created by internal Communist movements.

The Suez crisis promoted the spirit that enabled Nasser to unite Syria and Egypt in 1958 to form the United Arab Republic. In May, Nasser-supported rebels revolted in Lebanon, and the United Arab forces began to cross the Lebanese border. The pro-Western government in Baghdad was overthrown on July 14, an apparent prelude to Soviet domination of Iraq. Convinced radical action was necessary, President Eisenhower sent 8,000 American troops into Lebanon between July 15 and 19, 1958, while Britain dispatched 3,000 men to Jordan. As a result, Nasser flew to Moscow where Nikita Khrushchev, who had finally assumed the title of premier in March, 1958, after five years of sharing titles with G. M. Malenkov and Nikolai Bulganin, declared the world trembled on the brink of disaster. In August, 1958, the UN General Assembly unanimously approved an Arab-bloc resolution which requested the UN secretary general to make such arrangements in Lebanon and Jordan as would uphold the UN Charter. Under Secretary General Dag Hammarskjöld's direction, local control was restored and American and British troops were removed by November, 1958.

Russian connivance in the Suez crisis and its vicious suppression of the Hungarian revolt at approximately the same time, as well as later Anglo-American cooperation in the Middle East, did much to repair the strain in the Western alliance. Russian launching of the first *Sputnik* satellite in 1957 was combined with a threat of complete destruction of any country which permitted the launching of intercontinental missiles from its soil. To retain and reassure its allies, the United States, after obtaining amendment of the Atomic Energy Act in 1958, began to share additional nuclear information and atomic weapons. However, only Britain, Italy, and Turkey permitted the establishment

Dag Hammarskjöld

of missile bases on their soil. Of all the allies, France, where the militant nationalist Charles de Gaulle became president in 1958, proved most difficult. When his plans for a three-power directory for NATO were rejected, he restricted use of French troops in the organization. Yet NATO remained potent enough apparently to temper Russian policy in Germany, and European attempts at economic unity, warmly approved by the United States, made impressive gains.

The Common Market (European Economic Community) came into being partially as a result of American leadership. In order to utilize Marshall Plan aid, the sixteen non-Communist

European states formed the Organization for European Economic Cooperation. This was followed by the establishment in 1951 by France, West Germany, Italy, Belgium, Luxembourg, and the Netherlands of the European Coal and Steel Community, which in 1953 erected an effective common market in those commodities. After additional negotiations, provision was made for the gradual lowering of tariffs and trade restrictions on all goods traded between the member countries when the Common Market was established in 1958 by West Germany, France, the Netherlands, Belgium, Luxembourg, and Italy. Unsuccessful efforts were made to unite all sixteen members of the Organization for European Economic Cooperation in a free-trade arrangement in 1957 and 1958. In 1959, Great Britain, Portugal, Austria, Switzerland, Norway, Denmark, and Sweden formed the more loosely structured European Free Trade Association for the same purpose. Contests between the two areas became bitter but eventually in 1973, after years of intense controversy, the EEC and EFTA were merged. Their success as independent organizations contributed to European recovery, helped stifle Communist growth in the West, led the Russians to establish a comparable Eastern European organization, and resulted in an increase in U.S. deficits in its balance of payments.

In the Pacific, the Eisenhower administration relied heavily on Japan and the Philippines as firm U.S. allies. Red China remained militantly anti-American, confiscating U.S. property, imprisoning American citizens, and disgorging the most bitter invective against the United States. The U.S. led the opposition to seating the mainland Chinese in the United Nations and winced under violations of the 1953 Korean armistice.

In 1954, the final stages of "act one" in Indochina came to an end in the French puppet states of Laos, Cambodia, and Vietnam which had been created in 1947. Communist guerrillas had arisen in all three and, capitalizing on nationalism and reform, gained great strength, the most intense conflict emerging in Vietnam. On December 23, 1950, the Agreement for Mutual Defense Assistance in Indochina was signed by Cambodia, Laos, Vietnam, France, and the United States. President Truman began aid to the French, feeling Communist success would be most detrimental to the United States, and Eisenhower and Dulles increased this aid until by 1953 the United States was defraying about half the French war costs. Eisenhower defended aid to the French by enunciating the "falling domino" theory at a press conference in April, 1954. "You have a row of dominoes set up, you knock over the first one, and what will happen to the last is that it will go over very quickly. So you have the beginning of a disintegration that would have the most profound influence." Meanwhile, Red China and Russia furnished substantial aid to the rebels, and by early 1954 it was obvious France faced defeat unless the United States entered the conflict. Dulles favored congressional authorization of an air strike to aid the French defenders of Dien Bien Phu, but the plan was dropped when the Joint Chiefs of Staff and public opinion disapproved. Efforts to reach an agreement with Great Britain to form a strong military alliance like NATO in Southeast Asia also failed. Instead, the French withdrew and the representatives of Great Britain, Russia, France, Communist China, North Vietnam, South Vietnam, Cambodia, Laos, the Viet Minh (a largely Communist-dominated, Vietnamese nationalist group), and the United States met to attempt a settlement. The United States and South Vietnam would not become entangled in negotiations with the Communists, but the meeting took cognizance of the agreements reached, promised not to use force or the threat of force to disturb them, and stated that it would hold any violations of them to be a serious threat to international peace. The agreements provided for neutralization of Cambodia and Laos and division of Vietnam at the 17th parallel, with a Communist government in the North and a pro-Western regime in the South.

Before the 1954 agreements, the United States had taken several steps to aid Indochina. These included a mutual defense assistance agreement with the French states in December, 1950, economic cooperation agreements with Vietnam and Cambodia in 1951, and, under the United States Mutual Security Act of 1951, agreements on economic and military aid with Laos and Vietnam in 1951 and 1952. Arrangements providing for additional direct economic assistance were concluded with South Vietnam in March, 1955, and Laos in July, 1955. American aid and advisers supplied President Bao Dai in South Vietnam did not prevent his deposition in 1956, but they were continued to his successor, Ngo Dinh Diem. Instability increased, however, as Communist rebels, known as the Viet Cong, received support not only from North Vietnam but also from China and Russia. In 1956, Diem canceled the nationwide elections scheduled by the 1954 conference of the major powers and the Indochina states, and the conflict intensified.

Dulles was displeased with the Indochina settlement and, fearing additional aggression, pledged the United States would not stand by while the rest of Southeast Asia was overrun. To bring some security to the area and thwart Communist domination of Indochina, beginning in early 1954, he promoted an alliance of non-Communist powers interested in the region. In June, 1954, Asian defense was considered at five-power military staff talks in Washington between representatives of the United States, Great Britain, France, Australia, and New Zealand and in Anglo-American discussions. During the same months, the representatives of Australia, New Zealand and the United States (ANZUS) agreed immediate action should be taken to establish collective defense in Southeast Asia. As a result an eight-power conference was held in Manila in September, 1954, which created the Southeast Asia Treaty Organization (SEATO).

Under it, the United States, Great Britain, France, Australia, New Zealand, the Philippines, Pakistan, and Thailand (South Vietnam, Cambodia and Laos were added by protocol) agreed in case of military attack to "meet the common danger in accordance with constitutional processes" and to consult in case of subversion. The treaty was accompanied by a unilateral declaration of the United States, in the form of an "understanding," that the pact was directed against Communist aggression, and the conference delegates signed a Pacific Charter which bound their nations to support self-government in the region as a means of counteracting Communist charges of colonialism.

Although Dulles held SEATO was of major significance, it was not comparable to NATO; it lacked common military forces; an attack on one power was not treated as an attack on all; and most of its members were remote from Southeast Asia, where the major powers were nonaffiliates. Therefore, the organization gave the administration little of the leverage it sought in the region. In 1961, after three years of conflict in Laos, the United States was forced to seek a neutralist rather than a pro-Western government.

United States policies were somewhat more successful in other areas. On March 5, 1959, the United States signed bilateral agreements with Iran, Turkey, and Pakistan after six months of negotiations. Acting partially under the Eisenhower Doctrine, which pledged U.S. military aid to help countries resisting international Communism, the treaties committed the United States to take appropriate action in case of aggression. After Iraq withdrew from the

Baghdad Pact on March 24, 1959, the remaining members formed CENTO, the Central Treaty Organization. Though the United States was not a member, it gave strong support to the Ankara-based group which, like SEATO, lacked its own armed forces. CENTO aided in achieving improved conditions in the Middle East where Nasser, after his rebuff at American hands in Lebanon, concentrated on internal affairs; although he accepted some Russian loans, he suppressed Communism in Egypt. Jordan and Lebanon displayed a surprising degree of independency, while in the early 1960s Syria broke with Egypt and an anti-Communist government staged a successful coup in Iraq.

Struggles in Africa and Latin America

Meanwhile, a large number of new nations emerged in Africa, and intense nationalism arose to plague others. While generally approving these developments, American foreign policy remained largely passive. When Belgium granted independence to the Congo in 1960, a severe crisis emerged as the rich mineral province of Katanga attempted to secede. After the army removed the Soviet-backed Patrice Lumumba as Congolese premier, the contest became an international one as Russia supported him against both the central and Katangan governments. The contest was solved after 1961, when the moderate Premier Cyulle Adoula came to power. After being captured in Katanga, Lumumba was murdered and his forces rapidly declined. Only the presence of large UN forces prevented chaos, and they received much of their support from the United States since the Communist nations refused payments to the UN.

In the Western Hemisphere, strong anti-Americanism arose, a fact that was brought home to the American people in 1958 when Vice-President Nixon was attacked and spat upon while touring Latin America. A number of dictatorships which perpetuated the caste system and mass poverty had been overthrown in the 1950s, but rigid U.S. adherence to the principle of nonintervention made it appear as the friend of tyranny to many Latin liberals. Any other open action would probably have backfired, as demonstrated in 1954 at the Inter-American Conference in Caracas when the United States sought to direct the Latin American states in action against Guatemala. In 1953, following almost ten years of revolution, the Communist party came to power in Guatemala. Though Dulles pled for united action at Caracas, he only obtained a resolution stating the obvious fact that any Western government dominated by international Communism constituted a menace. Meanwhile, Guatemala proceeded to receive Czechoslovakian arms and foment strikes in Honduras. Dulles, who contended Guatemala was planning aggression, obtained arms for Honduras and Nicaragua which were used by Guatemalan exiles who moved into the country, overthrowing the Communist regime.

In response to public pressure and needs, other actions were taken in Latin America. Panamanian discontent led the United States to renegotiate the Canal Zone treaty with Panama, increasing its annual rent by more than 400 percent to $1,930,000 and granting it the right to tax workers in the Canal Zone. Following his unpleasant experiences in Latin America, Vice-President Nixon warned that opposition came from forces in addition to Communists and urged attention to problems that had been largely neglected. Regional free trade programs in Latin America were promoted, U.S. trade policies liberalized, and an

Inter-American Development Bank established with $1 billion capital, almost half of which was furnished or guaranteed by the United States.

The greatest crisis in Latin America began in January, 1959, when Cuba's dictator, Fulgencio Batista, was overthrown by Fidel Castro. Though Castro was critical of U.S. support of Batista and promised wholesale land confiscation and redistribution, the United States promptly extended recognition. With stunning speed, Castro became a militant Communist tool and began revolutionary activity in neighboring states. Despite this, Secretary of State Christian Herter could only obtain empty resolutions from the Inter-American Foreign Ministers at an August, 1959, meeting. For a year and a half, the Eisenhower administration waited patiently, but Cuba moved increasingly into the Russian sphere. A five-year trade agreement was signed with the Soviets in February, 1960, a possible prelude to a military alliance. American property was confiscated with impunity, including in June, 1960, a $25 million Texaco refinery to be used in processing Russian oil. Furious, the president cut American imports of sugar, denying Cuba its major source of income.

Premier Khrushchev entered the Cuban fray personally in July, 1960, asserting Russia could defend the island with rockets if it were attacked by the United States. Soon thereafter, he stated that the Monroe Doctrine was dead, to which the State Department replied it was as valid as when first issued and applied to Russia. When the Cuban question was referred to the Organization of American States, sympathy for Castro and anti-Americanism prevented action. In disgust, the U.S. government levied an embargo on all exports to Cuba except food and medicine in October, 1960, and established a naval patrol to prevent invasions of Central America in November. In January, 1961, diplomatic relations were broken with Cuba while training of Cuban exiles for an invasion was increased in Florida and Guatemala. Only time would tell what the outcome would be.

Eisenhower's Personal Diplomacy

Though he was a distinguished soldier, no man was more firmly dedicated to peace than President Eisenhower. He repeatedly explored, with little success, every feasible avenue for lessening tension with the Communist world while maintaining what he considered to be the essential American position. His frustration with the results mirrored that of the American people.

Following Stalin's death in 1953, the Russians supported efforts to end the Korean War, spoke of "peaceful coexistence," and loudly proclaimed that all disputes were negotiable. Eisenhower remained skeptical of the Soviets and, like President Truman before him, insisted on concrete evidence of a new attitude before he would heed British pleas for a summit meeting. This evidence came in May, 1955, at the Vienna Foreign Ministers' Conference, when the Russians at last agreed to end four-power occupation of Austria and negotiate a peace treaty; for the first time, they approved troop withdrawal from a major occupied area. As a result, Eisenhower consented to the Geneva summit meeting held from July 18 to July 23, 1955, with Premier Nikolai Bulganin of Russia, Premier Edgar Faure of France, Prime Minister Anthony Eden of Great Britain, and their foreign ministers. The Western leaders came to the sessions with the intention of discussing, among other questions, European security, disarmament, the future of Germany, and greater contact among the nations. The meeting was cordial in tone and effectively defined the issues which divided the major powers, however, in subsequent meetings of the foreign ministers, few steps were taken toward their resolution. For over a year, the meeting inspired hopes that some basic understandings would be reached, a dream enhanced by the polite correspondence Bulganin and Eisenhower exchanged, but the Hungarian and Suez crises in October, 1956, dissipated these illusions. Yet one positive result of the encounters was the opening of a greater number of contacts between the East and the West, especially in the cultural fields. Each year an increasing number of musicians, dancers, and artists have exchanged visits, exerting an incalculable influence in promoting improved relations.

In a shrewd effort to court world opinion, Russia revived efforts to obtain another summit shortly after launching *Sputnik I* in late 1957. Eisenhower agreed in March, 1958, but, after Khrushchev became prime minister, a virulent propaganda attack was launched against the United States and a Berlin crisis manufactured, which made the meeting impossible.

The Eisenhower administration consistently sought to reunify Germany through free elections and, failing this, to rearm Western Germany within NATO, plans which were anathema to the Communists. Beginning in 1958, Krushchev attempted to exploit the Berlin situation either to force the incorporation of the city into East Germany or, at least, force Western recognition of the East German government. As early as 1955, the Russians had given the East Germans supervision of the 110-mile surface routes through the Eastern zone to Berlin. The Western powers held Russia responsible for all decisions relative to Berlin, however.

In November, 1958, Khrushchev announced Russia would soon give all its controls in Berlin to East Germany; if the Western powers did not do the same, they would have to answer to the East German government. Shortly afterwards, he stated Russia did not recognize any Western rights in Berlin or any access rights to it. Khrushchev offered, as a compromise, to make Berlin a neutralized "free city"; otherwise, he proposed to sign a peace treaty with East Germany within six months which would give it complete sovereignty in all Russian-controlled German areas.

Confronted by the firmest Western resistance, including three separate presidential statements in late 1958, Khrushchev did not fulfill his threats, and talk was substituted for action. Deputy Premier Anastas Mikoyan came to the United States early in 1959, British Prime Minister Harold Macmillan visited Moscow, and a Foreign Ministers' Conference was held in Geneva from May to August, 1959. The six-month deadline for a Russian treaty with East Berlin passed without action, and in September, 1959, Khrushchev came for a widely publicized visit to the United States. At its conclusion, a cordial meeting with the president was held at Camp David, the executive retreat near Washington. Plans were consummated for Eisenhower to make a reciprocal visit to Russia in 1960 and another summit meeting in Paris in May, 1960, a session made possible by Khrushchev's agreement to withhold a time limit on his proposed Berlin solution.

Vice-President Nixon did visit Russia during which he had a celebrated public exchange of comments with Khrushchev regarding the merits of Communism and capitalism. But before the Eisenhower visit or another summit meeting occurred, the Russians, apparently concluding they would obtain nothing substantial from them, scuttled the plans by utilizing an unfortunate incident with telling propaganda effect. On May 1, 1960, a high-flying American reconnaissance aircraft, a U-2, was shot down in the interior of Russia. Unknown to the United States, both the pilot,

Francis Gary Powers, and the craft were captured. At first the U.S. government contended the plane was a weather observing craft which had strayed from its Turkish base. When confronted by the facts, the president astonished the diplomatic world by telling the truth and taking personal responsibility, saying similar flights had taken place since 1956 and were essential for the nation's safety. Though he suspended the flights, Eisenhower refused to apologize, and Khrushchev turned the Paris meeting into a forum for attacking U.S. duplicity. However, he did not renew the Berlin crisis and indicated he could hold another summit meeting with some president other than Eisenhower.

Failures at the summit were accompanied by comparable defeats for Eisenhower's efforts at disarmament and nuclear control. The president repeatedly attempted to obtain arms limitation, but the Russians would not agree to the inspection he felt essential. Following failure of the UN Disarmament Commission to achieve results, representatives from the four major powers and Canada held fruitless talks from 1955 to 1957 in London. At the Geneva summit, Eisenhower proposed an "open skies" plan under which aerial surveillance would check the military information furnished by both sides. In November, 1956, Russia announced qualified acceptance of the principle of mutual aerial inspection. After prolonged conferences, however, the Russians terminated further discussions in August, 1957. Yet the open skies proposal was significant, and the concept behind it helped prepare the way for a disarmament agreement fifteen years later.

Greater hopes were aroused by plans for a nuclear test ban than for general disarmament as many nations became concerned over atmospheric pollution, but here too, the snag was Western insistence on inspection. In March, 1958, Russia announced a unilateral suspension of testing, but, after a panel of international scientists proposed means of establishing detection stations with little penetration of countries by foreigners, Russia accepted an offer from Britain and the United States to end testing temporarily and work for a permanent ban. Negotiations began in Geneva in October, 1958, and continued for two years. No agreement could be reached, however, and Russia resumed testing in September, 1961, and the United States in March, 1962.

After repeated failures to reach disarmament agreements with Russia, the United States pursued with renewed zeal an effort to compete in the race for space. The U.S.'s first intercontinental ballistic missile, the air force's "Atlas," was successfully tested in November, 1958, and was ready for use in a missile squadron by 1960.

In 1958 the National Aeronautics and Space Agency (NASA) was organized to overtake and exceed an apparent Russian primacy in space. The Russians developed bigger rockets which could boost larger craft into orbit before the United States, and by 1960 they had launched one satellite into orbit around the moon as well as two spacecraft. Meanwhile, American spokesmen correctly contended that careful U.S. expansion, including launching of fifteen smaller earth satellites by October, 1960, were progressive steps which could result in America landing a man on the moon first. This victory was not apparent in November, 1960, and John F. Kennedy effectively indicted the Republican administration for its space program inadequacies in his successful bid for the presidency.

The Kennedy Foreign Policy

The new Democratic administration obtained increased funds for space exploration and soon began to garner the fruits of earlier efforts. In

April, 1961, Russia announced it had placed the first space satellite with a man aboard in earth orbit. This was followed, in May, 1961, by America's first suborbital flight, that of Astronaut Alan B. Shepard, Jr., and, in July, by that of Virgil I. Grissom. In August, a Russian astronaut made seventeen orbits of the earth, but in February, 1962, America began its route to primacy when John H. Glenn, Jr., made the nation's first manned orbital flight. This was followed later in the year by the orbital flights of M. Scott Carpenter and Walter M. Schirra, Jr., whose launching and landing was watched on television by millions around the world. By the fall of 1962, the United States had launched ninety-seven satellites and made ten space probes as opposed to the Russians' twenty-four launchings and four probes. Progress continued and the ultimate victory was attained by NASA's Apollo program when it won the race with Russia to first place a man on the moon. On July 16, 1969, Apollo 11 was launched and four days later Captain Neil A. Armstrong became the first human being to walk on the moon. As he stepped on the moon, Armstrong stated that he was making "one small step for man" but "one giant leap for mankind." This was followed in 1973 and 1974 by the fifty-eight and eighty-four day missions of Skylab 2 and 3 which docked with an orbiting space station.

Although the Kennedy administration correctly appraised the excellent possibilities for the United States in space, it encountered a severe reversal and a dangerous challenge in foreign affairs in 1961. Upon assuming office, the president was informed of Central Intelligence Agency plans to conduct an invasion of Cuba by refugees. Though skeptical, Kennedy approved the Bay of Pigs incursion without

Astronaut James Irwin saluting beside the flag on the Apollo 15 mission to the moon. Alfred Worden was the command module pilot and David Scott was the commander.

seeing that adequate force was used for success. Although Cuban airfields were bombed by refugee piloted planes, some 1,500 invaders moved ashore April 17, 1961, without naval or air support. They never made contact with the underground and were forced to surrender within three days. Throughout Latin America, the United States suffered a loss of prestige for its aggression, and Castro moved closer to Russia whose protection alone, he held, had saved his country. Significantly, America's Communist opponents were encouraged to believe the new U.S. government lacked the will to defend the country.

Russian contempt was obvious when in June, 1961, the president held a personal meeting with Khrushchev in Vienna. The Russian leader renewed demands for a peace treaty with East Germany and stated Russia would sign such a treaty with or without the West. In the crisis, Kennedy demonstrated a firmness which thereafter characterized his foreign policy. After consulting with other Western leaders, he stated unequivocally that the Western powers would not be driven from Berlin and implied that if necessary armed force would be used.

As both sides increased their military preparations, Russian troops virtually encircled Berlin, and, on August 13, 1961, the East Germans practically closed all movement between East and West Berlin. Before that time, the eighty crossings between the sections had become the principal escape routes from behind the "Iron Curtain," and the striking contrasts between living conditions in the free and Communist sections of the city were a constant humiliation. Therefore, all but seven heavily guarded exits were closed and the notorious "Berlin Wall" erected, despite strong Western protests of its illegality. In the following months, the free world was shocked when a number of people were killed in attempts to cross into West Berlin. In the meantime, Western traffic on the *autobahn* (expressway) was held up periodically and aircraft harassed while flying through the allocated air corridors to Berlin.

Under these provocations, the United States pursued policies which led Russia to back away from greater challenges. Kennedy sent General Lucius D. Clay, hero of the 1948–49 Berlin crisis, to the city as his personal representative, and Vice-President Lyndon Johnson was dispatched to reaffirm the U.S. commitment to its people. Some 1,500 American troops were sent into Berlin over the *autobahn*, a demonstration that the U.S. dared defend its rights. As a result, in October, 1961, Khrushchev stated there was no time limit on his proposed East German treaty, and by the spring of 1962 most challenges to the West in Berlin were stopped, although the hated wall remained.

The most direct confrontation with Russia did not come in Germany, however, but in Cuba, where Russian technicians erected missile bases in 1962. In January, Castro's government had come sufficiently under Russian control to frighten the Organization of American States into expelling Cuba, and the United States intensified its embargo on trade with the island. Despite pressure to invade Cuba, the president asserted this would not be done so long as it received only defensive weapons from Communist countries. On October 18, 1962, Soviet Foreign Minister Andrei Gromyko, who was in the United States, assured Kennedy that this was the case. Several days before, however, the president had learned from aerial photographs that Russia had delivered medium-range ballistic missiles to Cuba and that launching pads were being completed.

On October 22, 1962, the president presented the evidence he had received in a startling television address to the American people. He asserted offensive missile sites were being prepared in Cuba and demanded their immediate dismantling and withdrawal. To support his words, the president imposed a naval and air quarantine of unacceptable military equipment and called for an emergency meeting of the UN Security Council. So that no misunderstanding would exist, he stated that any missile attack from Cuba on any nation in the Western hemisphere would be regarded as an attack by Russia, against whom the United States would retaliate.

While the world hovered near nuclear disaster, the Russians backed down. Soviet vessels bound for Cuba with prohibited materials altered their course on October 24, while those with nonoffensive equipment permitted American inspection. Khrushchev quickly offered to remove the missile bases if the United States would dismantle its sites in Turkey. When Kennedy refused, Khrushchev agreed to the American demands on October 28 in return for a U.S. promise not to invade Cuba and removal of the blockade. A week after the crisis began, UN Secretary General U Thant was in Havana arranging for the implementation of the compromise.

President Kennedy's vigorous stand earned the United States new respect from Russia. Life was injected into the nuclear test ban conference which, under the United Nation's prodding, had been reconvened in November, 1961, and the Russians agreed to establish a "hot line" permitting direct communications between Washington and Moscow. Failing to agree on inspection to police underground explosions, the two powers signed a treaty in July, 1963, which most nations except Red China and France also accepted, banning nuclear tests in the atmosphere or in water.

Cognizant of some changes in attitude, President Kennedy called for a reappraisal of Russo-American relations in June, 1963, and proposed in September that the two powers join in a moon expedition. This action was soon followed by removal of restrictions which permitted the sale of American wheat to Russia. To many, a thaw appeared to have come in the Cold War which promised greater security than the world had known since 1946.

After 1963 some basic changes occurred in East-West relations which led many to conclude a break had come in the Cold War even though it was not over. Before this time, U.S. policy had been based on a strong Western Europe which required a settlement of the question of German reunification, an issue that perennially came up at foreign ministers conferences and summit meetings. After 1963, the United States no longer insisted on German reunification nor did it pursue the containment and massive retaliation policies as in the past. The confrontation with Russia under Kennedy impressed the American people with the fact that any massive attack on the United States would produce at least 70 million casualties. Although no sudden shift occurred in foreign policy, more emphasis began to be placed on tactical atomic weapons and conventional armaments.

As the menace of a massive, atomic war receded, the role of Europe in international affairs also changed. Instead of remaining aloof as a spectator in any direct clash between the two super powers, it became once again the potential battleground for smaller conflicts, a new status which interjected increased tension and uncertainty into the NATO and Warsaw Alliances.

Meanwhile, conditions in Indochina continued to deteriorate, and President Kennedy involved the United States more deeply. In Laos, he reluctantly concluded that the Eisenhower administration's plan for neutralization was the only feasible course. When the Pathet Lao guerrillas threatened to install Communists in power, Kennedy, in March, 1961, declared that the United States would not accept such a development, and soon afterwards, in April, 1961, the Russians agreed to a thirteen-nation conference on the question. For over a year the delegates, including those from three contending Laotian governments, the United States, and Russia, met in Geneva, but their plans for a neutral Laos were seriously jeopardized by the Pathet Lao, which even violated the borders of neighboring states. As a result, Kennedy ordered 5,000 marines and some naval forces into Thailand in May, 1962. The following month the conference obtained establishment of a coalition government in Laos after American pressure ousted the right-wing leader, Prince Boun Oum. American forces were withdrawn from Thailand in July, 1962, in accordance with the Geneva conference's request for removal of all foreign forces.

No comparable solution was found in South Vietnam. Viet Cong forces, augmented by additions from North Vietnam and Laos, gave the pro-Western government of Ngo Dinh Diem increasing difficulty. Kennedy obviously accepted the domino theory of President Eisenhower, believing that if South Vietnam fell to Communist control other Asian powers would also. Following a report made by Vice-President Johnson after a May, 1961, trip to South Vietnam, U.S. military and economic assistance was increased. The numbers of service personnel grew rapidly from 4,000 in January, 1962, to 11,000 in January, 1963, and over 16,000 by the time of the president's death. Although American troops were not used in combat, by November, 1963, 120 men had died. Tragically, South Vietnamese internal dissension and injustice contributed to the confusion. Many Buddhists especially were dissatisfied with President Diem, and, when they were denied freedom of expression, some burned themselves to dramatize their discontent. Diem was overthrown by a military coup in November, 1963, after which the internal situation approached chaos. Vietnam was a new experience for the United States, one whose complexity and gravity were grossly

underestimated. As the following years proved, additional military power alone did not provide a means to obtain peace.

The Johnson Agony

President Johnson continued to explore means of lessening the conflict with Khrushchev and with his successors after his deposition in the fall of 1964. Both Russia and the United States cut expenditures for their armed forces and mutually agreed to reduce production of fissionable material in 1964. At the same time, agreements were reached to open consulates and expand cultural and scientific exchanges.

By 1965, Soviet support of North Vietnam led to a cooling of cooperation, but the United States continued to seek a lessening of tension. Although the U.S. deplored failure of Russia and some of its own allies to pay UN assessments for peace-keeping operations, it did not press the issue. In 1966, Johnson took the initiative in improving relations with Eastern Europe by proposing a lessening of restrictions on trade, loans, and travel, a policy which was adopted in the following years. Another of his suggestions, direct air service from Moscow to New York, came after an agreement was signed in November, 1965. More significantly, the next month the United States and Russia proposed an international treaty excluding nuclear arms and other mass destruction weapons from outer space, the moon, and other planets. This was followed, in August, 1967, by another agreement, submitted to the Disarmament Conference in Geneva, to limit the spread of nuclear weapons. Although no method of inspection was outlined, the treaty was a major achievement.

In a number of instances, the United States during the Johnson years demonstrated notable restraint. Protests were lodged but the reaction kept low key in 1964 when the Russians shot down two U.S. aircraft and harassed others en route to Berlin. In the Congo, U.S. involvement was limited to aid in rescuing rebel-held prisoners and to economic and military help for the central government which proved able to overcome Communist-aided rebels. When the Six-Day War erupted between Israel and neighboring Arab states in 1967, the United States, while sympathetic with Israel, refrained from intervention. The president protested Arab blockade of the Gulf of Aqaba which denied Israel access to the Red Sea, but U.S. ships did not challenge it. Even though intensely embarrassed, the United States took no precipitate action when the navy intelligence ship *Pueblo* and its eighty-three-man crew were seized off North Korea in January, 1968. The North Koreans claimed the ship had been within the twelve-mile territorial waters area, which the United States denied. After lengthy negotiations, the crew was released in December, 1968, but the vessel was retained.

Rhetoric alone was the administration's reply to the invasion of Czechoslovakia by the armed forces of the Warsaw Pact nations in August, 1968. The president declared, "The Soviet Union and its allies have invaded a defenseless country to stamp out a resurgence of ordinary human freedom." Though the United States urged a prompt withdrawal of all foreign troops, no new sanctions were imposed against the Communist nations.

The United States was unable to stay out of some disputes nearer home, however. A rebellion erupted in Panama, in early 1964, that resulted in breaking of diplomatic relations which were restored only when President Johnson agreed to negotiate a new treaty for leasing the canal zone. Over 30,000 U.S. troops were sent into the Dominican Republic in April and May, 1964, when, the president declared, a rebellion was taken over by Communists. Pledging not to allow the establishment of another Communist government in the Western Hemisphere, he obtained reluctant approval of U.S. action by the Organization of American States, in May, 1965, and units from four other countries joined U.S. forces in the Dominican Republic. Withdrawal of American troops began in June, 1966, after peace was restored.

President Johnson made an effort to improve Latin American relations by declaring, in an address given during a 1966 Mexican visit, that the U.S. did not wish to impose its form of government on any other country, although he added, "despots are not welcome in this hemisphere." In other addresses, he stressed the need for a concerted effort to integrate the Latin American economies, pledging increased help through the Alliance for Progress, a ten-year program initiated under President Kennedy. Many were critical of its success, however, feeling that the monies made available were often used for purposes other than reform and economic growth.

Difficulties in the Western alliance furnished another challenge to the United States in the 1960s. France under President Charles de Gaulle, continuing its efforts to become a major power, pursued an increasingly unilateral policy. In January, 1964, it was the first of America's allies to recognize Red China, an action followed by proposals, rejected by the U.S., to neutralize all of Indochina. France vehemently objected to the American plan to share nuclear weapons with a NATO multilateral defense force and in 1966 announced all French troops would be withdrawn from NATO and all NATO installations and commands would be asked to leave French soil.

In the face of the French challenge, President Johnson and other NATO leaders successfully worked to save the Western alliance. Not only were headquarters relocated but also the finances of the organization were renegotiated, with West Germany assuming a larger role, and the NATO strategy was redefined. In 1967, NATO publicly renounced a massive retaliation policy, declaring that henceforth a Soviet attack would be countered by conventional methods. Following the 1968 invasion of Czechoslovakia, the members agreed to increase their forces in Germany, which had been reduced in recent years.

The unpopular role of the United States in Vietnam hurt its relations with its European allies and came to be the major concern of the Johnson administration. Inexorably, U.S. involvement was increased, and apparent vic-

tories and plans for a negotiated peace evaporated. Johnson's first major crisis came in August, 1964, when North Vietnamese patrol boats ineffectively attacked U.S. destroyers in the Gulf of Tonkin. The president ordered carrier-based jets to retaliate, and in sixty-four sorties they destroyed some two dozen patrol boats and their bases in North Vietnam, an action approved soon afterwards in resolutions passed by both houses of Congress.

The U.S. did not continue its attacks against North Vietnam, but, during 1964, service personnel in the South were increased to 22,000 and military and economic aid accelerated to

American troops press toward Viet Cong positions after being heliborne into battle positions.

an annual rate of $625 million. Meanwhile, Viet Cong insurgents continued to make gains in Cambodia, while the neutralist government of Laos proved incapable of maintaining peace. The fighting became intense in some areas of Laos, and the United States charged North Vietnam with aggression there.

In 1965 the United States took steps leading to total war in South Vietnam as the situation worsened. The Viet Cong with North Vietnamese support appeared to be near complete victory when two separate mortar attacks on American forces led the president to order air raids on North Vietnam. At first the targets were exclusively military, but gradually they were broadened to include much of the area. In April, 1965, a U.S. anti-aircraft battery was sent to defend South Vietnam's Da Nang airfield, and in July, 1965, the first army combat units arrived. Quickly, jungle conflict with extensive use of helicopters became a standard operating procedure. By the end of the year, there were 195,000 American troops in the country, and the administration asked for a $12 billion increase in military spending for fiscal 1966.

While escalating the war, President Johnson continued to search for peace. In April, 1965, in a speech at the Johns Hopkins University, he offered to engage in "unconditional discussions" with all concerned governments in an attempt to end the war; his one concern, he held, was the establishment of a free, unmenaced South Vietnam. Though the bombing was ended twice during 1965, no favorable response was received from North Vietnam. Some progress was made internally in South Vietnam when, after months of confusion, Air Marshal Nguyen Cao Ky was appointed premier by a military junta, a controlling council. Under pressure from President Johnson, Ky began extensive programs of economic and social reform, but many of his critics held these were inadequate. With approval of the Laotian

government, U.S. aircraft raided the Ho Chi Minh trail in Laos, which was used to provision Communist forces in South Vietnam. These attacks were largely made from Thailand where, by permission of its government, a number of American forces were stationed.

The magnitude of the Vietnam conflict was first realized by many Americans in 1966. The number of U.S. forces in the country was increased during the year to approximately 380,000; although the Communists' losses appeared to be four times as heavy as the allies', the U.S. had 4,500 men killed in combat and the South Vietnamese 8,500. Despite this, the war was far from won, and General William C. Westmoreland, the American commander, could only say that a Communist takeover was made impossible. World opinion was most critical of the U.S. when it resumed bombing of military targets in North Vietnam

President Johnson and General William C. Westmoreland inspecting the troops at Cam Ranh Bay, South Vietnam.

near Hanoi and Haiphong. It was not allayed when the Manila Conference of the U.S. and its Pacific allies, in October, 1966, pledged to remove all allied troops from South Vietnam within six months of Communist withdrawal to the North. At home a number of prominent Americans, including Senator J. William Fulbright, chairman of the Foreign Relations Committee, and House Majority Leader Mike Mansfield, became most critical of the administration's escalation policy.

The United States continued to press reforms on General Nguyen Van Thieu, South Vietnam's new president, who was chosen by popular vote in 1967 after the military junta gave him its support. Efforts were begun to place more of the war's responsibility on the 700,000 men in the South Vietnamese forces, but with little success during the Johnson years. The brunt of the fighting continued to be born by Americans who alternated between strange, debilitating guerrilla warfare and pitched battles. In September, 1967, the North Vietnamese attacked the U.S. outpost at Con Thien, two miles below the 17th parallel where, for a month, the Communists employed heavy artillery for the first time in Vietnam, and the United States used the heaviest bombardment in history as well as concentrated aerial bombing. The result, at most, was delay in a Communist offensive. By October, 1967, over 100,000 Americans had been killed or wounded in Vietnam and the Communists had lost many more. Yet the North Vietnamese rejected U.S. proposals to stop all naval and air bombardment in return for a guarantee they would not use the lull to reinforce their positions.

The Communists demonstrated their continued strength in January, 1968, when in their Tet (New Year) offensive they unleashed coordinated attacks against forty major South Vietnamese urban centers. Fighting was intense in Saigon and Hue, where even the presidential palace and the U.S. embassy compound were penetrated. Although the Communists suffered terrific casualties, their determination revealed once again the difficulties America faced in Vietnam. As a result, the president increased American forces there until they reached highs of 530,000 in November, 1968, and 543,000 in April, 1969.

In the meantime, on March 31, 1968, Johnson withdrew from the presidential race, and in a frantic search for a negotiated peace ended U.S. bombing except in the area north of the Demilitarized Zone where buildups threatened U.S. forces. In response to his overtures, after a month of wrangling, the North Vietnamese, in May, 1968, opened preliminary peace talks with the United States in Paris. When no progress was made after months of meetings, Johnson ended all bombardment on October 31, 1968. In return, the North Vietnamese permitted representatives of South Vietnam to take part in the talks. To expedite the discussions, the United States allowed members of the National Liberation Front, the political arm of the Viet Cong, to participate also, but endless bickering was the major consequence. While these events were occurring, Johnson suffered severe rebuffs at home when the foreign aid bill was cut by $1.2 billion to the lowest level in its history, and the Senate failed to ratify a carefully negotiated Treaty on the Non-Proliferation of Nuclear Weapons. The measure provided that non-nuclear powers would neither be given nor develop nuclear weapons and that a system would be instituted to insure that those nations possessing nuclear materials were not using them for military purposes. Failure was due to the Russian invasion of Czechoslovakia and opposition of the Republican presidential candidate.

Johnson left office repudiated by many of his own party for policies that did not attain their goals. The United States, which prided itself on humanity and love of freedom, found itself condemned by much of the world and divided at home because of its Vietnam policy.

The Nixon Foreign Policy

Few believed when President Nixon was inaugurated that he would take the initiative in reaching significant compromises with Russia and opening contact with the People's Republic of China (Red China). Nixon had first risen to national prominence as a Communist-fighter, and none could question his anti-Communist views. For that very reason, he had greater flexibility in dealing with the Communist world than more liberal opponents.

From his first days in office, Nixon gave top priority to ending the war in Vietnam, but he also reviewed American commitments throughout the world and refashioned the techniques of meeting them. To inform himself and elicit personal support, the president traveled extensively abroad. In February and March, 1969, he visited five Western European countries, demonstrating a notable effort to consult and learn from their governmental leaders. On a nine-day summer tour, he went to South Vietnam, Indonesia, Thailand, India, Pakistan, and became the first American president to visit behind the Iron Curtain by going to Rumania, where he received a cordial public reception.

Evidence of President Nixon's more realistic approach to foreign affairs came in October, 1969, when, in a statement on inter-American conditions, he called for more mature relationships among nations of the Western Hemisphere and indicated that Latin American states must take the initiative themselves in obtaining needed social and economic changes. Significantly, he held that the United States would "deal realistically with governments in the inter-American system as they are," apparently a return to recognizing *de facto* governments without moralistic evaluation of their merits.

In February, 1970, the president presented an important statement to Congress entitled "United States Foreign Policy for the 1970's: A Strategy for Peace." Though averring loyalty to the nation's treaty commitments, it called for reassessment to determine how they furthered U.S. interests. In every relationship, the United States proposed to be a partner rather than a dictator, and in foreign affairs generally cooperation was urged rather than domination by the major powers. The president clearly recognized the limits of American ability to implement and support change, declaring "America cannot—and will not—conceive *all* the plans, design *all* the programs, execute *all* the decisions and undertake *all* the defense of the free nations of the world."

Nixon's modification of American policy, despite reversals and disappointments, led to an improvement of relations with the Communist world. On November 24, 1969, at the same time as the Russians, he signed the Nuclear Non-Proliferation Treaty, eight months after Senate ratification. Concurrently, he opened preliminary talks with Russia on limitation of strategic armaments which led to the beginning of formal negotiations in April, 1970.

While pursuing cooperation, the president also threatened to use force if necessary when American interests warranted it. This was done most effectively in 1970 when the Near East seemed on the verge of eruption. Nixon publicly expressed a fear that the United States and Russia would be forced into a confrontation that neither desired nor supported. He advocated a ninety-day cease-fire during which a

UN mediator would conduct peace talks with Israel, Jordan, and the United Arab Republic, a proposal which the three countries accepted.

In September, 1970, after Palestinian guerrillas hijacked four airliners, civil war erupted in Jordan between the guerrillas and King Hussein's forces. When Syrian tanks crossed into Jordan to aid the guerrillas, the president threatened to intervene should they or Iraqi forces menace Hussein's control. After Syria was warned directly by the United States, its forces withdrew.

Not all U.S. extension of support had such salutary results. Its most notable failure in recent years came in December, 1971, when, though remaining technically neutral, it supported Pakistan against India in the brief war that resulted when India backed East Pakistan's revolt for independence. The United States charged India as the aggressor and canceled $87.6 million in loans to it. Indian victory and the conversion of East Pakistan into the independent state of Bangladesh was a blow to United States prestige in much of Asia, although not in the People's Republic of China, which had taken a similar position.

In 1971, the full extent of the Nixon reorientation of foreign affairs began to emerge. In a major message to Congress in February, the president described the nation as being at "the end of an era." The power structure that emerged at the end of World War II was gone, he declared. "With it are gone the conditions that have determined the assumptions and practices of United States foreign policy since 1945."

In July, 1971, the president startled the world with the announcement that he would go to Peking early in 1972 in an attempt to normalize relations between the two countries. This action was taken although, since its coming to power, the Red government of China had not only been unrecognized by the United States but also the intensity of conflict between the two powers had placed them at opposite ends of the diplomatic scale.

Immediately, speculation arose that Nixon's action was due to the increasing conflict between Russia and China, and many felt he was attempting to exploit the difficulties between the leaders of the Communist world. Much of this conjecture was ended in October, 1971, when the president announced that he would visit the Soviet Union in May, 1972, in an attempt to improve relations between the two countries and the prospects for peace. He declared emphatically that no effort was being made to profit from differences between China and Russia.

The new approach in foreign policy recognized that the People's Republic of China was a permanent establishment ruling the world's largest nation. To pretend it did not exist was to indulge in a moral luxury at the expense of the United States' best interest. Therefore, in August, 1971, Secretary of State William Rogers announced that, at the next session of the United Nations, the United States would support the seating of mainland China; simultaneously, it would oppose expulsion of Chiang Kai-shek's Republic of China. However, in October, over U.S. objections, the Republic of China was expelled when Red China was seated.

After consultation with Communist Chinese leaders by Henry Kissinger, the president's special adviser for National Security Affairs who had come to overshadow Secretary of State Rogers, the presidential visit was made in February, 1972. Much of the world watched the public aspects of the trip by television and was impressed by the courtesy of the major participants based on the obvious mutual respect and desire for improved relations which existed. The most immediate tangible gains were an improvement in attitude of each power toward the other and agreements for an increase in trade, travel, and communication.

The presidential visit to Russia was preceded by a mutual agreement of the powers to notify each other of objects sighted by their respective missile warning systems and by improvements in the hot line through the use of a satellite permitting instantaneous communication. Unlike the visit to China, the trip to Russia entailed lengthy negotiations and resulted in a resolution of differences over a Strategic Armament Limitation Treaty (SALT). Among other restrictions, it limited deployment of antiballistic missiles to two sites in each country and fixed the ratio of weapons. Senator Henry Jackson and others were critical of some aspects of the treaty, feeling it gave Russia advantages, and included, with Senate approval, a reservation requiring ultimate U.S. equality with Russia. World opinion hailed the agreement as a major stroke for peace and hoped it heralded other agreements between Russia and the Western world. President Nixon, through a series of visits before his trips to Peking and Moscow, fully consulted other allied leaders. As a result, except for the Republic of China, there was no disruption of the U.S. alliance system due to the new departure in American policy.

In the summer of 1974, Nixon made important visits to the troubled states of the Middle East and a second visit to Russia. He was cordially received everywhere and appeared to have advanced his image as a sincere advocate of peace.

The End of the Vietnam War

While pursuing a new relationship with the major Communist powers, the Nixon administration, under intense public and congressional pressure, devoted much time and effort to ending the war in Vietnam under conditions the president considered honorable. He refused to unilaterally withdraw American troops, feeling this would be a betrayal of the South Vietnamese and the American men who had fought and died there. Instead, he attempted to obtain North Vietnamese agreement to end the conflict, began to withdraw U.S. forces by stages, and prepared the South Vietnamese to assume an increasing portion of the fighting.

In May, 1969, Nixon presented an eight-point plan for Vietnam which included withdrawal of most U.S. and North Vietnamese forces, followed by an internationally supervised election which would see that all groups participated in choosing a government. When this plan proved unacceptable to North Vietnam, the president pushed ahead with his "Vietnamization" of the war. In November, 1969, he announced all American combat troops would ultimately be withdrawn. Earlier, he had disclosed 70,000 troops were being removed, and in December, 1969, he revealed 50,000 more would be withdrawn by April, 1970. These actions were taken despite the virtual collapse of the Paris peace talks in November, 1969.

The United States was on schedule with troop removals by April 20, 1970, at which time the president announced another 150,000 men would be removed by the spring of 1971. However, any hopes that the United States was ending its operations immediately were dispelled ten days later when U.S. forces moved into Cambodia. The president declared the only areas affected were those occupied by the North Vietnamese and the action was essential to remove them and the Viet Cong from sanctuaries which gave a decided combat advantage. He promised all forces would be withdrawn by the end of June; the last were removed June 29, and the Defense Department held the Cambodian operation a success.

Another indication that the United States was not surrendering came on November 21, 1970, when a U.S. task force landed near Hanoi in an effort to rescue U.S. prisoners. Discovering they had been removed, the force withdrew without casualties. At the same time, November 21–22, 1970, U.S. aircraft made extensive raids on North Vietnam, following attacks on unarmed U.S. reconnaissance craft. Soon thereafter, the president warned he would resume bombing of military targets in North Vietnam if the enemy insisted on increasing the tempo of fighting as U.S. troops departed.

In 1971 and 1972 bombing was stepped up and became an internal issue in the United States in 1972 after former Attorney General Ramsey Clark, who visited North Vietnam, and others charged that the dikes had been deliberately bombed. In 1971 Lieutenant William Calley, Jr., was convicted by a military court of the premeditated murder of twenty-two civilians in 1968 at My Lai in South Vietnam. Military trials of others accused of the massacre of over a hundred in the village resulted in not-guilty verdicts. Although the military authorities held the event was an isolated incident, it aroused much concern in the United States. Many began to give credence to reports of other atrocities committed in South Vietnam and wondered about the defensibility of a war which destroyed those it purported to save. Others sympathized with Lieutenant Calley, who they felt was victimized for carrying out orders, and a federal district court ordered his release from prison in September, 1974. The publication in 1971 of the "Pentagon Papers" led some to conclude the government's major desire was to protect its own image.

Though the speed of "Vietnamization" was slowed by the difficulty of teaching South Vietnamese soldiers to use complicated weapons, the process continued and with it the removal of U.S. troops. On April 7, 1971, the president announced that 100,000 troops would be withdrawn between May 1 and December 1, 1971. On November 12, he stated 45,000 more would be removed by February 1, 1972, which would reduce U.S. forces to 139,000 in Vietnam. After that time additional servicemen were recalled, with the last ground combat forces leaving in the summer of 1972. At the same time, the president announced draftees would not be sent to Vietnam and revealed plans to end the draft in July, 1973. (With the end of the Vietnam war, the draft was ended in January, 1973.)

Meanwhile, pressure for complete American withdrawal, which had abated with the deescalation of U.S. military activity, became intense during the 1972 presidential campaign. Two years before, in October, 1970, the president had presented a revised plan for peace which the Communist representatives at the resumed Paris peace talks had rejected. It proposed a cease-fire with all forces remaining where they were, a peace conference which would deal with Laos and Cambodia as well as South Vietnam, and an immediate release of all war prisoners. The question of the future of South Vietnam remained a critical one in the discussions, but the releasing of allied prisoners also became a significant issue. In the 1972 campaign, Senator George McGovern, the Democratic presidential candidate, promised to have all American forces out of Vietnam within ninety days of his inauguration, and, if necessary, to go to Hanoi and "beg" for the release of U.S. prisoners. President Nixon steadfastly refused to set a timetable for removal of all U.S. military personnel or agree to a coalition government in South Vietnam which could lead to a Communist takeover. Early in the campaign, he dispatched Henry Kissinger for talks with the North Vietnamese

negotiators in Paris and with the South Vietnamese government in Saigon.

Although an announcement of an impending peace settlement was made shortly before the elections, critics of the war were leaders in opposition to Nixon and Agnew's reelection. Though vocal, their effects were negligible, and the president and vice-president won a landslide victory. Soon after the election, massive bombing was resumed in North Vietnam, but a peace settlement was reached in late January, 1973—ironically immediately after the death of former President Johnson. It was agreed all U.S. troops would be withdrawn from South Vietnam within sixty days, during which time all American prisoners of war would be released and all foreign troops removed from Laos and Cambodia. Although no provision was made for the removal of some 145,000 North Vietnamese troops in South Vietnam, they were, in effect, neutralized and their reduction insured by the establishment of a demilitarized zone policed by the United Nations through which military supplies could not be taken. A Council on National Reconciliation and Concord was established to organize elections in South Vietnam, but its actions were subject to veto by any of the major participants. Clearly, a face-saving peace was negotiated, which some hopefully compared to that attained at the Congress of Vienna. Due to that fact, many Americans rejoiced not only because it ended the nation's longest war but also because it offered a basis for long-range accommodations of differences.

The Vietnam war resulted in a strong resurgence of isolationism in the United States, particularly among liberals who had championed internationalism since the late 1930s. Its end provided welcome opportunities for the country to concentrate both on internal problems and more creative relationships with other nations.

Kissinger Becomes Secretary of State

The end of the Vietnam war by no means ended America's international problems, although the achievement of peace was a welcome attainment, and Henry Kissinger, its chief architect, was confirmed in September, 1973, as secretary of state. He succeeded William Rogers and received the title which justly recognized his primacy in formulating and executing American policy. Kissinger, who had fled with his Jewish family to the United States from Germany in 1938, declared at his swearing-in ceremony, "There is no country in the world where it is conceivable that a man of my origin could be standing here next to the President of the United States."

Kissinger had scarcely assumed office when on October 6, 1973, which was also Yom Kippur, the Jewish Holy Day of Atonement, the fourth and largest Arab-Israeli war in twenty-five years erupted with the Egyptians moving across the Suez Canal at five points and Syrian forces attacking and seizing territory in two regions of the Golan heights. By October 12 the Israelis had driven the Syrian forces back to the cease-fire line of 1967 and by October 14 had stopped Egyptian attempts to break out of the bridgehead it had established in Sinai.

The war was ended and some stability brought to the Middle East in large part because of the policy pursued by Nixon and Kissinger. Sizable quantities of material, including much needed aircraft, were furnished the Israelis to counteract the extensive supplies airlifted to both the Egyptians and Syrians by Russia. On October 20, 1973, Kissinger discussed the situation with Soviet party leader Leonid A. Brezhnev in Moscow and obtained agreement to a resolution calling for a cease-fire which was adopted by the UN Security Council on October 22. The recommendation

Henry Kissinger

was immediately accepted by both sides, but the U.S. unequivocally rejected a proposal of Soviet representative to the UN Yakov A. Malik that the U.S. and Russia send military forces to enforce the peace, an agreement that would have given the Russians entry into the strategic Middle East.

On October 25, 1973, the United States startled the world by placing U.S. military forces on a worldwide "precautionary alert," an action Kissinger explained was designed to counteract a possible Russian intervention in the Middle East. Confronted by this dramatic expression of U.S. commitment, Russia joined the United States in supporting a UN Security Council vote barring the major powers from membership in a Middle East peace-keeping force. A confrontation comparable to the 1962 Cuban missile crisis had been successfully met.

Following the cease-fire, Kissinger continued to use his unique diplomatic ability in efforts to resolve problems created by the conflict. In January and June, 1974, he obtained Arab-Israeli agreement to disengagement of Israeli forces from a number of areas held by them in return for nonaggression agreements and policing by a United Nations force. This action was followed by Arab consent to loosen the oil embargoes levied against Western Europe, Japan, and the United States because of their support of Israel and Nixon's visits to the Middle East and Russia.

In a period of generally bleak outlook at home and abroad, the achievements of Kissinger and the Nixon administration in foreign affairs attested to American competence and its commitment to a world system based on order and justice. Upon assuming office following Nixon's resignation, President Ford immediately committed his administration to the policies that had achieved these results and asserted they would continue to be pursued. More than ever, the nation realized the extreme importance of foreign affairs in every aspect of American life whose continuance depended on its cooperative relationships with other nations.

Selected Bibliography

William G. Carleton, *The Revolution in American Foreign Policy, Its Global Range* (rev. ed., 1967), and Seyom Brown, *The Faces of Power: Constancy and Change in United States Foreign Policy from Truman to Johnson* (1968), provide overviews and comparisons for much of the period. Kennedy policies are the subject of Roger Hilsman, *To Move a Nation: The Politics of Foreign Policy in the Administration of John F. Kennedy* (1967), and the earlier Johnson foreign policy is surveyed in Philip L. Geyelin, *Lyndon B. Johnson and the World* (1966).

Dulles' important role is presented with approval in Louis L. Gerson, *John Foster Dulles* (1967), but is criticized in Cyrus L. Sulzberger, *What's Wrong With U.S. Foreign Policy* (1959), and Norman A. Graebner, *Cold War Diplomacy: American Foreign Policy, 1945–1960* (1962). On specific aspects of the Eisenhower policy see Robert E. Osgood, *NATO, The Entangling Alliance* (1962); Jean E. Smith, *The Defense of Berlin* (1963); J. C. Campbell, *Defense of the Middle East: Problems of American Policy* (rev. ed., 1960); Hugh Thomas, *Suez* (1967); and David Wise and Thomas B. Ross, *The U-2 Affair* (1962). Milton Eisenhower, the president's brother, revealingly traces the development of a new attitude toward Latin America in *The Wine is Bitter; The United States and Latin America* (1963). The race for space is described in Robert L. Rosholt, *An Administrative History of NASA, 1958–1963* (1966), and J. M. Logsdon, *The Decision to Go to the Moon* (1970).

Important analyses of major participants in formulating foreign policy are in John Kennedy, *The Strategy of Peace* (1960); Dean Rusk, *The Winds of Freedom, Selections from the Speeches and Statements of Secretary of State Dean Rusk, January 1961–August 1962* (1963); J. William Fulbright, *The Arrogance of Power* (1967) and *The Pentagon Propaganda Machine* (1970); Henry A. Kissinger, *Nuclear Weapons and Foreign Policy* (abr. ed., 1969) and *The Troubled Partnership: A Re-appraisal of the Atlantic Alliance* (1965); and Robert S. McNamara, *The Essence of Security: Reflections in Office* (1968).

Relations with Latin America are treated in Dexter Perkins, *The United States and Latin America* (1961); Nathan A. Haverstock, *"OAS": Organization of American States; The Challenge of the Americas* (1966); and Jerome Levinson and Juan De Onis, *The Alliance That Lost Its Way: A Critical Report on the Alliance for Progress* (1970). On relations with Cuba consult Robert F. Smith, *The United States and Cuba: Business and Diplomacy, 1917–1960* (1960); Haynes B. Johnson with Manuel Artime and others, *The Bay of Pigs; The Leaders' Story of Brigade 2506* (1964); Karl E. Meyer and Tad Szulc, *The Cuban Invasion: The Chronicle of a Disaster* (1962); and Robert F. Kennedy, *Thirteen Days: A Memoir of the Cuban Missile Crisis* (1971).

---

*Available in paperback.

The all-important relationship with Southeast Asia is the subject of many works. Gunnar Myrdal, *Asian Drama: An Inquiry Into the Poverty of Nations** (3 vols., 1968), presents the background for much Asian discontent. Russell H. Fifield deals with *Southeast Asia in United States Policy** (1963). A more recent presentation of great value is Frances FitzGerald, *Fire in the Lake: The Vietnamese and the Americans in Vietnam** (1972). Other works include Melvin Gurtov, *The First Vietnam Crisis: Chinese Communist Strategy and United States Involvement, 1953–1954** (1968), Bernard B. Fall, *Street Without Joy: From the Indochina War to the War in Viet-Nam* (4th ed., 1972) and *The Two Viet-Nams: A Political and Military Analysis* (2d rev. ed., 1967). Criticism of the U.S. role is found in Arthur M. Schlesinger, Jr., *The Bitter Heritage: Vietnam and American Democracy, 1941–1968** (rev. ed., 1968); Commission of Inquiry, *The Dellums Committee Hearings on War Crime in Vietnam** (1972); and Daniel Ellsberg, *Papers on the War** (1972).

Conditions leading to Nixon's reassessment of foreign policy are described in Harland B. Moulton, *From Superiority to Parity: The United States and the Strategic Arms Race, 1961–1971* (1973); Zbigniew K. Brzezinski, *Alternative to Partition; For a Broader Conception of America's Role in Europe** (1965); and David Horowitz, *Free World Colossus: A Critique of America's Foreign Policy in the Cold War** (rev. ed., 1971).

Appendix A

The Declaration of Independence

In Congress, July 4, 1776

THE UNANIMOUS DECLARATION OF THE THIRTEEN UNITED STATES OF AMERICA

When, in the course of human events, it becomes necessary for one people to dissolve the political bands which have connected them with another, and to assume, among the powers of the earth, the separate and equal station to which the laws of nature and of nature's God entitle them, a decent respect to the opinions of mankind requires that they should declare the causes which impel them to the separation.

We hold these truths to be self-evident, that all men are created equal; that they are endowed by their Creator with certain unalienable rights; that among these, are life, liberty, and the pursuit of happiness. That, to secure these rights, governments are instituted among men, deriving their just powers from the consent of the governed; that, whenever any form of government becomes destructive of these ends, it is the right of the people to alter or to abolish it, and to institute a new government, laying its foundation on such principles, and organizing its powers in such form, as to them shall seem most likely to effect their safety and happiness. Prudence, indeed, will dictate that governments long established, should not be changed for light and transient causes; and, accordingly, all experience hath shown, that mankind are more disposed to suffer, while evils are sufferable, than to right themselves by abolishing the forms to which they are accustomed. But, when a long train of abuses and usurpations, pursuing invariably the same object, evinces a design to reduce them under absolute despotism, it is their right, it is their duty, to throw off such government and to provide new guards for their future security. Such has been the patient sufferance of these colonies, and such is now the necessity which constrains them to alter their former systems of government. The history of the present King of Great Britain is a history of repeated injuries and usurpations, all having, in direct object, the establishment of an absolute tyranny over these States. To prove this, let facts be submitted to a candid world:—

He has refused his assent to laws the most wholesome and necessary for the public good.

He has forbidden his governors to pass laws of immediate and pressing importance, unless suspended in their operation till his assent should be obtained; and, when so suspended, he has utterly neglected to attend to them.

He has refused to pass other laws for the accommodation of large districts of people, unless those people would relinquish the right of representation in the legislature; a right inestimable to them, and formidable to tyrants only.

He has called together legislative bodies at places unusual, uncomfortable, and distant from the depository of their public records, for the sole purpose of fatiguing them into compliance with his measures.

He has dissolved representative houses repeatedly for opposing, with manly firmness, his invasions on the rights of the people.

He has refused, for a long time after such dissolutions, to cause others to be elected; whereby the legislative powers, incapable of annihilation, have returned to the people at large for their exercise; the state remaining, in the meantime, exposed to all the danger of invasion from without, and convulsions within.

He has endeavored to prevent the population of these States; for that purpose, obstructing the laws for naturalization of foreigners, refusing to pass others to encourage their migration hither, and raising the conditions of new appropriations of lands.

He has obstructed the administration of justice, by refusing his assent to laws for establishing judiciary powers.

He has made judges dependent on his will alone, for the tenure of their offices, and the amount and payment of their salaries.

He has erected a multitude of new offices, and sent hither swarms of officers to harass our people, and eat out their substance.

He has kept among us, in time of peace, standing armies, without the consent of our legislatures.

He has affected to render the military independent of, and superior to, the civil power.

He has combined, with others, to subject us to a jurisdiction foreign to our Constitution, and unacknowledged by our laws; giving his assent to their acts of pretended legislation:

For quartering large bodies of armed troops among us:

For protecting them by a mock trial, from punishment, for any murders which they should commit on the inhabitants of these States:

For cutting off our trade with all parts of the world:

For imposing taxes on us without our consent:

For depriving us, in many cases, of the benefit of trial by jury:

For transporting us beyond seas to be tried for pretended offenses:

For abolishing the free system of English laws in a neighboring province, establishing therein an arbitrary government, and enlarging its boundaries, so as to render it at once an example and fit instrument for introducing the same absolute rule into these colonies:

For taking away our charters, abolishing our most valuable laws, and altering, fundamentally, the powers of our governments:

For suspending our own legislatures, and declaring themselves invested with power to legislate for us in all cases whatsoever.

He has abdicated government here, by declaring us out of his protection, and waging war against us.

He has plundered our seas, ravaged our coasts, burnt our towns, and destroyed the lives of our people.

He is, at this time, transporting large armies of foreign mercenaries to complete the works of death, desolation, and tyranny, already begun, with circumstances of cruelty and perfidy scarcely paralleled in the most barbarous ages, and totally unworthy the head of a civilized nation.

He has constrained our fellow citizens, taken captive on the high seas, to bear arms against their country, to become the executioners of their friends, and brethren, or to fall themselves by their hands.

He has excited domestic insurrections amongst us, and has endeavored to bring on the inhabitants of our frontiers, the merciless Indian savages, whose known rule of warfare is an undistinguished destruction of all ages, sexes, and conditions.

In every stage of these oppressions, we have petitioned for redress, in the most humble terms; our repeated petitions have been answered only by repeated injury. A prince, whose character is thus marked by every act which may define a tyrant, is unfit to be the ruler of a free people.

Nor have we been wanting in attention to our British brethren. We have warned them, from time to time, of attempts made by their legislature to extend an unwarrantable jurisdiction over us. We have reminded them of the circumstances of our emigration and settlement here. We have appealed to their native justice and magnanimity, and we have conjured them, by the ties of our common kindred, to disavow these usurpations, which would inevitably interrupt our connections and correspondence. They, too, have been deaf to the voice of justice and consanguinity. We must, therefore, acquiesce in the necessity which denounces our separation, and hold them, as we hold the rest of mankind, enemies in war, in peace, friends.

We, therefore, the representatives of the United States of America, in general Congress assembled, appealing to the Supreme Judge of the world for the rectitude of our intentions, do, in the name, and by the authority of the good people of these colonies, solemnly publish and declare, that these united colonies are, and of right ought to be, free and independent states; that they are absolved from all allegiance to the British Crown, and that all political connection between them and the state of Great Britain is, and ought to be, totally dissolved; and that, as free and independent states, they have full power to levy war, conclude peace, contract alliances, establish commerce, and to do all other acts and things which independent states may of right do. And, for the support of this declaration, with a firm reliance on the protection of Divine Providence, we mutually pledge to each other our lives, our fortunes, and our sacred honor.

Appendix B

The Constitution

Preamble:

We, the people of the United States, in order to form a more perfect union, establish justice, insure domestic tranquility, provide for the common defense, promote the general welfare, and secure the blessings of liberty to ourselves and our posterity, do ordain and establish this Constitution for the United States of America.

The Congress:

ARTICLE I

Section 1

a. All legislative powers herein granted shall be vested in a Congress of the United States, which shall consist of a Senate and House of Representatives.

Section 2

a. The House of Representatives shall be composed of members chosen every second year by the people of the several states; and the electors in each state shall have the qualifications requisite for electors of the most numerous branch of the legislature.

b. No person shall be a Representative who shall not have attained to the age of twenty-five years, and been seven years a citizen of the United States, and who shall not, when elected, be an inhabitant of the State in which he shall be chosen.

c. Representatives and direct taxes shall be apportioned among the several States which may be included within this Union, according to their respective numbers, which shall be determined by adding to the whole number of free persons, including those bound to service for a term of years, and excluding Indians not taxed, three-fifths of all other persons. The actual enumeration shall be made within three years after the first meeting of the Congress of the United States, and within every subsequent term of ten years, in such manner as they shall by law direct. The number of Representatives shall not exceed one for every thirty thousand, but each State shall have at least one Representative; and until such enumeration shall be made, the State of New Hampshire shall be entitled to choose three; Massachusetts, eight; Rhode Island and Providence plantations, one; Connecticut, five; New York, six; New Jersey, four; Pennsylvania, eight; Delaware, one; Maryland, six; Virginia, ten; North Carolina, five; South Carolina, five; and Georgia, three.

d. When vacancies happen in the representation from any State, the executive authority thereof shall issue writs of election to fill such vacancies.

e. The House of Representatives shall choose their Speaker and other officers, and shall have the sole power of impeachment.

Section 3

a. The Senate of the United States shall be composed of two Senators from each State, chosen by the Legislature thereof, for six years; and each Senator shall have one vote.

b. Immediately after they shall be assembled consequence of the first election, they shall be divided as equally as may be into three classes. The seats of the Senators of the first class shall be vacated at the expiration of the second year, of the second class at the expiration of the fourth year, and of the third class at the expiration of the sixth year, so that one-third may be chosen every second year; and if vacancies happen, by resignation or otherwise, during the recess of the Legislature of any State, the executive thereof may make temporary appointments until the next meeting of the Legislature, which shall then fill such vacancies.

c. No person shall be a Senator who shall not have attained the age of thirty years, and been nine years a citizen of the United States, and who shall not, when elected, be an inhabitant of that State for which he shall be chosen.

d. The Vice-President of the United States shall be President of the Senate, but shall have no vote unless they be equally divided.

e. The Senate shall choose their other officers, and also President *pro tempore* in the absence of the Vice President or when he shall exercise the office of President of the United States.

f. The Senate shall have the sole power to try all impeachments. When sitting for that purpose, they shall be on oath or affirmation. When the President of the United States is tried, the Chief Justice shall preside; and no person shall be convicted without the concurrence of two-thirds of the members present.

g. Judgment in cases of impeachment shall not extend further than to removal from office, and disqualification to hold and enjoy any office of honor, trust or profit under the United States; but the party convicted, shall, nevertheless, be liable and subject to indictment, trial, judgment and punishment, according to law.

Section 4

a. The times, places and manner of holding elections for Senators and Representatives shall be prescribed in each State by the Legislature thereof, but the Congress may at any time by law make or alter such regulations, except as to the places of choosing Senators.

b. The Congress shall assemble at least once in every year, and such meeting shall be on the first Monday in December, unless they shall by law appoint a different day.

Section 5

a. Each House shall be the judge of the elections, returns and qualifications of its own members, and a majority of each shall constitute a quorum to do business; but a smaller number may adjourn from day to day, and may be authorized to compel the attendance of absent members, in such manner and under such penalties as each House may provide.

b. Each House may determine the rule of its proceedings, punish its members for disorderly behavior, and with the concurrence of two-thirds, expel a member.

c. Each House shall keep a journal of its proceedings, and from time to time publish the same, excepting such parts as may, in their judgment, require secrecy; and the yeas and nays of the members of either House on any question shall, at the desire of one-fifth of those present, be entered on the journal.

d. Neither House, during the session of Congress, shall, without the consent of the other, adjourn for more than three days, nor to any other place than that in which the two Houses shall be sitting.

Section 6

a. The Senators and Representatives shall receive a compensation for their services, to be ascertained by law, and paid out of the treasury of the United States. They shall, in all cases except treason, felony and breach of the of the peace, be privileged from arrest during their attendance at the session of their respective Houses, and in going to and returning from the same; and for any speech or debate in either House they shall not be questioned in any other place.

b. No Senator or Representative shall, during the time for which he was elected, be appointed to any civil office under the authority of the United States, which shall have been created, or the emoluments whereof shall have been increased, during such time; and no person holding any office under the United States shall be a member of either House during his continuance in office.

Section 7

a. All bills for raising revenue shall originate in the House of Representatives; but the Senate may propose or concur with amendments as on other bills.

b. Every bill which shall have passed the House of Representatives and the Senate shall, before it becomes a law, be presented to the President of the United States; if he approve, he shall sign it; but if not, he shall return it, with his objections, to that House in which it shall have originated; who shall enter the objections at large on their journal, and proceed to reconsider it. If, after such reconsideration, two-thirds of that House shall agree to pass the bill, it shall be sent, together with the objections, to the other House, by which it shall likewise be reconsidered; and, if approved by two-thirds of that House, it shall become a law. But in all such cases, the votes of both Houses shall be determined by yeas and nays, and the names of the persons voting for and against the bill shall be entered on the journal of each house respectively. If any bill shall not be returned by the President within ten days (Sundays excepted) after it shall have been presented to him, the same shall be a law in like manner as if he had signed it, unless the Congress, by their adjournment, prevent its return, in which case it shall not be a law.

c. Every order, resolution or vote, to which the concurrence of the Senate and House of Representatives may be necessary (except on a question of adjournment), shall be presented to the President of the United States; and, before the same shall take effect, shall be approved by him; or, being disapproved by him, shall be repassed by two-thirds of the Senate and House of Representatives, according to the rules and limitations prescribed in the case of a bill.

Powers Granted:

Section 8

The Congress shall have power:

a. To lay and collect taxes, duties, imposts, and excises; to pay the debts and provide for the common defense and general welfare of the United States; but all duties, imposts and excises shall be uniform throughout the United States.

b. To borrow money on the credit of the United States.

c. To regulate commerce with foreign nations, and among the several States, and with the Indian tribes.

d. To establish an uniform rule of naturalization, and uniform laws on the subject of bankruptcies throughout the United States.

e. To coin money, regulate the value thereof, and of foreign coin, and fix the standard of weights and measures.

f. To provide for the punishment of counterfeiting the securities and current coin of the United States.

g. To establish postoffices and post roads.

h. To promote the progress of science and useful arts, by securing for limited times, to authors and inventors, the exclusive right to their respective writings and discoveries.

i. To constitute tribunals inferior to the Supreme Court.

j. To define and punish piracies and felonies committed on the high seas, and offenses against the law of nations.

k. To declare war, grant letters of marque and reprisal, and make rules concerning capture on land and water.

l. To raise and support armies; but no appropriation of money to that use shall be for a longer term then two years.

m. To provide and maintain a navy.

n. To make rules for the government and regulation of the land and naval forces.

o. To provide for calling forth the militia to execute the laws of the Union, suppress insurrections, and repel invasions.

p. To provide for organizing, arming and disciplining the militia, and for governing such part of them as may be employed in the service of the United States; reserving to the States respectively the appointment of the officers and the authority of training the militia according to the discipline prescribed by Congress.

q. To exercise exclusive legislation in all cases whatsoever, over such district (not exceeding ten miles square) as may, by cession of particular States, and the acceptance of Congress, become the seat of government of the United States; and to exercise like authority over all places purchased, by the consent of the Legislature of the State in which the same shall be, for the erection of forts, magazines, arsenals, dockyards, and other needful buildings; and

r. To make all laws which shall be necessary and proper for carrying into execution the foregoing powers, and all other powers vested by this Constitution in the government of the United States, or in any department or officer thereof.

Powers Denied:

a. The migration or importation of such persons as any of the States now existing shall think proper to admit, shall not be prohibited by the Congress prior to the year one thousand eight hundred and eight; but a tax or duty may be imposed on such importation not exceeding ten dollars for each person.

b. The privilege of the writ of *habeas corpus* shall not be suspended, unless when, in cases of rebellion or invasion, the public safety may require it.

c. No bill of attainder, or *ex post facto* law, shall be passed.

d. No capitation or other direct tax shall be laid unless in proportion to the census or enumeration hereinbefore directed to be taken.

e. No tax or duty shall be laid on any articles exported from any State. No preference shall be given by any regulation of commerce or revenue to the ports of one State over those of another; nor shall vessels bound to or from one State be obliged to enter, clear or pay duties in another.

f. No money shall be drawn from the treasury but in consequence of appropriations made by law; and a regular statement and account of the receipts and expenditures of all public money shall be published from time to time.

g. No title of nobility shall be granted by the United States; and no person holding any office of profit or trust under them shall, without the consent of the Congress, accept of any present, emolument, office, or title of any kind whatever, from any king, prince, or foreign state.

Section 10

a. No State shall enter into any treaty, alliance or confederation; grant letters of marque and reprisal; coin money; emit bills of credit; make anything but gold and silver coin a tender in payment of debts; pass any bill of attainder, *ex post facto* law, or law impairing the obligation of contracts; or grant any title of nobility.

b. No State shall, without the consent of the Congress, lay any imposts or duties on imports or exports, except what may be absolutely necessary for executing its inspection laws, and the net produce of all duties and imposts laid by any State on imports or exports shall be for the use of the treasury of the United States, and all such laws shall be subject to the revision and control of the Congress. No State shall, without the consent of the Congress, lay any duty of tonnage, keep troops or ships of war in time of peace, enter into any agreement or compact with another State, or with a foreign power, or engage in war, unless actually invaded, or in such imminent danger as will not admit of delay.

The Presidency:

ARTICLE II

Section 1

a. The executive power shall be vested in the President of the United States of America. He shall hold his office during the term of four years; and, together with the Vice-President chosen for the same term, be elected as follows:

b. Each State shall appoint, in such manner as the Legislature thereof may direct, a number of Electors equal to the whole number of Senators and Representatives to which the State may be entitled in the Congress; but no Senator or Representative, or person holding an office of trust or profit under the United States, shall be appointed an Elector.

c. The Electors shall meet in their respective States, and vote by ballot for two persons, of whom one at least shall not be an inhabitant of the same State with themselves. And they shall make a list of all the persons voted for, and of the number of votes for each; which list they shall sign and certify, and transmit sealed to the seat of government of the United States, directed to the President of the Senate. The President of the Senate shall, in the presence of the Senate and House of Representatives, open all the certificates, and the votes shall then be counted. The person having the greatest number of votes shall be the President, if such number be a majority of the whole number of Electors appointed; and if there be more than one who have such majority, and have an equal number of votes, then the House of Representatives shall immediately choose, by ballot, one of them for President; and if no person have a majority, then from the five highest on the list, the said House shall, in like manner, choose the President. But in choosing the President, the vote shall be taken by States, the representation from each State having one vote; a quorum for this purpose shall consist of a member or members from two-thirds of the States, and a majority of all the States shall be necessary to a choice. In every case, after the choice of the President, the person having the greatest number of votes of the Electors shall be the Vice-President. But if there should remain two or more who have equal votes, the Senate shall choose from them, by ballot, the Vice-President.

d. The Congress may determine the time of choosing the Electors, and the day on which they shall give their votes, which day shall be the same throughout the United States.

e. No person, except a natural born citizen, or a citizen of the United States at the time of adoption of this Constitution, shall be eligible to the office of President; neither shall any person be eligible to that office who shall not have attained to the age of thirty-five years, and been fourteen years a resident within the United States.

f. In case of the removal of the President from office, or of his death, resignation, or inability to discharge the powers and duties of the said office, the same shall devolve on the Vice President; and the Congress may, by law, provide for the case of removal, death, resignation or inability, both of the President and Vice President, declaring what officer shall then act as President; and such officer shall act

accordingly, until the disability be removed, or a President shall be elected.

g. The President shall, at stated times, receive for his services a compensation which shall neither be increased nor diminished during the period for which he shall have been elected; and he shall not receive within that period any other emolument from the United States, or any of them.

h. Before he enter on the execution of his office, he shall take the following oath or affirmation: "I do solemnly swear (or affirm) that I will faithfully execute the office of President of the United States; and will, to the best of my ability, preserve, protect and defend the Constitution of the United States."

The Executive Power:

Section 2

a. The President shall be commander-in-chief of the army and navy of the United States, and of the militia of the several States, when called into the actual service of the United States. He may require the opinion, in writing, of the principal officer in each of the executive departments, upon any subject relating to the duties of their respective offices; and he shall have power to grant reprieves and pardons for offenses against the United States, except in cases of impeachment.

b. He shall have power, by and with the advice and consent of the Senate, to make treaties, provided two-thirds of the Senators present concur; and he shall nominate, and by and with the advice and consent of the Senate shall appoint, ambassadors, other public ministers and consuls, judges of the Supreme Court, and all other officers of the United States whose appointments are not herein otherwise provided for, and which shall be established by law. But the Congress may, by law, vest the appointment of such inferior officers as they think proper, in the President alone, in the courts of law, or in the heads of departments.

c. The President shall have power to fill up all vacancies that may happen during the recess of the Senate, by granting commissions which shall expire at the end of their next session.

a. He shall, from time to time, give to the Congress information of the state of the Union, and recommend to their consideration such measures as he shall judge necessary and expedient. He may on extraordinary occasions, convene both Houses, or either of them; and in case of disagreement between them, with respect to the time of adjournment, he may adjourn them to such time as he shall think proper. He shall receive ambassadors and other public ministers. He shall take care that the laws be faithfully executed, and shall commission all the officers of the United States.

Section 4

a. The President, Vice President and all civil officers of the United States shall be removed from office on impeachment for, and conviction of, treason, bribery or other high crimes and misdemeanors.

The Judicial Power:

ARTICLE III

Section 1

a. The judicial power of the United States shall be vested in one Supreme Court, and in such inferior courts as the Congress may, from time to time, ordain and establish. The judges, both of the Supreme and inferior courts, shall hold their offices during good behavior; and shall, at stated times, receive for their services a compensation, which shall not be diminished during their continuance in office.

Section 2

a. The judicial power shall extend to all cases in law and equity arising under this Constitution, the laws of the United States, and treaties made, or which shall be made under their authority; to all cases affecting ambassadors, other public ministers and consuls; to all cases of admiralty and maritime jurisdiction; to controversies to which the United States shall be a party; to controversies between two or more States, between a State and citizens of another State, between citizens of different States, between citizens of the same State claiming lands under grants of different States, and between a State, or the citizens thereof, and foreign States, citizens or subjects.

b. In all cases affecting ambassadors, other public ministers and consuls, and those in which a State shall be a party, the Supreme Court shall have original jurisdiction. In all the other cases before mentioned, the Supreme Court shall have appellate jurisdiction, both as to law and fact, with such exceptions and under such regulations as the Congress shall make.

c. The trial of all crimes, except in cases of impeachment, shall be by jury, and such trial shall be held in the State where the said crimes shall have been committed, but when not committed within any State, the trial shall be at such place or places as the Congress may by law have directed.

Section 3

a. Treason against the United States shall consist only in levying war against them or in adhering to their enemies, giving them aid and comfort. No person shall be convicted of treason, unless on the testimony of two witnesses to the same overt act, or on confession in open court.

b. The Congress shall have power to declare the punishment of treason; but no attainder of treason shall work corruption of blood, or forfeiture, except during the life of the person attainted.

Concerning the States:

ARTICLE IV

Section 1

a. Full faith and credit shall be given in each State to the public acts, records and judicial proceedings of every other State; and the Congress may, by general laws, prescribe the manner in which such acts, records and proceedings shall be proved, and the effect thereof.

Section 2

a. The citizens of each State shall be entitled to all privileges and immunities of citizens in the several States.

b. A person charged in any State with treason, felony or other crime, who shall flee from justice, and be found in another State, shall on demand of the executive authority of the State from which he fled, be delivered up, to be removed to the State having jurisdiction of the crime.

c. No person held to service or labor in one State under the laws thereof, escaping into another, shall, in consequence of any law or regulation therein, be discharged from such service or labor, but shall be delivered up on claim of the party to whom such service or labor may be due.

Section 3

a. New States may be admitted by the Congress into this Union; but no new State shall be formed or erected within the jurisdiction of any other State, nor any State be formed by the junction of two or more States or parts of States, without the consent of the Legislatures of the States concerned, as well as of the Congress.

b. The Congress shall have the power to dispose of, and make all needful rules and regulations respecting the territory or other property belonging to the United States; and nothing in this Constitution shall be so construed as to prejudice any claims of the United States or of any particular State.

Section 4

a. The United States shall guarantee to every State in this Union a republican form of government, and shall protect each of them against invasion; and, on application of the Legislature, or of the executive (when the Legislature cannot be convened), against domestic violence.

Final Provisions:

ARTICLE V

a. The Congress, whenever two-thirds of both Houses shall deem it necessary, shall propose amendments to this Constitution, or, on the application of the Legislatures of two-thirds of the several States, shall call a convention for proposing amendments, which, in either case, shall be valid to all intents and purposes, as part of this Constitution, when ratified by the Legislatures of three-fourths of the several States, or by conventions in three-fourths thereof, as the one or the other mode of ratification may be proposed by the Congress; provided that no amendment, which may be made prior to the year one thousand eight hundred and eight, shall in any manner affect the first and fourth clauses in the ninth section of the first article; and that no State, without its consent, shall be deprived of its equal suffrage in the Senate.

ARTICLE VI

a. All debts contracted and engagements entered into before the adoption of this Constitution shall be as valid against the United States under this Constitution, as under the Confederation.

b. This Constitution, and the laws of the United States which shall be made in pursuance thereof, and all treaties made, or which shall be made, under the authority of the United States, shall be the supreme law of the land; and the judges in every State shall be bound thereby, anything in the Constitution or laws of any State to the contrary notwithstanding.

c. The Senators and Representatives before mentioned, and the members of the several State Legislatures, and all executive and judicial officers, both of the United States and of the several States, shall be bound by oath or affirmation to support this Constitution; but no religious test shall ever be required as a qualification to any office or public trust under the United States.

ARTICLE VII

The ratification of the Conventions of nine States shall be sufficient for the establishment of this Constitution between the States so ratifying the same.

Done in convention, by the unanimous consent of the States present, the seventeenth day of September, in the year of our Lord one thousand seven hundred and eighty-seven, and of the independence of the United States of America the twelfth.

In witness whereof, we have hereunto subscribed our names.

GEORGE WASHINGTON,
President, and Deputy from Virginia

New Hampshire

John Langdon
Nicholas Gilman

Massachusetts

Nathaniel Gorham
Rufus King

Connecticut

William Samuel Johnson
Roger Sherman

New York

Alexander Hamilton

New Jersey

William Livingston
David Brearley
William Paterson
Jonathan Dayton

Pennsylvania

Benjamin Franklin
Thomas Mifflin
Robert Morris
George Clymer
Thomas Fitzsimmons
Jared Ingersoll
James Wilson
Gouverneur Morris

Delaware

George Read
Gunning Bedford, Jr.
John Dickinson
Richard Bassett
Jacob Broom

Maryland

James M'Henry
Daniel of St. Thomas Jenifer
Daniel Carroll

Virginia

John Blair
James Madison, Jr.

North Carolina

William Blount
Richard Dobbs Spaight
Hugh Williamson

South Carolina

John Rutledge
Charles C. Pinckney
Charles Pinckney
Pierce Butler

Georgia

William Few
Abraham Baldwin

Attest:

William Jackson, Secretary

The Amendments:

[The following ten amendments were proposed at the first session of the first Congress of the United States and were ratified by December, 1791.]

AMENDMENT I

Congress shall make no law respecting an establishment of religion, or prohibiting the free exercise thereof, or abridging the freedom of speech or of the press, or the right of the people peaceably to assemble, and to petition the government for a redress of grievances.

AMENDMENT II

A well regulated militia, being necessary to the security of a free State, the right of the people to keep and bear arms shall not be infringed.

AMENDMENT III

No soldier shall, in time of peace, be quartered in any house without the consent of the owner; nor in time of war but in a manner to be prescribed by law.

AMENDMENT IV

The right of the people to be secure in their persons, houses, paper and effects, against unreasonable searches and seizures shall not be violated; and no warrants shall issue but upon probable cause, supported by oath or affirmation, and particularly describing the place to be searched, and the persons or things to be seized.

AMENDMENT V

No person shall be held to answer for a capital or otherwise infamous crime, unless on a presentment or indictment of a grand jury, except in cases arising in the land or naval forces, or in the militia, when in actual service in time of war or public danger; nor shall any person be subject for the same offense to be twice put in jeopardy of life or limb; nor shall be compelled, in any criminal case, to be a witness against himself, nor be deprived of life, liberty or property, without due process of law; nor shall private property be taken for public use without just compensation.

AMENDMENT VI

In all criminal prosecutions, the accused shall enjoy the right to a speedy and public trial, by an impartial jury of the State and district wherein the crime shall have been committed, which district shall have been previously ascertained by law; and to be informed of the nature and cause of the accusation; to be confronted with the witnesses against him; to have compulsory process for obtaining witnesses in his favor, and to have the assistance of counsel for his defense.

AMENDMENT VII

In suits at common law, where the value in controversy shall exceed twenty dollars, the right of trial by jury shall be preserved; and no fact tried by a jury shall be otherwise reexamined in any court of the United States, than according to the rules of the common law.

AMENDMENT VIII

Excessive bail shall not be required, nor excessive fines imposed, nor cruel and unusual punishments inflicted.

AMENDMENT IX

The enumeration in the Constitution of certain rights shall not be construed to deny or disparage others retained by the people.

AMENDMENT X

The powers not delegated to the United States by the Constitution, nor prohibited by it to the States, are reserved to the States respectively, or to the people.

AMENDMENT XI

[Submitted by Congress to the state legislatures in March, 1794, duly ratified, and proclaimed in January, 1798.]

The judicial power of the United States shall not be construed to extend to any suit in law or equity, commenced or prosecuted against one of the United States by citizens of another State, or by citizens or subjects of any foreign State.

AMENDMENT XII

[Submitted by Congress to the state legislatures in December, 1803, duly ratified, and proclaimed in September, 1804.]

1. The Electors shall meet in their respective States, and vote by ballot for President and Vice-President, one of whom at least shall not be an inhabitant of the same State with themselves. They shall name in their ballots the person voted for as President, and in distinct ballots the person voted for as Vice-President; and they shall make distinct lists of all persons voted for as President, and of all persons voted for as Vice-President, and of the number of votes for each, which lists they shall sign and certify, and transmit sealed to the seat of the government of the United States, directed to the President of the Senate. The President of the Senate shall, in the presence of the Senate and House of Representatives, open all the certificates and the votes shall then be counted. The person having the greatest number of votes for President shall be the President, if such number be a majority of the whole number of Electors appointed; and if no person have

such majority, then from the persons having the highest numbers, not exceeding three, on the list of those voted for as President, the House of Representatives shall choose immediately, by ballot, the President. But in choosing the President, the votes shall be taken by State, the representation from each State having one vote; a quorum for this purpose shall consist of a member or members from two-thirds of the States, and a majority of all the States shall be necessary to a choice. And if the House of Representatives shall not choose a President, whenever the right of choice shall devolve upon them, before the fourth day of March next following, then the Vice-President shall act as President as in the case of the death or other constitutional disability of the President.

2. The person having the greatest number of votes as Vice-President shall be the Vice-President, if such number be a majority of the whole number of Electors appointed, and if no person have a majority, then from the two highest numbers on the list the Senate shall choose the Vice-President. A quorum for the purpose shall consist of two-thirds of the whole number of Senators, and a majority of the whole number shall be necessary to a choice.

3. But no person constitutionally ineligible to the office of President shall be eligible to that of Vice-President of the United States.

AMENDMENT XIII

[Submitted by Congress to the state legislatures in February, 1865, duly ratified and proclaimed in December, 1865.]

1. Neither slavery nor involuntary servitude, except as a punishment for crime, whereof the party shall have been duly convicted, shall exist within the United States, or any place subject to their jurisdiction.

2. Congress shall have power to enforce this article by appropriate legislation.

AMENDMENT XIV

[Submitted by Congress to the state legislatures in June, 1866, duly ratified, and proclaimed in July, 1868.]

1. All persons born or naturalized in the United States, and subject to the jurisdiction thereof, are citizens of the United States and of the State wherein they reside. No State shall make or enforce any law which shall abridge the privileges or immunities of citizens of the United States; nor shall any State deprive any person of life, liberty or property, without due process of law, nor deny to any person within its jurisdiction the equal protection of the laws.

2. Representatives shall be apportioned among the several States according to their respective numbers, counting the whole number of persons in each State, excluding Indians not taxed. But when the right to vote at any election for the choice of Electors for President and Vice-President of the United States, Representatives in Congress, the executive and judicial officers of a State, or the members of the Legislature thereof, is denied to any of the male inhabitants of such State, being twenty-one years of age, and citizens of the United States, or in any way abridged, except for participation in rebellion or other crime, the basis of representation therein shall be reduced in the proportion which the number of such male citizens shall bear to the whole number of male citizens twenty-one years of age in such State.

3. No person shall be a Senator or Representative in Congress, or Elector of President and Vice-President, or hold any office, civil or military, under the United States, or under any State, who having previously taken an oath as a member of Congress, or as an officer of the United States, or as a member of any State Legislature, or as an executive or judical officer of any State, to support the Constitution of the United States, shall have engaged in insurrection or rebellion against the same, or given aid or comfort to the enemies thereof. But Congress may, by a vote of two-thirds of each House, remove such disability.

4. The validity of the public debt of the United States authorized by law, including debts incurred for payment of pensions and bounties for services in suppressing insurrection or rebellion, shall not be questioned. But neither the United States nor any State shall assume or pay any debt or obligation incurred in aid of insurrection or rebellion against the United States, or any claim for the loss or emancipation of any slave; but all such debts, obligations, and claims shall be held illegal and void.

5. The Congress shall have the power to enforce, by appropriate legislation, the provisions of this article.

AMENDMENT XV

[Submitted by Congress to the state legislatures in February, 1869, duly ratified, and proclaimed in March, 1870.]

1. The rights of citizens of the United States to vote shall not be denied or abridged by the United States or by any State on account of race, color, or previous condition of servitude.

2. The Congress shall have power to enforce this article by appropriate legislation.

AMENDMENT XVI

[Submitted by Congress to the state legislatures in July, 1909, duly ratified, and proclaimed in February, 19_3.]

The Congress shall have power to lay and collect taxes on incomes, from whatever source derived, without apportionment among the several States, and without regard to any census or enumeration.

AMENDMENT XVII

[Submitted by Congress to the state legislatures in May, 1912, duly ratified, and proclaimed in May, 1913.]

1. The Senate of the United States shall be composed of two Senators from each State, elected by the people thereof, for six years; and each Senator shall have one vote. The Electors in each State shall have the qualifications requisite for Electors of the most numerous branch of the State Legislatures.

2. When vacancies happen in the representation of any State in the Senate, the executive authority of such State shall issue writs of election to fill such vacancies: Provided, That the Legislature of any State may empower the executive thereof to make temporary appointment until the people fill the vacancies by election as the Legislature may direct.

3. This amendment shall not be so construed as to affect the election or term of any Senator chosen before it becomes valid as part of the Constitution.

AMENDMENT XVIII

[Submitted by Congress to the state legislatures in December, 1917, duly ratified and proclaimed in January 1919, as going into full force and effect January 16, 1920.]

1. After one year from the ratification of this article the manufacture, sale or transportation of intoxicating liquors within, the importation thereof into, or the exportation thereof from the United States and all territory subject to the jurisdiction thereof for beverage purposes is hereby prohibited.

2. The Congress and the several States shall have concurrent power to enforce this article by appropriate legislation.

3. This article shall be inoperative unless it shall have been ratified as an amendment to the Constitution by the Legislatures of the several States, as provided by the Constitution, within seven years from the date of the submission hereof to the States by the Congress.

AMENDMENT XIX

[Submitted by Congress to the state legislatures in June, 1919, duly ratified, and proclaimed in August, 1920.]

1. The rights of citizens of the United States to vote shall not be denied or abridged by the United States or by any State on account of sex.

2. Congress shall have the power, by appropriate legislation, to enforce the provisions of this article.

AMENDMENT XX

[Submitted by Congress to the state legislatures in March, 1932, duly ratified, and proclaimed in January, 1933.]

1. The terms of the President and Vice-President shall end at noon on the 20th day of January, and the terms of Senators and Representatives at noon on the 3rd day of January of the years in which such terms would have ended if this article had not been ratified; and the terms of their successors shall then begin.

2. The Congress shall assemble at least once in every year, and such meeting shall begin at noon on the 3rd day of January, unless they shall by law appoint a different day.

3. If, at the time fixed for the beginning of the term of the President, the President elect shall have died, the Vice-President elect shall become President. If a President shall not have been chosen before the time fixed for the beginning of his term, or if the President elect shall have failed to qualify, then the Vice-President elect shall act as President until a President shall have qualified; and the Congress may by law provide for the case wherein neither a President elect or a Vice-President elect shall have qualified, declaring who shall then act as President, or the manner in which one who is to act shall be selected, and such person shall act accordingly until a President or Vice-President shall have qualified.

4. The Congress may by law provide for the case of the death of any of the persons from whom the House of Representatives may choose a President whenever the right of choice shall have devolved upon them, and for the case of the death of any of the persons from whom the Senate may choose a Vice-President whenever the right of choice shall have devolved upon them.

5. Sections 1 and 2 shall take effect on the 15th day of October following the ratification of this article.

6. This article shall be inoperative unless it shall have been ratified as an amendment to the Constitution by the Legislatures of three-fourths of the several States within seven years from the date of its submission.

AMENDMENT XXI

[Submitted by Congress to state conventions in February, 1933, duly ratified, and proclaimed in December, 1933.]

1. The eighteenth article of amendment to the Constitution of the United States is hereby repealed.

2. The transportation or importation into any State, Territory, or Possession of the United States for delivery or use therein of intoxicating liquors, in violation of the laws thereof, is hereby prohibited.

3. This article shall be inoperative unless it shall have been ratified as an amendment to the Constitution by conventions in the several States, as provided in the Constitution, within seven years from the date of the submission hereof to the States by the Congress.

AMENDMENT XXII

[Submitted by Congress to the state legislatures in March, 1947, duly ratified, and proclaimed in March, 1951.]

No person shall be elected to the office of the President more than twice, and no person who has held the office of President, or acted as President, for more than two years of a term to which some other person was elected President shall be elected to the office of the President more than once. But this Article shall not apply to any person holding the office of President when this Article was proposed by the Congress, and shall not prevent any person who may be holding the office of President, or acting as President, during the term within which this Article becomes operative from holding the office of President or acting as President during the remainder of such term.

AMENDMENT XXIII

[Submitted by Congress to the state legislatures in June, 1960, duly ratified, and proclaimed in April, 1961.]

1. The District constituting the seat of Government of the United States shall appoint in such manner as the Congress may direct: A number of electors of President and Vice-President equal to the whole number of Senators and Representatives in Congress to which the District would be entitled if it were a State, but in no event more than the least populous State; they shall be in addition to those appointed by the States, but they shall be considered, for the purposes of the election of President and Vice-President, to be electors appointed by a State; and they shall meet in the District and perform such duties as provided by the twelfth article of amendment.

2. The Congress shall have power to enforce this article by appropriate legislation.

AMENDMENT XXIV

[Submitted by Congress to the state legislatures August 27, 1962, duly ratified and proclaimed in January, 1964.]

1. The right of citizens of the United States to vote in any primary or other election for President or Vice-President, for electors for President or Vice-President, or for Senator or Representative in Congress, shall not be denied or abridged by the United States or any State by reason of failure to pay any poll tax or other tax.

2. The Congress shall have the power to enforce this article by appropriate legislation.

AMENDMENT XXV

[Submitted by Congress to the State Legislatures in July, 1965, duly ratified, and proclaimed in April, 1967.]

1. In case of the removal of the President from office or his death or resignation, the Vice-President shall become President.

2. Whenever there is a vacancy in the office of the Vice-President, the President shall nominate a Vice-President who shall take the office upon confirmation by a majority vote of both houses of Congress.

3. Whenever the President transmits to the President *pro tempore* of the Senate and the Speaker of the House of Representatives his written declaration that he is unable to discharge the powers and duties of his office, and until he transmits to them a written declaration to the contrary, such powers and duties shall be discharged by the Vice-President as Acting President.

4. Whenever the Vice-President and a majority of either the principal officers of the executive departments or of such other body as Congress may by law provide, transmit to the President *pro tempore* of the Senate and the Speaker of the House of Representatives their written declaration that the President is unable to discharge the powers and duties of his office, the Vice-President shall immediately assume the powers and duties of the office as Acting President.

Thereafter, when the President transmits to the President *pro tempore* of the Senate and the Speaker of the House of Representatives his written declaration that no inability exists, he shall resume the powers and duties of his office unless the Vice-President and a majority of either the principal officers of the executive department or of such other body as Congress may by law provide, transmit within four days to the President *pro tempore* of the Senate and the Speaker of the House of Representatives their written declaration that the President is unable to discharge the powers and duties of his office. Thereupon Congress shall decide the issue, assembling within forty-eight hours for that purpose if not in session. If the Congress, within twenty-one days after receipt of the latter written declaration, or, if Congress is not in session, within twenty-one days after Congress is required to assemble, determines by two-thirds vote of both houses that the President is unable to discharge the powers and duties of his office, the Vice-President shall continue to discharge the same as Acting President; otherwise, the President shall resume the powers and duties of his office.

AMENDMENT XXVI

[Ratified June 30, 1971]

Section 1. The right of citizens of the United States, who are eighteen years of age or older, to vote shall not be denied or abridged by the United States or by any State on account of age.

Section 2. The Congress shall have power to enforce this article by appropriate legislation.

Appendix C

Presidential Elections 1880-1972

Year	Candidates	Party	Vice-President
1880	**James A. Garfield** Winfield S. Hancock James B. Weaver	Republican Democratic Greenback-Labor	**Chester A. Arthur** (1881)
1884	**Grover Cleveland** James G. Blaine Benjamin F. Butler	Democratic Republican Greenback-Labor	Thomas A. Hendricks
1888	**Benjamin Harrison** Grover Cleveland	Republican Democratic	Levi P. Morton
1892	**Grover Cleveland** Benjamin Harrison James B. Weaver	Democratic Republican People's	Adlai E. Stevenson
1896	**William McKinley** William J. Bryan	Republican Democratic: People's	Garret A. Hobart
1900	**William McKinley** William J. Bryan	Republican Democratic: Populist	**Theodore Roosevelt** (1901)
1904	**Theodore Roosevelt** Alton B. Parker Eugene V. Debs	Republican Democratic Socialist	Charles W. Fairbanks
1908	**William H. Taft** William J. Bryan Eugene V. Debs	Republican Democratic Socialist	James S. Sherman
1912	**Woodrow Wilson** Theodore Roosevelt William H. Taft Eugene V. Debs	Democratic Progressive Republican Socialist	Thomas R. Marshall
1916	**Woodrow Wilson** Charles E. Hughes A. L. Benson	Democratic Republican Socialist	Thomas R. Marshall

Year	Candidates	Party	Vice-President
1920	**Warren G. Harding** James M. Cox Eugene V. Debs	Republican Democratic Socialist	**Calvin Coolidge** (1923)
1924	**Calvin Coolidge** John .W. Davis Robert M. La Follette	Republican Democratic Progressive	Charles G. Dawes
1928	**Herbert C. Hoover** Alfred E. Smith	Republican Democratic	Charles Curtis
1932	**Franklin D. Roosevelt** Herbert C. Hoover Norman Thomas	Democratic Republican Socialist	John Nance Garner
1936	**Franklin D. Roosevelt** Alfred M. Landon William Lemke	Democratic Republican Union	John Nance Garner
1940	**Franklin D. Roosevelt** Wendell L. Willkie	Democratic Republican	Henry A. Wallace
1944	**Franklin D. Roosevelt** Thomas E. Dewey	Democratic Republican	**Harry S Truman** (1945)
1948	**Harry S Truman** Thomas E. Dewey J. Strom Thurmond Henry A. Wallace	Democratic Republican States' Rights Progressive	Alben W. Barkley
1952	**Dwight D. Eisenhower** Adlai E. Stevenson	Republican Democratic	Richard M. Nixon
1956	**Dwight D. Eisenhower** Adlai E. Stevenson	Republican Democratic	Richard M. Nixon
1960	**John F. Kennedy** Richard M. Nixon	Democratic Republican	**Lyndon B. Johnson** (1963)
1964	**Lyndon B. Johnson** Barry M. Goldwater	Democratic Republican	Hubert H. Humphrey
1968	**Richard M. Nixon** Hubert H. Humphrey George C. Wallace	Republican Democratic American Independent	Spiro T. Agnew
1972	**Richard M. Nixon** George McGovern	Republican Democratic	Spiro T. Agnew **Gerald R. Ford** (1974)

Index

Belknap, William W., 21
Bell, Alexander Graham, 62
Bellamy, Edward, 74, 75
Belleau Wood, 176
Belmont, August, 99, 152
Benét, Stephen Vincent, 203
Benson, Ezra Taft, 304
Benton, Thomas Hart, 311
Benton, William, 297
Berle, Adolf A., Jr., 223
Berlin, 112, 268, 361; 1958 crisis, 358
"Berlin Wall," 361
Bernadotte, Folke, 280
Bernstein, Leonard, 311–12
Bernstorff, Count Johann von, 169, 170
Bessemer process, 58
Beveridge, Albert, 144, 148
Bevin, Ernest, 282
Bible, 196–97; reading in schools, 334
Big Four, at Paris Peace Conference, 179
Bill of Rights, 9
Birmingham, Ala., 44, 58, 308, 314
"Birmingham Differential" system, 44
Bizerte, Tunisia, 262
Black, Hugo, 234, 338
Black Belt, 98, 323, 336
Black Codes, in postwar South, 6, 9
Black Hills: gold rush, 33, 36; Indian reservations, 33
"Black International," 67
"Black Monday" (1935), 233
"Black Friday": 1869, 20; 1873, 22
Black Muslims, 335
Black Panthers, 335
"Black Power," 325–26
Black Star line, 204
"Black Tuesday" (1929), 210
Blacks, 197; abuse following W.W. I, 184; B. T. Washington's influence, 46–47; chauvinism of M. W. Garvey, 204; condition after Civil War, 4–6; continued discrimination against, 335, 336; during Kennedy's adm., 314–15; during W.W. II, 259, 304; effect of Court decisions (1938–55), 304–5; Force Bill, 95; gains during Eisenhower years, 305–6; gains under LBJ, 322–24; gains under Truman, 294, 296; leadership of King, 307–8; in literature, 75, 203–4; naturalization rights, 130; post-W.W. II frustration, 292; role in Radical Reconst., 11, 14–15; segregated in govt., 158; support Truman in 1948, 295; treatment in New South, 45–46
"Blacks and Tans," 158
Blackmun, Harry A., 334
Blaine, James G., 24, 88; 1884 election, 91–92; sec. of state, 89, 95, 110–12
Blair, Francis P., 13
Blair Bill, 72
Bland, Richard, 87, 100
Bland-Allison Act, 87–88, 95–96, 101
Blount, James H., 113
Board of Governors of Federal Reserve System, 226
Board of Indian Commissioners, 34
Bolivia, 237
Borah, William E., 180
Borglum, Gutzon, 205
Bosnia, 167
Boston, Mass., 77, 91, 244, 312
Boston, 113
Boxer Rebellion, 122
Bozeman Trail, 33
Bradley, Joseph P., 25
"Brain Trust," 214, 233

Brandeis, Louis D., 65, 224, 233; advises Wilson in 1912 campaign, 152; advises Wilson on antitrust policy, 156; appointment to Supreme Court, 157; in conservation controversy, 149
Brannan, Charles, 296
Braun, Eva, 269
Brazil, 19, 166
Bremer, Arthur, 339
Brezhnev, Leonid A., 373
Briand, Aristide, 195
Bricker, John W., 266
Bristow, Benjamin H., 21
British Guiana, 112, 244
Brotherhood of Railway Conductors, 141
Brotherhood of Railway Engineers, 293
Brotherhood of Railway Trainmen, 293
Browder, Earl, 297
Brown, B. Gratz, 22
Brown v. *Board of Education of Topeka*, 305, 306
Bruce, Blanche K., 14
Brussels, Belgium, 241
Brussels Pact, 282, 283
Bryan, Charles, 192
Bryan, William Jennings, 100, 115, 143, 155, 192; candidate for president (1908), 147; fundamentalist leader, 196, 197; 1896 campaign, 100, 102; 1900 campaign, 123; 1912 convention, 152; opposes Peace of Paris, 119; opposes neutral rights, 170, 171; sec. of state, 154, 164, 167, 169, 170
Buckner, Simon B., 102
Buddhists, 363
Buffalo, Indian reliance on, 32, 33–34
Bulganin, Nikolai, 353, 357
Bulgaria, 179, 277
Bulge, battle of, 265
"Bull Moose" party, 152, 223, 232
Bunau-Varilla, Philippe, 125, 126
Bunche, Ralph J., 280
Bunshaft, Gordon, 311
Bunting v. *Oregon*, 65
Bureau of Corporations, 142
Burger, Warren E., 334
Burke-Wadsworth Act, 256
Burleson, Albert S., 154, 158
Burma, 262–63
Business: attitude toward New Deal, 223, 231; influence in 1920s, 191, 197–99
Butler, Benjamin F., 24, 92
Butler, Pierce, 232
Butterfield, Alexander, 342
Byrne, William M., 341
Byrnes, James F.: FDR's choice for vice-president, 267; sec. of state, 277; W.W. II economic czar, 258

Caball, James Branch, 202
Cable, George Washington, 75
Cairo Conference, 263
California, 32, 35, 36, 38, 75, 76, 94, 98, 125, 129, 130, 138, 139, 151, 172, 190, 207, 231, 293, 298, 302, 324, 327, 329, 335, 338, 340
Calles, Plutarcho Elias, 194
Calley, William, Jr., 371
Cambodia, 330, 354, 355, 371, 372
Canada, 19, 32, 39, 111–12, 129, 150–51, 281; Alaskan boundary dispute, 128
Canal Zone, 356
Canary, "Calamity Jane," 36
Cannon, James, Jr., 209–10
Cannon, Joseph, 142, 148, 149
Capone, Al, 201

Cárdenas, Lázaro, 239
Cardozo, Benjamin N., 233
Caribbean Sea, 77, 114, 124; dollar diplomacy in, 130–31
Carnegie, Andrew, 58–59, 73
Carnegie Steel Co., 58–59, 68–69
Carpenter, M. Scott, 360
Carpetbaggers, 14, 16
Carranza, Venustiano, 166
Carrizal, Mexico, 166
Carswell, G. Harrold, 334
Casablanca, Morocco, 261
Cassatt, Mary, 78
Castro, Cipriano, 126
Castro, Fidel, 335; Bay of Pigs, 360–61
Cather, Willa, 202
Cattle drives, 39–41
Central Intelligence Agency, 340, 360
Central Pacific Railroad, 37
Central Powers, 168
Central Treaty Organization, 356
Cervera, Pascual, 117, 118
Cézanne, Paul, 205
Chamberlain, Neville, 241, 252
Chambers, Wittaker, 297
Champion v. *Ames*, 140
Charities, 65
Chase, Salmon P., 12
Chateau-Thierry, 176
Chattanooga, Tenn., 44
Chautauqua movement, 73
Chavez, Cesar, 337
Che Guevara, 335
Cherokee Nation v. *Georgia*, 35
Cherokee Outlet, 43
Cheyenne Indians, 33
Chiang Kai-shek, 253, 351, 370; Cairo conference, 263; Korean War, 283, 284; Nationalist loss of mainland, 278–79
Chicago, Ill., 58, 63, 65, 67, 69, 70, 78, 100, 138, 145, 172, 184, 201, 204, 207, 214, 236, 241, 309, 327, 335, 340
Chicago, Burlington and Quincy Railroad, 141
Chicago Daily News, 232
Chicago, Milwaukee and St. Paul Railway Co. v. *Minnesota*, 50
Chicanos, struggle for civil rights, 337
Child labor: Beveridge bill, 145; Children's Bureau, 145, 228; in New South, 45
Children's Bureau, 145, 228
Chile, 111, 165
China (*see also* People's Republic of China), 114, 119, 128, 130, 131, 164, 193, 239, 251, 267, 274; Hull demands regarding, 253; Open Door Policy, 121–22; significance in coming of war with Japan, 253, 254; U.S. defeat in, 278–79; war with Japan, 241
"China Lobby," 279
Chinese, 24, 37
Chinese Exclusion Act, 130
Chisholm Trail, 40, 41
Chivington, John M., 33
Chou En-lai, 284
Christianity, 110
Christian Science, 71
Christian Socialists, 71
Churches, 1919–29 development, 206–7
Churchill, Winston: obtains Am. aid, 242–43, 250–51; post-W.W. II leadership, 279; meetings with Roosevelt, 260, 262–63, 268
Cincinnati, O., 96, 229
Cities, continued segregation in, 336–37